ACCA

STUDY TEXT

PAPER F8

AUDIT AND ASSURANCE (INTERNATIONAL)

In this edition approved by ACCA

- We **discuss** the **best strategies** for studying for ACCA exams
- We **highlight** the **most important elements** in the syllabus and the **key skills** you will need
- We **signpost** how each chapter links to the syllabus and the study guide
- We **provide** lots of **exam focus points** demonstrating what the examiner will want you to do
- We **emphasise key points** in regular **fast forward summaries**
- We **test your knowledge** of what you've studied in **quick quizzes**
- We **examine your understanding** in our **exam question bank**
- We **reference all the important topics** in our **full index**

BPP's **i-Learn** and **i-Pass** products also support this paper.

FOR EXAMS IN 2010

BPP LEARNING MEDIA

First edition 2007
Fourth edition September 2009

ISBN 9780 7517 7609 6
(Previous ISBN 9870 7517 6372 0)

British Library Cataloguing-in-Publication Data
A catalogue record for this book
is available from the British Library

Published by

BPP Learning Media Ltd
BPP House, Aldine Place
London W12 8AA

www.bpp.com/learningmedia

Printed in the United Kingdom

We are grateful to the Association of Chartered Certified Accountants for permission to reproduce past examination questions. The suggested solutions in the exam answer bank have been prepared by BPP Learning Media Ltd, unless otherwise stated.

Contents

A note about copyright

Dear Customer

What does the little © mean and why does it matter?

Your market-leading BPP books, course materials and e-learning materials do not write and update themselves. People write them: on their own behalf or as employees of an organisation that invests in this activity. Copyright law protects their livelihoods. It does so by creating rights over the use of the content.

Breach of copyright is a form of theft – as well as being a criminal offence in some jurisdictions, it is potentially a serious breach of professional ethics.

With current technology, things might seem a bit hazy but, basically, without the express permission of BPP Learning Media:

- Photocopying our materials is a breach of copyright
- Scanning, ripcasting or conversion of our digital materials into different file formats, uploading them to facebook or emailing them to your friends is a breach of copyright

You can, of course, sell your books, in the form in which you have bought them – once you have finished with them. (Is this fair to your fellow students? We update for a reason.) But the e-products are sold on a single user licence basis: we do not supply 'unlock' codes to people who have bought them second-hand.

And what about outside the UK? BPP Learning Media strives to make our materials available at prices students can afford by local printing arrangements, pricing policies and partnerships which are clearly listed on our website. A tiny minority ignore this and indulge in criminal activity by illegally photocopying our material or supporting organisations that do. If they act illegally and unethically in one area, can you really trust them?

How the BPP ACCA-approved Study Text can help you pass your exams – AND help you with your Practical Experience Requirement!

NEW FEATURE – the PER alert!

Before you can qualify as an ACCA member, you do not only have to pass all your exams but also fulfil a three year **practical experience requirement** (PER). To help you to recognise areas of the syllabus that you might be able to apply in the workplace to achieve different performance objectives, we have introduced the '**PER alert**' feature. You will find this feature throughout the Study Text to remind you that what you are **learning to pass** your ACCA exams is **equally useful to the fulfilment of the PER requirement**.

Tackling studying

Studying can be a daunting prospect, particularly when you have lots of other commitments. The **different features** of the text, the **purposes** of which are explained fully on the **Chapter features** page, will help you whilst studying and improve your chances of **exam success**.

Developing exam awareness

Our Texts are completely **focused** on helping you pass your exam.

Our advice on **Studying F8** outlines the **content** of the paper, the **necessary skills** the examiner expects you to demonstrate and any **brought forward knowledge** you are expected to have.

Exam focus points are included within the chapters to highlight when and how specific topics were examined, or how they might be examined in the future.

Using the Syllabus and Study Guide

You can find the syllabus, Study Guide and other useful resources for F8 on the ACCA website:

www.accaglobal.com/students/study_exams/qualifications/acca_choose/acca/fundamental/aa/

At the time of publication the Syllabus and Study Guide for the 2010 exams were not available and so references to and extracts from these documents in this Study Text are to the Syllabus and Study Guide for the 2009 exams. This Study Text has been fully updated to reflect the 2010 versions, however, and these will be available on the ACCA website in due course.

The Study Text covers **all aspects** of the syllabus to ensure you are as fully prepared for the exam as possible.

Testing what you can do

Testing yourself helps you develop the skills you need to pass the exam and also confirms that you can recall what you have learnt.

We include **Questions** – lots of them - both within chapters and in the **Exam Question Bank**, as well as **Quick Quizzes** at the end of each chapter to test your knowledge of the chapter content.

Chapter features

Each chapter contains a number of helpful features to guide you through each topic.

Topic list

Topic list	Syllabus reference

Tells you what you will be studying in this chapter and the relevant section numbers, together the ACCA syllabus references.

Introduction — Puts the chapter content in the context of the syllabus as a whole.

Study Guide — Links the chapter content with ACCA guidance.

Exam Guide — Highlights how examinable the chapter content is likely to be and the ways in which it could be examined.

Knowledge brought forward from earlier studies — What you are assumed to know from previous studies/exams.

FAST FORWARD — Summarises the content of main chapter headings, allowing you to preview and review each section easily.

Examples — Demonstrate how to apply key knowledge and techniques.

Key terms — Definitions of important concepts that can often earn you easy marks in exams.

Exam focus points — Tell you when and how specific topics were examined, or how they may be examined in the future.

Formula to learn — Formulae that are not given in the exam but which have to be learnt.

This is a new feature that gives you a useful indication of syllabus areas that closely relate to performance objectives in your Practical Experience Requirement (PER).

Question — Give you essential practice of techniques covered in the chapter.

Case Study — Provide real world examples of theories and techniques.

Chapter Roundup — A full list of the Fast Forwards included in the chapter, providing an easy source of review.

Quick Quiz — A quick test of your knowledge of the main topics in the chapter.

Exam Question Bank — Found at the back of the Study Text with more comprehensive chapter questions. Cross referenced for easy navigation.

Studying F8

The F8 Audit and Assurance exam tests students' knowledge of auditing and assurance theory but also, very importantly, their ability to apply that knowledge to scenarios that they might well come across in their auditing careers.

There will be a new examiner for F8 from **June 2010**, **Pami Bahl**, who will be issuing her examiner's approach article to F8 later in 2009. You should look out for this article on the ACCA's website as it will provide useful information about the F8 exam from her perspective.

All questions on this paper are **compulsory** so any topic from across the syllabus could be examined. As stated above, it is essential that students possess both the **knowledge** of auditing and the ability to **apply that knowledge** to situations that could arise in real life.

1 What F8 is about

The purpose of the F8 syllabus is to develop **knowledge and understanding** of the process of carrying out the assurance engagement and its **application** in the context of the professional regulatory framework.

The syllabus is divided into **seven** main sections:

(a) **Audit framework and regulation**

The syllabus introduces the concept of assurance engagements such as the external audit and the different levels of assurance that can be provided. You need to understand the **purpose** of an external audit and the respective **roles** of auditors and management. This part of the syllabus also explains the importance of good **corporate governance** within an entity. The **regulatory framework** is also explained, as well as the key area of **professional ethics**.

(b) **Internal audit**

In this part of the syllabus we explain the nature of internal audit and describe its role as part of overall **performance management** and good **corporate governance** within an entity. It is essential that you understand the differences between internal and external audit at this stage.

(c) **Planning and risk assessment**

Planning and risk assessment are key stages of the external audit because it is the information and knowledge gained at this time that determine the audit approach to take. We also develop further the concept of **materiality** which was introduced briefly in the first part of the syllabus.

(d) **Internal control**

In this part of the syllabus you need to be able to describe and evaluate information systems and **internal controls** to identify and communicate **control risks** and their potential consequences to the entity's management, making appropriate recommendations to mitigate those risks. We cover key areas of purchases, sales, payroll, inventory, cash and non-current assets.

(e) **Audit evidence**

Audit conclusions need to be supported by **sufficient** and **appropriate** audit evidence. This area of the syllabus assesses the **reliability** of various types and sources of audit evidence and also examines in detail the audit of specific items (non-current assets, inventory, receivables, bank and cash and payables). We also look at the special considerations for the audit of not-for-profit organisations such as charities, which could come up in a scenario-based question.

(f) **Review**

Towards the end of an external audit, the auditor needs to consider the concept of **going concern** and **subsequent events** which could impact on the financial statements. We also look at the audit evidence provided by **written representations from management** and consider the impact of any **unadjusted errors** on the accounts.

(g) **Reporting**

The outcome of the external audit is the **audit report** which sets out the **auditor's opinion** on the financial statements. This section of the syllabus looks at the various types of audit report that can be issued and what each of them means. It also looks at **reports to management**, which are a by-product of the audit but nevertheless very important for high-lighting areas of weakness to management.

2 What skills are required?

F8 builds on the knowledge and understanding gained from Paper F3 *Financial Accounting.*

You must possess good technical knowledge of audit and financial reporting but one of the key skills you will need to is to be able to **apply** your knowledge to the question.

Another important skill you will need is to be able to **explain key ideas, techniques or approaches**. Explaining means providing simple definitions and including the reasons why these approaches have been developed. Your explanations need to be clearly focused on the particular scenario in the question.

Question 1 of the paper will be scenario-based for 30 marks, broken down into several parts. It is important to read the question requirements carefully and make sure that you answer the question set. This applies equally to all the other questions in the paper too. Question 2 is a knowledge-based question for 10 marks but here again, make sure you answer the question set, bearing in mind also the number of marks available for each part of the question – it's far too easy to be tempted to write down everything you know about a particular aspect of the syllabus but this is counter-productive if the question is only worth three marks and you have spent 15 minutes on it.

3 How to improve your chances of passing

Cover the whole syllabus

All the questions in paper F8 are **compulsory**. It is therefore very important that you cover the whole syllabus in your studies – question spotting is unwise and not recommended. Question 2 on the paper is a knowledge-based question for 10 marks which could be drawn from across the syllabus and is an opportunity for you to score the more straightforward marks on this paper.

Question practice

Question practice is a **key** part of your revision and will allow you to develop your application skills. Use the questions in the question bank in this Study Text and later in the BPP *Practice and Revision Kit* for F8.

Analysis and answering of questions

You need to consider the question **requirements** carefully so that you answer the question set. For example, if the requirements ask you to 'explain', make sure that you do so, rather than just produce a list of bullet points.

When answering questions, you need to ensure that your answers are **relevant** to the scenario in the question – do not just produce a general answer covering everything you know about a particular area. This is an inefficient use of your time and will not score you many marks.

Employ good exam technique

The following aspects of exam technique are particularly relevant in this paper.

- **Sub-headings** and leaving **spaces between paragraphs** help to demonstrate that your answer is clearly structured and emphasise the points you are making.
- **Short paragraphs** (2-3 sentences) help you keep to the point, but avoid 2-3 word bullet points.
- **Time management** is key in this paper but less likely to be a problem if you do the longest question (Question 1) first.
- **Reading the question carefully** first is important in ensuring that you answer the question set.

4 Brought forward knowledge

The F8 syllabus assumes knowledge brought forward form F3 *Financial Accounting*. It's important to be comfortable with your financial reporting studies because such aspects are likely to come up in scenario-based questions such as subsequent events. ACCA therefore recommends that you sit papers in order so you have the knowledge from Paper F7 *Financial Reporting* which will also be an advantage when taking Paper F8. However, please note that you do **not** have to have passed F7 in order to sit F8.

The exam paper

Format of the paper

The exam is a three-hour paper consisting of five compulsory questions. You also have 15 minutes for reading and planning.

The majority of the questions will be discursive but some questions involving computational elements could be set from time to time. The questions will cover all areas of the syllabus.

Question 1 will be a scenario-based question worth 30 marks. Question 2 will be a knowledge-based question worth 10 marks. The remaining three questions will be worth 20 marks each.

Guidance

Question 1 is very likely to test areas from the statement of comprehensive income and the statement of financial position. Internal audit/review could be examined in questions 1 or 4. Audit completion and audit reports will possibly be tested in question 5 in a scenario context. Question 2 is a knowledge-based question worth 10 marks and split into parts. This question can test topics from across the F8 syllabus.

Other key areas are:

- Application of professional ethics
- Audit planning
- Risk identification in systems and reporting weaknesses to management
- Engagement risk

Analysis of past papers – F8 Audit and Assurance

The table below provides details of when each element of the syllabus has been examined and the question number and section in which each element appeared. Further details can be found in the Exam Guide sections and Exam Focus Points in the relevant chapters.

Covered in Text chapter		June 2009	Dec 2008	June 2008	Dec 2007	Pilot Paper
	AUDIT FRAMEWORK AND REGULATION					
1	Audit and other assurance engagements			5d		
2	Statutory audit and regulation		2b			
3	Corporate governance	4b				3b, c
4	Professional ethics	5b	3a		2a	2a, 3a
	INTERNAL AUDIT					
5	Internal audit	4a	3b	4	3a	4b, c
	PLANNING AND RISK ASSESSMENT					
6	Risk assessment	3, 5b	4		4c	
7	Audit planning and documentation	1a				
8	Introduction to audit evidence	2b	1d	2a, c		
	INTERNAL CONTROL					
9	Internal control			1a	1c, d	1c, 4a
10	Tests of controls	1b	1a, b	1b	1c	1c, 4a
	AUDIT EVIDENCE					
11	Audit procedures and sampling	1c, 2a, 3	1c, 2a	3a, b	1d, 4	1d, 2b
12	Non-current assets		2c			
13	Inventory				1b	
14	Receivables	1d		1c, d	4a	
15	Cash and bank			3c	3b	
16	Liabilities and capital				1a	1a, b
17	Not-for-profit organisations		4b, c			
	REVIEW					
18	Audit review and finalisation	5a	5	2b, 5	2b, 5a	5
	REPORTING					
19	Reports	2c			5	2c, 5

P A R T

A

Audit framework and regulation

Audit and other assurance engagements

1

Topic list	Syllabus reference
1 The purpose of external audit engagements	A1
2 Accountability, stewardship and agency	A1
3 Types of assurance services	A1
4 Assurance and reports	A1, A2

Introduction

In the first section of this chapter we consider why there is a need for assurance in relation to financial and non-financial information. The main reason an assurance service such as external audit is required is the fact that the ownership and management of a company are not necessarily one and the same.

In Section 2 we introduce the concepts of agency, accountability and stewardship and consider reporting as a means of communication to the different stakeholders who are interested in the financial statements of the company.

It is important to understand what other assurance services exist in addition to the external audit. The key assurance services which the F8 syllabus concentrates on are the external audit (statutory and non-statutory), review engagements and internal audit assignments.

The effect of audits and reviews is that the stakeholders of an entity are given a level of assurance as to the quality of the information in the accounts. The degrees of assurance provided by external audits and other engagements are discussed in Section 4.

The remainder of the Study Text builds on the themes introduced in this chapter.

Study guide

		Intellectual level
A1	The concept of audit and other assurance engagements	
(a)	Identify and describe the objective and general principles of external audit engagements	2
(b)	Explain the nature and development of audit and other assurance engagements	1
(c)	Discuss the concepts of accountability, stewardship and agency	2
(d)	Discuss the concepts of materiality, true and fair presentation and reasonable assurance	2
(e)	Explain reporting as a means of communication to different stakeholders	1
(f)	Explain the level of assurance provided by audit and other review assignments	1
A2	Statutory audits	
(f)	Describe the limitations of statutory audits	1

Exam guide

This chapter explains the basis of auditing and the distinction between audit and other review assignments. The mechanics of these issues are expanded in more detail throughout the text. Questions in the exam could draw on matters in this chapter, in conjunction with the knowledge you will obtain later in the Study Text. The June 2007 paper had a four mark question for explaining what negative assurance is and how it differs from the assurance provided by a statutory audit.

1 The purpose of external audit engagements

FAST FORWARD

An **external audit** is a type of **assurance engagement** that is carried out by an auditor to give an independent opinion on a set of financial statements.

1.1 Objective of external audit

Key term

The objective of an **audit** of financial statements is to enable the auditor to express an opinion on whether the financial statements are prepared, in all material respects, in accordance with an applicable financial reporting framework. An audit of financial statements is an example of an assurance engagement.

The purpose of an external audit is to enable auditors to **give an opinion** on the financial statements. Whilst an audit might produce by-products such as advice to the directors on how to run the business, its objective is **solely to report to shareholders.**

1.1.1 Statutory and non-statutory audits

In most countries, audits are required under national statute for many undertakings, including limited liability companies. Other organisations and entities requiring a statutory audit may include charities, investment businesses and trade unions. In the UK for example, under registered companies' legislation (currently the Companies Act 2006), most companies are required to have an audit.

The statutory audit can bring various advantages to the company and shareholders. The key benefit to shareholders is the impartial view provided by the auditors. However, the company also benefits from professional accountants reviewing the accounts and system as part of the audit. Advantages might include recommendations being made in relation to accounting and control systems and the possibility that auditors might detect fraud and error.

Non-statutory audits are performed by independent auditors because the company's owners, proprietors, members, trustees, professional and governing bodies or other interested parties want them, rather than because the law requires them. In consequence, **auditing may extend** to every type of undertaking which produces accounts, including clubs, charities (some of these will require statutory audits as well), sole traders and partnerships. Some of these organisations do not operate for profit, and this has a specific impact on the nature of their audit. The audit of not-for-profit organisations will be considered in more detail in Chapter 17.

1.1.2 Advantages of the non-statutory audit

In addition to the advantages common to all forms of audit, a non-statutory audit can bring other advantages. For example, the audit of the accounts of a **partnership** may be seen to have the following advantages.

(a) It can provide a means of **settling accounts** between the partners.

(b) Where audited accounts are available this may make the **accounts more acceptable** to the **taxation authorities** when it comes to agreeing an individual partner's liability to tax.

(c) The **sale** of the business or the **negotiation of loan or overdraft facilities** may be facilitated if the firm is able to produce audited accounts.

(d) An audit on behalf of a **'sleeping partner'** is useful since generally such a person will have little other means of checking the accounts of the business or confirming the share of profits due to him or her.

2 Accountability, stewardship and agency

FAST FORWARD

An audit provides **assurance** to the shareholders and other stakeholders of a company on the financial statements because it is **independent and impartial.**

2.1 The nature and development of audit and other assurance engagements

The accounting and auditing professions have come under the public spotlight for many years now and as a result of certain events, many changes have occurred in relation to audit and assurance engagements.

As a result of the stock market bubble of the late 1990s and speculation over the future of 'dotcom' companies, many countries experienced huge **corporate financial scandals and frauds**. The bubble burst in 2000 and was followed by the revelation that senior management at **Enron**, a US energy company, had been deceiving investors by fraudulently overstating profitability. Its auditor, **Arthur Andersen**, was shown to have lacked objectivity in evaluating its accounting methods. This led to the demise of Arthur Andersen in 2002.

Other companies that were also involved in corporate frauds included WorldCom, Parmalat, Cable & Wireless and Xerox, to name but a few. The subsequent fallout of these frauds was a lack of confidence in the way companies were run and audited. In the USA, this resulted in the **Sarbanes-Oxley Act 2002** which has radically changed the **regulation** of the accounting profession in the USA and influenced such issues worldwide.

The above events illustrate the importance of auditing and other assurance engagements to companies. We will go on to demonstrate this below.

2.2 Accountability and stewardship

The key reason for having an audit or review can be seen by working through the following case study.

Case Study

Vera decides to set up a business selling flowers. She gets up early in the morning, visits the market, and then sets up a stall by the side of the road. For the first year, all goes well. She sells all the flowers she is able to buy and she derives some income from the business.

However, Vera feels that she could sell more flowers if she was able to transport more to the place where she sells them, and she also knows that there are several other roads nearby where she could sell flowers, if she could be in two places at once. She could achieve these two things by buying a van and by employing other people to sell flowers in other locations.

Vera needs more money to achieve this expansion of her business. She decides to ask her rich friend Peter to invest in the business.

Peter can see the potential of Vera's business and wants to invest, but he doesn't want to be involved in the management of the business. He also does not want to have ultimate liability for the debts of the business if it fails. He therefore suggests that they set up a limited company. He will own the majority of the shares and be entitled to dividends. Vera will be managing director and be paid a salary for her work.

At the end of the first year of trading as a limited company, Peter receives a copy of the financial statements. Profits are lower than expected, so his dividend will not be a large as he had hoped. He knows that Vera is paid a salary so does not care as much as him that profits are low.

Peter is concerned by the level of profits and feels that he wants further assurance on the accounts. He doesn't know whether they give a true reflection on the last year's trading, particularly as the profits do not seem as high as those Vera had predicted when he agreed to invest.

The solution is that the **assurance** Peter is seeking can be given by an independent **audit or review** of the financial statements. An auditor can provide the two things that Peter requires:

- A **knowledgeable review** of the company's business and of the accounts
- An **impartial view**, since Vera's view might be biased

Other people will also view the company's accounts with interest, for example:

- Creditors of the company
- Taxation authorities

The various parties interested in the accounts of a company are sometimes referred to as **stakeholders**. Although they will each judge the accounts by different criteria, they will all **gain assurance** from learning that the accounts they are reading have been subject to an independent report.

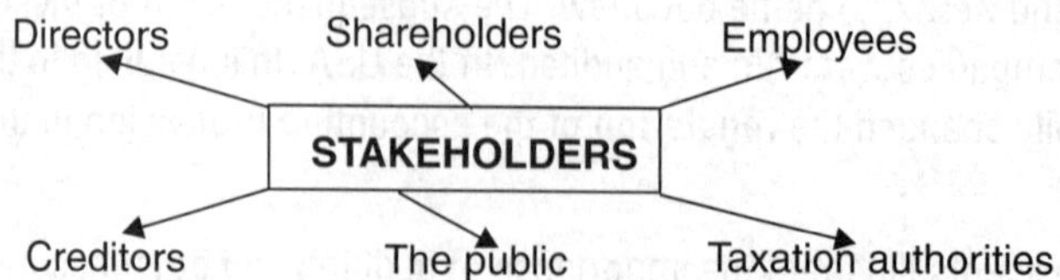

The example above is a simple one. In practice companies may have thousands of shareholders and may not know the management personally. It is therefore important that directors are **accountable** to shareholders. Directors act as **stewards** of the shareholders' investments. They are **agents** of the shareholders.

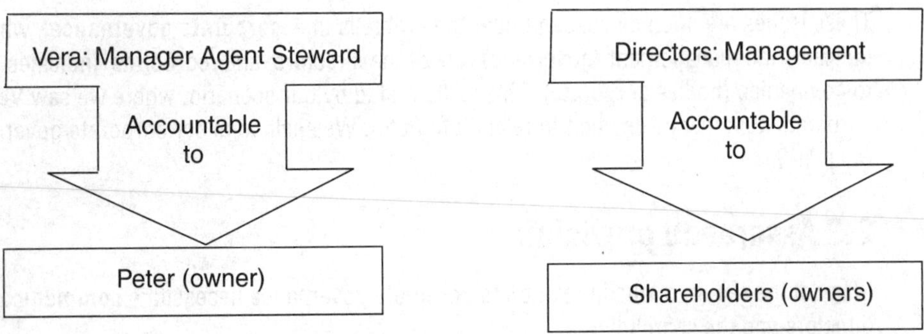

Key terms

Accountability is the quality or state of being accountable, that is, being required or expected to justify actions and decisions. It suggests an obligation or willingness to accept responsibility for one's actions.

Stewardship refers to the duties and obligations of a person who manages another person's property.

Agents are people employed or used to provide a particular service. In the case of a company, the people being used to provide the service of managing the business also have the second role of being people in their own right trying to maximise their personal wealth.

You may ask, 'what are the directors accountable for?' It is important to understand the answer to this question. The directors are accountable for the **shareholders' investment**. The shareholders have bought shares in that company (they have invested). They **expect a return** from their investment. As the **directors** manage the company, they are **in a position to affect that return.**

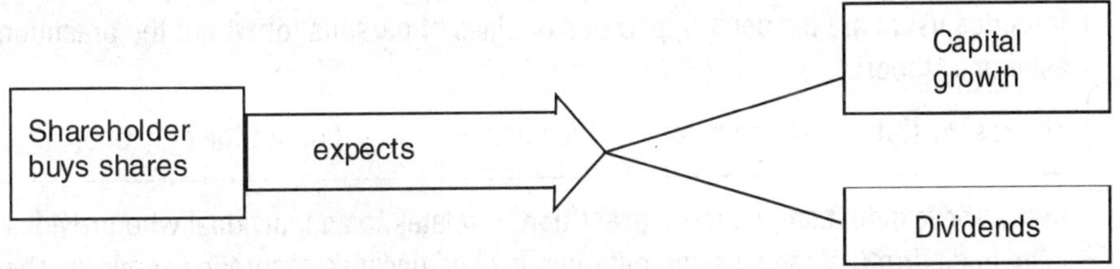

The exact nature of the return expected by the shareholder will depend on the type of company he or she has chosen to invest in: that is part of his or her investment risk analysis. Certain issues are true of any such investment, however. For example, if the directors **mismanage** the company, and it goes **bankrupt**, it will neither provide a source of future dividends, nor will it create capital growth in the investment – indeed, the opposite is true and the original investment may even be lost.

Accountability therefore covers a range of issues:

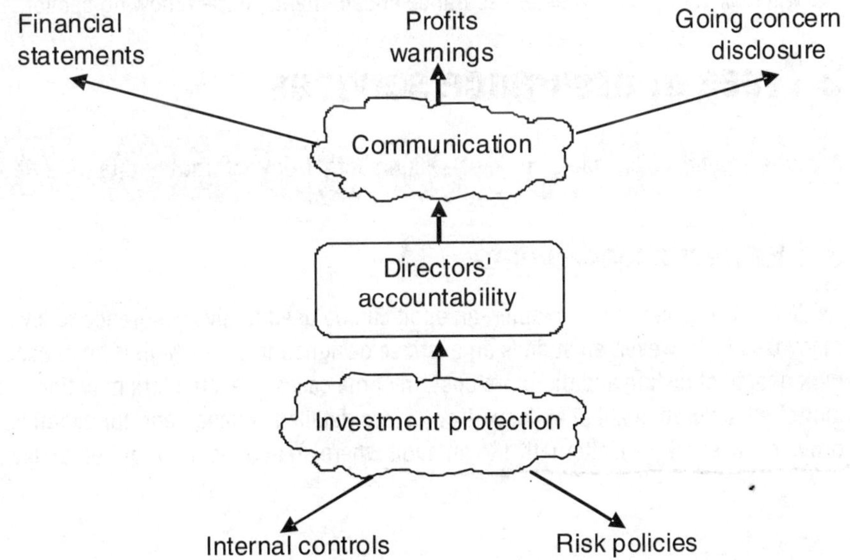

These issues are often discussed under the umbrella title '**corporate governance'**, where 'governance' indicates the management (governing) role of the directors, and 'corporate' indicates that the issue relates to companies (bodies corporate). This is illustrated by our scenario, where we saw Vera taking up a corporate governance position in relation to Peter. We shall consider corporate governance further in Chapter 3.

2.3 Assurance provision

Many of the requirements in relation to corporate governance necessitate **communication** between the directors and the shareholders.

As discussed in Section 1, **directors** of all companies are usually **required to produce financial statements** annually which give a **true and fair view** of the affairs of the company and its profit or loss for the period. They are also **encouraged** to **communicate with shareholders** on matters relating to **directors' pay** and **benefits** (this is required by law in the case of public limited companies), **going concern** and **management of risks**.

But how will the shareholders know whether the directors' communications are **accurate**, or present a **fair picture?** We are back to the problem that Peter had in the scenario we presented at the beginning of this section. He knew that Vera's view might be **biased** in a different way to his own, and he sought **assurance** on the information he was presented with.

Key terms

An **assurance engagement** is one in which a practitioner expresses a conclusion designed to enhance the degree of confidence of the intended users other than the responsible party about the outcome of the evaluation or measurement of a subject matter against criteria. The outcome of the evaluation or measurement of a subject matter is the information that results from applying the criteria.

Intended users are the person, persons or class of persons for whom the practitioner prepares the assurance report.

The **responsible party** can be one of the intended users, but not the only one.

In the above definition, the term '**practitioner**' relates to an individual who provides professional services in an audit firm (i.e. the term 'practitioner' is used because assurance services other than external audits are also provided by audit firms).

The '**responsible party**' is the person (or persons) who is responsible for the subject matter (in a direct reporting engagement) or subject matter information of the assurance engagement. Subject matter can take many forms which include financial performance (e.g. historical financial information), non-financial performance (e.g. key performance indicators), processes (e.g. internal control) and behaviour (e.g. compliance with laws and regulations).

We will look at different types of assurance engagements in the following section.

3 Types of assurance services

FAST FORWARD

Assurance services include a range of assignments, from **external audits** to **review engagements**.

3.1 Review engagements

As discussed earlier in this chapter, an audit can be used to give assurance to a variety of stakeholders on many issues. However, an audit is an exercise designed to give a high level of assurance and involves a high degree of testing and therefore cost. In some cases, stakeholders may find that they receive **sufficient assurance** about an issue from a less detailed engagement, for example, a **review**. A review can provide a cost-efficient alternative to an audit where an audit is not required by law.

Key term

> The objective of a **review engagement** is to enable an auditor to state whether, on the basis of procedures which do not provide all the evidence that would be required in an audit, anything has come to the auditor's attention that causes the auditor to believe that the financial statements are not prepared, in all material respects, in accordance with an applicable financial reporting framework.

The major outcome for recipients of a review engagement is that the **level of assurance** they gain from it is not as high as from an audit, although the procedures carried out in a review engagement are similar to an audit.

3.2 Internal audit reviews

FAST FORWARD

> **Internal auditors** are employed as part of an organisation's system of controls. Their responsibilities are determined by management and may be wide-ranging.

Key term

> **Internal auditing** is an appraisal or monitoring activity established or provided as a service to the entity. Its functions include examining, evaluating and monitoring the adequacy and effectiveness of internal control.

Up to now we have discussed assurance services where an independent outsider provides an opinion on financial information. Assurance can also be provided to management (and by implication, to other parties) by **internal auditors**.

As we shall see in Chapter 3, as part of good corporate governance all directors are advised to review the effectiveness of the company's risk management and internal control systems. They should also consider the need for an **internal audit function to help them carry out their duties.**

Larger organisations may therefore appoint full-time staff whose **function is to monitor and report on the running of the company's operations**. Internal audit staff members are one type of control. Although some of the work carried out by internal auditors is similar to that performed by external auditors, there are **important distinctions** between the two functions in terms of their responsibilities, scope and relationship with the company, and we will examine these in more detail in Chapter 5.

4 Assurance and reports

FAST FORWARD

> The auditors' report on company financial statements is expressed in terms of **truth** and **fairness**. This is generally taken to mean that financial statements:
>
> - Are factual
> - Are free from bias
> - Reflect the commercial substance of the business's transactions

4.1 Truth and fairness

Below is an example of an auditor's report on an entity's financial statements. This is an **unmodified** report (which means the financial statements are true and fair and properly prepared).

INDEPENDENT AUDITOR'S REPORT

[Appropriate addressee]

Report on the financial statements

We have audited the financial statements of ABC company, which comprise the balance sheet* as at 31 December, 20X1, and the income statement*, statement of changes in equity and cash flow statement* for the year then ended, and a summary of significant accounting policies and other explanatory information.

Management's responsibility for the financial statements

Management is responsible for the preparation and fair presentation of these financial statements in accordance with International Financial Reporting Standards, and for such internal control as management determines is necessary to enable the preparation of financial statements that are free from material misstatement, whether due to fraud or error.

Auditor's responsibility

Our responsibility is to express an opinion on these financial statements based on our audit. We conducted our audit in accordance with International Standards on Auditing. Those standards require that we comply with ethical requirements and plan and perform the audit to obtain reasonable assurance about whether the financial statements are free from material misstatement.

An audit involves performing procedures to obtain audit evidence about the amounts and disclosures in the financial statements. The procedures selected depend on the auditor's judgement, including the assessment of the risks of material misstatement of the financial statements, whether due to fraud or error. In making those risk assessments, the auditor considers internal control relevant to the entity's preparation and fair presentation of the financial statements in order to design audit procedures that are appropriate in the circumstances, but not for the purpose of expressing an opinion on the effectiveness of the entity's internal control. An audit also includes evaluating the appropriateness of accounting policies used and the reasonableness of accounting estimates made by management, as well as evaluating the overall presentation of the financial statements.

We believe that the audit evidence we have obtained is sufficient and appropriate to provide a basis for our audit opinion.

Opinion

In our opinion the financial statements present fairly, in all material respects, (or *give a true and fair view of*) the financial position of ABC Company as at December 31, 20X1, and (*of*) its financial performance and its cash flows for the year then ended in accordance with International Financial Reporting Standards.

Report on other legal and regulatory requirements

[Form and content of this section of the auditor's report will vary depending on the nature of the auditor's other reporting responsibilities.]

[Auditor's signature]

[Date of the auditor's report]

[Auditor's address]

*Note: This example of an auditor's report is in accordance with the relevant auditing standard. However, you may also come across the term 'statement of financial position' (for 'balance sheet'), 'statement of comprehensive income' (for 'income statement') and 'statement of cash flows' (for 'cash flow statement') in accordance with IAS 1 *Presentation of financial statements.*

Modified audit reports may arise because of a number of different reasons and are discussed in greater depth in Chapter 19.

External auditors give an opinion on the **truth and fairness** of financial statements. This is not an opinion of absolute correctness. 'True' and 'fair' are not defined in law or audit guidance, but the following definitions are generally accepted.

Key terms

> **True:** Information is factual and conforms with reality. In addition the information conforms with required standards and law. The financial statements have been correctly extracted from the books and records.
>
> **Fair:** Information is free from discrimination and bias and in compliance with expected standards and rules. The accounts should reflect the commercial substance of the company's underlying transactions.

The auditor's report refers to the fact that the audit is planned and performed to obtain 'reasonable assurance' whether the financial statements are free from material misstatement. This is because the auditor cannot check everything and therefore can only provide 'reasonable' not 'absolute' assurance.

Key term

> An audit gives the reader **reasonable assurance** on the truth and fairness of the financial statements, which is a high, but not absolute, level of assurance. The auditor's report does not guarantee that the financial statements are correct, but that they are true and fair within a reasonable margin of error.

One of the reasons that an auditor does not give absolute assurance is because of the **inherent limitations** of audit. We discuss these limitations below.

4.2 Limitations of audit and materiality

FAST FORWARD

> External audits give **reasonable assurance** that the financial statements are free from material misstatement.

The assurance given by auditors is governed by the fact that auditors use **judgement** in deciding what audit procedures to use and what conclusions to draw, and also by the **limitations** of every audit. These are illustrated in the following diagram.

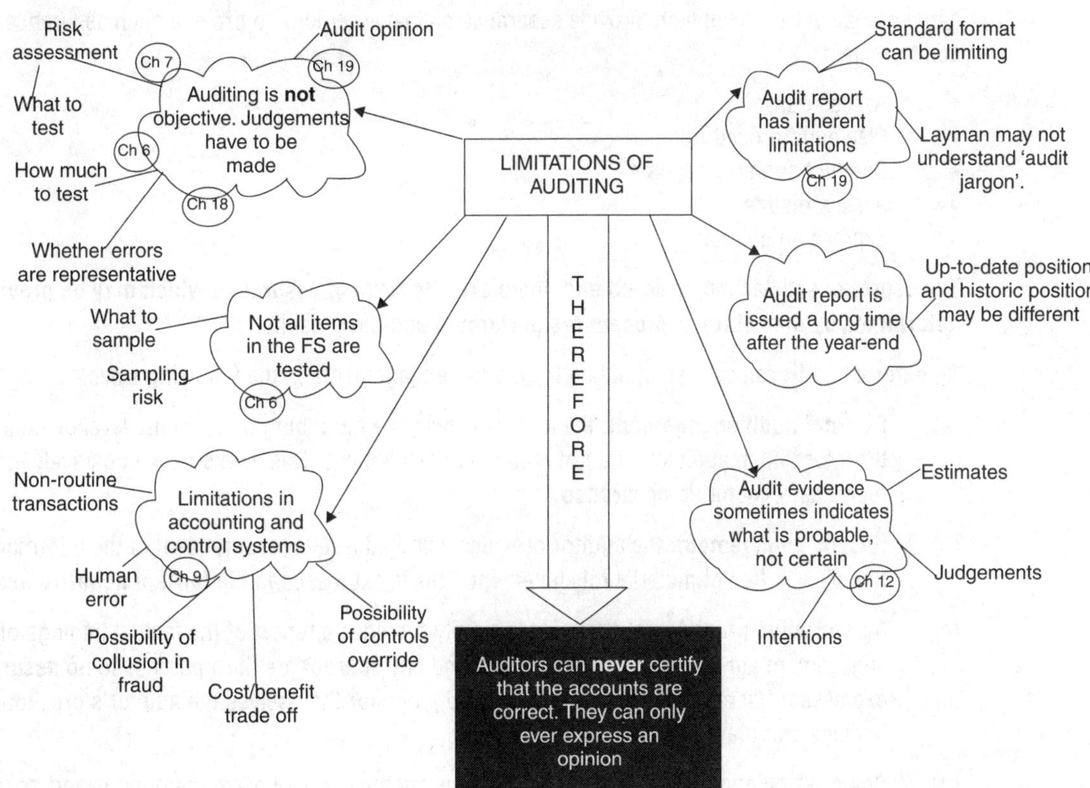

Misstatements which are significant to readers may exist in financial statements and auditors will plan their work on this basis, that is, with **professional scepticism**. The concept of '**significance to readers**' is the concept of **materiality** (which will be discussed in more detail in Chapter 6).

Key term

Materiality is an expression of the relative significance or importance of a particular matter in the context of the financial statements as a whole. A matter is material if its omission or misstatement would reasonably influence the economic decisions of users taken on the basis of the financial statements. Materiality depends on the size of the item or error judged in the particular circumstances of its omission or misstatement.

The auditors' task is to decide whether the financial statements show a **true and fair view**. The auditors are not responsible for establishing whether the financial statements are correct in every particular. This is because it can take a great deal of time and trouble to check the accuracy of even a very small transaction and the resulting benefit may not justify the effort. Also financial accounting inevitably involves a degree of estimation which means that financial statements can never be completely precise.

Although the definition of materiality refers to the decisions of the addressees of the audit report (the company's members), their decisions may well be influenced by other entities who use the financial statements, for example, the bank.

4.3 Levels of assurance

FAST FORWARD

The **degree of assurance** given by the impartial professional will depend on the nature of the exercise being carried out.

'Assurance' here means **the auditors' satisfaction as to the reliability of the assertion made by one party for use by another party**.

Key term

Negative assurance is when an auditor gives an assurance that nothing has come to his attention which indicates that the financial statements have not been prepared according to the framework. In other words, he gives his assurance in the absence of any evidence to the contrary.

Directors prepare financial statements for the benefit of members. They **assert** that the financial statements give a true and fair view. The auditors provide **assurance** on that assertion. To provide such assurance, the auditors must:

- Assess risk
- Plan audit procedures
- Conduct audit procedures
- Assess results
- Express an opinion

The degree of satisfaction achieved and, therefore, **the level of assurance which may be provided**, is **determined by** the **nature** of **procedures performed** and their results.

An **external audit** can be distinguished from other engagements in the following ways.

(a) **External audit engagement:** the auditor provides a high, but not absolute, level of assurance that the information audited is free of material misstatement. This is expressed positively in the audit report as **reasonable assurance.**

(b) **Review engagement:** the auditor provides a limited level of assurance that the information subject to review is free of material misstatement. This is expressed in the form of **negative assurance.**

(c) **Agreed-upon procedures:** the auditor simply provides a report of the factual findings of the engagement agreed by the auditor, entity and any appropriate third parties, so **no assurance** is expressed. Users of the report must instead judge for themselves the auditor's procedures and findings and draw their own conclusions.

(d) **Compilation engagement:** the practitioner is engaged to use his accounting expertise (as opposed to auditing expertise) to collect, classify and summarise financial information. **No assurance** is expressed.

The following table summarises the different types of engagement that can be carried out by practitioners.

Engagement	Type of assurance provided	Examples
External audit	Reasonable	– Statutory external audit
Review	Negative	– Review of interim financial statements
Agreed-upon procedures	None	– Examination of statement of financial position – Examination of segmental sales and profit
Compilation	None	– Preparation of financial statements – Preparation of tax returns

Exam focus point

You must understand the levels of assurance provided by different types of engagement as you could be asked to explain this in the exam.

Chapter Roundup

- An **external audit** is a type of **assurance engagement** that is carried out by an auditor to give an independent opinion on a set of financial statements.
- An audit provides **assurance** to the shareholders and other stakeholders of a company on the financial statements because it is **independent and impartial**.
- Assurance services include a range of assignments, from **external audits** to **review engagements**.
- **Internal auditors** are employed as part of an organisation's system of controls. Their responsibilities are determined by management and may be wide-ranging.
- The auditors' report on company financial statements is expressed in terms of **truth** and **fairness**. This is generally taken to mean that financial statements:
  - Are factual
  - Are free from bias
  - Reflect the commercial substance of the business's transactions
- External audits give **reasonable assurance** that the financial statements are free from material misstatement.
- The **degree of assurance** given by the impartial professional will depend on the nature of the exercise being carried out.

Quick Quiz

1 Complete the IFAC definition of an audit:

The objective of an .... of .... is to enable the auditor to .... an .... on whether the financial statements are prepared, in all .... respects, in accordance with an identified financial reporting framework.

2 Link the correct definition to each term.

(i)	Accountable	(iv)	True
(ii)	Steward	(v)	Fair
(iii)	Agent	(vi)	Materiality

(a) An expression of the relative significance or importance of a particular matter in the context of the financial statements as a whole.

(b) A person employed to provide a particular service.

(c) Factual and conforming with reality. In conformity with relevant standards and law and correctly extracted from accounting records.

(d) A person employed to manage other people's property.

(e) Free from discrimination and bias and in compliance with expected standards and rules. Reflecting the commercial substance of underlying transactions.

(f) Being required or expected to justify actions and decisions.

3 What level of assurance is provided by a review engagement?

4 Which of the following is not an assurance engagement?

- External audit
- Compilation engagement
- Review engagement
- Agreed-upon procedures

Answers to Quick Quiz

1 Audit, financial statements, express, opinion, material

2 (i) (f) (iv) (c)
(ii) (d) (v) (e)
(iii) (b) (vi) (a)

3 Negative assurance

4 Compilation engagements and agreed-upon procedures are not assurance engagements.

Now try the question below from the Exam Question Bank

Number	Level	Marks	Time
Q1	Introductory	n/a	n/a

Statutory audit and regulation

2

Topic list	Syllabus reference
1 Objective of statutory audits and the audit opinion	A2
2 Appointment, removal and resignation of auditors	A2
3 Regulation of auditors	A2
4 International Standards on Auditing	A3

Introduction

This chapter describes the aims and objectives of the statutory audit and the regulatory environment within which it takes place.

The regulatory framework for auditors discussed in this chapter and the regulation of auditors by bodies such as the ACCA are very important.

This chapter considers in detail the regulatory aspects of the appointment, removal and resignation of auditors.

It ends with an examination of International Standards on Auditing which auditors must comply with when carrying out an external audit.

Study guide

		Intellectual level
A2	**Statutory audits**	
(a)	Describe the regulatory environment within which statutory audits take place	1
(b)	Discuss the reasons and mechanisms for the regulation of auditors	2
(c)	Explain the statutory regulations governing the appointment, removal and resignation of auditors	1
(d)	Discuss the types of opinion provided in statutory audits	2
(e)	State the objectives and principle activities of statutory audit and assess its value (eg in assisting management to reduce risk and improve performance)	1
(f)	Describe the limitations of statutory audits	1
A3	**The regulatory environment and corporate governance**	
(a)	Explain the development and status of International Standards on Auditing	1
(b)	Explain the relationship between International Standards on Auditing and national standards	1

Exam guide

An understanding of the overall regulatory regime is essential to an understanding of external audit and could be examined as part of a longer question on audit planning or in conjunction with a question on professional ethics. It could also come up as a short factual part in question 2 as it did in December 2008 as a three mark question on the rights of auditors.

1 Objective of statutory audits and the audit opinion

FAST FORWARD

Most companies are required to have an external audit by law, but some small companies are exempt. The outcome of the audit is the **audit report**, which sets out the auditor's **opinion** on the financial statements

1.1 The statutory audit opinion

As introduced in Chapter 1, the purpose of an audit is for the auditor to express an opinion on the financial statements.

The audit opinion may also **imply** certain things are true, because otherwise the audit report would have mentioned them. For example, in the UK, such implications include the following:

- **Adequate accounting records** have been kept.
- **Returns** adequate for the audit have been received from branches not visited.
- The **accounts agree** with the **accounting records** and **returns**.
- **All information and explanations** have been **received** that the auditor believes are necessary for the purposes of the audit.
- **Details** of **directors' emoluments** and **other benefits** have been correctly **disclosed** in the financial statements.
- Particulars of **loans** and **other transactions** in favour of **directors** and others have been correctly in the financial statements.

1.1.1 The value of the statutory audit

We have discussed already the principal aim of the external audit – to provide an independent opinion on the truth and fairness of the financial statements. However, an external audit can be invaluable to an entity because it may **enhance the credibility** of the financial statements because they will have been examined independently.

The external audit can also highlight other issues as a result of work relating to the financial statements in respect of **deficiencies in the internal control system** of the entity, which can be improved by the entity's management. We will look at this aspect later in this Study Text.

For these reasons, even where entities are not obliged to undergo an external audit, they may choose to do so, regardless of the costs involved (time and money) because the benefits outweigh those costs.

1.2 Small company audit exemption

The majority of companies are required by national law to have an audit. A key exception to this requirement is that given to small companies. Many EC countries have a small company exemption from audit that is based on the turnover and total assets at the year-end.

Note that unless otherwise stated, companies in the F8 paper will require an audit.

In most countries, the majority of companies are very small, employing few staff (if any) and are often owner-managed. This is very different from a large business where the owners (the shareholders) devolve the day-to-day running of the business to a group of managers or directors.

Key term

A **small entity** is any enterprise in which:

(a) There is concentration of ownership and management in a small number of individuals (often a single individual), and

(b) One or more of the following are also found:

- (i) Few sources of income and uncomplicated activities
- (ii) Unsophisticated record-keeping
- (iii) Limited internal controls together with the potential for management override of internal controls

There has long been a debate over the benefits of audit to small entities. Where such entities are owned by the same people that manage them, there is significantly less value in an independent review of the stewardship of the managers than where management and ownership are separate.

The case for retaining the small company audit rests on the value of the statutory audit to those who have an interest in audited financial statements, that is, the users of the financial statements. From the viewpoint of each type of user, the arguments for and against abolition are summarised in the table below.

User	For abolition	Against abolition
Shareholders	Benefit may not be worth the cost	Provides reassurance to shareholders not involved in managing. Assists in fair valuation of share in unquoted companies
Bank and other institutions or lenders	Doubt over whether banks rely on audited financial statements more than unaudited ones	Banks may rely on audited financial statements for making loans and reviewing value of security
Other payables	Limited reliance in practice as financial statements filed too late	Provides opportunity to assess strength of customers

User	For abolition	Against abolition
Taxation authorities	Little evidence whether reliance placed on audited financial statements	Taxation authorities may rely on audited financial statements to calculate corporation tax and check returns
Employees	Little evidence that employees make assessments of financial statements for wage negotiations	Employees entitled to assess financial statements for wage negotiations and considering future viability of their employer
Management	System review and management consultancy review would be of greater benefit and less or similar cost to audit	Useful independent check on accounting systems and recommendations for improving those systems

1.3 Auditor rights and duties

The law gives auditors both rights and duties. This allows auditors to have sufficient power to carry out an independent and effective audit.

The audit is primarily a statutory concept, and eligibility to conduct an audit is often set down in statute. Similarly, the rights and duties of auditors can be set down in law, to ensure that the auditors have sufficient power to carry out an effective audit. In this section we look at the rights and duties of auditors in the **UK as an example** (but bear in mind that these may be different in other jurisdictions). The relevant legislation in the UK is the **Companies Act 2006**.

1.3.1 Duties

The auditors are required to report on every balance sheet (statement of financial position) and profit and loss account (statement of comprehensive income) laid before the company in general meeting.

The auditors must consider the following.

Compliance with legislation	Whether the financial statements have been prepared in accordance with the relevant legislation
Truth and fairness of accounts	Whether the balance sheet shows a true and fair view of the company's affairs at the end of the period and the profit and loss account (and cash flow statement) show a true and fair view of the results for the period
Adequate accounting records and returns	Whether adequate accounting records have been kept and returns adequate for the audit received from branches not visited by the auditor
Agreement of accounts to records	Whether the accounts are in agreement with the accounting records and returns
Consistency of other information	Whether the information in the directors' report is consistent with the financial statements
Directors' benefits	Whether disclosure of directors' benefits has been made in accordance with the Companies Act 2006

1.3.2 Rights

The auditors must have certain rights to enable them to carry out their duties effectively.

The principal rights auditors should have, excepting those dealing with resignation or removal, are set out in the table below.

Access to records	A right of access at all times to the books, accounts and vouchers of the company (in whatever form they are held)
Information and explanations	A right to require from the company's officers such information and explanations as they think necessary for the performance of their duties as auditors
Attendance at/notices of general meetings	A right to attend any general meetings of the company and to receive all notices of and other communications relating to such meetings which any member of the company is entitled to receive
Attendance at/notices of general meetings	A right to be heard at general meetings which they attend on any part of the business that concerns them as auditors
Rights in relation to written resolutions	A right to receive a copy of any written resolution proposed

If auditors have not received all the information and explanations they consider necessary, they should state this fact in their audit report.

The Companies Act 2006 makes it an offence for a company's officer knowingly or recklessly to make a statement in any form to an auditor which:

- Conveys or purports to convey any information or explanation required by the auditor and
- Is misleading, false or deceptive in a material particular

2 Appointment, removal and resignation of auditors

FAST FORWARD

There are various legal and professional requirements on appointment, resignation and removal of auditors which must be followed.

2.1 Appointment

The auditors should be appointed by and therefore **answerable** to the **shareholders**. The table below shows what the position should ideally be, again using the **UK as an example**. The Companies Act 2006 sets out the rules for appointment of auditors. An auditor must be appointed for each financial year unless the directors reasonably resolve otherwise on the grounds that audited financial statements are unlikely to be required. The table summarises the appointment of auditors for UK public companies.

AUDITOR APPOINTMENT (UK)	
Directors	Can appoint auditor: (a) Before company's **first period for appointing auditors** (b) Following a period during which the company **did not have an** auditor (as exempt), at any time before the next period for appointing auditors (c) To fill a **casual vacancy**
Members	Can appoint auditor by ordinary resolution: (a) During a **period for appointing auditors** (b) If company **should have** appointed auditor during a period for appointing auditors **but failed to do so** (c) If directors **failed to do so**
Secretary of State	Can appoint auditors if **no auditors** are **appointed** per above

2.1.1 Remuneration

The remuneration of the auditors, which will include auditors' expenses, will be fixed by whoever made the appointment.

However the auditors' remuneration is fixed, in many countries it must be disclosed in the annual financial statements of the company.

2.2 Resignation and removal

The legal requirements for resignation and removal of auditors using the **UK as an example** are discussed below.

It is important that auditors know the procedures because as part of their client acceptance, they have a duty to ensure the old auditors were properly removed from office.

RESIGNATION OF AUDITORS (UK)		
1	Resignation procedures	Auditors deposit **written notice** together with **statement of circumstances** relevant to members/creditors or statement that no circumstances exist. A statement of circumstance must always be submitted for a quoted company, even if the auditor considers that there are no circumstances that should be brought to the attention of members or creditors.
2	Notice of resignation	Sent by **company** to regulatory authority
3	Statement of circumstances	Sent by: (a) Auditors to regulatory authority (b) Company to everyone entitled to receive a copy of accounts
4	Convening of general meeting	**Auditors** can **require directors** to call an **extraordinary general meeting** to discuss circumstances of resignation. Directors must send out notice for meeting within **21 days** of having received requisition by auditors.
5	Statement prior to general meeting	**Auditors** may require company to circulate (different) **statement of circumstances** to everyone entitled to notice of meeting.
6	Other rights of auditors	Can **receive all notices** that relate to: (a) A general meeting at which their term of office would have expired (b) A general meeting where casual vacancy caused by their resignation to be filled Can **speak** at these meetings on **any matter** which **concerns them as auditors**

REMOVAL OF AUDITORS (UK)		
1	Notice of removal	**Either special notice** (28 days) with copy sent to auditor **Or** if elective resolution in place, **written resolution** to terminate auditors' appointment Directors must convene meeting to take place within reasonable time.
2	Representations	**Auditors** can make **representations** on why they ought to stay in office, and may require company to state in notice that representations have been made and send copy to members.
3	If resolution passed	(a) Company must **notify** regulatory authority (b) Auditors must **deposit statement of circumstances** at company's registered office **within 14 days** of ceasing to hold office. Statement must be sent to regulatory authority.
4	Auditor rights	Can **receive notice** of and **speak** at: (a) General meeting at which their term of office would have expired (b) General meeting where casual vacancy caused by their removal is to be filled

The UK's Companies Act 2006 places a requirement on auditors to notify the appropriate audit authority in certain circumstances on leaving office.

If it is a **major audit** (quoted company or major public interest company), the notification must be given **whenever** an auditor ceases to hold office.

If it is **not a major audit**, the notification is only required if the auditor is leaving **before** the end of his term of office.

The appropriate audit authority is:

- Secretary of State or delegated body (such as the UK Professional Oversight Board) if a major audit
- Recognised Supervisory Body (eg ACCA) for other audits

Notice must inform the appropriate audit authority that the auditor has ceased to hold office and be accompanied by a statement of circumstances or no circumstances.

3 Regulation of auditors

FAST FORWARD

Requirements for the **eligibility**, **registration** and **training** of auditors are extremely important as they are designed to maintain standards in the auditing profession.

3.1 National level

The accounting and auditing profession varies in structure from country to country. In some countries accountants and auditors are subject to strict legislative regulation, while in others the profession is allowed to regulate itself. We cannot look at every country, but some of the examples below will show you the divergence of structure and we can make some general points.

3.1.1 United Kingdom

In the UK there are a number of different accountancy, or accountancy-related, institutes and associations, such as the Association of Chartered Certified Accountants (ACCA), the Institute of Chartered Accountants in England and Wales (ICAEW) and the Institute of Chartered Accountants of Scotland (ICAS). All these bodies vary from each other but they are all characterised by various attributes:

- Stringent entrance requirements (examinations and practical experience)
- Strict code of ethics
- Technical updating of members

3.1.2 France

In France, the accounting profession is split into two distinct organisations:

- Accountants (Ordre des Experts Comptables et des Comptables Agréés)
- Auditors (Compagnie Nationale des Commissaires aux Comptes)

Most members of the auditors' organisation are also members of the more important accountants' organisation. Examinations, work experience and articles are similar to those of the UK accountancy bodies. The profession's main influence is through the issue of non-mandatory opinions and recommendations of accounting principles relevant to the implementation of the National Plan.

3.1.3 Germany

The main professional body in Germany is the Institute of Certified Public Accountants (Institut der Wirtschaftsprüfer). Members of this institute carry out all the statutory audits, and are required to have very high educational and experience qualifications. The Institute issues a form of auditing standard but this is tied very closely to legislation. As well as auditing, members are mainly involved in tax and business management, with no obvious significant role in establishing financial accounting principles and practices. There is no independent accounting standard-setting body.

3.1.4 USA

In America, accountants are members of the American Institute of Certified Public Accountants (AICPA), a private sector body. Although the Securities and Exchange Commission in the USA can prescribe accounting standards for listed companies, it relies on the Financial Accounting Standards Board (FASB), an independent body, to set such standards. In turn, FASB keeps in close contact with the AICPA, which issues guidance on US standards and which is closely involved in their development.

3.1.5 Ghana

In Ghana, the Institute of Chartered Accountants (Ghana), established in 1963, is the sole body charged with the regulation of the accountancy profession. Its members are the only persons recognised under the country's companies' legislation to carry out the audit of company financial statements. The institute is governed by a council of 11 chartered accountants.

3.1.6 Singapore

The Institute of Certified Public Accountants of Singapore (ICPAS) is the national organisation of the accountancy profession in Singapore. It was established in 1963 and its objective is to develop, support and enhance the integrity, status and interests of the accountancy profession in Singapore. ICPAS has a Joint Scheme of Examination agreement in place with ACCA.

3.1.7 General points

It can be seen from the above paragraphs that the accounting and auditing profession in most Western Countries is regulated by legislation to some extent. In the UK and the USA the profession effectively regulates itself, ie regulation is devolved from statute to the private bodies involved in the accountancy profession. In many European countries, statutory control by governments is much more direct.

3.2 EC member states

Persons carrying out audits in EC member states must have the permission of the relevant authorities. In the UK the relevant authorities are **Recognised Supervisory Bodies** (RSBs). As well as giving authority, RSBs in the UK supervise and monitor auditors. In other countries however supervising and monitoring is carried out by a state body or by the national government.

The Companies Act 2006 defines an RSB as a body established in the UK which maintains and enforces rules as to the

- Eligibility of persons for appointment as a statutory auditor
- Conduct of statutory audit work

The following bodies are all RSBs:

- ACCA
- ICAEW
- ICAS
- ICAI (Institute of Chartered Accountants in Ireland)
- AAPA (Association of Authorised Public Accountants)

Professional qualifications, which will be prerequisites for membership of an RSB, are offered by **Recognised Qualifying Bodies** (RQBs) approved by the government. RQBs include ACCA, ICAEW and ICAS amongst others.

3.3 International level

Regulations governing auditors will, in most countries, be most important at the national level. International regulation, however, can play a major part by:

(a) Setting **minimum standards** and **requirements** for auditors
(b) Providing **guidance** for those countries without a **well-developed national regulatory framework**
(c) Aiding **intra-country recognition** of professional accountancy qualifications

3.3.1 International Federation of Accountants (IFAC)

IFAC, based in New York, is a non-profit, non-governmental, non-political international organisation of accountancy bodies. The ACCA is a member of IFAC.

IFAC came into being in the 1970s as a result of proposals put forward and eventually approved by the International Congress of Accountants. IFAC's mission is:

> 'The development and enhancement of the profession to enable it to provide services of consistently high quality in the public interest'.

IFAC co-operates with member bodies, regional organisations of accountancy bodies and other world organisations. Through such co-operation, IFAC initiates, co-ordinates and guides efforts to achieve international technical, ethical and educational pronouncements for the accountancy profession.

Any accountancy body may join IFAC if it is recognised by law or general consensus within its own country as a substantial national organisation of good standing within the accountancy profession. Members of IFAC automatically become members of the International Accounting Standards Committee Foundation, which is an independent not-for-profit, private sector organisation which sets international financial reporting standards through its standard-setting body, the International Accounting Standards Board.

3.4 Regulation, monitoring and supervision

Each country's regulation of external audits will differ. Most regimes do have certain common elements, which we examine in detail below. Briefly these are as follows.

(a) **Education and work experience**: the IFAC has issued guidance on this.
(b) **Eligibility**: there may well be statutory rules determining who can act as auditors. Membership of an appropriate body is likely to be one criteria.
(c) **Supervision and monitoring**: these activities came under particular scrutiny in a number of countries during the 1990s. Questions were asked about why auditors have failed to identify impending corporate failures, and whether therefore they were being regulated strongly enough. The supervision regime has come under particular scrutiny in countries where regulation and supervision is by the auditors' own professional body (self-regulation). Suggestions have been made in these countries that supervision ought to be by external government agencies.

3.5 Education, examinations and experience

IFAC issued the Statement of Policy of Council *Recognition of Professional Accountancy Qualifications* primarily to tackle the problems of intra-country recognition of qualifications. It sets minimum standards for accountancy qualifications. It looks at three main areas.

3.5.1 Education

The theoretical knowledge to be contained in the body of knowledge of accountants should include compulsory subjects (such as audit, consolidated accounts and general accounting) and relevant subjects (such as law and economics). Accountants should have covered these subjects in a breadth and depth sufficient to enable them to perform their duties to the expected standard.

3.5.2 Examinations

Accountants should demonstrate that they have passed an examination of professional competence. This examination must assess not only the necessary level of **theoretical** knowledge but also the ability to apply that knowledge competently in a **practical** situation. Objective evaluation of professional examinations is a key requirement.

3.5.3 Experience

It is crucial to any professional to have not only a sound theoretical knowledge but also to be able to apply that knowledge competently in the world of work.

It is suggested that, prior to qualification, an individual should have completed a *minimum* of two years approved and properly supervised practical experience primarily in the area of audit and accountancy and in a suitable professional environment.

3.6 Eligibility to act as auditor

Eligibility to act as an auditor is likely to arise from membership of some kind of regulatory body.

Bodies of this type will offer qualifications and set up rules to ensure compliance with any statutory requirements related to auditors. In this way national governments will control who may act as an auditor to limited liability companies, or to any other body requiring a statutory audit.

In some countries, regulation is devolved to professional accountancy bodies by the statutory authorities. On the other hand, the regulatory body could be a direct extension of national government.

The regulatory body should have rules to ensure that those eligible for appointment as a company auditor are either:

- **Individuals** holding an **appropriate qualification** or
- **Firms controlled** by **qualified persons**

Regulatory bodies should also have procedures to maintain the competence of members. The regulatory body's rules should:

- Ensure that only **fit and proper** persons are appointed as company auditors
- Ensure that company audit work is conducted **properly** and with **professional integrity**
- Include rules as to the **technical standards** of company audit work (eg following International Standards on Auditing)
- Ensure that **eligible persons** maintain an appropriate level of **competence**
- Ensure that all firms eligible under its rules have arrangements to prevent:
  - Individuals not holding an **appropriate qualification**
  - Persons who are **not members** of the firm from being able to exert influence over an audit which would be likely to affect the independence or integrity of the audit

The regulatory body's rules should provide for adequate monitoring and enforcement of compliance with its rules and should include provisions relating to:

- **Admission** and **expulsion** of members
- **Investigation of complaints** against members
- **Compulsory professional indemnity insurance**

Up-to-date lists of approved auditors and their names and addresses should be maintained by the regulatory body. This register of auditors should be made available to the public.

Membership of a regulatory body is the main prerequisite for eligibility as an auditor. Some countries allow a 'firm' to be appointed as a company auditor. A firm may be either a body corporate (such as a company) or a partnership.

A person should be **ineligible** for appointment as a company auditor if he or she is:

- An **officer or employee** of the company
- A **partner or employee** of such a person
- A **partnership** in which such a person is a partner

There may be further rules about connections between the company or its officers and the auditor, depending on local statutory rules.

3.7 Supervisory and monitoring roles

Some kind of supervision and monitoring regime should be implemented by the regulatory body. This should inspect auditors on a regular basis.

The frequency of inspection will depend on the number of partners, number of offices and number of listed company audits (these factors may also be reflected in the size of annual registration fees payable by approved audit firms).

The following features should be apparent in each practice visited by the monitoring regulatory body.

(a) A **properly structured audit approach**, suitable for the range of clients served and work undertaken by the practice.

(b) **Carefully instituted quality control procedures**, revised and updated constantly, to which the practice as a whole is committed. This will include:
   - Staff recruitment
   - Staff training
   - Continuing professional development
   - Frequent quality control review

(c) Commitment to **ethical guidelines**, with an emphasis on independence issues

(d) An emphasis on **technical excellence**

(e) Adherence to the **'fit and proper' criteria** by checking personnel records and references

(f) Use of internal and, if necessary, external **peer reviews**, consultations etc

(g) **Appropriate fee** charging per audit assignment

4 International Standards on Auditing

FAST FORWARD

International Standards on Auditing are set by the **International Auditing and Assurance Standards Board**.

4.1 Rules governing audits

We discussed in Chapter 1 the various stakeholders in a company, and the various people who might read a company's financial statements. Consider also that some of these readers will not just be reading a single company's financial statements, but will also be looking at those of a large number of companies, and making comparisons between them.

Readers want **assurance** when making comparisons that the **reliability** of the financial statements **does not vary from company to company**. This assurance will be obtained not just from knowing that each set of financial statements has been audited, but knowing that this has been done to **common standards**.

Hence there is a need for audits to be **regulated** so that auditors follow the same standards. As we see in this chapter, auditors have to follow rules issued by a variety of bodies. Some obligations are imposed by governments in law, or statute. Some obligations are imposed by the professional bodies to which auditors are required to belong, such as the ACCA.

International Standards on Auditing (ISAs) are produced by the **International Auditing and Assurance Standards Board (IAASB)**, a technical standing committee of IFAC, which also issues standards relating to review engagements, other assurance engagements, quality control and related services. An explanation of the workings of the IAASB, the authority of ISAs and so on are laid out in the *Preface to the International*

Standards on Quality Control, Auditing, Review, Other Assurance and Related Services, and we will look at this below.

4.2 Preface

The preface states that the IAASB's objective is the development of a set of international standards that are accepted worldwide. The IAASB's pronouncements relate to audit, other assurance and related services that are conducted in accordance with international standards.

Within each country, local laws and regulations govern, to a greater or lesser degree, the practices followed in the auditing of financial or other information. Such regulations may be either of a statutory nature, or in the form of statements issued by the regulatory or professional bodies in the countries concerned. For example, in the UK, the Auditing Practices Board (APB) sets ISAs, and the Companies Act 2006 provides legislative regulations.

4.2.1 The authority attached to ISAs and other pronouncements

The preface also lays out the authority attached to international standards issued by the IAASB:

IAASB Pronouncements	
International Standards on Auditing (ISAs)	To be applied in the audit of historical financial information
International Standards on Review Engagements (ISREs)	To be applied in the review of historical financial information
International Standards on Assurance Engagements (ISAEs)	To be applied in assurance engagements dealing with subject matters other than historical financial information
International Standards on Related Services (ISRSs)	To be applied to compilation engagements, engagements to apply agreed upon procedures to information and other related services engagement as specified by the IAASB
International Standards on Quality Control (ISQCs)	To be applied for all services falling under the IAASB's engagement standards (ISAs, ISREs, ISAEs, ISRSs)
International Auditing Practice Statements (IAPSs)	Provide interpretive guidance and practical assistance to professional accountants in implementing ISAs and to promote good practice

Any **limitation** of the applicability of a specific ISA is made very clear in the Preface.

ISAs do **not** override the local regulations referred to above governing the audit of financial or other information in a particular country.

(a) To the extent that ISAs **conform** with local regulations on a particular subject, the audit of financial or other information in that country in accordance with local regulations will automatically comply with the ISA regarding that subject.

(b) In the event that the local regulations **differ from**, or conflict with, ISAs on a particular subject, member bodies should comply with the obligations of members set forth in the IFAC Constitution as regards these ISAs (ie **encourage changes** in local regulations to comply with ISAs).

The IAASB also publishes other papers, such as **Discussion Papers**, to promote discussion on auditing, review, other assurance and related services and quality control issues affecting the accounting profession, present findings, or describe matters of interest relating to these engagements.

4.2.2 Working procedures of the IAASB

A rigorous due process is followed by the IAASB to ensure that the views of all those affected by its guidance are taken into account. The following diagram summarises the process followed in the development of IAASB standards.

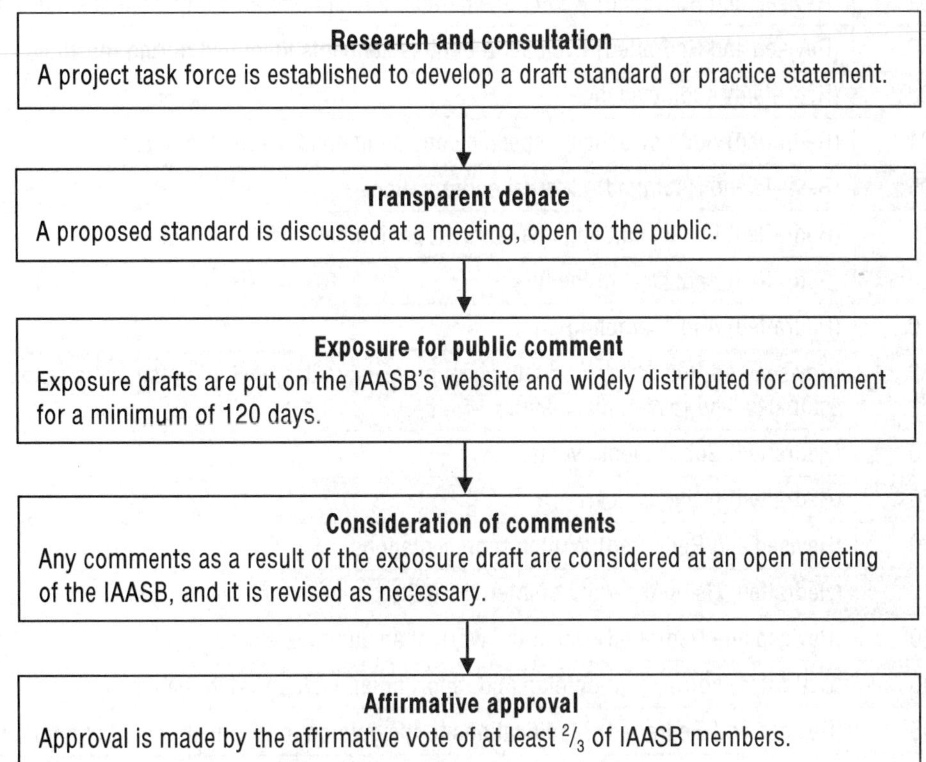

Research and consultation
A project task force is established to develop a draft standard or practice statement.
Transparent debate
A proposed standard is discussed at a meeting, open to the public.
Exposure for public comment
Exposure drafts are put on the IAASB's website and widely distributed for comment for a minimum of 120 days.
Consideration of comments
Any comments as a result of the exposure draft are considered at an open meeting of the IAASB, and it is revised as necessary.
Affirmative approval
Approval is made by the affirmative vote of at least $^{2}/_{3}$ of IAASB members.

4.3 Current ISAs and other standards

The following table sets out those ISAs and other pronouncements that are examinable in accordance with the **F8 syllabus**.

No	Title
200	(Revised and Redrafted) Overall objectives of the independent auditor and the conduct of an audit in accordance with International Standards on Auditing
210	(Redrafted) Agreeing the terms of audit engagements
230	(Redrafted) Audit documentation
240	(Redrafted) The auditor's responsibilities relating to fraud in an audit of financial statements
250	(Redrafted) Consideration of laws and regulations in an audit of financial statements
260	(Revised and Redrafted) Communication with those charged with governance
265	Communicating deficiencies in internal control to those charged with governance and management
300	(Redrafted) Planning an audit of financial statements
315	(Redrafted) Identifying and assessing the risks of material misstatement through understanding the entity and its environment

No	Title
320	(Revised and Redrafted) Materiality in planning and performing an audit
330	(Redrafted) The auditor's responses to assessed risks
402	(Revised and Redrafted) Audit considerations relating to an entity using a service organisation
450	(Revised and Redrafted) Evaluation of misstatements identified during the audit
500	(Redrafted) Audit evidence
501	(Redrafted) Audit evidence – specific considerations for selected items
505	(Revised and Redrafted) External confirmations
510	(Redrafted) Initial audit engagements – opening balances
520	(Redrafted) Analytical procedures
530	(Redrafted) Audit sampling
540	(Revised and Redrafted) Auditing accounting estimates, including fair value accounting estimates, and related disclosures
560	(Redrafted) Subsequent events
570	(Redrafted) Going concern
580	(Revised and Redrafted) Written representations
610	(Redrafted) Using the work of internal auditors
620	(Revised and Redrafted) Using the work of an auditor's expert
700	(Redrafted) Forming an opinion and reporting on financial statements
705	(Revised and Redrafted) Modifications to the opinion in the independent auditor's report
706	(Revised and Redrafted) Emphasis of matter paragraphs and other matter paragraphs in the independent auditor's report
710	(Redrafted) Comparative information – corresponding figures and comparative financial statements
720	(Redrafted) The auditor's responsibilities relating to other information in documents containing audited financial statements

The following IAASB pronouncements are also examinable:

International Auditing Practice Statements	
IAPS 1000	Inter-bank confirmation procedures
IAPS 1013	Electronic commerce: effect on the audit of financial statements
IAPS 1014	Reporting by auditors on compliance with International Financial Reporting Standards
International Standards on Assurance Engagements	
ISAE 3000	Assurance engagements other than audits or reviews of historical financial information
International Standards on Review Engagements	
ISRE 2400	Engagements to review financial statements

Exam focus point

ISAs are quoted throughout this text and you must understand how they are applied in practice. You do not therefore need to know the names of the standards or the details off by heart – it's your ability to **apply** them in the exam that will be tested.

4.4 Application of ISAs to smaller entities

You should refer back to the definition of small entities given earlier in this chapter. Although ISAs apply to the audit of historical financial information of any entity regardless of its size, small businesses possess a combination of characteristics which makes it necessary for the auditors to adapt their audit approach to the circumstances surrounding the small business engagement. ISAs include an indication of how they would be applied to smaller entities.

4.5 The IAASB Clarity project

This section highlights an important current issue regarding ISAs issued by the IAASB, known as the **Clarity project**. Although the background of the Clarity project is not examinable under the F8 syllabus, you must be aware of it, particularly because all the clarified ISAs issued as a result of it which are relevant to F8 are examinable from the June 2010 exam onwards. It will certainly impact on your further auditing studies in Paper P7 and in practice if you work in the auditing profession. Below we provide some background to the Clarity project.

In 2004, the IAASB began a comprehensive program to **enhance the clarity** of its ISAs by setting an **overall objective** for each ISA and improving the **overall readability and understandability** through structural and drafting improvements.

At the end of 2008, the IAASB had finalised all its clarified ISAs, and auditors all over the world now have access to 36 newly updated and clarified ISAs and a clarified ISQC.

The improvements arising from the Clarity project can be summarised below:

- Identifying the auditor's **overall objectives** when conducting an audit
- **Setting an objective** in each ISA and establishing the auditor's obligation in relation to that objective
- **Clarifying the obligations** imposed on auditors by the requirements of ISAs and the language used to communicate these requirements
- **Eliminating** any possible **ambiguity** about the auditor's requirements
- Improving the **overall readability and understandability** of the ISAs through structural and drafting improvements

Chapter Roundup

- Most companies are required to have an audit by law, but some small companies are exempt. The outcome of the audit is the **audit report**, which sets out the auditor's **opinion** on the financial statements.
- The law gives auditors both rights and duties. This allows auditors to have sufficient power to carry out an independent and effective audit.
- There are various legal and professional requirements on appointment, resignation and removal of auditors which must be followed.
- Requirements for the **eligibility**, **registration** and **training** of auditors are extremely important as they are designed to maintain standards in the auditing profession.
- **International Standards on Auditing** are set by the **International Auditing and Assurance Standards Board.**

Quick Quiz

1 What makes a person ineligible for appointment as a company auditor?

2 A person does not have to satisfy membership criteria to become a member of an RSB.

True ☐

False ☐

3 Using the UK as an example, who can appoint an auditor?

4 The ACCA has its own monitoring unit which inspects registered auditors on a regular basis.

True ☐

False ☐

5 What is the function of IFAC?

6 Which of the following are not engagement standards issued by the IAASB?

- International Standards on Auditing
- International Standards on Quality Control
- International Auditing Practice Statements
- International Standards on Related Services
- International Standards on Assurance Engagements
- International Standards on Review Engagements

Answers to Quick Quiz

1 An officer or employee of the company
A partner or employee of such a person
A partnership in which such a person is a partner

2 False. All RSBs have stringent membership requirements.

3 Members can appoint the auditors (at each general meeting where accounts are laid).

Directors can appoint the auditors (before the first general meeting where accounts are laid or to fill a casual vacancy).

The Secretary of State can appoint the auditors (if no auditors are appointed/reappointed at the general meeting where accounts are laid).

4 True

5 The function of IFAC is to initiate, co-ordinate and guide efforts to achieve international technical, ethical and educational pronouncements for the accountancy profession.

6 International Standards on Quality Control and International Auditing Practice Statements are not engagement standards issued by the IAASB. The others are all classed as engagement standards.

Now try the questions below from the Exam Question Bank

Number	Level	Marks	Time
Q2	Examination	10	18 mins
Q3	Introductory	n/a	n/a

Corporate governance

3

Topic list	Syllabus reference
1 Codes of corporate governance	A3
2 Audit committees	A3
3 Internal control effectiveness	A3
4 Communication with those charged with governance	A3

Introduction

The concept of corporate governance was introduced in Chapter 1. In this chapter we will look at the codes of practice that have been put in place to ensure that companies are well managed and controlled. The UK's Combined Code on Corporate Governance is an internationally recognised code which we will use as an example of a code of best practice. The audit carried out by the external auditors is a very important part of corporate governance, as it is an independent check on what the directors are reporting to the shareholders.

Auditors of all kinds have most contact with the audit committee, a sub-committee of the board of directors. External auditors liaise with the audit committee over the audit, and internal auditors will report their findings about internal control effectiveness to it. We shall look at audit committees in Section 2 and internal control effectiveness in Section 3.

We end this chapter with a consideration of the importance of auditors communicating with those charged with governance in an entity. ISA 260 *Communication with those charged with governance* provides guidance to auditors in this respect.

Study guide

		Intellectual level
A3	**The regulatory environment and corporate governance**	
(c)	Discuss the objective, relevance and importance of corporate governance	2
(d)	Discuss the need for auditors to communicate with those charged with governance	2
(e)	Discuss the provisions of international codes of corporate governance (such as OECD) that are most relevant to auditors	2
(f)	Describe good corporate governance requirements relating to directors' responsibilities (eg for risk management and internal control) and the reporting responsibilities of auditors	1
(g)	Analyse the structure and roles of audit committees and discuss their drawbacks and limitations	2
(h)	Explain the importance of internal control and risk management	1
(i)	Compare the responsibilities of management and auditors for the design and operation of systems and controls	2

Exam guide

Questions on corporate governance could be either knowledge-based or application-based and may be part of a scenario question on ethics. The pilot paper had 10 marks on a question on corporate governance in the context of meeting corporate governance requirements and communication with the audit committee by the auditors. The June 2009 paper had a 12 mark part on the benefits of forming an audit committee (scenario question).

1 Codes of corporate governance **Pilot paper**

FAST FORWARD

Corporate governance is the system by which companies are **directed and controlled**. Good corporate governance is important because the owners of a company and the people who manage the company are not always the same.

1.1 The importance of corporate governance

Key term

Corporate governance is the system by which companies are directed and controlled.

There are various stakeholders in companies, as we discussed in Chapter 1. The **Cadbury Report** on financial aspects of corporate governance commissioned by the UK government in the early 1990s identified the following:

- **Directors**: responsible for corporate governance
- **Shareholders**: linked to the directors by the financial statements
- **Other relevant parties**: such as employees, customers and suppliers (stakeholders)

In some companies, the **shareholders** are **fully informed about** the **management** of the business because they are directors themselves, whereas in other companies, the **shareholders** only have an opportunity to find out about the management of the company at the **AGM (annual general meeting)**.

The **day-to-day running of a company is the responsibility of the directors** and other management staff to whom they delegate, and although the company's results are submitted for shareholders' approval at the AGM, there is often apathy and acquiescence in directors' recommendations.

AGMs are often very poorly attended. For these reasons, there is the **potential** for **conflicts of interest** between management and shareholders.

Corporate governance is important because it ensures that stakeholders with a relevant interest in the company's business are fully taken into account.

In other words, it is necessary for structures to be in place to ensure that every stakeholder in the company is not disadvantaged. As it is the directors that manage the company, the burden of good corporate governance falls on them. It is important that they manage the company in the best way for the shareholders, employees and other parties.

1.2 OECD Principles of Corporate Governance

FAST FORWARD

The **OECD Principles of Corporate Governance** set out the rights of shareholders, the importance of disclosure and transparency and the responsibilities of the board of directors.

An important question to consider is 'will the same way of managing companies be the best method for all companies?' The answer is likely to be no. Companies are different from each other, and globally, they operate in different legal systems with different institutions, frameworks and traditions. It would not be possible to construct one single way of operating companies that could be described as good practice for all.

The key issue in corporate governance is that 'a high degree of priority [is] placed on the interests of shareholders, who place their trust in corporations to use their investment funds wisely and effectively'. Shareholders in a company might be a family, they might be the general public or they might be institutional investors representing, in particular, people's future pensions. These shareholders will vary in their degree of interaction with the company and their directors.

In the context of this great variety in the basic element of these companies, the Organisation for Economic Co-operation and Development (OECD) has established a number of **Principles of Corporate Governance**, which were issued in 1999 and reviewed in 2004, and which serve as a **reference point** for countries (to develop corporate governance codes if they wish) and companies. They were developed in response to a mandate given to the OECD to develop a set of standards and guidelines on good corporate governance.

OECD Principles of Corporate Governance	
I	The corporate governance framework should promote transparent and efficient markets, be consistent with the rule of law and clearly articulate the division of responsibilities among different supervisory, regulatory and enforcement authorities.
II	The corporate governance framework should protect shareholders' rights.
III	The corporate governance framework should ensure the equitable treatment of all shareholders, including minority and foreign shareholders. All shareholders should have the opportunity to obtain effective redress for violation of their rights.
IV	The corporate governance framework should recognise the rights of stakeholders established by law or through mutual agreements and encourage active co-operation between corporations and stakeholders in creating wealth, jobs and the sustainability of financially sound enterprises.
V	The corporate governance framework should ensure that timely and accurate disclosure is made on all material matters regarding the corporation, including the financial situation, performance, ownership, and governance of the company.
VI	The corporate governance framework should ensure the strategic guidance of the company, the effective monitoring of management by the board, and the board's accountability to the company and the shareholders.

In order to obtain the best of the advantages and avoid the worst disadvantages, countries may take a hybrid approach and make some elements of corporate governance mandatory and some voluntary. For instance, in the UK, companies are required to comply with **legislation** (such as the Companies Act) and there is also a **voluntary corporate governance code**, the Combined Code on Corporate Governance, which contains some **mandatory elements** for listed companies. We discuss the provisions of the Combined Code below.

1.3 The Combined Code on Corporate Governance

FAST FORWARD

The **Combined Code on Corporate Governance** contains detailed guidance for UK companies on good corporate governance.

1.3.1 A history of corporate governance in the UK

Before we discuss the provisions of the Combined Code in detail, it is useful to provide a short history of corporate governance in the UK.

As a result of several accounting scandals in the 1980s and 1990s (Mirror Group, BCCI, PollyPeck), the **Cadbury** committee produced a report entitled *Financial aspects of corporate governance.*

In 1995, the **Greenbury** report added a set of principles on the remuneration of executive directors. The **Hampel** report in 1998 brought the Cadbury and Greenbury reports together to form the first Combined Code. In 1999, **Turnbull** produced a report relating to risk management and internal control.

In 2002, the **Higgs** report (*Review of the role and effectiveness of non-executive directors*) was commissioned to produce a single comprehensive code, which was refined by the FRC to produce the Combined Code. At the same time, the **Smith** report was produced on the role of audit committees, and the recommendations of this were incorporated into the new Combined Code.

1.3.2 Principles of the Combined Code

The Combined Code is produced by the FRC and sets out standards of good practice regarding board composition, remuneration, accountability and audit, and relations with shareholders.

All companies incorporated in the UK and listed on the London Stock Exchange are required under the Listing Rules to report on how they have applied the code in their annual report and accounts.

The Combined Code contains broad principles and more specific provisions. Listed companies have to report how they have applied the principles, and either confirm that they have applied the provisions or if they have not, to provide an explanation.

The code was first issued in 1998 and has been updated regularly. The current edition is from 2008, although it is currently being reviewed by the FRC.

Principles of the Combined Code (for listed UK companies)

The board

- Every company should be headed by an effective board, which is collectively responsible for the success of the company.
- There should be a clear division of responsibilities at the head of the company between the running of the board and the executive responsibility for the running of the company's business. No one individual should have unfettered powers of decision.
- The board should include a balance executive and non-executive directors (and in particular independent non-executive directors) such that no individual or small group of individuals can dominate the board's decision taking.
- There should be a formal, rigorous and transparent procedure for the appointment of new directors to the board.
- The board should be supplied in a timely manner with information in a form and of a quality appropriate to enable it to discharge its duties.
- All directors should receive induction on joining the board and should regularly update and refresh their skills and knowledge.
- The board should undertake a formal and rigorous annual evaluation of its own performance and that of its committees and individual directors.
- All directors should be submitted for re-election at regular intervals, subject to continued satisfactory performance. The board should ensure planned and progressive refreshing of the board.

Remuneration

- Levels of remuneration should be sufficient to attract, retain and motivate directors of the quality required to run the company successfully, but a company should avoid paying more than is necessary for this purpose. A significant proportion of executive directors' remuneration should be structured so as to link rewards to corporate and individual performance.
- There should be a formal and transparent procedure for developing policy on executive remuneration and for fixing the remuneration packages of individual directors. No director should be involved in deciding his or her remuneration.

Accountability and audit

- The board should present a balanced and understandable assessment of the company's position and prospects.
- The board should maintain a sound system of internal control to safeguard shareholders' investment and the company's assets.
- The board should establish formal and transparent arrangements for considering how they should apply the financial reporting and internal control principles and for maintaining an appropriate relationship with the company's auditors.

Relations with shareholders

- There should be a dialogue with shareholders based on the mutual understanding of objectives. The board as a whole has responsibility for ensuring that satisfactory dialogue with shareholders takes place.
- The board should use the AGM to communicate with investors and to encourage their participation.

Institutional shareholders

- Institutional shareholders should enter into a dialogue with companies based on the mutual understanding of objectives.
- Institutional shareholders have a responsibility to make considered use of their votes.

1.3.3 Auditors and the Combined Code

There are three key issues in relation to auditors suggested by the principles of the Combined Code.

- They strongly recommend that all companies have an **annual**, **independent audit** of financial statements.
- They state that information should be disclosed and audited according to high quality standards. This is in order to increase **reliability** and **comparability** of reporting, allowing investors to make better investment decisions.
- They imply that shareholders will benefit if other information is subject to **checks** by auditors.

So for example, auditors could be asked to check whether companies are applying certain aspects of corporate governance codes. Auditors in the UK are required to report on whether **listed companies** comply with the following aspects of the Combined Code:

- Directors' responsibility for preparing financial statements explained in report
- System of internal control reviewed and reported on
- Audit committee of at least three non-executive directors set up
- Audit committee terms of reference set out in writing
- Audit committee terms of reference available/described in report
- Audit committee arranges methods for staff to report impropriety in financial reporting
- Audit committee monitors and reviews effectiveness of internal control
- Audit committee has primary responsibility for appointment of external auditors
- If external audit provides non-audit services, annual report sets out how independence maintained

1.3.4 Directors

The directors of a company should set company policy, including risk policy, and are responsible for the company's systems and controls.

Policy

Directors are responsible ultimately for managing the company, and this includes setting strategy, budgets, managing the company's people, maintaining company assets, and ensuring corporate governance rules are kept. An important element of setting strategies is determining and managing risks. We shall outline in Chapter 5 how internal audit may have a role in this area. The Combined Code requires that there is clear division of responsibility at the head of a company between the chairman and the chief executive. It requires that no one individual has unfettered powers of decision.

The board should be supplied with information in a timely manner to enable it to carry out its duties and directors should receive induction on joining the board and should regularly update and refresh their skills.

Systems, controls and monitoring

Directors are responsible for the systems put in place to achieve the company policies and the controls put in place to mitigate risks. These issues will be considered further later in this chapter. Under the Combined Code, UK boards are required to consider annually whether an internal audit department is required.

They are also responsible for **monitoring** the effectiveness of systems and controls. **Internal auditors** have an important role in this area as we shall discuss in Chapter 5, but remember it is the directors that are responsible for determining whether to have an internal audit department to assist them in monitoring in the first place.

In the UK, the **Turnbull** report on internal control made the following recommendations:

Turnbull Guidelines
Have a **defined process** for the effectiveness of internal control
Review **regular reports** on internal control
Consider **key risks** and how they have been managed
Check the **adequacy** of **action taken** to remedy weaknesses and incidents
Consider the **adequacy** of **monitoring**
Conduct an **annual assessment** of risks and the effectiveness of internal control
Make a **statement** on this process in the **annual report**

Non-executive directors

Key term

Non-executive directors are directors who do not have day-to-day operational responsibility for the company. They are not employees of the company or affiliated with it in any other way.

An important recommendation of the principles of the Combined Code is that the board contains some non-executive directors to ensure that it exercises **objective judgement**. The Combined Code requires 'a balance' of executive and non-executive directors on the board and recommends that the board is made up of at least half non-executive directors.

Such non-executive directors may have a particular role in some sensitive areas such as company reporting, nomination of directors and remuneration of executive directors. Often companies will set up sub-committees of the board to deal with such issues. We are now going on to consider one such sub-committee, the **audit committee**, in more detail.

2 Audit committees — Pilot paper, June 2009

FAST FORWARD

An **audit committee** can help a company maintain objectivity with regard to financial reporting and the audit of financial statements.

2.1 Role and function of audit committees

An **audit committee** is a sub-committee of the board of directors, usually containing a number of non-executive directors. The role and function of the audit committee is described by the Cadbury report, which sets out the following advantages of having an audit committee.

- Improve the quality of financial reporting, by reviewing the financial statements on behalf of the Board
- Create a climate of discipline and control which will reduce the opportunity for fraud
- Enable the non-executive directors to contribute an independent judgement and play a positive role
- Help the finance director, by providing a forum in which he can raise issues of concern, and which he can use to get things done which might otherwise be difficult
- Strengthen the position of the external auditor, by providing a channel of communication and forum for issues of concern
- Provide a framework within which the external auditor can assert his independence in the event of a dispute with management
- Strengthen the position of the internal audit function, by providing a greater degree of independence from management
- Increase public confidence in the credibility and objectivity of financial statements

One of the principles of the Combined Code is that the board should establish formal and transparent arrangements for considering how it should apply the financial reporting and internal control principles for maintaining an appropriate relationship with the company's auditors. The provisions relating to this principle are set out in the following table.

Combined Code provisions relating to the audit committee
The board should establish an audit committee of at least three, or in the case of smaller companies, two members, who should all be **independent non-executive directors**. The main role and responsibilities should be set out in **written terms of reference** and should include: (a) To monitor the integrity of the financial statements of the company and any formal announcements relating to the company's financial performance, reviewing significant financial reporting issues and judgements contained in them (b) To review the company's internal financial controls and, unless expressly addressed by a separate board risk committee composed of independent directors or by the board itself, the company's control and risk management systems (c) To monitor and review the effectiveness of the company's internal audit function (d) To make recommendations to the board for it to put to the shareholders for their approval in general meeting in relation to the appointment of the external auditor and to approve the remuneration and terms of engagement of the external auditors (e) To monitor and review the external auditor's independence, objectivity and effectiveness, taking into consideration relevant UK professional and regulatory requirements (f) To develop and implement policy on engagement of the external auditor to supply non-audit services, taking into account relevant ethical guidance regarding the provisions of non-audit services by the external audit firm and to report to the board, identifying any matters in respect of which it considers that action or improvement is needed, and making recommendations as to the steps to be taken
The terms of reference of the audit committee, including its role and the authority delegated to it by the board, should be made available. A separate section of the annual report should describe the work of the committee in discharging those responsibilities.
The audit committee should review arrangements by which staff of the company may, in confidence, raise concerns about possible improprieties in matters of financial reporting or other matters. The audit committee's objective should be to ensure that arrangements are in place for the proportionate and independent investigation of such matters and for appropriate follow-up action.
The audit committee should monitor and review the effectiveness of the internal audit activities. Where there is no internal audit function, the audit committee should consider annually whether there is a need for an internal audit function and make a recommendation to the board, and the reasons for the absence of such a function should be explained in the relevant section of the annual report.
The audit committee should have primary responsibility for making a recommendation on the appointment, reappointment and removal of the external auditors. If the board does not accept the audit committee's recommendation, it should include in the annual report, and in any papers recommending appointment or re-appointment, a statement from the audit committee explaining the recommendation and should set out reasons why the board has taken a different position. The annual report should explain to shareholders how, if the auditor provides non-audit services, auditor objectivity and independence is safeguarded.

2.2 Drawbacks of audit committees

We discussed the possible benefits of the audit committee above.

Opponents of audit committees argue that:

(a) The executive directors may **not understand** the purpose of an audit committee and may perceive that it detracts from their authority.

(b) There may be **difficulty selecting** sufficient non-executive directors with the necessary competence in auditing matters for the committee to be really effective.

(c) The establishment of such a **formalised reporting procedure** may **dissuade** the **auditors** from raising matters of judgement and limit them to reporting only on matters of fact.

(d) **Costs** may be **increased**.

3 Internal control effectiveness

FAST FORWARD

The **directors** of a company are **responsible** for ensuring that a company's **system of controls is effective**.

3.1 Importance of internal control and risk management

Internal controls are essential to management, as they contribute to:

- Safeguarding the company's **assets**
- Helping to prevent and detect **fraud**
- Safeguarding the shareholders' **investment**

Good internal control helps the business to run efficiently. A control system reduces identified risks to the business. It also helps to ensure reliability of reporting, and compliance with laws.

3.2 Directors' responsibilities for internal control

The **ultimate responsibility** for a company's system of internal controls lies with the **board of directors**. It should set procedures of internal control and regularly monitor that the system operates as it should.

Part of setting up an internal control system will involve **assessing the risks** facing the business, so that the **system** can be **designed** to ensure those **risks are avoided**.

Internal control systems will always have **inherent limitations**, the most important being that a system of internal control cannot eliminate the possibility of human error, or the chance that staff will collude in fraud.

Once the directors have set up a system of internal control, they are responsible for **reviewing** it regularly, to ensure that it **still meets its objectives**.

The board may decide that in order to carry out their review function properly they have to employ an **internal audit function** to undertake this task. When deciding whether an internal audit function is required, directors will need to consider the extent of systems and controls, and the relative expense of obtaining checks from other parties, such as the external auditors. These issues will be considered in more detail in Chapter 5.

If the board does not see the need for an internal audit function, in the UK, the Combined Code requires companies to consider the need for one annually, so that the **need for internal audit is regularly reviewed**.

The Combined Code also recommends that the board of directors **reports** on its **review of internal controls** as part of the annual report.

The statement should be based on an annual assessment of internal control which should confirm that the board has considered **all significant aspects** of internal control. In particular the assessment should cover:

(a) The **changes** since the last **assessment** in **risks** faced, and the company's **ability** to **respond** to **changes** in its business environment

(b) The **scope** and **quality** of management's monitoring of risk and internal control, and of the work of internal audit, or consideration of the need for an internal audit function if the company does not have one

(c) The **extent** and **frequency** of reports to the board

(d) **Significant controls**, **failings** and **weaknesses** which have or might have material impacts upon the accounts

(e) The **effectiveness** of the **public reporting** processes

3.3 Auditors' responsibilities for internal control

The auditors' detailed responsibilities with regard to reporting on the requirements of the Combined Code are set out in a bulletin issued by the UK's Auditing Practices Board, which is not examinable. However, in summary, the auditors should review the statements made concerning internal control in the annual report to ensure that they appear true and are not in conflict with the audited financial statements.

4 Communication with those charged with governance

Pilot paper

FAST FORWARD

Auditors shall **communicate** specific matters to **those charged with governance** and ISA 260 provides guidance to auditors in this area.

4.1 The importance of communicating with those charged with governance

ISA 260 *Communication with those charged with governance* sets out guidance for auditors on the communication of audit matters arising from the audit of the financial statements of an entity with those charged with governance.

'Those charged with governance' is defined by ISA 260 as 'the person(s) or organisation(s) with responsibility for **overseeing the strategic direction** of the entity and obligations related to the **accountability** of the entity'.

'Management' is defined by ISA 260 as 'the person(s) with executive responsibility for the conduct of the entity's operations'.

Communication with those charged with governance is important because:

- It assists the auditor and those charged with governance to **understand** audit-related matters in context and allows them to **develop a constructive working relationship.**
- It allows the auditor to **obtain information** relevant to the audit.
- It assists those charged with governance to fulfil their **responsibility** to oversee the financial reporting process, thus reducing the risks of material misstatement in the financial statements.

4.2 Matters to be communicated by auditors to those charged with governance

The following matters shall be communicated to those charged with governance:

The auditor's responsibilities in relation to the financial statement audit

Including that the auditor is responsible for forming and expressing an opinion on the financial statements and that the audit does not relieve management or those charged with governance of their responsibilities

Planned scope and timing of the audit

An overview of the planned scope and timing of the audit

Significant findings from the audit

The auditor shall communicate the following:

- The auditor's views about significant qualitative aspects of the entity's accounting practices, including accounting policies, accounting estimates and financial statement disclosures
- Significant difficulties encountered during the audit
- Material weaknesses in the design, implementation or operating effectiveness of internal control that have come to the auditor's attention and have been communicated to management
- Significant matters arising from the audit that were discussed or subject to correspondence with management
- Written representations requested by the auditor
- Other matters that, in the auditor's professional judgement, are significant to the oversight of the financial reporting process

Auditor independence

The auditor shall communicate the following for **listed** entities:

- A statement that the engagement team and others in the firm, the firm, and network firms have complied with relevant ethical requirements regarding independence
- All relationships between the firm and entity that may reasonably be thought to bear on independence
- Related safeguards that have been applied to eliminate identified threats to independence or reduce them to an acceptable level

4.3 The communication process

The auditor shall communicate with those charged with governance the **form, timing and expected general content** of communications. The auditor shall communicate with those charged with governance on a **timely basis**.

Exam focus point

A question on corporate governance is most likely to come up in a scenario-based question, perhaps in conjunction with internal audit (which we cover in Chapter 5) as the two are linked.

Chapter Roundup

- **Corporate governance** is the system by which companies are **directed and controlled**. Good corporate governance is important because the owners of a company and the people who manage the company are not always the same.
- The **OECD Principles of Corporate Governance** set out the rights of shareholders, the importance of disclosure and transparency and the responsibilities of the board of directors.
- The **Combined Code on Corporate Governance** contains detailed guidance for UK companies on good corporate governance.
- An **audit committee** can help a company maintain objectivity with regard to financial reporting and the audit of financial statements.
- The **directors** of a company are **responsible** for ensuring that a company's **system of controls is effective**.
- Auditors shall **communicate** specific matters to **those charged with governance** and ISA 260 provides guidance to auditors in this area.

Quick Quiz

1 Briefly explain the meaning of the term 'corporate governance'.

2 The OECD principles strongly recommend:

A An annual audit
B Internal audit
C Directors should not receive pay
D Directors should be non-executive

3 Complete the blanks

An audit.............is a sub-committee of the............. ...., usually containing a number of...........................directors.

4 When a company cannot easily find non-executive directors it should not have an audit committee.

True ☐

False ☐

5 Why are internal controls important in a company?

Answers to Quick Quiz

1 'Corporate governance' is the system by which companies are directed and controlled.

2 A

3 An audit **committee** is a sub-committee of the **board of directors**, usually containing a number of **non-executive** directors.

4 False. It should have an audit committee if required, or if the directors feel it is in the best interests of the shareholders, even if it is difficult to find non-executive directors.

5 Internal controls contribute to:

- Safeguarding company assets
- Preventing and detecting fraud
- Safeguarding the shareholder's investment

Now try the question below from the Exam Question Bank

Number	Level	Marks	Time
Q4	Introductory	n/a	n/a

4

Professional ethics

Topic list	Syllabus reference
1 Fundamental principles of professional ethics	A4
2 Accepting audit appointments	A4
3 Agreeing the terms of the engagement	A4

Introduction

In Chapter 2 we looked at some of the regulations surrounding the audit. Here we look at the ethical requirements of the RSBs, specifically the ACCA's *Code of ethics and conduct*, which is based on IFAC's *Code of ethics for professional accountants.*

The ethical matters covered in this chapter are very important. They could arise in almost every type of exam question and you must be able to apply the ACCA's guidance on ethical matters to any given situation, but remember that common sense is usually a good guide.

First we examine the five fundamental principles of professional ethics as defined in the ACCA's *Code of ethics and conduct.* We then look at the five main threats to compliance with these principles and the sorts of safeguards that can be put in place to mitigate these threats.

Sections 2 and 3 of this chapter are concerned with obtaining audit engagements and agreeing the terms of the engagement.

Study guide

		Intellectual level
A4	**Professional ethics and ACCA's Code of Ethics and Conduct**	
(a)	Define and apply the fundamental principles of professional ethics of integrity, objectivity, professional competence and due care, confidentiality and professional behaviour	2
(b)	Define and apply the conceptual framework	2
(c)	Discuss the sources of, and enforcement mechanisms associated with, ACCA's Code of ethics and conduct	2
(d)	Discuss the requirements of professional ethics and other requirements in relation to the acceptance of new audit engagements	2
(e)	Discuss the process by which an auditor obtains an audit engagement	2
(f)	Explain the importance of engagement letters and state their contents	1

Exam guide

Questions about auditor independence and objectivity may involve discussion of topical, controversial issues in a scenario-based question, such as the provision of services other than the audit to audit clients. Exam questions will generally require you to consider the possible threats and to suggest appropriate safeguards to mitigate those threats. Other questions may include knowledge-based questions on topics such as the audit engagement letter as in the pilot paper. The December 2007 paper had a five mark part for explaining each of the fundamental principles of professional ethics in question 2. In the December 2008 paper, there was a 12 mark scenario-based question on ethical threats and safeguards to mitigate those threats. The June 2009 had a four mark part on safeguards to overcome intimidation.

1 Fundamental principles of professional ethics

Pilot paper, Dec 07, Dec 08, June 09

FAST FORWARD

The ACCA's *Code of ethics and conduct* sets out the five **fundamental principles** of professional ethics and provides a **conceptual framework** for applying them.

The ACCA's *Code of ethics and conduct* sets out five fundamental principles of professional ethics and provides a conceptual framework for applying those principles. Members must apply this conceptual framework to identify threats to compliance with the principles, evaluate their significance and apply appropriate safeguards to eliminate or reduce them so that compliance is not compromised.

1.1 The fundamental principles

FAST FORWARD

Members of the ACCA must comply with the fundamental principles set out in the *Code of ethics and conduct* (**integrity, objectivity, professional competence and due care, confidentiality and professional behaviour**).

The five fundamental principles are summarised in the table below:

The ACCA's fundamental principles of professional ethics	
Integrity	Members should be straightforward and honest in all professional and business relationships.
Objectivity	Members should not allow bias, conflicts of interest or undue influence of others to override professional or business judgements.

The ACCA's fundamental principles of professional ethics	
Professional competence and due care	Members have a continuing duty to maintain professional knowledge and skill at a level required to ensure that a client or employer receives competent professional service based on current developments in practice, legislation and techniques. Members should act diligently and in accordance with applicable technical and professional standards when providing professional services.
Confidentiality	Members should respect the confidentiality of information acquired as a result of professional and business relationships and should not disclose any such information to third parties without proper or specific authority or unless there is a legal or professional right or duty to disclose. Confidential information acquired as a result of professional and business relationships should not be used for the personal advantage of members or third parties.
Professional behaviour	Members should comply with relevant laws and regulations and should avoid any action that discredits the profession.

1.2 Confidentiality

FAST FORWARD

Although auditors have a professional duty of **confidentiality**, they may be compelled by **law** or consider it necessary in the **public interest** to disclose details of clients' affairs to third parties.

Confidentiality requires members to refrain from disclosing information acquired in the course of professional work except where:

- **Consent has been obtained** from the client, employer or other proper source, or
- There is a **public duty** to disclose, or
- There is a **legal** or **professional right or duty** to disclose

A member acquiring information in the course of professional work should neither use nor appear to use that information for his **personal advantage** or for the **advantage of a third party**.

In general, where there is a right (as opposed to a duty) to disclose information, a member should only make disclosure in pursuit of a public duty or professional obligation.

A member must make clear to a client that he may only act for him if the client agrees to disclose in full to the member all information relevant to the engagement.

Where a member agrees to serve a client in a professional capacity both the member and the client should be aware that it is an **implied term** of that agreement that the **member will not disclose** the client's affairs to any other person save with the client's consent or within the terms of certain **recognised exceptions,** which fall under **obligatory** and **voluntary** disclosures.

If a member knows or suspects his client to have committed **money-laundering**, **treason**, **drug-trafficking** or **terrorist** offences, he is obliged to disclose all the information at his disposal to a competent authority. Auditing standards require auditors to consider whether **non-compliance** with laws and regulations affects the accounts.

Voluntary disclosure may be applicable in the following situations:

- Disclosure is reasonably necessary to **protect** the **member's interests**, for example to enable him to sue for fees or defend an action for, say, negligence.
- Disclosure is **compelled** by **process of law**, for example where in an action a member is required to give evidence of discovery of documents.
- There is a **public duty** to disclose, say where an offence has been committed which is contrary to the public interest.
- **Disclosure** is to **non-governmental bodies** which have statutory powers to compel disclosure.

If an ACCA member is requested to assist the police, the taxation or other authorities by providing information about a client's affairs in connection with enquiries being made, he should first enquire under what **statutory authority** the information is demanded.

Unless he is satisfied that such statutory authority exists he should decline to give any information until he has obtained his client's authority. If the client's authority is not forthcoming and the demand for information is pressed the member should not accede unless advised by his legal advisor.

If a member knows or suspects that a client has committed a wrongful act he must give careful thought to his own position. He must ensure that he has not prejudiced himself by, for example, relying on information given by the client which subsequently proves to be incorrect.

However, it would be a **criminal offence** for a **member to act positively**, without lawful authority or reasonable excuse, in such a manner as **to impede with intent** the arrest or prosecution of a client whom he knows or believes to have committed an 'arrestable offence'.

1.3 Integrity, objectivity and independence

The fundamental principles require that members behave with integrity in all professional and business relationships and they strive for objectivity in all their professional and business judgements. Objectivity is a state of mind but in certain roles the preservation of objectivity has to be shown by the maintenance of **independence** from those influences which could impair objectivity.

It is very important that the auditor is **impartial**, and **independent** of management, so that he can give an **objective** view on the financial statements of an entity. The onus is always on the auditor not only to be ethical but also to be **seen** to be ethical.

Independence and objectivity matter because of:

(a) The **expectations** of those directly affected, particularly the members of the company. The audit should be able to provide **objective** assurance on the truth and fairness of the financial statements that the directors can never provide.

(b) The **public interest**. Companies are public entities, governed by rules requiring the disclosure of information.

What can the auditor do to preserve objectivity? The simple answer is to **withdraw from any engagement** where there is the **slightest threat** to objectivity. However there are disadvantages in this strict approach.

- Clients may lose an auditor who knows their business.
- It denies clients the freedom to be advised by the accountant of their choice.

A better approach would be to **consider** whether the **auditors' own objectivity** and the **general safeguards** operating in the professional environment are **sufficient** to offset the threat and to **consider** whether **safeguards over and above** the general safeguards are required, for example specified partners or staff not working on an assignment.

However the ultimate option must always be withdrawing from an engagement or refusing to act.

1.4 Threats to independence and objectivity

FAST FORWARD

Threats to independence and objectivity may arise in the form of **self-review, self-interest, advocacy, familiarity and intimidation threats**. Appropriate **safeguards** must be put in place to eliminate or reduce such threats to acceptable levels.

Compliance with the fundamental principles of professional ethics may potentially be threatened by a wide range of different circumstances. These generally fall into five categories:

- Self-interest (discussed in Section 1.4.1)
- Self-review (discussed in Section 1.4.2)
- Advocacy (discussed in Section 1.4.3)
- Familiarity (discussed in Section 1.4.4)
- Intimidation (discussed in Section 1.4.5)

1.4.1 Self-interest

The ACCA *Code of ethics and conduct* highlights a number of areas in which a self-interest threat might arise. These may arise as a result of the financial or other interests of members or of immediate or close family and are summarised in the diagram below.

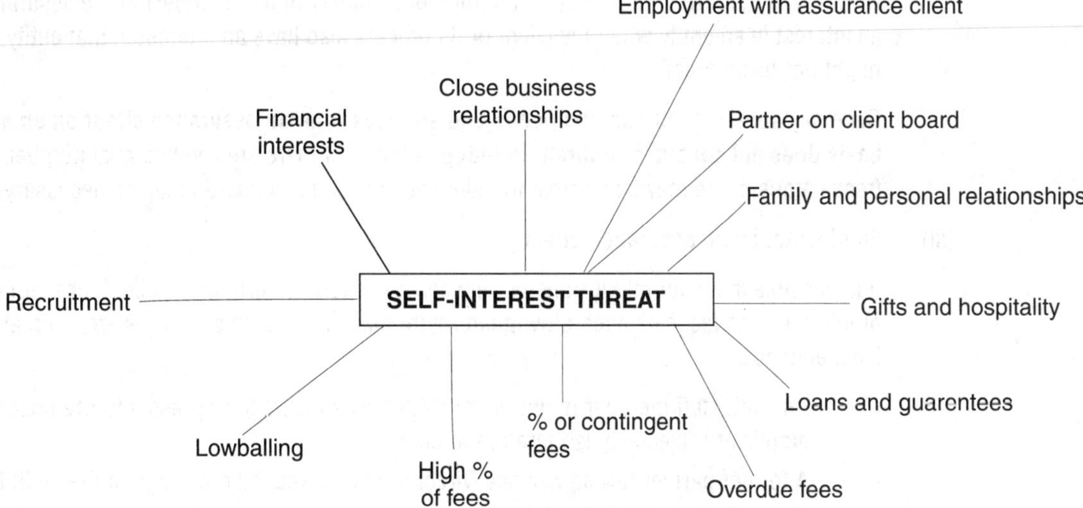

We will look at each of theses areas in turn.

(i) **Financial interests**

Key term

> A **financial interest** exists where an audit firm has a financial interest in a client's affairs, for example, the audit firm owns shares in the client, or is a trustee of a trust that holds shares in the client.

The ACCA does not allow the following to own a direct financial interest or an indirect material financial interest in a client:

- The **assurance** firm
- A **member** of the assurance team
- An **immediate family member of a member** of the assurance team

The following safeguards will therefore be relevant:

- Disposing of the interest
- Removing the individual from the team if required
- Keeping the client's audit committee informed of the situation
- Using an independent partner to review work carried out if necessary

Audit firms should have quality control procedures requiring staff to disclose relevant financial interests for themselves and close family members. They should also foster a culture of voluntary disclosure on an ongoing basis so that any potential problems are identified in a timely manner.

(ii) **Close business relationships**

Examples of when an audit firm and an audit client have an inappropriately close business relationship include:

- Having a material financial interest in a joint venture with the assurance client
- Arrangements to combine one or more services or products of the firm with one or more services or products of the assurance client and to market the package with reference to both parties
- Distribution or marketing arrangements under which the firm acts as distributor or marketer of the assurance client's products or services or vice versa

It will be necessary for the partners to judge the materiality of the interest and therefore its significance. However, **unless the interest is clearly insignificant, an assurance provider should**

not participate in such a venture with an assurance client. Appropriate safeguards are therefore to end the assurance provision or to terminate the (other) business relationship.

If an individual member of an assurance team has such an interest, he should be removed from the assurance team.

However, if the firm or a member (and immediate family of the member) of the assurance team has an interest in an entity when the client or its officers also have an interest in that entity, the threat might not be so great.

Generally speaking, **purchasing goods and services from an assurance client on an arm's length basis does not constitute a threat to independence**. If there are a substantial number of such transactions, there may be a threat to independence and safeguards may be necessary.

(iii) **Employment with assurance client**

It is possible that staff might transfer between an assurance firm and a client, or that negotiations or interviews to facilitate such movement might take place. Both situations are a threat to independence:

- An audit staff member might be motivated by a desire to impress a future possible employer (objectivity is therefore affected)
- A former partner turned Finance Director has too much knowledge of the audit firm's systems and procedures

The extent of the threat to independence depends on various factors, such as the role the individual has taken up at the client, the extent of his influence on the audit previously, the length of time that has passed between the individual's connection with the audit and the new role at the client.

Various safeguards might be:

- Considering modifying the assurance plan
- Ensuring the audit is assigned to someone of sufficient experience
- Involving an additional professional accountant not involved with the engagement to review the work done
- Carrying out a quality control review of the engagement

In respect of audit clients, a partner should not accept a key management position at an audit client until at least **two years** have elapsed since the conclusion of the audit he was involved with.

An individual who has moved from the firm to a client should not be entitled to any benefits or payments from the firm unless these are made in accordance with pre-determined arrangements. If money is owed to the individual, it should not be so much as to compromise the independence of the assurance engagement.

A firm should have quality control procedures setting out that an individual involved in serious employment negotiations with an audit client should notify the firm and that this person would then be removed from the engagement.

(iv) **Partner on client board**

A partner or employee of an assurance firm should not serve on the board of an assurance client.

It may be acceptable for a partner or an employee of an assurance firm to perform the role of company secretary for an assurance client, if the role is essentially administrative.

(v) **Family and personal relationships**

Family or close personal relationships between assurance firm and client staff could seriously threaten independence. Each situation has to be evaluated individually. Factors to consider are:

- The individual's responsibilities on the assurance engagement
- The closeness of the relationship
- The role of the other party at the assurance client

When an immediate family member of a member of the assurance team is a director, an officer or an employee of the assurance client in a position to exert direct and significant influence over the subject matter information of the assurance engagement, the individual should be removed from the assurance team.

The audit firm should also consider whether there is any threat to independence if an employee who is not a member of the assurance team has a close family or personal relationship with a director, an officer or an employee of an assurance client.

A firm should have quality control policies and procedures under which staff should disclose if a close family member employed by the client is promoted within the client.

If a firm inadvertently violates the rules concerning family and personal relationships they should apply additional safeguards, such as undertaking a quality control review of the audit and discussing the matter with the audit committee of the client, if there is one.

(vi) **Gifts and hospitality**

Unless the value of the gift/hospitality is **clearly insignificant**, a firm or a member of an assurance team should not accept. Threats to independence in such circumstances cannot be reduced to an acceptable level by the application of any safeguard.

(vii) **Loans and guarantees**

The advice on loans and guarantees falls into two categories:

- The client is a bank or other similar institution
- Other situations

If a lending institution client lends an immaterial amount to an audit firm or member of assurance team on normal commercial terms, there is no threat to independence. If the loan is material it will be necessary to apply appropriate safeguards to bring the risk to an acceptable level. A suitable safeguard is likely to be an independent review (by a partner from another office in the firm).

Loans to members of the assurance team from a bank or other lending institution client are likely to be material to the individual, but provided that they are on normal commercial terms, these do not constitute a threat to independence.

An audit firm or individual on the assurance engagement should not enter into any loan or guarantee arrangement with a client that is not a bank or similar institution. The self-interest threat created by entering into such an arrangement would be so significant that no safeguard would be able to reduce the threat to an acceptable level.

(viii) **Overdue fees**

In a situation where there are overdue fees, the auditor runs the risk of, in effect, **making a loan** to a client, whereupon the guidance above becomes relevant.

Audit firms should guard against significant fees building up by discussing the issues with those charged with governance, and, if necessary, the possibility of resigning if overdue fees are not paid.

(ix) **Contingent fees**

Contingent fees are fees calculated on a predetermined basis relating to the outcome or result of a transaction or the result of the work performed.

A firm should not enter into any fee arrangement for an assurance engagement under which the amount of the fee is contingent on the result of the assurance work or on items that are the subject matter of the assurance engagement.

It would also usually be inappropriate to accept a contingent fee for non-assurance work from an assurance client. Factors to consider in deciding whether a contingent fee is acceptable or not include:

- The range of possible fee outcomes
- The degree of variability in the fee
- The basis on which the fee is to be determined
- Whether the transaction is to be reviewed by an independent third party
- The effect of the transaction on the assurance engagement

In other circumstances it may be appropriate to accept a contingent fee for non-assurance work if suitable safeguards are in place. Examples include:

- Making disclosures to the audit committee about the fees
- Reviewing or determination of the fee by an unrelated third party
- Quality control policies and procedures

(x) **High percentage of fees**

A firm should be alert to the situation arising where the total fees generated by an assurance client represent a large proportion of a firm's total fees. Factors such as the structure of the firm and the length of time it has been trading will be relevant in determining whether there is a threat to independence. It is also necessary to beware of situations where the fees generated by an assurance client present a large proportion of the revenue of an individual partner.

Safeguards in these situations might include:

- Discussing the issues with the audit committee
- Taking steps to reduce the dependency on the client
- Obtaining external/internal quality control reviews
- Consulting a third party such as the ACCA

The public may perceive that a member's objectivity is likely to be in jeopardy where the fees for audit and recurring work paid by one client or group of connected clients exceed 15% of the firm's total fees. Where the entity is listed or a public interest company, this figure should be 10%.

It will be difficult for new firms establishing themselves to keep outside of these limits and firms in this situation should make use of the safeguards outlined.

(xi) **Lowballing**

When a firm quotes a significantly lower fee level for an assurance service than would have been charged by the predecessor firm, there is a significant self-interest threat. If the firm's tender is successful, the firm must apply safeguards such as:

- Maintaining records such that the firm is able to demonstrate that appropriate staff and time are spent on the engagement
- Complying with all applicable assurance standards, guidelines and quality control procedures

(xii) **Recruitment**

Recruiting senior management for an assurance client, particularly those able to affect the subject matter of an assurance engagement, creates a self-interest threat for the assurance firm.

Assurance providers must not make management decisions for the client. Their involvement could be limited to reviewing a shortlist of candidates, providing that the client has drawn up the criteria by which they are to be selected.

1.4.2 Self-review threat

Self-review threats may occur when a previous judgement needs to be re-evaluated by members responsible for that judgement. Circumstances that may give rise to such threats include the following:

The key area in which there is likely to be a self-review threat is where a firm provides services other than assurance services to an assurance client (providing multiple services). There is a great deal of guidance in the ACCA and IFAC rules about various other services accountancy firms could provide their clients and these are discussed below.

(i) **Recent service with an assurance client**

Individuals who have been a **director or officer of the client, or an employee in a position to exert direct and significant influence** over the subject matter information of the assurance engagement in the period under review or the previous two years should not be assigned to the assurance team.

If an individual had been closely involved with the client prior to the time limits set out above, the assurance firm should consider the threat to independence arising and apply appropriate safeguards, such as:

- Obtaining a quality control review of the individual's work on the assignment
- Discussing the issue with the audit committee

(ii) **General other services**

For assurance clients, accountants are not allowed to:

- **Authorise, execute or consummate a transaction**
- **Determine which recommendation of the company should be implemented**
- **Report in a management capacity to those charged with governance**

Having custody of an assurance client's assets, supervising client employees in the performance of their normal duties, and preparing source documents on behalf of the client also pose significant self-review threats which should be addressed by safeguards such as the following:

- Ensuring non-assurance team staff are used for these roles
- Involving an independent professional accountant to advise
- Quality control policies on what staff are and are not allowed to do for clients
- Making appropriate disclosures to those charged with governance
- Resigning from the assurance engagement

(iii) **Preparing accounting records and financial statements**

There is clearly a significant risk of self-review if a firm prepares accounting records and financial statements and then audits them. However, in practice, auditors routinely assist management with the preparation of financial statements and give advice about accounting treatments and journal entries.

Assurance firms must therefore analyse the risks arising and put safeguards in place to ensure that the risk is at an acceptable level. Safeguards include:

- Using staff members other than assurance team members to carry out work
- Obtaining client approval for work undertaken

The rules are more stringent when the client is listed or public interest. **Firms should not prepare accounts or financial statements for listed or public interest clients**, unless an emergency arises.

For any client, assurance firms are also not allowed to:

- Determine or change journal entries without client approval
- Authorise or approve transactions
- Prepare source documents

(iv) **Valuation services**

Key term

A **valuation** comprises the making of assumptions with regard to future developments, the application of certain methodologies and techniques, and the combination of both in order to compute a certain value, or range of values, for an asset, a liability or for a business as a whole.

If an audit firm performs a valuation for which will be included in financial statements audited by the firm, a self-review threat arises.

Audit firms should not carry out valuations on matters which will be material to the financial statements. If the valuation is for an immaterial matter, the audit firm should apply safeguards to ensure that the risk is reduced to an acceptable level. Matters to consider when applying safeguards are the extent of the audit client's knowledge of the relevant matters in making the valuation and the degree of judgement involved, how much use is made of established methodologies and the degree of uncertainty in the valuation. Safeguards include:

- Second partner review
- Confirming that the client understands the valuation and the assumptions used
- Ensuring the client acknowledges responsibility for the valuation
- Using separate personnel for the valuation and the audit

(v) **Taxation services**

In many jurisdictions, the assurance firm may be asked to provide taxation services to its client. These encompass a wide range of services, including compliance, planning, provision of formal taxation opinions and assistance in the resolution of tax disputes. The provision of taxation services is generally not seen to threaten independence.

(vi) **Internal audit services**

A firm may provide internal audit services to an audit client. However, it should ensure that the client acknowledges its responsibility for establishing, maintaining and monitoring the system of internal control. It may be appropriate to use safeguards such as ensuring that an employee of the client is designated responsible for internal audit activities and that the client approves all the work that internal audit does.

(vii) **Corporate finance**

Certain aspects of corporate finance will create self-review threats that cannot be reduced to an acceptable level by safeguards. Therefore, **assurance firms are not allowed to promote, deal in or underwrite an assurance client's shares. They are also not allowed to commit an assurance client to the terms of a transaction or consummate a transaction on the client's behalf**.

Other corporate finance services, such as assisting a client in defining corporate strategies, assisting in identifying possible sources of capital and providing structuring advice may be acceptable, providing that safeguards, such as using different teams of staff, are used and ensuring no management decisions are taken on behalf of the client.

(viii) **Other services**

The audit firm might sell a variety of other services to audit clients, such as:

- IT services
- Temporary staff cover
- Litigation support
- Legal services

The assurance firm should consider whether there are any barriers to independence, such as if the firm were asked to design internal control IT systems, which it would then review as part of its audit, or if the firm were asked to provide an accountant to cover the chief accountant's maternity leave. The firm should consider whether the threat to independence could be reduced to an acceptable level by appropriate safeguards.

1.4.3 Advocacy threat

Advocacy threats arise in those situations where the assurance firm promotes a position or opinion to the point that subsequent objectivity is compromised. Examples include commenting publicly on future events in particular circumstances, having made assertions without detailing the assumptions, or acting as an advocate on behalf of an assurance client in litigation or disputes with third parties. Advocacy threats might also arise if the firm promoted shares in a listed audit client.

Relevant safeguards might include using different departments to carry out the work and making disclosures to the audit committee. Remember, the ultimate option is always to withdraw from an engagement if the risk to independence is too high.

1.4.4 Familiarity threat

A familiarity threat occurs when, because of a close relationship, members become too sympathetic to the interests of others. There is a substantial risk of loss of professional scepticism in such circumstances.

We have already discussed some examples of when this risk arises, because very often a familiarity threat arises in conjunction with a self-interest threat. These include situations where there are family and personal relationships between the client and firm, long association with a client, employment with a client and recent service with a client.

Independence may be threatened significantly if senior members of staff at an audit firm have a long association with a client. All firms should therefore monitor the relationship between staff and established clients and use safeguards such as rotating senior staff off the assurance team, obtaining second partner reviews and independent (but internal) quality control reviews.

In addition, the *Code of ethics and conduct* sets out specific rules for listed and other public interest entities in this situation:

- The engagement partner should be rotated after a pre-defined period, normally no more than **five years**, and should not return to the engagement until a period of five years has elapsed.
- Other key audit partners should be rotated after a pre-defined period, normally no more than **seven years**, and should not return to the engagement until a period of two years (or five years if returning as engagement partner) has elapsed.
- The individual responsible for the engagement quality control review should be rotated after a pre-defined period, normally no more than **seven years**, and should not return to the engagement until a period of two years has elapsed

When an entity becomes a listed entity, the length of time the staff involved with the audit have been involved should be taken into consideration, but **the engagement partner, other key partners and quality control person should only continue in those positions for another two years**.

1.4.5 Intimidation threat

An intimidation threat arises when members of the assurance team may be deterred from acting objectively by threats, actual or perceived. These could arise from family and personal relationships, litigation, or close business relationships. These are also examples of self-interest threats, largely because intimidation may only arise significantly when the assurance firm has something to lose.

The most obvious example is when the client threatens to sue, or does sue, the assurance firm for work that has been done previously. The firm is then faced with the risk of losing the client, bad publicity and the possibility that it will be found to have been negligent. This could lead to the firm being under pressure to produce an unqualified audit report when it has been qualified in the past, for example.

Generally, assurance firms should seek to avoid such situations arising. If they do arise, factors to consider are:

- The materiality of the litigation
- The nature of the assurance engagement
- Whether the litigation relates to a prior assurance engagement

The following safeguards could be considered:

- Disclosing to the audit committee the nature and extent of the litigation
- Removing specific affected individuals from the engagement team
- Involving an additional professional accountant on the team to review work

However, if the litigation is at all serious, it may be necessary to resign from the engagement, as the threat to independence is so great.

1.5 Conflicts of interest

In some ways conflict of interest issues are similar to the difficulties firms have in maintaining independence. They can arise in a variety of circumstances and each problem has to be dealt with on its own merits. There are no rules to deal with most of the situations, outside the ACCA's rules about independence and integrity, and the solution will usually be based on common sense as much as ethical behaviour.

We have already dealt with conflicts of interest in terms of auditor independence, particularly in situations where there is a financial or personal interest in a client company.

Conflicts of interest can arise when a firm has two (or more) audit clients, both of which have reason to be unhappy that their auditors are also auditors of the other company. This situation frequently arises when the companies are in **direct competition** with each other, and particularly when the **auditors have access to** particularly **sensitive information**.

In general, where conflicts of interest arise, there should be **full** and **frank explanation** to those involved by the audit firm, coupled with any action necessary to disengage from one or both positions.

Conflicts should, so far as possible, be avoided by **not accepting** any appointment or assignment in which they seem likely to occur.

This avoidance of clients causing a conflict of interest is more important for smaller audit firms. The larger firms can overcome a conflict by building a **'Chinese wall'** within the firm. This would mean that the respective audits are undertaken by different audit 'groups', the engagement partners are different and all the other audit staff are allowed to work on one of the clients only.

Case Study

British Telecom was not happy when its auditors merged with the firm which audited Cable and Wireless. The new firm was forced to drop one of the audits. Legal cases such as Prince Jefri of Brunei and KPMG, and in connection with the merger of Robson Rhodes and Parnell Kerr Forster, have also cast doubt on the ability of accountants to rely on Chinese walls.

Whenever accountants are acting for two clients who are in a **directly adversarial** situation, both should be **informed** and asked to **give consent** for the accountant to continue to act for both.

Other situations, for example clients in competition, might be covered by a paragraph in the **audit engagement letter** (the audit engagement letter is covered in section 3 of this chapter).

If consent has not been given, a Chinese wall may be effective, providing the departments concerned are **physically separated** and there are **strict procedures** and **monitoring** in place. The Chinese wall needs to be part of the organisational culture of the firm.

The guidance suggests firms can avoid the need for a Chinese wall in these circumstances by a paragraph in the audit engagement letter saying that information will be kept confidential except as required by law, regulatory or ethical guidance, and the client permits the firm to take such steps as it thinks fit to preserve confidentiality.

It would be better to advise the companies to obtain arbitration from an independent accountant. The auditors should not investigate one client on behalf of another, nor pass on any knowledge of either client in such a situation. This is not always easy, particularly when the auditors can see the whole picture, but the companies cannot. The auditors must be extremely tactful and firm.

1.6 Enforcement mechanisms

In this section we briefly consider how ACCA enforces the *Code of ethics and conduct.* Members are liable to disciplinary action if they breach the ethical guidance.

The professional conduct department first investigates the potential breach and if liability is indicated, it prepares a report for consideration by an external assessor. If the assessor concludes there is a case to answer, he or she may refer the matter to the ACCA's Disciplinary Committee.

The Disciplinary Committee hears the case and if the complaint is proved wholly or in part, the member concerned could be excluded from membership of the ACCA, severely reprimanded or fined for example.

Members can appeal to the Appeal Committee which will consider the appeal at a hearing.

Members have to confirm in their annual Continuing Professional Development (CPD) returns that they have kept their professional ethics up to date. ACCA does monitor CPD returns by checking a sample on an annual basis.

1.7 Country-specific ethical guidance

Although the ACCA and IFAC have produced detailed ethical guidance for professional accountants, countries may have their own additional ethical guidance.

For example, in the UK, the Auditing Practices Board of the Financial Reporting Council has issued five ethical standards, an ethical standard specific to small entities and an ethical standard for reporting accountants, which provide an additional source of guidance. These are not examinable under your syllabus, but are simply mentioned here as an example.

2 Accepting audit appointments

FAST FORWARD

The present and proposed auditors must **communicate** with each other prior to the audit being accepted, however if the client refuses to give **permission** to the proposed auditors to make contact, the proposed auditors must **decline nomination**.

2.1 Tendering and obtaining work

Members are entitled to advertise their services and products. The advertising medium should not reflect adversely on the member, ACCA or the accountancy profession. Adverts should not:

- Bring ACCA into disrepute or bring discredit to the member, firm or accountancy profession
- Discredit the services of others
- Be misleading
- Fall short of local regulatory or legislative requirements

2.1.1 Fee negotiation and lowballing

The audit fee is a sensitive subject for most companies. It represents a cost for something the company often does not really want and the fees may be perceived as too high just for this reason. The auditors must ensure that they can provide a quality audit for the price.

Many large companies invite **tenders** for their audit work. The directors then have the opportunity to compare directly a range of offers.

Generally, a tender will take the form of detailed written proposals and a presentation. Factors include:

- The **level** of **expertise** each firm has in the industry
- **Similar companies** audited by each firm (good for expertise, bad for confidentiality?)
- **National** and **international presence**
- The proposed **fee**

Audit firms which tender for such audits will usually give at least an indication of the level of fees in the next few years, including likely overall rate rises. Fee levels are very important to most companies and are often the determining factor.

In all situations, the auditors should quote a fee based on the estimated hours worked by each member of staff required on the audit, multiplied by the hourly rate plus any travel and other expenses to be incurred during the audit. They may also charge a premium for more complex audits.

Sometimes it appears that firms are charging less than 'market rate' for an audit, especially when tendering for new clients. This practice is known as **lowballing**, and we discussed it in Section 1.4.1.

It is not considered ethically wrong to charge a low price for an audit in itself. However, the auditors must ensure that they carry out an audit of the quality demanded by auditing standards and that the 'cut-price' audit fee does not call their independence into question.

This is always going to be a topical debate, but in terms of negotiating the audit fee the following factors need to be taken into account.

(a) The audit is perceived to have a **fluctuating 'market price'** as any other commodity or service.

(b) Companies can reduce external audit costs through various **legitimate measures:**

  - Extending the size and function of internal audit
  - Reducing the number of different audit firms used world-wide
  - Selling off subsidiary companies leaving a simplified group structure to audit
  - The tender process itself simply makes auditors more competitive
  - Exchange rate fluctuations in audit fees

(c) Auditing firms have **increased productivity**, partly through the use of more sophisticated information technology techniques in auditing.

In any case, an auditing firm lays itself open to accusations of loss of independence if it reduces its fees to below a certain level, particularly if it is difficult to see how such fees will cover direct labour costs. This is also true of firms which use the audit as a 'loss leader' to obtain profitable consultancy work from audit clients.

When such non-audit services are offered to a client by the auditors, there can, of course, be an apparent loss of independence. The allegation may arise that the price of an 'acceptable' audit opinion is lucrative taxation or consulting work.

2.2 Appointment ethics

This section covers the procedures that the auditors must undertake to ensure that their appointment is valid and that they are clear to act.

2.2.1 Before accepting nomination

Before a new audit client is accepted, the auditors must ensure that there are no **independence** or **other ethical problems** likely to cause conflict with the ethical code. Furthermore, new auditors should ensure that they have been appointed in a proper and legal manner.

The nominee auditors must carry out the following procedures:

ACCEPTANCE PROCEDURES	
Ensure **professionally qualified** to act	Consider whether disqualified on legal or ethical grounds
Ensure **existing resources adequate**	Consider available time, staff and technical expertise
Obtain references	Make independent enquiries if directors not personally known
Communicate with present auditors	Enquire whether there are reasons/circumstances behind the change which the new auditors ought to know, also courtesy

An appointment decision chart is shown below.

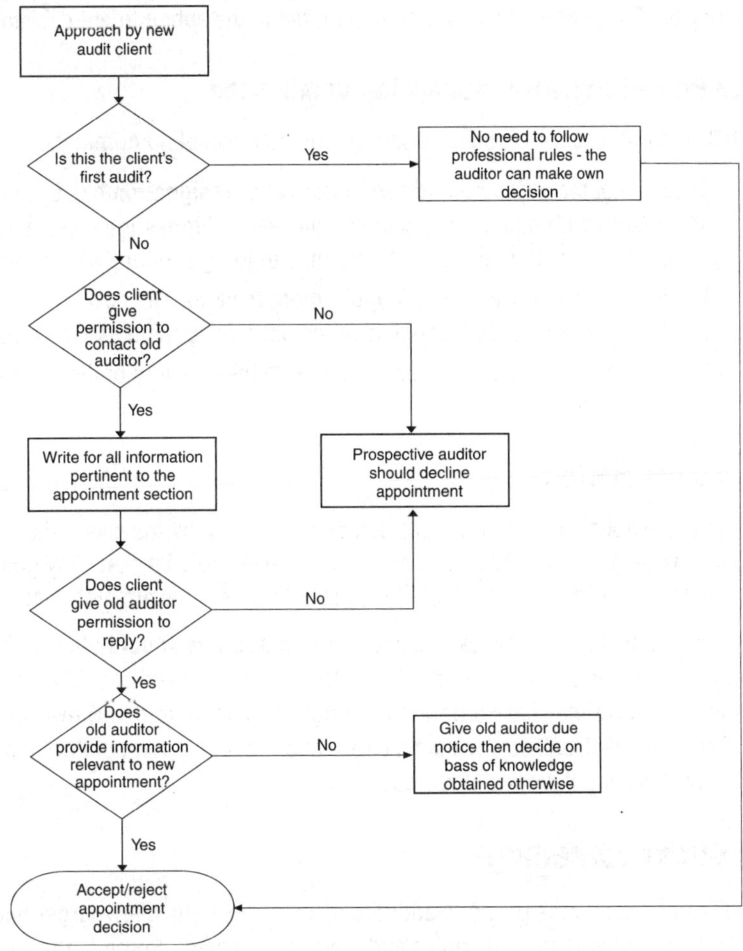

2.2.2 Example nomination letter

This is an example of an initial communication.

To: Retiring & Co
Certified Accountants

Dear Sirs

Re: New Client Co Ltd

We have been asked to allow our name to go forward for nomination as auditors of the above company, and we should therefore be grateful if you would let us know whether there are any professional reasons why we should not accept nomination ....

Acquiring & Co

Certified Accountants

Having negotiated these steps the auditors will be in a position to accept the nomination, or not, as the case may be. These procedures are demonstrated in the appointment decision chart.

2.2.3 Procedures after accepting nomination

The following procedures should be carried out after accepting nomination.

(a) **Ensure** that the **outgoing auditors' removal** or **resignation** has been **properly conducted** in accordance with national legislation. The new auditors should see a valid notice of the outgoing auditors' resignation, or confirm that the outgoing auditors were properly removed.

(b) **Ensure** that the **new auditors' appointment is valid**. The new auditors should obtain a copy of the resolution passed at the general meeting appointing them as the company's auditors.

(c) Set up and **submit a letter of engagement** to the directors of the company. Letters of engagement are discussed in the next section.

2.2.4 Other matters

Where the previous auditors have fees still owing to them by the client, the new auditors need not decline appointment solely for this reason. They should decide how far they may go in aiding the former auditors to obtain their fees, as well as whether they should accept the appointment.

Once a new appointment has taken place, the **new auditors should obtain all books and papers which belong to the client from the old auditors**. The former auditors should ensure that all such documents are transferred, **unless** they have a **lien** (a legal right to hold on to them) over the books because of unpaid fees. They should also pass any useful information onto the new auditors if it will be of help, without charge, unless a lot of work is involved.

2.3 Client screening

As well as contacting the previous auditors many firms, particularly larger ones, carry out **stringent checks** on potential client companies and their management. Some of the basic factors for consideration are given below.

2.3.1 Management integrity

The integrity of those managing a company will be of great importance, particularly if the company is controlled by one or a few dominant personalities.

2.3.2 Risk

The following table contrasts low and high risk clients.

LOW RISK	HIGH RISK
Good long-term prospects	Poor recent or forecast performance
Well-financed	Likely lack of finance
Strong internal controls	Significant control weaknesses
Conservative, prudent accounting policies	Evidence of questionable integrity, doubtful accounting policies
Competent, honest management	Lack of finance director
Few unusual transactions	Significant related party or unexplained transactions

Where the risk level of a company's audit is determined as anything other than low, then the specific risks should be identified and documented. It might be necessary to assign specialists in response to these risks, particularly industry specialists, as independent reviewers. Some audit firms have procedures for closely monitoring audits which have been accepted, but which are considered high risk.

2.3.3 Engagement economics

Generally, the expected fees from a new client should reflect the **level of risk** expected. They should also offer the same sort of return expected of clients of this nature and reflect the overall financial strategy of the audit firm. Occasionally, the audit firm will want the work to gain entry into the client's particular industry, or to establish better contacts within that industry. These factors will all contribute to a total expected economic return.

2.3.4 Relationship with client

The audit firm will generally want the relationship with a client to be **long-term**. This is not only to enjoy receiving fees year after year but to allow the audit work to be enhanced by better knowledge of the client and thereby offer a better service.

Conflict of interest problems are significant here; the firm should establish that no existing clients will cause difficulties as competitors of the new client. Other services to other clients may have an impact here, not just audit.

2.3.5 Ability to perform the work

The audit firm must have the **resources** to perform the work properly, as well as any **specialist knowledge or skills**. The impact on existing engagements must be estimated, in terms of staff time and the timing of the audit.

2.4 Approval

Once all the relevant procedures and information gathering has taken place, the company can be put forward for approval. The engagement partner will have completed a **client acceptance form** and this, along with any other relevant documentation, will be submitted to the partner who is in overall charge of accepting clients.

Exam focus point

In the exam you may be given a 'real-life' client situation and asked what factors you would consider in deciding whether to accept appointment.

3 Agreeing the terms of the engagement

Pilot paper

FAST FORWARD

The **terms** of the audit engagement shall be **agreed** with management and **recorded** in an audit engagement letter.

3.1 Preconditions for an audit

ISA 210 *Agreeing the terms of audit engagements* states that the objective of the auditor is to accept or continue an audit engagement only when the basis on which it is to be carried out has been agreed by establishing whether the **preconditions for an audit** are present and confirming that there is a common understanding between the auditor and management of the terms of the engagement.

Key term

The **preconditions for an audit** are the use by management of an acceptable financial reporting framework in the preparation of the financial statements and the agreement of management and, where appropriate, those charged with governance to the premise on which an audit is conducted.

To determine whether the preconditions for an audit are present, the auditor shall do the following:

- Determine whether the **financial reporting framework is acceptable**. Factors to consider include the nature of the entity, the purpose of the financial statements, the nature of the financial statements, and whether law or regulation prescribes the applicable financial reporting framework.
- Obtain management's agreement that it **acknowledges and understands** its **responsibilities** for the following.
  - **Preparing the financial statements** in accordance with the applicable financial reporting framework
  - **Internal control** that is necessary to enable the preparation of financial statements which are free from material misstatement
  - **Providing the auditor with access to all information** of which management is aware that is relevant to the preparation of the financial statements, with **additional information** that the auditor may request, and with **unrestricted access** to entity staff from whom the auditor determines it necessary to obtain audit evidence

If these preconditions are not present, the auditor shall **discuss** the matter with management. The auditor **shall not accept** the audit engagement if:

- The auditor has determined that the **financial reporting framework** to be applied is **not acceptable**.
- **Management's agreement** referred to above has **not been obtained**.

3.2 The audit engagement letter

Key term

The **engagement letter** is the written terms of an engagement in the form of a letter.

The auditor shall agree the terms of the engagement with management or those charged with governance and these shall be recorded in an **audit engagement letter** or other suitable form of written agreement. This has to be done before the audit engagement begins so as to **avoid misunderstandings** regarding the audit.

3.2.1 Form and content of the audit engagement letter

The audit engagement letter shall include the following:

- The **objective and scope** of the audit
- The **auditor's responsibilities**
- **Management's responsibilities**

- Identification of the **applicable financial reporting framework** for the preparation of the financial statements
- Reference to the **expected form and content of any reports** to be issued by the auditor and a statement that there may be circumstances in which a report may differ from its expected form and content

3.2.2 Additional matters that may be included

The audit engagement letter may also make reference to the following:

- **Elaboration of scope of audit**, including reference to legislation, regulations, ISAs, ethical and other pronouncements
- Form of **any other communication** of results of the engagement
- The fact that due to the inherent limitations of an audit and those of internal control, there is an **unavoidable risk that some material misstatements may not be detected**, even though the audit is properly planned and performed in accordance with ISAs
- **Arrangements regarding planning and performance**, including audit team composition
- Expectation that management will provide **written representations**
- **Agreement** of management to provide **draft financial statements** and other information in time to allow auditor to complete the audit in accordance with proposed timetable
- **Agreement** of management to inform auditor of **facts** that may affect the financial statements, of which management may become aware from the date of the auditor's report to the date of issue of the financial statements
- **Fees and billing arrangements**
- Request for management to **acknowledge receipt** of the letter and agree to the terms outlined in it
- Involvement of **other auditors and experts**
- Involvement of **internal auditors and other staff**
- Arrangements to be made with **predecessor auditor**
- Any **restriction of auditor's liability**
- Reference to **any further agreements** between auditor and entity
- Any **obligations to provide audit working papers** to other parties

Appendix 1 of ISA 210 includes an example of an audit engagement letter.

3.3 Recurring audits

On recurring audits, the auditor shall assess whether the terms of the engagement need to be revised and whether there is a need to remind the entity of the existing terms. The following factors may indicate that it would be appropriate to revise the terms of the engagement or remind the entity of the existing terms.

- Any indication that the entity **misunderstands** the objective and scope of the audit
- Any **revised or special terms** of the audit engagement
- A recent change of **senior management**
- A significant change in **ownership**
- A significant change in **nature or size** of the entity's business
- A change in **legal or regulatory requirements**
- A change in the **financial reporting framework**
- A change in **other reporting requirements**

3.4 Acceptance of a change in terms

A change in the terms of audit engagement prior to completion may result from:

(a) A **change in circumstances** affecting the need for the service

(b) A **misunderstanding** as to the nature of an audit or of the related service originally requested

(c) A **restriction on the scope** of the audit engagement, whether imposed by management or caused by circumstances

The auditor shall not agree to a change in the terms of the audit engagement where there is no **reasonable justification** for doing so. In the case of (a) and (b) above, these might be acceptable reasons for requesting a change in the engagement. A change may not be considered reasonable, however, if it seems to relate to information that is incorrect, incomplete or otherwise unsatisfactory. An example of this would be if the auditor could not obtain sufficient appropriate audit evidence for receivables and the entity then asks the auditor to change the engagement from an audit to a review so as to avoid a qualification of the auditor's report.

If the auditor is asked to **change** the audit engagement before it is completed to an engagement providing a **lower level of assurance** such as a review or a related service, the auditor shall determine whether there is **reasonable justification** for doing so because there may be legal or contractual implications.

If the terms are **changed**, the auditor and management shall **agree and record** the new terms in an engagement letter. However, to avoid confusing users, the report on the related service will not include reference to the original audit engagement or any procedures performed in the original audit engagement (unless the engagement is changed to a agreed-upon procedures engagement, where reference to procedures performed is included in the report).

However, if the auditor **cannot agree** to a change of terms and management does not allow the auditor to carry on with the original audit engagement, the auditor shall **withdraw** from the engagement and determine whether there is an **obligation to report** this to other parties (e.g. those charged with governance, owners, regulators).

Question — **New auditors**

You are a partner in Messrs Borg, Connors & Co, Certified Accountants. You are approached by Mr Nastase, the managing director of Navratilova Enterprises Ltd, who asks your firm to become auditors of his company. In return for giving you this appointment Mr Nastase says that he will expect your firm to waive 50 per cent of your normal fee for the first year's audit. The existing auditors, Messrs Wade, Austin & Co, have not resigned but Mr Nastase informs you that they will not be re-appointed in the future.

Required

(a) What action should Messrs Borg, Connors & Co take in response to the request from Mr Nastase to reduce their first year's fee by 50 per cent?

(b) Are Messrs Wade, Austin & Co within their rights in not resigning when they know Mr Nastase wishes to replace them? Give reasons for your answer.

Answer

(a) The request by Mr Nastase that half of the first year's audit fee should be waived is quite improper. If this proposal were to be accepted it could be held that Borg Connors & Co had sought to procure work through the quoting of lower fees. This would be unethical and would result in disciplinary proceedings being taken against the firm.

Mr Nastase should be informed that the audit fee will be determined by reference to the work involved in completion of a satisfactory audit, taking into account the nature of the audit tasks involved and the resources required to carry out those tasks in an efficient manner. He should also be told that if he is not prepared to accept an audit fee arrived at in this way and insists on there being a reduction then regrettably the nomination to act as auditor will have to be declined.

(b) Wade, Austin & Co have every right not to resign even though they may be aware that Mr Nastase wishes to replace them. The auditors of a company are appointed by, and report to, the members of a company and the directors are not empowered to remove the auditors. If the reason for the proposed change arises out of a dispute between management and the auditors then the auditors have a right to put forward their views as seen above and to insist that any decision should be made by the members, but only once they have been made aware of all pertinent facts concerning the directors' wishes to have them removed from office.

Chapter Roundup

- The ACCA's *Code of ethics and conduct* sets out the five **fundamental principles** of professional ethics and provides a **conceptual framework** for applying them.
- Members of the ACCA must comply with the fundamental principles set out in the *Code of ethics and conduct* (**integrity, objectivity, professional competence and due care, confidentiality and professional behaviour**).
- Although auditors have a professional duty of **confidentiality,** they may be compelled by **law** or consider it necessary in the **public interest** to disclose details of clients' affairs to third parties.
- Threats to independence and objectivity may arise in the form of **self-review, self-interest, advocacy, familiarity and intimidation threats**. Appropriate **safeguards** must be put in place to eliminate or reduce such threats to acceptable levels.
- The present and proposed auditors must **communicate** with each other prior to the audit being accepted, however if the client refuses to give **permission** to the proposed auditors to make contact, the proposed auditors must **decline nomination**.
- The **terms** of the audit engagement shall be **agreed** with management and **recorded** in an audit engagement letter.

Quick Quiz

1 Match each ethical principle to the correct definition.

(a) Integrity
(b) Objectivity
(c) Professional competence and due care
(d) Confidentiality
(e) Professional behaviour

(i) Not allow bias, conflicts of interest or undue influence of others to override professional or business judgements.

(ii) Have a continuing duty to maintain professional knowledge and skill at a level required to ensure that a client or employer receives competent professional service based on current developments in practice, legislation and techniques. Act diligently and in accordance with applicable technical and professional standards when providing professional services.

(iii) Be straightforward and honest in all business and professional relationships.

(iv) Comply with relevant laws and regulations and avoid any action that discredits the profession.

(v) Respect the confidentiality of information acquired as a result of professional and business relationships and should not disclose any such information to third parties without proper or specific authority or unless there is a legal or professional right or duty to disclose. Confidential information acquired as a result of professional and business relationships should not be used for the personal advantage of members or third parties.

2 ACCA's *Code of ethics and conduct* applies only to statutory audits.

True ☐

False ☐

3 Fill in the blanks:

In general, the recurring work paid by the client or group of connected clients should not exceed ....% of the gross practice income.

In the case of .... or other .... companies, the figure should be ....% of gross practice income.

4 (a) Which of the following are legitimate reasons for breach of client confidentiality?

(i) Auditor **suspects** client has committed treason
(ii) Disclosure **needed** to protect auditor's own interests
(iii) Information is **required** for the auditor of another client
(iv) Auditor **knows** client has committed terrorist offence
(v) There is a **public duty** to disclose
(vi) Auditor **considers** there to be non-compliance with law and regulations
(vii) Auditor **suspects** client has committed fraud

(b) Of the above reasons, which are voluntary disclosures and which are obligatory disclosures?

5 An engagement letter is only ever sent to a client before the first audit.

True ☐

False ☐

Answers to Quick Quiz

1 (a) (iii)
(b) (i)
(c) (ii)
(d) (v)
(e) (iv)

2 False. The spirit of the guidance applies equally to other audit situations.

3 15, listed, public interest, 10

4 (a) (i), (ii), (iv), (v), (vi)

(b) (i) Obligatory
(ii) Voluntary
(iv) Obligatory
(v) Voluntary
(vi) Obligatory

(*NB.* In the case of (vii), the auditor should not take action outside the company until he is certain. When he is certain, he should seek legal advice.)

5 False. It should be re-issued if there is a change in circumstances.

Now try the questions below from the Exam Question Bank

Number	Level	Marks	Time
Q5	Introductory	n/a	n/a
Q6	Examination	20	36 mins

PART B

Internal audit

Internal audit

Topic list	Syllabus reference
1 Internal audit and corporate governance	B1
2 Distinction between internal and external audit	B2
3 Scope of the internal audit function	B3
4 Internal audit assignments	B5
5 Internal audit reports	B2, B3, G3
6 Outsourcing the internal audit function	B4

Introduction

Internal audit is a function established by management to assist in corporate governance by assessing internal controls and helping in risk management. It can be a department of employees or can be outsourced to expert service providers.

Internal auditing is different from external auditing, although the techniques used by both are very similar. While the techniques used may be similar, the focus and reasons behind the audit are different.

Various assurance assignments may be undertaken by internal auditors and these are outlined in Section 4. The role of internal audit with regard to fraud is also discussed briefly.

The chapter ends with a consideration of outsourcing the internal audit function – this is very common in the real world and we discuss the potential benefits and drawbacks of doing so.

Study guide

		Intellectual level
B1	**Internal audit and corporate governance**	
(a)	Discuss the factors to be taken into account when assessing the need for internal audit	2
(b)	Discuss the elements of best practice in the structure and operations of internal audit with reference to appropriate international codes of corporate governance	2
B2	**Differences between external and internal audit**	
(a)	Compare and contrast the role of external and internal audit regarding audit planning and the collection of audit evidence	2
(b)	Compare and contrast the types of report provided by internal and external audit	2
B3	**The scope of the internal audit function**	
(a)	Discuss the scope of internal audit and the limitations of the internal audit function	2
(b)	Explain the types of audit report provided in internal audit assignments	1
(c)	Discuss the responsibilities of internal and external auditors for the prevention and detection of fraud and error	2
B4	**Outsourcing the internal audit department**	
(a)	Explain the advantages and disadvantages of outsourcing internal audit	1
B5	**Internal audit assignments**	
(a)	Discuss the nature and purpose of internal audit assignments including value for money, IT, best value and financial	2
(b)	Discuss the nature and purpose of operational internal audit assignments including procurement, marketing, treasury and human resources management	2
G3	**Internal audit reports**	
(a)	Describe and explain the format and content of internal audit review reports and other reports dealing with the enhancement of performance	1
(b)	Explain the process for producing an internal audit report	1

Exam guide

Internal audit has featured in every sitting of the F8 paper to date so it is therefore very important that you understand what internal auditing is and how it differs from external auditing, as there is a good chance it could come up again.

The pilot paper had a question worth six marks on the responsibilities of internal and external auditors to detect fraud. In December 2007, there were eight marks available on the independence of internal audit in a scenario question. In June 2008, question 4 was wholly devoted to internal audit – part (a) was knowledge-based for eight marks on the advantages and disadvantages of outsourcing the internal audit function, and part (b) was for 12 marks on the reasons for having an internal audit function (scenario context). There was a similar question in December 2008 on the benefits of having an internal audit department, worth eight marks and in a scenario context. The June 2009 paper had an eight mark question on comparing and contrasting the role of internal and external auditors.

1 Internal audit and corporate governance **Pilot paper**

FAST FORWARD

Internal audit assists management in achieving the entity's corporate objectives, particularly in establishing good corporate governance.

1.1 Introduction

The following definition of internal auditing was given in Chapter 1, for comparison with other forms of assurance service and providers:

Key term

Internal auditing is an appraisal or monitoring activity established within an entity as a service to the entity. It functions by, amongst other things, examining, evaluating and reporting to management and the directors on the adequacy and effectiveness of components of the accounting and internal control systems.

Internal audit is generally a feature of large companies. It is a function, provided either by employees of the entity or sourced from an external organisation, to assist management in **achieving corporate objectives**. An entity's corporate objectives will vary from company to company, and will be found in a company's mission statement and strategic plan. However, other corporate objectives will not vary so much between companies, and are linked to a key issue we have already discussed in Chapter 3 on **good corporate governance**.

1.2 Internal audit and corporate governance

Established codes of corporate governance such as the UK's Combined Code highlight the need for businesses to maintain **good systems of internal control** to manage the risks the company faces. **Internal audit** can play a key role in assessing and monitoring internal control policies and procedures.

The internal audit function can assist the board in other ways as well:

- By, in effect, acting as auditors for board reports not audited by the external auditors
- By being the experts in fields such as auditing and accounting standards in the company and assisting in implementation of new standards
- By liaising with external auditors, particularly where external auditors can use internal audit work and reduce the time and therefore cost of the external audit.

One of the principles of the Combined Code that was set out in Chapter 3 is that:

The board should establish formal and transparent arrangements for considering how they should apply the financial reporting and internal control principles for maintaining an appropriate relationship with the company's auditors.

Part of achieving this principle requires the audit committee to:

- Monitor and review the effectiveness of internal audit activities
- Where there is no internal audit function, to consider annually whether there is a need for this function and make a recommendation to the board
- Where there is no internal audit function, to explain in the annual report the absence of such a function

2 Distinction between internal and external audit

June 09

FAST FORWARD

Although many of the techniques internal and external auditors use may be similar, the basis and reasoning of their work is different.

The **external audit** is focused on the **financial statements**, whereas the **internal audit** is focused on the **operations of the entire business**.

The following table highlights the key differences between internal and external audit.

	Internal audit	External audit
Objective	Designed to add value and improve an organisation's operations.	An exercise to enable auditors to express an opinion on the financial statements.
Reporting	Reports to the board of directors, or other people charged with governance, such as the audit committee. Reports are private and for the directors and management of the company.	Reports to the shareholders or members of a company on the truth and fairness of the accounts. Audit report is publicly available to the shareholders and other interested parties.
Scope	Work relates to the operations of the organisation.	Work relates to the financial statements.
Relationship	Often employees of the organisation, although sometimes the function is outsourced.	Independent of the company and its management. Usually appointed by the shareholders.
Planning and collection of evidence	Strategic long term planning carried out, to achieve objective of assignments, with no materiality level being set. Some audits may be procedural, rather than risk-based. Evidence mainly from interviewing staff and inspecting documents (ie not external).	Planning carried out to achieve objective regarding truth and fairness of financial statements. Materiality level set during planning (may be amended during course of audit). External audit work is risk-based. Evidence collected using a variety of procedures per ISAs to obtain sufficient appropriate audit evidence.

The table demonstrates that the **whole basis and reasoning** of internal audit work is **fundamentally different** to that of external audit work.

Exam focus point

It is vital that you understand the difference between the role of internal and external audit. Questions from either perspective could come up in the exam, so your understanding of the respective roles of internal and external auditors will assist you in answering the question set.

2.1 Regulation of internal auditors

Internal auditing is not regulated in the same way as statutory external auditing (which we covered in Chapter 2). There are **no legal requirements** associated with becoming an internal auditor. The **scope** and **nature** of **internal audit's work** is more likely to be set by **company policy** than by any external guidelines.

In contrast to external auditors, internal auditors are not required to be members of a professional body such as the ACCA. However, this does not mean they cannot be, and many are. There is also a global Institute of Internal Auditors (IIA) which internal auditors may become members of. It issues 'Standards for the Professional Practice of Internal Auditing'. These are not examinable, so are not detailed in this Study Text, but you should be aware of the them as being another Code of Good Practice that internal auditors can follow, providing a framework for a wide range of internal audit services.

3 Scope of the internal audit function   Pilot paper, Dec 07

FAST FORWARD

Internal audit has two key roles to play in relation to organisational risk management:

- Ensuring the company's risk management system operates effectively
- Ensuring that strategies implemented in respect of business risks operate effectively

3.1 Business risk

The UK's Turnbull guidance on internal control assists companies in applying the section of the Combined Code relating to internal control. This guidance refers to the management of risks that are significant to the fulfilment of the company's objectives which is known as **business risk**.

Key term

Business risk is a risk resulting from significant conditions, events, circumstances, actions or inactions that could adversely affect an entity's ability to achieve its objectives and execute its strategies, or from the setting of inappropriate objectives and strategies.

Business risk cannot be eliminated, but it must be **managed** by the company:

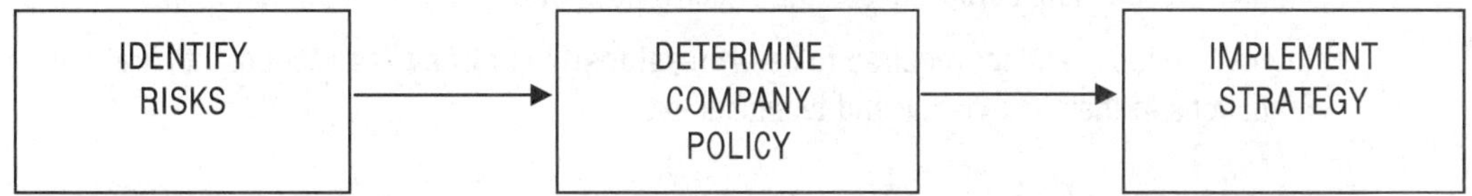

Designing and operating internal control systems is a key part of a company's risk management. This will often be done by employees in their various departments, although sometimes (particularly in the case of specialised computer systems) the company will hire external expertise to design systems.

3.2 The role of internal audit

The internal audit department has a two-fold role in relation to risk management.

- It monitors the company's overall risk management policy to ensure it operates effectively.
- It monitors the strategies implemented to ensure that they continue to operate effectively.

As a significant risk management policy in companies is to implement internal controls, internal audit has a key role in assessing systems and testing controls.

Internal audit may assist in the development of systems. However, its key role will be in **monitoring the overall process** and in **providing assurance** that the **systems** which the departments have designed **meet objectives** and **operate effectively**.

It is important that the internal audit department retains its **objectivity** towards these aspects of its role, which is another reason why internal audit would generally not be involved in the assessment of risks and the design of the system.

3.3 Responsibility for fraud and error

FAST FORWARD

It is the responsibility of management and those charged with governance to prevent and detect fraud, and in this respect, internal auditors may have a role to play.

Fraud is a **key business risk**. It is the responsibility of the **directors** to prevent and detect fraud. As the internal auditor has a role in risk management he is involved in the process of managing the risk of fraud. It is not the responsibility of the external auditors to prevent and detect fraud, although they may unearth fraud as part of their audit of the financial statements, and they shall be aware of the risks of fraud while carrying out the audit. (We look at the external auditor's responsibilities for fraud and error in more detail in Chapter 6.)

The internal auditor can help to **prevent** fraud by carrying out work on **assessing the adequacy and effectiveness of control systems**. The internal auditor can help to **detect** fraud by **being mindful** when carrying out his work and **reporting any suspicions**.

The very **existence of an internal audit** department may act as a **deterrent** to fraud. The internal auditors might also be called upon to undertake **special projects** to investigate a suspected fraud.

3.4 Limitations of the internal audit function

Although the presence of an internal audit department within an organisation is indicative of good internal control, by its very nature, there are some **limitations** of the internal audit function.

Internal auditors are employed by the organisation and this can **impair their independence and objectivity** and ability to report fraud/error to senior management because of perceived threats to their continued employment within the company.

To ensure transparency, best practice indicates that the internal audit function should have a **dual reporting relationship**, i.e. report both to management and those charged with governance (the audit committee). If this reporting structure is not in place, management may be able to unduly influence the internal audit plan, scope, and whether issues are reported appropriately. This results in a serious conflict, limits the scope and compromises the effectiveness of the internal audit function.

Internal auditors are not required to be **professionally qualified** (as accountants are) and so there may be limitations in their knowledge and technical expertise.

Question

Internal control procedures

The growing recognition by management of the benefits of good internal control and the complexities of an adequate system of internal control have led to the development of internal auditing as a form of control over all other internal controls. The emergence of internal auditors as experts in internal control is the result of an evolutionary process similar in many ways to the evolution of external auditing.

Required

(a) Explain why the internal and independent external auditors' review of internal control procedures differ in purpose.

(b) Explain the reasons why internal auditors should or should not report their findings on internal control to the following company officials:

 (i) The board of directors
 (ii) The chief accountant

Answer

(a) Internal auditors review and test the system of internal control and report to management in order to improve the information received by managers and to help in their task of running the company. They will recommend changes to the system to ensure that management receives objective information which is efficiently produced. They also have a duty to search for and discover fraud. The external auditors review the system of internal control in order to determine the extent of the substantive work required on the year-end accounts.

The external auditors report to the shareholders rather than the managers or directors. They report on the truth and fairness of the financial statements, not directly on the system of internal control. External auditors usually however issue a report to management, laying out any areas of weakness and recommendations for improvement in the system of internal control. They do not have a specific duty to detect fraud, although they should plan their audit procedures so as to detect any material misstatements in the accounts on which they give an opinion.

(b) (i) *Board of directors*

A high level of independence is achieved by the internal auditors if they report directly to the board. There may be problems with this approach.

(1) The members of the board may not understand all the implications of the internal audit reports when accounting or technical information is required.

(2) The board may not have enough time to spend considering the reports in sufficient depth. Important recommendations might therefore remain unimplemented.

A way around these problems might be to delegate the review of internal audit reports to an audit committee, which would act as a sub-committee to the main board. The audit committee should be made up largely of non-executive directors who have more time and independence from the day-to-day running of the company.

(ii) *Chief accountant*

It would be inappropriate for internal audit to report to the chief accountant, who is in charge of running the system of internal control. It may be feasible for him or her to receive the report as well as the board. Otherwise, the internal audit function cannot be effectively independent as the chief accountant may suppress unfavourable reports or may just not act on the recommendations of such reports.

4 Internal audit assignments

FAST FORWARD

Internal audit can be involved in many different assignments as directed by management. These can range from **value for money** projects to **operational** assignments looking at specific parts of the business.

In the next section we will consider a number of the detailed assignments which an internal auditor could get involved in.

4.1 Value for money audits

Value for money (VFM) audits examine the **economy**, **efficiency** and **effectiveness** of activities and processes. These are known as the **three Es** of VFM audits. For example, in Singapore, the Auditor-General's Office carries out VFM audits on the economic, efficient and effective use of public resources.

The three Es can be defined as follows.

(a) **Economy**: attaining the appropriate quantity and quality of physical, human and financial resources (**inputs**) at lowest cost. An activity would not be economic, if, for example, there was over-staffing or failure to purchase materials of requisite quality at the lowest available price.

(b) **Efficiency**: this is the relationship between goods or services produced (**outputs**) and the resources used to produce them. An efficient operation produces the maximum output for any given set of resource inputs, or it has minimum inputs for any given quantity and quality of product or service provided.

(c) **Effectiveness**: this is concerned with how well an activity is achieving its policy objectives or other intended effects.

The internal auditors will **evaluate** these three factors for any given business system or operation in the company. Value for money can often only be judged by **comparison.** In searching for value for money, present methods of operation and uses of resources must be **compared with alternatives.**

The following list identifies areas of an organisation, process or activity where there might be scope for significant value for money improvements. Each of these should be reviewed within individual organisations.

- Service delivery (the actual provision of a public service)
- Management process
- Environment

An alternative approach is to look at areas of spending. A value for money assessment of economy, efficiency and effectiveness would look at whether:

- Too much money is being spent on certain items or activities, to achieve the targets or objectives of the overall operation
- Money is being spent to no purpose, because the spending is not helping to achieve objectives
- Changes could be made to improve performance

An illustrative list is shown below of the sort of spending areas that might be looked at, and the aspects of spending where value for money might be improved.

- Employee expenses
- Premises expenses
- Suppliers and services
- Establishment expenses
- Capital expenditure

Problems with VFM auditing	
Measuring outputs	For example, the outputs of a fire brigade can be measured by the number of call-outs, but it is not satisfactory to compare a call-out to individuals stuck in a lift with a call-out to a small house fire or a major industrial fire or a road accident etc.
Defining objectives	In not-for-profit organisations the quality of the service provided will be a significant feature of their service. For example, a local authority has, amongst its various different objectives, the objective of providing a rubbish collection service. The effectiveness of this service can only be judged by establishing what standard or quality of service is required.
Sacrifice of quality	Economy and efficiency can be achieved by sacrificing quality. Neither outputs nor impacts are necessarily measured in terms of quality. For example, the cost of teaching can be reduced by increasing the pupil:teacher ratio in schools, but it is difficult to judge the consequences of such a change on teaching standards and quality.
Measuring effectiveness	For example, the effectiveness of the health service could be said to have improved if hospitals have greater success in treating various illnesses and other conditions, or if the life expectancy of the population has increased, but a consequence of these changes will be overcrowded hospitals and longer waiting lists.
Over-emphasis in cost control	There can be an emphasis with VFM audits on costs and cost control rather than on achieving more benefits and value, so that management might be pressurised into 'short-term' decisions, such as abandoning capital expenditure plans which would create future benefits in order to keep current spending levels within limits.
Measuring efficiency	In profit-making organisations, the efficiency of the organisation as a whole can be measured in terms of return on capital employed. Individual profit centres or operating units within the organisation can also have efficiency measured by relating the quantity of output produced, which has a **market value** and therefore a quantifiable financial value, to the inputs (and their cost) required to make the output. In not-for-profit organisations, output does not usually have a market value, and it is therefore more difficult to measure efficiency. This difficulty is compounded by the fact that, since such organisations often have many different activities or operations, it is difficult to compare the efficiency of one operation with the efficiency of another. For example, with the police force, it might be difficult to compare the efficiency of a serious crimes squad with the efficiency of the traffic police.

4.2 Information technology audits

An information technology (IT) audit is a test of controls in a specific area of the business, the computer systems. Increasingly in modern business, computers are vital to the functioning of the business, and therefore the controls over them are key to the business.

It is likely to be necessary to have an IT specialist in the internal audit team to undertake an audit of the controls, as some of them will be programmed into the computer system.

The diagram below shows the various areas of IT in the business which might be subject to a test of controls by the auditors.

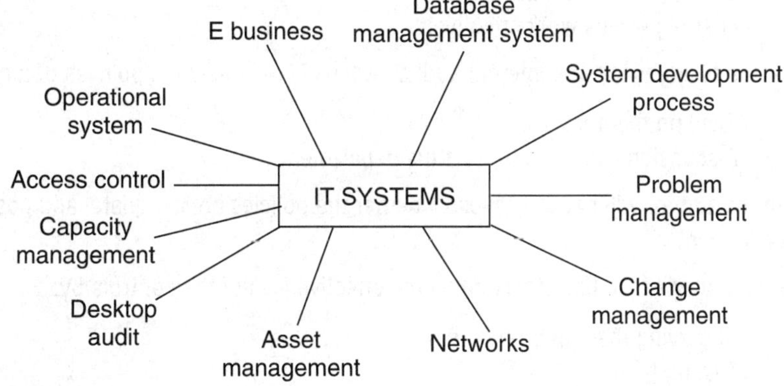

4.3 Best value audits

'Best value' is a performance framework introduced into local authorities by the UK government. They are required to publish annual best value performance plans and review all of their functions over a five year period.

As part of best value authorities are required to strive for continuous improvement by implementing the '4 Cs':

- **Challenge**. How and why is a service provided?
- **Compare**. Make comparisons with other local authorities and the private sector.
- **Consult**. Talk to local taxpayers and services users and the wider business community in setting performance targets.
- **Compete**. Embrace fair competition as a means of securing efficient and effective services.

One of internal audit's standard roles in a company is to provide assurance that internal control systems are adequate to promote the effective use of resources and that risks are being managed properly.

This role can be extended to ensure that the local authority has arrangements in place to achieve best value, that the risks and impacts of best value are incorporated into normal audit testing and that the authority keeps abreast of best value developments.

As best value depends on assessing current services and setting strategies for development, internal audit can take part in the 'position audit', as they should have a good understanding of how services are currently organised and relate to each other.

As assurance providers, internal audit will play a key part in giving management assurance that its objectives and strategies in relation to best value are being met.

4.4 Financial

The financial audit is internal audit's traditional role. It involves reviewing all the available evidence (usually the company's records) to substantiate information in management and financial reporting.

This role in many ways echoes that of the external auditor, and is not one in which the internal auditors can add any particular value to the business. Increasingly, it is a minor part of the function of internal audit.

4.5 Operational audits

Key term

Operational audits are audits of the operational processes of the organisation. They are also known as management or efficiency audits. Their prime objective is the monitoring of management's performance, ensuring company policy is adhered to.

4.5.1 Approaching operational internal audit assignments

There are two aspects of an operational assignment:

- Ensure policies are adequate
- Ensure policies work effectively

In terms of adequacy, the internal auditor will have to review the policies of a particular department by:

- Reading them
- Discussion with members of the department

Then the auditor will have to assess whether the policies are adequate, and possibly advise the board of improvement.

The auditor will then have to examine the effectiveness of the controls by:

- Observing them in operation
- Testing them

This will be done on similar lines to the testing of controls by external auditors which is discussed in Section D of this Study Text, even though the controls being tested may differ.

4.5.2 Procurement audits

Procurement is the process of **purchasing** for the business. A procurement audit will therefore concentrate on the **systems** of the purchasing department(s). The internal auditor will be checking that the system achieves key objectives and that it operates according to company guidelines.

4.5.3 Marketing audits

Marketing is the **process of assessing and enhancing demand for the company's products**. Marketing and associated sales are very important for the business and also therefore for the internal auditor but as the **associated systems do not directly impact on the financial statements**, they do not usually concern the external auditor.

It is important for the internal auditor to review the marketing processes to ensure:

- The process is **managed efficiently**
- **Information is freely available** to manager demand
- **Risks** are being **managed** correctly

An audit may be especially critical for a marketing department which may be complex with several different teams, for example:

- Research
- Advertising
- Promotions
- After-sales

It is vital to ensure that information is passed on properly within the department and that activities are streamlined.

4.5.4 Treasury audits

Treasury is a function within the finance department of a business. It **manages the funds** of a business so that cash is available when required.

There are risks associated with treasury, in terms of interest rate risk and foreign currency risk, and the internal auditor must ensure that the **risk is managed in accordance with company procedures.**

As with marketing audits, it is vital to ensure that **information is available** to the treasury department, so that they can **ensure funds are available when required**.

4.5.5 Human resources audits

The human resources department both procures a human resource (employee) for the operation of the business and supports that employee in developing within the organisation.

It is important to ensure that the processes in place ensure that people are available to work as the business requires them and that the overall development of the business is planned and controlled.

Again, **ensuring company policies are maintained** and **information is freely available** are key factors for internal audit to assess.

5 Internal audit reports

The internal auditors' report may take any form as there are no formal reporting requirements for these reports as there are for the external auditor's report.

5.1 Reporting on internal audit assignments

Internal auditors produce reports for directors and management as a result of work performed. These reports are internal to the business and are unlikely to be shared with third parties other than the external auditors.

We have looked in detail at the types of assignment internal audit will carry out. These may be summarised as '**risk-based'**, where the internal auditors consider internal and external risks and discuss company operations and systems in place in respect of them or **'performance enhancement'** where internal auditors consider risk and strategy on a higher level.

For the most part work is likely to be **risk-based**. Regardless of the nature of the assignment, however, all internal audits are likely to result in a formal report.

Usually at the end of the audit fieldwork, the internal auditors produce a draft report which is sent out for consideration by the relevant management. Once this has been approved, the internal auditors will meet with management to discuss the work and the findings and recommendations. After the meeting, the internal auditors then produce a formal report which, once approved by the relevant people, is used to produce the final report for distribution.

5.2 Contents of the report

There are **no formal requirements** for internal audit reports as there are for the external audit report. The external audit report is a highly stylised document which is substantially the same for any audit. A report from the internal auditors in relation to an assignment can take essentially any form. However, some points should be borne in mind.

There is a generally accepted format for reports in business, which is laid out below. This format makes reports useful to readers as it highlights the conclusions drawn and gives easy reference to the user.

Standard report format
TERMS OF REFERENCE
EXECUTIVE SUMMARY
BODY OF THE REPORT
APPENDICES FOR ANY ADDITIONAL INFORMATION

The report will also be dated, marked as draft or final and have a 'distribution list' attached.

Some internal audit reports will be modified as responses are made to them by various members of staff. If this is the case, the report should clearly state which version it is. The distribution list may also be annotated to show who has commented on the report at any time.

The **executive summary** of an internal audit report should give the following information.

- Background to the assignment
- Objectives of the assignment
- Major outcomes of the work
- Key risks identified
- Key action points
- Summary of the work left to do

The **main body** of the report will contain the detail such as the audit tests carried out and their findings, full lists of action points, including details of who has responsibility for carrying them out, the future time-scale and costs.

6 Outsourcing the internal audit function June 08

FAST FORWARD

Internal audit departments may consist of employees of the company, or may be **outsourced** to external service providers. The **advantages** of outsourcing the internal audit function include speed, cost and a tailored answer to internal audit requirements. One of the main **disadvantages** may include threats to independence and objectivity if the external audit service is provided by the same firm.

6.1 What is outsourcing?

Key term

Outsourcing is the use of external suppliers as a source of finished products, components or services. It is also known as sub-contracting.

Whilst the scope of the internal auditor's work is different to that of the external auditor, there are many features that can link them. One of the key factors is that the **techniques** which are used to carry out audits are the same for internal and external auditors.

It can be expensive to maintain an internal audit function consisting of employees of the company. It is possible that the monitoring and review required by a certain company could be done in a small amount of time and full-time employees cannot be justified.

It is also possible that a number of internal audit staff are required, but the cost of recruitment is prohibitive, or the directors are aware that the need for internal audit is only short-term.

In such circumstances, it is possible to **outsource** the internal audit function, that is, purchase the service from outside.

In this respect, many of the larger accountancy firms offer internal audit services. It is likely that the same firm might offer one client both internal and external audit services. In such circumstances the firm would have to be aware of the **independence issues** this would raise for the external audit team and **implement safeguards** to ensure that its independence and objectivity were not impaired. We discussed such issues in Chapter 4 when we looked at professional ethics.

6.2 Advantages and disadvantages of outsourcing

The advantages and disadvantages of outsourcing the internal audit function are set out in the following table.

Advantages of outsourcing	Disadvantages of outsourcing
• Staff do not need to be recruited, as the **service provider has good quality staff.** • The service provider has different **specialist skills** and can assess what management require them to do. • Outsourcing can provide an **immediate** internal audit department. • **Associated costs**, such as staff training, are **eliminated**. • The service contract can be for the **appropriate time scale**. • Because the time scale is **flexible**, a **team of staff** can be provided if required. • It can be used on a **short-term basis**.	• There will be **independence** and **objectivity** issues if the company uses the same firm to provide both internal and external audit services. • The **cost** of outsourcing the internal audit function might be high enough to make the directors choose not to have an internal audit function at all. • Company staff may oppose outsourcing if it results in **redundancies**. • There may be a **high staff turnover** of internal audit staff. • The outsourced staff may only have a **limited knowledge** of the company. • The company will **lose** in-house skills.

6.3 Managing an outsourced department

A company will need to establish **controls** over the outsourced internal audit department. These would include:

- Setting **performance measures** in terms of cost and areas of the business reviewed and investigating any variances
- Ensuring appropriate **audit methodology** (working papers/reviews) is maintained
- **Reviewing** working papers on a sample basis to ensure they meet internal standards/guidelines
- **Agreeing** internal audit work plans in advance of work being performed
- If external auditor is used, ensuring the firm has suitable controls to keep the two functions separate so that **independence and objectivity** is not impaired

Chapter Roundup

- Internal audit assists management in achieving the entity's corporate objectives, particularly in establishing good corporate governance.
- Although many of the techniques internal and external auditors use may be similar, the basis and reasoning of their work is different.
- Internal audit has two key roles to play in relation to organisational risk management:
  - Ensuring the company's risk management system operates effectively
  - Ensuring that strategies implemented in respect of business risks operate effectively
- It is the responsibility of management and those charged with governance to prevent and detect fraud, and in this respect, internal auditors may have a role to play.
- Internal audit can be involved in many different assignments as directed by management. These can range from **value for money** projects to **operational** assignments looking at specific parts of the business.
- The internal auditors' report may take any form as there are no formal reporting requirements for these reports as there are for the external auditor's report.
- Internal audit departments may consist of employees of the company, or may be **outsourced** to external service providers. The **advantages** of outsourcing the internal audit function include speed, cost and a tailored answer to internal audit requirements. One of the main **disadvantages** may include threats to independence and objectivity if the external audit service is provided by the same firm.

Quick Quiz

1 What is an internal audit?

2 Name three key differences between internal and external audit.

(1) ....

(2) ....

(3) ....

3 Link the value for money 'E' with its definition.

(a) Economy

(b) Efficiency

(c) Effectiveness

(i) The relationships between the goods and services produced (outputs) and the resources used to produce them.

(ii) The concern with how well an activity is achieving its policy objectives or other intended effects.

(iii) Attaining the appropriate quantity and quality of physical, human and financial resources (inputs) at lowest cost.

4 Name five areas of the computer system which might benefit from an IT audit.

(1) ....

(2) ....

(3) ....

(4) ....

(5) ....

5 There are formal statutory rules governing the format of internal audit reports.

True ☐

False ☐

6 It is possible to buy in an internal audit service from an external organisation.

True ☐

False ☐

Answers to Quick Quiz

1 Internal audit is an appraisal or monitoring activity established by the entity as a service to the entity.

2 (1) External auditors report to members, internal auditors report to directors.

(2) External auditors report on financial statements, internal auditors report on systems, controls and risks.

(3) External auditors are independent of the company, internal auditors are often employed by it.

3 (a) (iii), (b) (i), (c) (ii)

4 Five from e-business, operational system, access control, capacity management, desktop audit, asset management, networks, change management, problem management, system development process, database management system.

5 False

6 True – this is known as outsourcing.

Now try the question below from the Exam Question Bank

Number	Level	Marks	Time
Q7	Examination	20	36 mins

PART C

Planning and risk assessment

Risk assessment

Topic list	Syllabus reference
1 Introduction to risk	C1
2 Materiality	C3
3 Understanding the entity and its environment	C2, C4
4 Assessing the risks of material misstatement	C1, C2
5 Responding to the risk assessment	C1, C2
6 Fraud, law and regulations	C3
7 Documentation of risk assessment	C1, C2, C3, C4

Introduction

This chapter covers the aspects of the external audit which will be considered at the earliest stages, during planning.

Firstly we introduce the concept of risk and look in detail at audit risk and its components (control risk, inherent risk and detection risk) and at how audit risk is managed by the auditor. The distinction between audit risk and business risk is also made.

We discuss the concept of materiality for the financial statements as a whole and performance materiality and the methods used for calculating them. It is important to understand that the calculation of materiality is a matter of judgement and that materiality must be reviewed during the course of the audit and revised if necessary.

The importance of understanding the entity being audited and its environment is a key aspect of audit planning and helps the auditor to identify potential risk areas to focus on. Various techniques can be used here such as inquiry, analytical procedures, observation and inspection. The risk assessment stage allows the auditor to respond with a proposed audit approach which may be controls based or totally substantive.

The auditor also needs to consider the risks of fraud and non-compliance with laws and regulations in the audit and this is examined towards the end of this

Study guide

		Intellectual level
C1	**Objective and general principles**	
(a)	Identify and describe the need to plan and perform audits with an attitude of professional scepticism	2
(b)	Identify and describe engagement risks affecting the audit of an entity	1
(c)	Explain the components of audit risk	1
(d)	Compare and contrast risk based, procedural and other approaches to audit work	2
(e)	Discuss the importance of risk analysis	2
(f)	Describe the use of information technology in risk analysis	1
C2	**Understanding the entity and knowledge of the business**	
(a)	Explain how auditors obtain an initial understanding of the entity and knowledge of its business environment	2
C3	**Assessing the risks of material misstatement and fraud**	
(a)	Define and explain the concepts of materiality and tolerable error	2
(b)	Compute indicative materiality levels from financial information	2
(c)	Discuss the effect of fraud and misstatements on the audit strategy and extent of audit work	2
C4	**Analytical procedures**	
(a)	Describe and explain the nature and purpose of analytical procedures in planning	2
(b)	Compute and interpret key ratios used in analytical procedures	2

Exam guide

Audit planning is a very important stage of the audit because it helps direct the focus of the audit. Within planning, risk is a key topic area. You may be asked in the exam to explain various terms such as risk and materiality. This involves not merely learning the definitions but also being able to show how in practice the auditor uses these techniques in planning an audit. You might also have to identify the risks from a given scenario – in such a question it's important to explain fully why any factors you have identified are risks, otherwise you will not attain the maximum marks available.

The June 2008 paper had a question on analytical procedures used during planning, with an eight mark knowledge-based part and a nine mark part requiring the application of analytical procedures to income statement figures.

The December 2008 paper had a question on audit risk and a 12 mark part on the identification of inherent risk areas in a charity.

The June 2009 had a question worth six marks, on the external auditor's responsibilities for the detection of fraud, and a ten mark question on risks relating to the audit of a new audit client.

1 Introduction to risk

1.1 Professional scepticism, professional judgement and ethical requirements

FAST FORWARD

Auditors are required to carry out the audit with an attitude of **professional scepticism,** exercise **professional judgement** and comply with **ethical requirements**.

Key terms

Professional scepticism is an attitude that includes a questioning mind, being alert to conditions which may indicate possible misstatement due to error or fraud, and a critical assessment of audit evidence.

Professional judgement is the application of relevant training, knowledge and experience in making informed decisions about the courses of action that are appropriate in the circumstances of the audit engagement.

1.1.1 Professional scepticism

ISA 200 *Overall objectives of the independent auditor and the conduct of an audit in accordance with International Standards on Auditing* states that auditors must plan and perform an audit with an attitude of **professional scepticism** recognising that circumstances may exist that cause the financial statements to be materially misstated.

This requires the auditor to be alert to:

- Audit evidence that **contradicts** other audit evidence obtained
- Information that brings into question the **reliability** of documents and responses to inquiries to be used as audit evidence
- Conditions that may indicate **possible fraud**
- Circumstances that suggest the need for **audit procedures in addition** to those required by ISAs

Professional scepticism needs to be maintained throughout the audit to reduce the risks of overlooking unusual transactions, over-generalising when drawing conclusions, and using inappropriate assumptions in determining the nature, timing and extent of audit procedures and evaluating the results of them.

Professional scepticism is also necessary to the critical assessment of audit evidence. This includes questioning contradictory audit evidence and the reliability of documents and responses from management and those charged with governance.

1.1.2 Professional judgement

ISA 200 also requires the auditor to exercise **professional judgement** in planning and performing an audit of financial statements. Professional judgement is required in the following areas:

- Materiality and audit risk
- Nature, timing and extent of audit procedures
- Evaluation of whether sufficient appropriate audit evidence has been obtained
- Evaluating management's judgements in applying the applicable financial reporting framework
- Drawing conclusions based on the audit evidence obtained

1.1.3 Ethical requirements

ISA 200 states that the auditor must comply with the relevant ethical requirements, including those relating to independence, that are relevant to financial statement audit engagements. We discussed professional ethics in Chapter 4 of this Study Text.

1.2 Overall audit risk

Auditors usually follow a **risk-based approach** to auditing as required by ISAs. In this approach, auditors analyse the risks associated with the client's business, transactions and systems which could lead to misstatements in the financial statements, and direct their testing to risky areas. This is in contrast to a procedural approach which is not in accordance with ISAs. In a procedural approach, the auditor would perform a set of standard tests regardless of the client and its business. The risk of the auditor providing an incorrect opinion on the truth and fairness of the financial statements might be higher if a procedural approach was adopted.

1.3 Audit risk **Dec 08**

FAST FORWARD

Audit risk is the risk that the auditor expresses an inappropriate audit opinion when the financial statements are materially misstated. It is a function of the risk of material misstatement (**inherent risk** and **control risk**) and the risk that the auditor will not detect such misstatement (**detection risk**).

Key term

Audit risk is the risk that the auditor expresses an inappropriate audit opinion when the financial statements are materially misstated.

Audit risk has two elements, the risk that the financial statements contain a material misstatement and the risk that the auditors will fail to detect any material misstatements.

Audit risk has two major components. One is dependent on the entity, and is the risk of material misstatement arising in the financial statements (**inherent risk** and **control risk**). The other is dependent on the auditor, and is the risk that the auditor will not detect material misstatements in the financial statements (**detection risk**). We shall look in detail at the concept of materiality in the next section of this chapter. Audit risk can be represented by the **audit risk model**:

Audit risk = Inherent risk × control risk × detection risk

1.3.1 Inherent risk

Key term

Inherent risk is the susceptibility of an assertion to a misstatement that could be material individually or when aggregated with other misstatements, assuming there were no related internal controls.

Inherent risk is the risk that items will be misstated due to the characteristics of those items, such as the fact they are estimates or that they are important items in the accounts. The auditors must use their professional judgement and all available knowledge to assess inherent risk. If no such information or knowledge is available then the inherent risk is **high**.

Inherent risk is affected by the nature of the entity; for example, the industry it is in and the regulations it falls under, and also the nature of the strategies it adopts. We shall look at more examples of inherent risks later in this chapter.

1.3.2 Control risk

The other element of the risk of material misstatements in the financial statements is control risk.

Key term

Control risk is the risk that a material misstatement that could occur in an assertion and that could be material, individually or when aggregated with other misstatements, will not be prevented or detected and corrected on a timely basis by the entity's internal control.

We shall look at control risk in more detail in Chapter 9 when we discuss internal controls.

1.3.3 Detection risk

Key term

> **Detection risk** is the risk that the procedures performed by the auditor to reduce audit risk to an acceptably low level will not detect a misstatement that exists and that could be material, individually or when aggregated with other misstatements.

The third element of audit risk is detection risk. This is the component of audit risk that the auditors have a degree of control over, because, if risk is too high to be tolerated, the auditors can carry out more work to reduce this aspect of audit risk, and therefore audit risk as a whole. **Sampling risk** and **non-sampling risk** are components of detection risk, and will be examined further in chapter 11.

1.4 Management of audit risk

ISA 200 states that 'to obtain reasonable assurance, the auditor shall obtain sufficient appropriate audit evidence to reduce audit risk to an acceptably low level and thereby enable the auditor to draw reasonable conclusions on which to base the auditor's opinion.'

Auditors will want their overall audit risk to be at an acceptable level, or it will not be worth them carrying out the audit. In other words, if the chance of them giving an inappropriate opinion and being sued is high, it might be better not to do the audit at all.

The auditors will obviously consider how risky a new audit client is during the acceptance process, and may decide not to go ahead with the relationship. However, they will also consider audit risk for each individual audit, and will seek to manage the risk.

As we have seen above, it is not in the auditors' power to affect inherent or control risk. These are risks integral to the client, and the auditor cannot change the level of these risks.

The auditors therefore manage overall audit risk by manipulating detection risk, the only element of audit risk they have control over. This is because the more audit work the auditors carry out, the lower detection risk becomes, although it can never be entirely eliminated due to the inherent limitations of audit.

The auditors will decide what level of overall risk is acceptable, and then determine a level of audit work so that detection risk is as low as possible.

It is important to understand that there is not a standard level of audit risk which is generally considered by auditors to be acceptable. This is a matter of **audit judgement**, and so will vary from firm to firm and audit to audit. Audit firms are likely to charge higher fees for higher risk clients. Regardless of the risk level of the audit, however, it is vital that audit firms always carry out an audit of **sufficient quality**.

Question — **Audit risk**

Hippo Co is a long established client of your firm. It manufactures bathroom fittings and fixtures, which it sells to a range of wholesalers, on credit.

You are the audit senior and have recently been sent the following extract from the draft statement of financial position by the finance director.

	Budget		*Actual*	
	$'000s	$'000s	$'000s	$'000s
Non-current assets		453		367
Current assets				
Trade accounts receivable	1,134		976	
Bank	–		54	
Current liabilities				
Trade accounts payable	967		944	
Bank overdraft	9		–	

During the course of your conversation with the finance director, you establish that a major new customer the company had included in its budget went bankrupt during the year.

Required

Identify any potential risks for the audit of Hippo and explain why you believe they are risks.

Answer

Potential risks relevant to the audit of Hippo

(1) **Credit sales**. Hippo makes sales on credit. This increases the risk that Hippo's sales will not be converted into cash. Trade receivables is likely to be a risky area and the auditors will have to consider what the best evidence that customers are going to pay is likely to be.

(2) **Related industry**. Hippo manufactures bathroom fixtures and fittings. These are sold to wholesalers, but it is possible that Hippo's ultimate market is the building industry. This is a notoriously volatile industry, and Hippo may find that their results fluctuate too, as demand rises and falls. This suspicion is added to by the bankruptcy of the wholesaler in the year. The auditors must be sure that accounts which present Hippo as a viable company are in fact correct.

(3) **Controls**. The fact that a major new customer went bankrupt suggests that Hippo did not undertake a very thorough credit check on that customer before agreeing to supply them. This implies that the controls at Hippo may not be very strong.

(4) **Variance**. The actual results are different from budget. This may be explained by the fact that the major customer went bankrupt, or it may reveal that there are other errors and problems in the reported results, or in the original budget.

(5) **Bankrupt wholesaler**. There is a risk that the result reported contains balances due from the bankrupt wholesaler, which are likely to be irrecoverable.

1.5 Business risk

The other major category of risk which the auditor must be aware of is **business risk**. As you shall see in more detail in Chapter 9 when we look at internal control, the auditor is required to consider the company's process of business risk management.

We briefly introduced the concept of business risk in Chapter 5 in the context of internal audit's role in risk management and organisational control. Remember business risk is the risk inherent to the company in its operations.

Exam focus point

It is important that you do not confuse the concepts of audit and business risks. Remember – audit risk is focused on the financial statements of a company, whereas business risk is related to the company as a whole. If an exam question asks you to identify audit risks, make sure you explain them in relation to the financial statements.

2 Materiality

FAST FORWARD

Materiality for the financial statements as a whole and **performance materiality** must be calculated at the planning stages of all audits. The calculation or estimation of materiality should be based on experience and judgement. Materiality for the financial statements as a whole must be **reviewed throughout** the audit and **revised if necessary**.

ISA 320 *Materiality in planning and performing an audit* provides guidance to auditors on this area. The objective of the auditor is to apply the concept of materiality appropriately in planning and performing the audit. Information is generally consider to be material if its omission or misstatement could influence the economic decisions of users taken on the basis of the financial statements.

2.1 Determining materiality and performance materiality when planning the audit

Key term

> **Performance materiality** is the amount or amounts set by the auditor at less than materiality for the financial statements as a whole to reduce to an appropriately low level the probability that the aggregate of uncorrected and undetected misstatements exceeds materiality for the financial statements as a whole. Performance materiality also refers to the amount or amounts set by the auditor at less than the materiality level or levels for particular classes of transactions, account balances or disclosures.

During planning, the auditor must establish materiality for the financial statements as a whole. However, if there are classes of transactions, account balances or disclosures for which misstatements less than materiality for the financial statements as a whole could reasonably be expected to influence the economic decisions of users taken on the basis of the financial statements, the auditor must also determine materiality levels to be applied to these.

The auditor must also determine performance materiality in order to assess the risks of material misstatement and to determine the nature, timing and extent of further audit procedures.

Determining materiality for the financial statements as a whole involves the exercise of professional judgement (which we covered in section 1 of this chapter). Generally, a percentage is applied to a chosen benchmark as a starting point for determining materiality for the financial statements as a whole. The following factors may affect the identification of an appropriate benchmark:

- **Elements** of the financial statements (e.g. assets, liabilities, equity, revenue, expenses)
- Whether there are items on which **users tend to focus**
- **Nature of the entity**, **industry** and **economic environment**
- Entity's **ownership structure and financing**
- Relative **volatility** of the benchmark

The following **benchmarks and percentages** may be appropriate in the calculation of materiality for the financial statements as a whole.

Value	%
Profit before tax	5
Gross profit	½ – 1
Revenue	½ – 1
Total assets	1 – 2
Net assets	2 – 5
Profit after tax	5 – 10

The determination of **performance materiality** involves the exercise of **professional judgement** and is affected by the auditor's understanding of the entity and the nature and extent of misstatements identified in prior audits.

Exam focus point

> Bear in mind that materiality has qualitative, as well as quantitative, aspects. You must not simply think of materiality as being a percentage of items in the financial statements.

2.2 Revision of materiality

The level of materiality must be revised for the financial statements as a whole if the auditor becomes aware of information during the audit that would have caused the auditor to have determined a different amount during planning.

If the auditor concludes that a lower amount of materiality for the financial statements as a whole is appropriate, the auditor must determine whether performance materiality also needs to be revised, and whether the nature, timing and extent of further audit procedures are still appropriate. A revision to

materiality might be required for example if during the audit it appears that actual results are going to be significantly different from the expected results, which were used to calculate materiality for the financial statements as a whole during planning.

2.3 Documentation of materiality

ISA 320 requires the following to be documented:

- Materiality for the financial statements as a whole
- Materiality level or levels for particular classes of transactions, account balances or disclosures if applicable
- Performance materiality
- Any revision of the above as the audit progresses

3 Understanding the entity and its environment **June 08**

FAST FORWARD

The auditor is required to obtain an **understanding** of the entity and its environment in order to be able to assess the risks of material misstatements.

3.1 Why do we need an understanding?

ISA 315 *Identifying and assessing the risks of material misstatement through understanding the entity and its environment* states that the objective of the auditor is to identify and assess the risks of material misstatement, whether due to fraud or error, through understanding the entity and its environment, including the entity's internal control, thereby providing a basis for designing and implementing responses to the assessed risks of material misstatement.

The following table summarises this simply.

OBTAINING AN UNDERSTANDING OF THE ENTITY AND ITS ENVIRONMENT	
Why?	– To identify and assess the risks of material misstatement in the financial statements – To enable the auditor to design and perform further audit procedures – To provide a frame of reference for exercising audit judgement, for example, when setting audit materiality
What?	– Industry, regulatory and other external factors, including the applicable financial reporting framework – Nature of the entity, including operations, ownership and governance, investments, structure and financing – Entity's selection and application of accounting policies – Objectives and strategies and related business risks that might cause material misstatement in the financial statements – Measurement and review of the entity's financial performance – Internal control (which we shall look at in detail in Chapter 9)
How?	– Inquiries of management and others within the entity – Analytical procedures – Observation and inspection – Prior period knowledge – Client acceptance or continuance process – Discussion by the audit team of the susceptibility of the financial statements to material misstatement – Information from other engagements undertaken for the entity

As can be seen in the table, the reasons the auditor has to obtain an understanding of the entity and its environment are very much bound up with assessing risks and exercising audit judgement. We shall look at these aspects more in the next two sections of this chapter.

3.2 What do we need an understanding of?

The ISA sets out a number of requirements about what the auditors shall consider in relation to obtaining an understanding of the business. The general areas are shown in the following diagram.

UNDERSTANDING THE ENTITY AND ITS ENVIRONMENT

Nature of the entity
Investments
Financial reporting
Business operations
Financing

Objectives and strategies and relating business risks
Expansion
Use of IT
Industry developments
New products and services

Selection and application of accounting policies

Industry, regulatory and other external factors
Taxation
Regulatory framework
Cyclical or seasonal activity
The market and competition
Accounting principles
Energy supply and cost
Interest rates
Product technology

Internal control
Information system
Entity's risk assessment process
The control environment
Monitoring of controls
Control activities

Financial performance
Key performance indicators
Financial analysis
Competitors
Budgets, forecasts etc
Employee performance measures

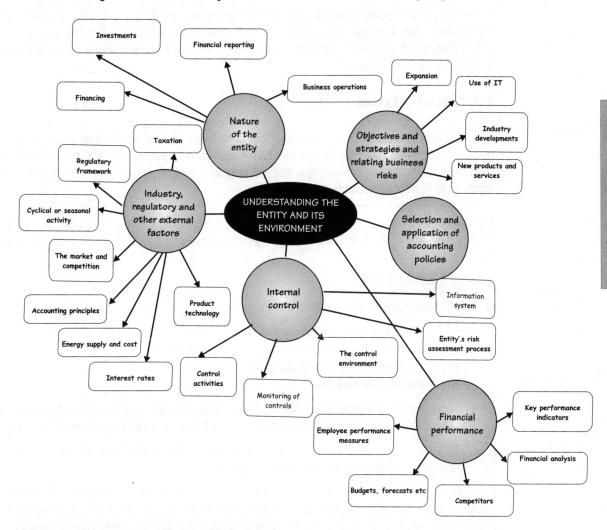

3.3 How do we gain an understanding?

ISA 315 sets out the methods that the auditor shall use to obtain the understanding and they were shown in the table in Section 3.1. A combination of these procedures should be used.

- **Inquiries** of management and others within the entity
- **Analytical procedures**
- **Observation** and **inspection**

ISA 315 also states the auditor shall consider whether information obtained from client acceptance or continuance processes is relevant.

If the engagement partner has performed other engagements for the entity, he/she shall consider whether information from these is relevant to identifying risks of material misstatement.

ISA 315 states that if the auditor is going to use information from prior year audits, the auditor shall determine whether changes have occurred that could affect the relevance to the current year's audit.

ISA 315 also requires the engagement partner and other key team members to discuss the susceptibility of the financial statements to material misstatement, and the application of the applicable financial

reporting framework to the entity's facts and circumstances. The engagement partner shall determine what matters are to be communicated to team members not involved in the discussion.

3.3.1 Inquiry

The auditors will usually obtain most of the information they require from staff in the accounts department, but may also need to make enquiries of other personnel, for example, internal audit, production staff or those charged with governance.

Those charged with governance may give insight into the environment in which the financial statements are prepared. In-house legal counsel may help with understanding matters such as outstanding litigation, or compliance with laws and regulations. Sales and marketing personnel may give information about marketing strategies and sales trends.

3.3.2 Analytical procedures

Key term

> **Analytical procedures** consist of the evaluations of financial information made by a study of plausible relationships among both financial and non-financial data. They also encompass the investigation of identified fluctuations and relationships that are consistent with other relevant information or deviate significantly from predicted amounts.

Analytical procedures can be used at all stages of the audit. ISA 315 requires their use during the risk assessment stage of the audit. Their use during other stages of the audit is considered in Chapters 11 and 18.

Analytical procedures include:

(a) The consideration of comparisons with:

- **Similar information** for prior periods
- **Anticipated results** of the entity, from budgets or forecasts
- **Predictions** prepared by the auditors
- **Industry information**

(b) Those between elements of financial information that are expected to conform to a predicted pattern based on the entity's experience, such as the relationship of gross profit to sales.

(c) Those between financial information and relevant non-financial information, such as the relationship of payroll costs to number of employees.

A variety of methods can be used to perform the procedures discussed above, ranging from **simple comparisons** to **complex analysis** using statistics, on a company level, branch level or individual account level. The choice of procedures is a matter for the auditors' professional judgement. The use of information technology may be extensive when carrying out analytical procedures during risk assessment.

Auditors may also use specific industry information or general knowledge of current industry conditions to assess the client's performance.

As well as helping to determine the nature, timing and extent of other audit procedures, such analytical procedures may also indicate aspects of the business of which the auditors were previously unaware. Auditors are looking to see if developments in the client's business have had the expected effects. They will be particularly interested in changes in audit areas where problems have occurred in the past.

Analytical procedures at the risk assessment stage of the audit are usually based on interim financial information, budgets or management accounts.

3.3.3 Observation and inspection

These techniques are likely to confirm the answers made to inquiries made of management. They will include observing the normal operations of a company, reading documents or manuals relating to the client's operations or visiting premises and meeting staff.

3.3.4 Companies that use e-business

IAPS 1013 *Electronic commerce – effect on the audit of financial statements* provides guidance to auditors auditing entities that engage in e-commerce. The IAPS identifies specific matters to assist the auditor when considering the significance of e-commerce to the entity's business and the effect on the auditor's risk assessment.

The auditor needs to consider whether the **skills and knowledge** of team members are appropriate to perform the audit, and also whether an **expert** is required.

The auditor also needs to have a good **understanding of the business** to assess the significance of e-commerce and its effect on audit risk. The auditor should consider the following:

- The entity's **business activities and industry**
- The entity's **e-commerce strategy**
- The **extent** of e-commerce activities
- **Outsourcing** arrangements

The IAPS identifies specific business risks affecting entities that engage in e-commerce, which are outlined below.

- Loss of transaction integrity
- Security risks
- Improper accounting policies (e.g. capitalisation of expenditure, translation of foreign currency, allowances for warranties and returns, revenue recognition)
- Non-compliance with taxation and other laws and regulations
- Failure to ensure that contracts are binding
- Over-reliance on e-commerce
- Systems and infrastructure failures or crashes

The auditor uses the knowledge of the business gained to identify events, transactions and practices related to business risks arising from e-commerce activities that may result in material misstatements in the financial statements.

The auditor also considers the control environment and control procedures that are relevant to the financial statement assertions, in accordance with ISA 315, in particular those relating to **security, transaction integrity** and **process alignment**.

Question — Analytical procedures

You are auditing the financial statements of Pumpkin Co for the year ended 31 March 20X9. Pumpkin Co is a chain of bakeries operating in 5 locations. The bakeries sell a range of cakes, pastries, bread, sandwiches, pasties and drinks which customers purchase in cash. The company has had a 'challenging' year, according to its directors, and is renegotiating its bank overdraft facility with its bank. The income statement for the year ended 31 March 20X8 is shown below together with the draft income statement for the year ended 31 March 20X9.

Pumpkin Co: income statements

	31 March 20X9	**31 March 20X8**
	$000	**$000**
Revenue	4,205	3,764
Cost of sales	(1,376)	(1,555)
Gross profit	2,829	2,209
Operating expenses		
Administration	(667)	(798)
Selling and distribution	(423)	(460)
Interest payable	(50)	(49)
Profit/(loss) before tax	1,689	902

Required

As part of your risk assessment procedures for the audit of Pumpkin Co, perform analytical procedures on the draft income statement to identify possible risk areas requiring further audit work.

Answer

In total, Pumpkin's profit for the year has increased by 87% which appears at odds with the revenue figure, which has only increased by 12% in comparison to the previous year. This may indicate that revenue has been inflated or incorrect cut-off applied, especially given the fact that the directors of Pumpkin have described the year as 'challenging'.

Revenue has increased overall by 12% but cost of sales has fallen by 12% - we would expect an increase in revenue to be matched by a corresponding increase in cost of sales. Again this may indicate incorrect allocation of revenue in order for the bank to look favourably on the company and increase its overdraft facility. It could also indicate an error in the valuation of closing inventory.

The gross profit has increased by 28% compared to the previous period. The audit will need to focus on this change which is significant, focusing on the revenue and costs of sales figures to establish the reasons for the increase.

Administration expenses have fallen in comparison to the previous year (decrease of 16%) which is unusual given that revenue has increased by 12%. We would expect an increase in costs to be in line with the increase in the revenue figure. This could indicate that expenses may be understated through incorrect cut-off or incorrectly capitalising expenditure which should be written off to the income statement for the year.

A similar issue applies to selling and distribution costs which have fallen by 8% - they have not increased as expected in line with revenue. There could be legitimate reasons for the change but this area needs to be investigated further during the audit fieldwork stage.

Interest payable has stayed in line with the previous year (increase of 2%). This figure can be verified easily during the audit fieldwork by inspecting bank statements and other relevant documentation from the bank.

4 Assessing the risks of material misstatement

FAST FORWARD

When the auditor has obtained an understanding of the entity, he shall assess the risks of material misstatement in the financial statements, also identifying significant risks.

4.1 Identifying and assessing the risks of material misstatement

ISA 315 says that the auditor shall identify and assess the risks of material misstatement at the financial statement level and at the assertion level for classes of transactions, account balances and disclosures.

It requires the auditor to take the following steps:

- Identify risks throughout the process of obtaining an understanding of the entity and its environment
- Assess the identified risks, and evaluate whether they relate more pervasively to the financial statements as a whole
- Relate the risks to what can go wrong at the assertion level
- Consider the likelihood of the risks causing a material misstatement

Key term

Assertions are representations by management, explicit or otherwise, that are embodied in the financial statements, as used by the auditors to consider the different types of potential misstatements that may occur. We look at these in detail in Chapter 8.

4.2 Significant risks

FAST FORWARD

Significant risks are complex or unusual transactions that may indicate fraud, or other special risks.

Key term

Significant risks are those that require special audit consideration.

As part of the risk assessment described above, the auditor shall determine whether any of the risks are **significant risks**.

The following factors indicate that a risk might be significant:

- Risk of fraud (see Section 6)
- Its relationship with recent economic, accounting or other developments
- The degree of subjectivity in the financial information
- It is an unusual transaction
- It is a significant transaction with a related party
- The complexity of the transaction

Routine, non-complex transactions are less likely to give rise to significant risk than unusual transactions or matters of management judgement. This is because unusual transactions are likely to have more:

- Management intervention
- Complex accounting principles or calculations
- Manual intervention
- Opportunity for control procedures not to be followed

When the auditor identifies a significant risk, if he has not done so already, he shall obtain an understanding of the entity's controls relevant to that risk.

Question — Assessing the risks of material misstatement

You are involved with the audit of Tantpro Co, a small company. You have been carrying out procedures to gain an understanding of the entity. The following matters have come to your attention:

The company offers standard credit terms to its customers of 60 days from the date of invoice. Statements are sent to customers on a monthly basis. However, Tantpro does not employ a credit controller, and other than sending the statements on a monthly basis, it does not otherwise communicate with its customers on a systematic basis. On occasion, the sales ledger clerk may telephone a customer if the company has not received a payment for some time. Some customers pay regularly according to the credit terms offered to them, but others pay on a very haphazard basis and do not provide a remittance advice. Sales ledger receipts are entered onto the sales ledger but not matched to invoices remitted. The company does not produce an aged list of balances.

Required

From the above information, assess the risks of material misstatement arising in the financial statements. Outline the potential materiality of the risks and discuss factors in the likelihood of the risks arising.

Answer

The key risk arising from the above information is that trade receivables will not be carried at the appropriate **value** in the financial statements, as some may be irrecoverable. Where receipts are not matched against invoices in the ledger, the balance on the ledger may include old invoices that the customer has no intention of paying.

It is difficult to assess at this stage whether this will be material. Trade receivables is likely to be a material balance in the financial statements, but the number of irrecoverable balances may not be material. Analytical procedures, for example, to see if the level of receivables has risen year-on-year, in a manner that is not explained by price rises or levels of production, might help to assess this.

A key factor that affects the likelihood of the material misstatement arising is the poor controls over the sales ledger. The fact that invoices are not matched against receipts increases the chance of old invoices not having been paid and not noticed by Tantpro. It appears reasonably likely that the trade receivables balance is overstated in this instance.

5 Responding to the risk assessment

FAST FORWARD

The auditor shall **formulate an approach** to the assessed risks of material misstatement.

The main objective of ISA 330 *The auditor's responses to assessed risks* is to obtain sufficient appropriate audit evidence regarding the assessed risks of material misstatement, through designing and implementing appropriate responses to those risks.

5.1 Overall responses

Overall responses include issues such as emphasising to the team the importance of professional scepticism, allocating more staff, using experts or providing more supervision.

Overall responses to address the risks of material misstatement at the financial statement level will be changes to the general audit strategy or re-affirmations to staff of the general audit strategy. For example:

- Emphasising to audit staff the need to maintain professional scepticism
- Assigning additional or more experienced staff to the audit team
- Providing more supervision on the audit
- Incorporating more unpredictability into the audit procedures
- Making general changes to the nature, timing or extent of audit procedures

The evaluation of the control environment that will have taken place as part of the assessment of the client's internal control systems will help the auditor determine what type of audit approach to take.

5.2 Responses to the risks of material misstatement at the assertion level — Dec 07

The ISA says that the auditor shall design and perform further audit procedures whose **nature**, **timing** and **extent** are based on and are responsive to the assessed risks of material misstatement at the assertion level. 'Nature' refers to the purpose and the type of test that is carried out, which include **tests of controls** and **substantive tests**.

5.2.1 Tests of controls

Key term

Tests of controls are audit procedures designed to evaluate the operating effectiveness of controls in preventing, or detecting and correcting, material misstatements at the assertion level.

When the auditor's risk assessment includes an expectation that controls are operating effectively, the auditor shall design and perform tests of controls to obtain sufficient appropriate audit evidence that the controls were operating.

The auditor shall also undertake tests of control when it will not be possible to obtain sufficient appropriate audit evidence simply from substantive procedures. This might be the case if the entity conducts its business using IT systems which do not produce documentation of transactions.

In carrying out tests of control, auditors shall use **inquiry**, but shall also use other procedures. **Re-performance** and **inspection** will often be helpful procedures.

When considering timing in relation to tests of controls, the purpose of the test will be important. For example, if the company carries out a year-end inventory count, controls over the inventory count can only be tested at the year-end. Other controls will operate all year round, and the auditor may need to test that those controls have been effective throughout the period.

Some controls may have been tested in prior audits and the auditor may choose to rely on that evidence of their effectiveness. If this is the case, the auditor shall obtain evidence about any changes since the controls were last tested and shall test the controls if they have changed. In any case, controls shall be tested for effectiveness at least once in every three audits.

If the related risk has been designated a significant risk, the auditor shall not rely on testing done in prior years, but shall perform testing in the current year.

5.2.2 Substantive procedures

Substantive procedures are audit procedures designed to detect material misstatements at the assertion level. They consist of tests of details of classes of transactions, account balances and disclosures, and substantive analytical procedures.

The auditor shall always carry out substantive procedures on material items. The ISA says that irrespective of the assessed risk of material misstatement, the auditor shall design and perform substantive procedures for each material class of transactions, account balance and disclosure.

In addition, the auditor shall carry out the following substantive procedures:

- Agreeing or reconciling the financial statements to the underlying accounting records
- Examining material journal entries
- Examining other adjustments made in preparing the financial statements

Substantive procedures fall into two categories: analytical procedures and tests of details. The auditor must determine when it is appropriate to use which type of substantive procedure. We discuss these in more detail in Chapter 11 but they are introduced below.

Analytical procedures as substantive procedures tend to be appropriate for large volumes of predictable transactions (for example, wages and salaries). **Tests of detail** may be appropriate to gain information about account balances for example, inventory or trade receivables.

Tests of detail rather than analytical procedures are likely to be more appropriate with regard to matters which have been identified as **significant risks**, but the auditor must develop procedures that are specifically responsive to that risk, which may include analytical procedures. Significant risks are likely to be the most difficult to obtain sufficient appropriate audit evidence about.

6 Fraud, law and regulations **Pilot paper, June 09**

FAST FORWARD

When carrying out risk assessment procedures, the auditor shall also consider the risk of fraud or non-compliance with law and regulations causing a misstatement in the financial statements.

6.1 What is fraud?

Key terms

Fraud is an intentional act by one or more individuals among management, those charged with governance, employees or third parties involving the use of deception to obtain an unjust or illegal advantage. Fraud may be perpetrated by an individual, or colluded in, with people internal or external to the business.

Fraud risk factors are events or conditions that indicate an incentive or pressure to commit fraud or provide an opportunity to commit fraud.

Fraud is a wide legal concept, but the auditor's main concern is with fraud that causes a material misstatement in financial statements. It is distinguished from error, which is when a material misstatement is caused by mistake, for example, in the misapplication of an accounting policy.

Specifically, there are two types of fraud causing material misstatement in financial statements:

- Fraudulent financial reporting
- Misappropriation of assets

6.1.1 Fraudulent financial reporting

Key term

Fraudulent financial reporting involves intentional misstatements, including omissions of amounts or disclosures in financial statements, to deceive financial statement users.

This may include:

- Manipulation, falsification or alteration of accounting records/supporting documents
- Misrepresentation (or omission) of events or transactions in the financial statements
- Intentional misapplication of accounting principles

Such fraud may be carried out by overriding controls that would otherwise appear to be operating effectively, for example, by recording fictitious journal entries or improperly adjusting assumptions or estimates used in financial reporting.

6.1.2 Misappropriation of assets

Key term

Misappropriation of assets involves the theft of an entity's assets and is often perpetrated by employees in relatively small and immaterial amounts. However, it can also involve management who are usually more capable of disguising or concealing misappropriations in ways that are difficult to detect.

This is the theft of the entity's assets (for example, cash, inventory). Employees may be involved in such fraud in small and immaterial amounts, but it can also be carried out on a larger scale by management who may then conceal the misappropriation, for example by:

- Embezzling receipts (for example, diverting them to private bank accounts)
- Stealing physical assets or intellectual property (inventory, selling data)
- Causing an entity to pay for goods not received (payments to fictitious vendors)
- Using assets for personal use

6.2 Fraud and the auditor

ISA 240 *The auditor's responsibilities relating to fraud in an audit of financial statements* provides guidance to auditors in this area.

6.2.1 Responsibilities of management and auditors

The primary responsibility for the prevention and detection of fraud is with those charged with governance and the management of an entity. This is effected by having a commitment to creating a **culture of honesty and ethical behaviour** and **active oversight** by those charged with governance.

The auditor is responsible for obtaining reasonable assurance that the financial statements are free from material misstatement, whether caused by fraud or error. The risk of not detecting a material misstatement from fraud is higher than from error because of the following reasons:

- Fraud may involve **sophisticated schemes** designed to conceal it.
- Fraud may be perpetrated by individuals in **collusion**.
- Management fraud is harder to detect because management is in a position to **manipulate accounting records** or **override control procedures.**

The auditor is responsible for maintaining **professional scepticism** throughout the audit, considering the possibility of management override of controls, and recognising that audit procedures effective for detecting errors may not be effective for detecting fraud.

6.2.2 Risk assessment

ISA 315 requires a **discussion** among team members that places particular emphasis on how and where the financial statements may be susceptible to fraud.

Risk assessment procedures to obtain information in identifying the risks of material misstatement due to fraud shall include the following:

- **Inquiries of management** regarding:
  - **Management's assessment** of the risk that the financial statements may be misstated due to fraud
  - **Management's process** for identifying and responding to the risk of fraud
  - **Management's communication to those charged with governance** in respect of its process for identifying and responding to the risk of fraud
  - **Management's communication to employees** regarding its views on business practices and ethical behaviour
  - **Knowledge** of any actual, suspected or alleged fraud
- **Inquiries of internal audit** for knowledge of any actual, suspected or alleged fraud, and its views on the risks of fraud
- Obtaining an **understanding** of how those charged with governance **oversee** management's processes for identifying and responding to the risk of fraud and the internal control established to mitigate these risks
- **Inquiries of those charged with governance** for knowledge of any actual, suspected or alleged fraud
- Evaluating whether any unusual relationships have been identified in performing **analytical procedures** that may indicate risk of material misstatement due to fraud
- Considering whether any **other information** may indicate risk of material misstatement due to fraud
- Evaluating whether any **fraud risk factors** are present

In accordance with ISA 315, the auditor shall identify and assess the risks of material misstatement due to fraud at the financial statement level and at the assertion level for classes of transactions, account balances and disclosures. These risks shall be treated as **significant risks**.

In accordance with ISA 330, the auditor shall determine **overall responses** to address the assessed risks of material misstatement due to fraud at the financial statement level. In this regard, the auditor shall:

- **Assign and supervise** staff responsible taking into account their knowledge, skill and ability.
- Evaluate whether the **accounting policies** may be indicative of fraudulent financial reporting.
- Incorporate **unpredictability** in the selection of the nature, timing and extent of audit procedures.

As we mentioned above, management fraud is more difficult to detect than employee fraud because of management's ability to override controls and therefore manipulate accounting records. ISA 240 states that irrespective of the auditor's assessment of the risks of management override of controls, the auditor shall design and perform audit procedures to:

- Test the appropriateness of **journal entries and other adjustments**.
- Review **accounting estimates for bias**.
- For **significant transactions** outside the normal course of business, evaluate whether they have been entered into to engage in fraudulent financial reporting or to conceal misappropriation of assets.

6.2.3 Written representations

ISA 240 requires the auditor to obtain **written representations** from management and those charged with governance that:

- They acknowledge their **responsibility** for the design, implementation and maintenance of internal control to prevent and detect fraud.
- They have disclosed to the auditor **management's assessment** of the risk of fraud in the financial statements.
- They have disclosed to the auditor their **knowledge of fraud/suspected fraud** involving management, employees with significant roles in internal control, and others where fraud could have a material effect on the financial statements.
- They have disclosed to the auditor their **knowledge of any allegations of fraud/suspected fraud** communicated by employees, former employees, analysts, regulators or others.

We shall look at written representations from management in more detail in Chapter 18 of this Study Text.

6.2.4 Communication to management and those charged with governance

If the auditor identifies fraud or receives information that a fraud may exist, the auditor shall report this on a **timely basis** to the **appropriate level of management**.

If the auditor identifies or suspects fraud involving management, employees with significant roles in internal control, and others where fraud could have a material effect on the financial statements, he shall communicate this on a **timely basis** to **those charged with governance**.

The auditor also needs to consider whether there is a responsibility to report to the **regulatory or enforcement authorities** – the auditor's professional duty of **confidentiality** may be **overridden** by **laws and statutes** in certain jurisdictions.

6.3 Law and regulations

The auditor is also required to consider the issue of law and regulations in the audit. Auditors are given guidance in ISA 250 *Consideration of laws and regulations in an audit of financial statements*, the objectives of the auditor are:

- To obtain sufficient appropriate audit evidence regarding compliance with the provisions of those laws and regulations that have a **direct effect** on the determination of material amounts and disclosures in the financial statements
- To perform specified audit procedures to help identify non-compliance with other laws and regulations that may have a **material effect** on the financial statements
- To respond appropriately to **non-compliance/suspected non-compliance** identified during the audit

6.3.1 Responsibilities of management and auditors

It is management's responsibility to ensure that the entity complies with the relevant laws and regulations. It is not the auditor's responsibility to prevent or detect non-compliance with laws and regulations.

The auditor's responsibility is to obtain reasonable assurance that the financial statements are free from material misstatement, and in this respect, the auditor must take into account the legal and regulatory framework within which the entity operates.

ISA 250 distinguishes the auditor's responsibilities in relation to compliance with two different categories of laws and regulations:

- Those that have a **direct effect** on the determination of **material amounts** and disclosures in the financial statements
- Those that **do not have a direct effect** on the determination of material amounts and disclosures in the financial statements but where compliance may be fundamental to the **operating aspects**, ability to **continue in business**, or to avoid **material penalties**

For the first category, the auditor's responsibility is to obtain sufficient appropriate audit evidence about **compliance** with those laws and regulations.

For the second category, the auditor's responsibility is to undertake specified audit procedures to help **identify non-compliance** with laws and regulations that may have a **material effect** on the financial statements. These include inquiries of management and inspecting correspondence with the relevant licensing or regulatory authorities.

6.3.2 Audit procedures

In accordance with ISA 315, the auditor shall obtain a general understanding of:

- The applicable legal and regulatory framework
- How the entity complies with that framework

The auditor can achieve this understanding by using his/her **existing understanding** and updating it, and making **inquiries of management** about other laws and regulations that may affect the entity, about its policies and procedures for ensuring compliance, and about its policies and procedures for identifying, evaluating and accounting for litigation claims.

The auditor shall remain alert throughout the audit to the possibility that **other audit procedures** may bring instances of non-compliance or suspected non-compliance to the auditor's attention. These audit procedures could include:

- Reading minutes
- Making inquiries of management and in-house/external legal advisors regarding litigation, claims and assessments
- Performing substantive tests of details of classes of transactions, account balances or disclosures

The auditor shall request **written representations** from management that all known instances of non-compliance or suspected non-compliance with laws and regulations whose effects should be considered when preparing the financial statements have been disclosed to the auditor.

6.3.3 Audit procedures when non-compliance is identified or suspected

The following factors may indicate non-compliance with laws and regulations:

- Investigations by regulatory authorities and government departments
- Payment of fines or penalties
- Payments for unspecified services or loans to consultants, related parties, employees or government employees
- Sales commissions or agents' fees that appear excessive
- Purchasing at prices significantly above/below market price
- Unusual payments in cash
- Unusual transactions with companies registered in tax havens
- Payment for goods and services made to a country different to the one in which the goods and services originated
- Payments without proper exchange control documentation
- Existence of an information system that fails to provide an adequate audit trail or sufficient evidence
- Unauthorised transactions or improperly recorded transactions
- Adverse media comment

The following table summarises audit procedures to be performed when non-compliance is identified or suspected.

Non-compliance: audit procedures
Obtain understanding of nature of act and circumstances.
Obtain further information to evaluate possible effect on financial statements.
Discuss with management and those charged with governance.
Consider need to obtain legal advice if sufficient information not provided and matter is material.
Evaluate effect on auditor's opinion if sufficient information not obtained.
Evaluate implications on risk assessment and reliability of written representations.

6.3.4 Reporting identified or suspected non-compliance

The auditor shall communicate with **those charged with governance**, but if the auditor suspects that those charged with governance are involved, the auditor shall communicate with the next higher level of authority such as the **audit committee or supervisory board**. If this does not exist, the auditor shall consider the need to obtain **legal advice.**

The auditor shall consider the impact on the **auditor's report** if he/she concludes that the non-compliance has a material effect on the financial statements and has not been adequately reflected or is prevented by management and those charged with governance from obtaining sufficient appropriate audit evidence to evaluate whether non-compliance is material to the financial statements.

The auditor shall determine whether identified or suspected non-compliance has to be reported to the **regulatory and enforcement authorities**. Although the auditor must maintain the fundamental principle of **confidentiality**, in some jurisdictions the duty of confidentiality may be **overridden** by law or statute.

7 Documentation of risk assessment

AST FORWARD

Auditors must ensure they have **documented** the work done at the risk assessment stage, such as the discussion among the audit team of the susceptibility of the financial statements to material misstatements, significant risks, and overall responses.

The need for auditors to document their audit work is discussed in the next chapter where we will look in particular at the **audit plan** and the **audit strategy**, two documents for planning. ISAs 315 and 330 contain a number of general requirements about documentation, and we shall briefly run through those here.

The following matters shall be documented during planning

- The discussion among the audit team concerning the susceptibility of the financial statements to material misstatements, including any significant decisions reached
- Key elements of the understanding gained of the entity regarding the elements of the entity and its internal control components specified in ISA 315, the sources of the information gained and the risk assessment procedures carried out
- The identified and assessed risks of material misstatement at the financial statement level and at the assertion level
- Risks identified and related controls evaluated
- The overall responses to address the risks of material misstatement at the financial statement level
- Nature, extent and timing of further audit procedures linked to the assessed risks at the assertion level
- Results of audit procedures
- If the auditors have relied on evidence about the effectiveness of controls from previous audits, conclusions about how this is appropriate
- Demonstration that the financial statements agree or reconcile with the underlying accounting records

Chapter Roundup

- Auditors are required to carry out the audit with an attitude of **professional scepticism**, exercise **professional judgement** and comply with **ethical requirements**.
- **Audit risk** is the risk that the auditor expresses an inappropriate audit opinion when the financial statements are materially misstated. It is a function of the risk of material misstatement (**inherent risk** and **control risk**) and the risk that the auditors will not detect such misstatement (**detection risk**).
- **Materiality for the financial statements as a whole** and **performance materiality** must be calculated at the planning stages of all audits. The calculation or estimation of materiality should be based on experience and judgement. Materiality for the financial statements as a whole must be **reviewed throughout** the audit and **revised if necessary**.
- The auditor is required to obtain an **understanding** of the entity and its environment in order to be able to assess the risks of material misstatements.
- When the auditor has obtained an understanding of the entity, he shall assess the risks of material misstatement in the financial statements, also identifying significant risks.
- **Significant risks** are complex or unusual transactions that may indicate fraud, or other special risks.
- The auditor shall **formulate an approach** to the assessed risks of material misstatement.
- When carrying out risk assessment procedures, the auditor shall also consider the risk of fraud or non-compliance with law and regulations causing a misstatement in the financial statements.
- Auditors must ensure they have **documented** the work done at the risk assessment stage, such as the discussion among the audit team of the susceptibility of the financial statements to material misstatements, significant risks, and overall responses.

Quick Quiz

1 Complete the definitions.

.... risk is the risk that .... may give an ....opinion on the financial statements.

.... risk is the .... of an assertion to a .... that could be material, assuming there were no related ....

2 If control risk and inherent risk are assessed as sufficiently low, substantive procedures can be abandoned completely.

True ☐

False ☐

3 Which procedures might an auditor use in gaining an understanding of the entity?

4 The audit team is required to discuss the susceptibility of the financial statements to material misstatements.

True ☐

False ☐

5 Auditors have a duty to detect fraud.

True ☐

False ☐

Answers to Quick Quiz

1 Audit, auditors, inappropriate

Inherent, susceptibility, misstatement, internal controls

2 False

3 Inquiry, analytical procedures, observation and inspection

4 True

5 False

Now try the question below from the Exam Question Bank

Number	Level	Marks	Time
Q8	Examination	20	36 mins

7

Audit planning and documentation

Topic list	Syllabus reference
1 Audit planning	C5
2 Audit documentation	C6

Introduction

In the chapter we look at the contents of the overall audit strategy and the detailed audit plan.

We also look at how auditors document their work in general. Audit documentation is important because it provides the evidence of the work performed by the auditors in carrying out the audit.

Study guide

		Intellectual level
C5	**Planning an audit**	
(a)	Identify and explain the need for planning an audit	2
(b)	Identify and describe the contents of the overall audit strategy and audit plan	2
(c)	Explain and describe the relationship between the overall audit strategy and the audit plan	2
(d)	Develop and document an audit plan	2
(e)	Explain the difference between interim and final audit	1
C6	**Audit documentation**	
(a)	Explain the need for and the importance of audit documentation	1
(b)	Describe and prepare working papers and supporting documentation	2
(c)	Explain the procedures to ensure safe custody and retention of working papers	1

Exam guide

Audit planning is a very important part of the audit process because it sets the direction for the audit, based on an assessment of the risks relevant to the entity. Questions on planning could come up in a scenario-based setting, asking you to identify risks relevant to planning the audit of the entity. You might also be asked to discuss the advantages and disadvantages of standardised working papers in a knowledge-based part to a question. The June 2009 paper had an eight mark part on the overall audit strategy document in question 1.

1 Audit planning

June 09

FAST FORWARD

The auditors formulate an **overall audit strategy** which is translated into a **detailed audit plan** for audit staff to follow.

1.1 The importance of planning

An effective and efficient audit relies on proper planning procedures. The planning process is covered in general terms by ISA 300 *Planning an audit of financial statements* which states that the auditor shall plan the audit so that the engagement is performed in an effective manner.

Audits are planned to:

- Help the auditor devote appropriate attention to important areas of the audit.
- Help the auditor identify and resolve potential problems on a timely basis.
- Help the auditor properly organise and manage the audit so it is performed in an effective manner.
- Assist in the selection of appropriate team members and assignment of work to them.
- Facilitate the direction, supervision and review of work.
- Assist in coordination of work done by auditors of components and experts.

Audit procedures should be discussed with the client's management, staff and/or audit committee in order to co-ordinate audit work, including that of internal audit. However, all audit procedures remain the responsibility of the external auditors.

A structured approach to planning will include:

Step 1 Ensuring that ethical requirements are met, including independence

Step 2 Ensuring the terms of the engagement are understood

Step 3 Establishing the overall audit strategy that sets the scope, timing and direction of the audit and guides the development of the audit plan

- Identify the characteristics of the engagement that define its scope.
- Ascertain the reporting objectives to plan the timing of the audit and nature of communications required.
- Consider significant factors in directing the team's efforts.
- Consider results of preliminary engagement activities.
- Ascertain nature, timing and extent of resources necessary to perform the engagement.

Step 4 Developing an audit plan that includes the nature, timing and extent of planned risk assessment procedures and further audit procedures

1.2 The overall audit strategy and the audit plan

FAST FORWARD

The overall audit strategy and audit plan shall be updated and changed as necessary during the course of the audit.

1.2.1 The audit strategy

Key term

The overall **audit strategy** sets the scope, timing and direction of the audit, and guides the development of the more detailed audit plan.

The matters the auditor may consider in establishing an overall audit strategy are set out in the table below.

THE OVERALL AUDIT STRATEGY: MATTERS TO CONSIDER	
Characteristics of the engagement	• Financial reporting framework • Industry-specific reporting requirements • Expected audit coverage • Nature of business segments • Availability of internal audit work • Use of service organisations • Effect of information technology on audit procedures • Availability of client personnel and data
Reporting objectives, timing of the audit and nature of communications	• Entity's timetable for reporting • Organisation of meetings with management and those charged with governance • Discussions with management and those charged with governance • Expected communications with third parties
Significant factors, preliminary engagement activities, and knowledge gained on other engagements	• Determination of materiality • Areas identified with higher risk of material misstatement • Results of previous audits • Need to maintain professional scepticism • Evidence of management's commitment to design, implementation and maintenance of sound internal control • Volume of transactions • Significant business developments • Significant industry developments • Significant changes in financial reporting framework • Other significant recent developments
Nature, timing and extent of resources	• Selection of engagement team • Assignment of work to team members • Engagement budgeting

Examples of items to include in the overall audit strategy could be:

- Industry-specific financial reporting requirements
- Number of locations to be visited
- Audit client's timetable for reporting to its members
- Communication between the audit team and the client

1.2.2 The audit plan

Key term

> The **audit plan** converts the audit strategy into a more detailed plan and includes the nature, timing and extent of audit procedures to be performed by engagement team members in order to obtain sufficient appropriate audit evidence to reduce audit risk to an acceptably low level.

The audit plan shall include the following:

- A description of the nature, timing and extent of planned risk assessment procedures
- A description of the nature, timing and extent of planned further audit procedures at the assertion level
- Other planned audit procedures required to be carried out for the engagement to comply with ISAs

The planning for these procedures occurs over the course of the audit as the audit plan develops.

Examples of items included in the audit plan could be:

- Timetable of planned audit work
- Allocation of work to audit team members
- Audit procedures for each major account area (eg inventory, receivables, cash etc)
- Materiality for the financial statements as a whole and performance materiality

Any changes made during the audit engagement to the overall audit strategy or audit plan, and the reasons for such changes, shall be included in the audit documentation.

1.3 Interim and final audits

Auditors usually carry out their audit work for a financial year in one or more sittings. These are referred to as the **interim audit(s)** and the **final audit**.

The interim audit visits are carried out during the period of review and work focuses on planning and risk assessment and tests of controls and systems, although substantive audit procedures may also be carried out. The final audit visit is at the year-end or shortly after and work focuses on the audit of the financial statements.

ISA 330 *The auditor's responses to assessed risks* states that the higher the risk of material misstatement, the more likely it is that the auditor will decide that it is more effective to undertake substantive procedures nearer to, or at, the period-end rather than earlier. However, performing audit procedures before the period-end can assist in identifying significant matters at an early stage of the audit and being able to resolve them with management's assistance or developing an effective audit approach to address them.

Auditors must obtain evidence that controls have operated effectively throughout the period. ISA 330 states that when the auditor obtains evidence about the operating effectiveness of controls during an interim audit visit, the auditor must determine what additional audit evidence should be obtained for the remaining period.

The ISA makes a similar observation with regard to substantive procedures: when substantive procedures are performed at an interim audit visit, the auditor shall perform further substantive procedures or substantive procedures combined with tests of controls to cover the remaining period that provide a reasonable basis for extending the audit conclusions from the interim date to the period-end.

Some audit procedures can only be performed at the final audit visit, such as agreeing the financial statements to the accounting records and examining adjustments made during the process of preparing the financial statements.

2 Audit documentation

FAST FORWARD

It is important to document audit work performed in working papers to:

- Enable reporting partner to ensure all planned work has been completed adequately
- Provide details of work done for future reference
- Assist in planning and control of future audits
- Encourage a methodical approach

2.1 The objective of audit documentation

Key term

Audit documentation is the record of audit procedures performed, relevant audit evidence obtained and conclusions reached. The term 'working papers' or 'work papers' are also sometimes used.

All audit work must be documented: the working papers are the tangible evidence of the work done in support of the audit opinion. ISA 230 *Audit documentation* states that the auditor shall prepare audit documentation on a **timely basis**.

Audit documentation is necessary for the following reasons:

- It provides evidence of the auditor's basis for a conclusion about the achievement of the overall objective.
- It provides evidence that the audit was planned and performed in accordance with ISAs and other legal and regulatory requirements.
- It assists the engagement team to plan and perform the audit.
- It assists team members responsible for supervision to direct, supervise and review audit work.
- It enables the team to be accountable for its work.
- It allows a record of matters of continuing significance to be retained.
- It enables the conduct of quality control reviews and inspections (both internal and external).

2.2 Form and content of working papers

The ISA requires working papers to be sufficiently complete and detailed to provide an overall understanding of the audit. Auditors cannot record everything they consider. Therefore judgement must be used as to the extent of working papers, based on the following general rule:

What would be necessary to provide an experienced auditor, with no previous connection with the audit, with an understanding of the work performed, the results of audit procedures, audit evidence obtained, significant matters arising during the audit and conclusions reached.

The form and content of working papers are affected by matters such as:

- The **size and complexity** of the entity
- The **nature** of the audit procedures to be performed
- The **identified risks** of material misstatement
- The **significance** of the audit evidence obtained
- The nature and extent of **exceptions** identified
- The need to document a **conclusion** or the basis for a conclusion not readily determinable from the documentation of the work performed or audit evidence obtained
- The audit **methodology and tools** used

2.2.1 Examples of working papers

- Information obtained in understanding the entity and its environment, including its internal control, such as the following:
  - Information concerning the legal documents, agreements and minutes
  - Extracts or copies of important legal documents, agreements and minutes
  - Information concerning the industry, economic environment and legislative environment within which the entity operates.
  - Extracts from the entity's internal control manual
- Evidence of the planning process including audit programs and any changes thereto
- Evidence of the auditor's consideration of the work of internal audit and conclusions reached
- Analyses of transactions and balances
- Analyses of significant ratios and trends
- Identified and assessed risks of material misstatements
- A record of the nature, timing, extent and results of audit procedures
- Evidence that the work performed was supervised and reviewed
- An indication as to who performed the audit procedures and when they were performed
- Details of audit procedures applied regarding components whose financial statements are audited by another auditor
- Copies of communications with other auditors, experts and other third parties
- Copies of letters or notes concerning audit matters communicated to or discussed with management or those charged with governance, including the terms of the engagement and material weaknesses in internal control
- Letters of representation received from the entity
- Conclusions reached by the auditor concerning significant aspects of the audit, including how exceptions and unusual matters, if any, disclosed by the auditor's procedures were resolved or treated.
- Copies of the financial statements and auditors' reports
- Notes of discussions about significant matters with management and others
- In exceptional circumstances, the reasons for departing from a basic principle or essential procedure of an ISA and how the alternative procedure performed achieve the audit objective

The following is an illustration of a typical audit working paper.

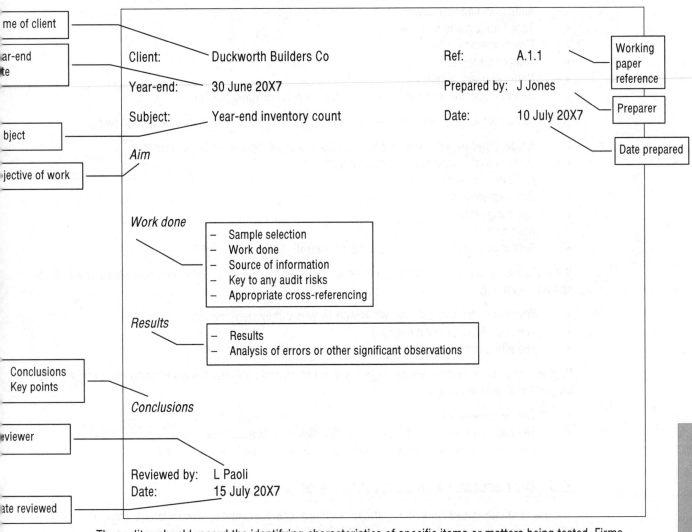

The auditor should record the identifying characteristics of specific items or matters being tested. Firms should have standard **referencing** and **filing** procedures for working papers, to facilitate their review.

2.2.2 Audit files

For recurring audits, working papers may be split between:

Permanent audit files (containing information of **continuing importance** to the audit). These contain:

- Engagement letters
- New client questionnaire
- The memorandum and articles
- Other legal documents such as prospectuses, leases, sales agreement
- Details of the history of the client's business
- Board minutes of continuing relevance
- Previous years' signed accounts, analytical review and management letters
- Accounting systems notes, previous years' control questionnaires

Current audit files (containing information of relevance to the **current year's audit**). These should be compiled on a timely basis after the completion of the audit and should contain:

- Financial statements
- Accounts checklists
- Management accounts details
- Reconciliations of management and financial accounts
- A summary of unadjusted errors
- Report to partner including details of significant events and errors

- Review notes
- Audit planning memorandum
- Time budgets and summaries
- Representation letter
- Management letter
- Notes of board minutes
- Communications with third parties such as experts or other auditors

They also contain working papers covering each audit area. These should include the following:

- A lead schedule including details of the figures to be included in the accounts
- Problems encountered and conclusions drawn
- Audit programmes
- Risk assessments
- Sampling plans
- Analytical review
- Details of substantive tests and tests of control

If it is necessary to modify/add new audit documentation to a file after it has been assembled, the auditor should document:

- Who made the changes, and when, and by whom they were reviewed
- The reasons for making changes
- The effect of changes on the auditors' conclusions

If, in exceptional circumstances, changes are made to an audit file after the audit report has been signed, the auditor should document:

- The circumstances
- The audit procedures performed, evidence obtained, conclusions drawn
- When and by whom changes to audit documents were made and reviewed

2.3 Standardised and automated working papers

The use of **standardised** working papers, for example, checklists and specimen letters, may improve the efficiency of audit work but they can be dangerous because they may lead to auditors mechanically following an approach without using audit judgement.

Automated working paper packages have been developed which can make the documenting of audit work much easier. Such programs aid preparation of working papers, lead schedules, the trial balance and the financial statements themselves. These are automatically cross-referenced, adjusted and balanced by the computer.

The **advantages** of automated working papers are as follows.

- The risk of errors is reduced.
- The working papers will be neater and easier to review.
- The time saved will be substantial as adjustments can be made easily to all working papers, including those summarising the key analytical information.
- Standard forms do not have to be carried to audit locations.
- Audit working papers can be transmitted for review via a modem or fax facilities.

2.4 Safe custody and retention of working papers

Judgement may have to be used in deciding the length of holding working papers, and further consideration should be given to the matter before their destruction. The ACCA recommends **seven years** as a minimum period.

Working papers are the property of the auditors. They are not a substitute for, nor part of, the entity's accounting records.

Auditors must follow ethical guidance on the confidentiality of audit working papers. They may, at their discretion, release parts of or whole working papers to the entity, as long as disclosure does not undermine 'the independence or validity of the audit process'. Information should not be made available to third parties without the permission of the entity.

xam focus oint

> You must understand the difference between the audit strategy and the audit plan. A question on this area of the syllabus could come up as part of a longer scenario question or as a short factual question in question 2.

Chapter Roundup

- The auditors formulate an **overall audit strategy** which is translated into a **detailed audit plan** for audit staff to follow.
- The overall audit strategy and audit plan shall be updated and changed as necessary during the course of the audit.
- It is important to document audit work performed in working papers to:
  - Enable reporting partner to ensure all planned work has been completed adequately
  - Provide details of work done for future reference
  - Assist in planning and control of future audits
  - Encourage a methodical approach

Quick Quiz

1 Complete the definitions:

An .... is the formulation of a general strategy for the audit.

An .... is a set of instructions to the audit team that sets out the further audit procedures to be carried out.

2 Changes to the overall audit strategy or audit plan do not need to be documented.

True ☐

False ☐

3 What is the general rule for audit documentation?

4 State two advantages of standardised working papers.

(1) ....

(2) ....

5 Complete the table, using the working papers given below.

Current audit file	Permanent audit file

Engagement letters	New client questionnaire
Financial statements	Management letter
Accounts checklists	Audit planning memorandum
Board minutes of continuing relevance	Accounting systems notes

Answers to Quick Quiz

1 Overall audit strategy, audit plan.

2 False – any changes shall be fully documented in accordance with ISA 300 *Planning an audit of financial statements*.

3 What would be necessary to provide an experienced auditor, with no previous connection with the audit, with an understanding of the nature, timing and extent of the audit procedures performed, the results of audit procedures, audit evidence obtained, significant matters arising during the audit and conclusions reached.

4 Advantages of standardised working papers

(1) Facilitate the delegation of work
(2) Means of quality control

5

Current audit file	**Permanent audit file**
Financial statements	Engagement letters
Management letter	New client questionnaire
Accounts checklists	Board minutes of continuing relevance
Audit planning memorandum	Accounting systems notes

Now try the question below from the Exam Question Bank

Number	Level	Marks	Time
Q9	Examination	10	18 mins

Introduction to audit evidence

Topic list	Syllabus reference
1 Audit evidence	E2
2 Financial statement assertions	E1

Introduction

In this chapter, we introduce the fundamental auditing concept of audit evidence. Audit evidence is required to enable the auditor to form an opinion on the financial statements. Therefore such evidence has to be sufficient and appropriate.

We also explain the financial statement assertions for which audit evidence is required. These will be particularly important when we consider detailed testing later in this Study Text, since audit tests are designed to obtain sufficient appropriate evidence about the assertions for each balance or transaction in the financial statements.

Study guide

		Intellectual level
E1	**The use of assertions by auditors**	
(a)	Explain the assertions contained in the financial statements	2
(b)	Explain the principles and objectives of transaction testing, account balance testing and disclosure testing	1
(c)	Explain the use of assertions in obtaining audit evidence	2
E2	**Audit procedures**	
(a)	Discuss the sources and relative merits of the different types of evidence available	2
(e)	Discuss the quality of evidence obtained	2

Exam guide

The issues of audit evidence and financial statement assertions will underpin exam questions about detailed audit testing which we look at later in this Study Text. In addition, you could be asked a question on the theory of evidence such as the different types of evidence that can be obtained by auditors.

The pilot paper had 12 marks for audit procedures to confirm assertions relating to purchases in the long scenario question, as well as four knowledge-based marks available to explain types of audit evidence that could be obtained by the auditor.

The December 2007 paper had a question on the aims of a test of control and a substantive procedure.

The June 2008 exam had four marks for explaining assertions relating to the confirmation of receivables as part of question 1, and four marks in question 2 on factors that would influence the auditor's judgement regarding the sufficiency of evidence obtained.

The December 2008 paper had eight marks available in question 1 for explaining audit procedures used in collecting audit evidence. Question 2 had four marks for listing four assertions relevant to the audit of tangible non-current assets.

The June 2009 paper had four marks in question 2 on assertions relating to classes of transactions.

1 Audit evidence — Pilot paper, Dec 07, June 08

FAST FORWARD

Auditors must design and perform audit procedures to obtain **sufficient appropriate** audit evidence.

1.1 The need for audit evidence

Remember that the objective of an audit of financial statements is to enable the auditor to express an opinion on whether the financial statements are prepared, in all material respects, in accordance with an identified financial reporting framework. In this section, we shall look at the **audit evidence** gathered, which enables the auditor to express his opinion.

Key term

Audit evidence is all of the information used by the auditor in arriving at the conclusions on which the auditor's opinion is based.

Audit evidence includes the information contained in the accounting records underlying the financial statements, and other information gathered by the auditors, such as confirmations from third parties. Auditors are **not expected to look at all the information** that might exist. They will often select **samples** to test, as we shall see in Chapter 11.

1.2 Sufficient appropriate audit evidence

Key terms

The **appropriateness** of audit evidence is the measure of the quality of it, that is, its relevance and its reliability in providing support for the conclusions on which the auditor's opinion is based.

The **sufficiency** of audit evidence is the measure of the quantity of audit evidence. The quantity of audit evidence required is affected by the auditor's assessment of the risks of material misstatement and also by the quality of such audit evidence.

ISA 500 *Audit evidence* requires auditors to 'design and perform audit procedures that are appropriate in the circumstances for the purposes of obtaining **sufficient appropriate** audit evidence'. 'Sufficiency' and 'appropriateness' are interrelated and apply to both tests of controls and substantive procedures.

- **Sufficiency** is the measure of the **quantity** of audit evidence.
- **Appropriateness** is the measure of the **quality** or **reliability** of the audit evidence.

The **quantity** of audit evidence required is affected by the **level of risk** in the area being audited. It is also affected by the **quality** of evidence obtained. If the evidence is high quality, the auditor may need less than if it were poor quality. However, obtaining a high quantity of poor quality evidence will not cancel out its poor quality. The ISA requires auditors to consider the **relevance and reliability** of the information to be used as audit evidence when designing and performing audit procedures.

Relevance deals with the logical connection with the purpose of the audit procedure and the assertion under consideration (we look at assertions in the next section). The relevance of information may be affected by the direction of testing.

Reliability is influenced by the source and nature of the information, including the controls over its preparation and maintenance. The following generalisations may help in assessing the **reliability** of audit evidence.

QUALITY OF EVIDENCE	
External	Audit evidence from **external sources** is more reliable than that obtained from the entity's records because it is from an independent source.
Auditor	Evidence obtained **directly by auditors** is more reliable than that obtained indirectly or by inference
Entity	Evidence obtained from the entity's records is more reliable when the related **control system operates effectively**
Written	Evidence in the form of **documents (paper or electronic)** or **written representations** are more reliable than oral representations, since oral representations can be retracted.
Originals	**Original documents** are more reliable than photocopies or facsimiles, which can easily be altered by the client.

1.2.1 Management's expert

Key term

A **management's expert** is an individual or organisation possessing expertise in a field other than auditing or accounting, whose work is used by the entity to assist in the preparation of the financial statements.

ISA 500 considers the use of a management's expert by management and states that if information to be used as audit evidence has been prepared by a management's expert, the auditor must evaluate the competence, capabilities and objectivity of the expert, obtain an understanding of the work done, and evaluate the appropriateness of the work done as audit evidence.

1.2.2 Information produced by the entity

If information produced by the entity is to be used by the auditor, the auditor needs to evaluate whether it is sufficiently reliable for the auditor's purposes, including obtaining audit evidence regarding its accuracy and completeness, and evaluating whether it is sufficiently precise and detailed.

1.2.3 Selecting items to test

ISA 500 states that the auditor must determine the means of selecting items for testing that are effective in meeting the purpose of the audit procedure. The auditor could either select **all items**, select **specific items** or use **audit sampling**. We look at these in more detail in Chapter 11.

1.2.4 Inconsistencies and doubts over reliability

If audit evidence from one source is inconsistent with that from another, or the auditor has doubts over the reliability of information, the auditor must determine what modifications or additions to audit procedures are necessary to resolve the issues and must consider the effect on other aspects of the audit.

Objective 17 of the PER performance objectives is to prepare for and collect evidence for audit. You can apply the knowledge you gain from this and subsequent chapters to assist in achieving this objective.

2 Financial statement assertions — June 08, Dec 08, June 09

FAST FORWARD

Audit tests are designed to obtain evidence about the **financial statement assertions**. Assertions relate to **classes of transactions and events**, **account balances** at the period-end, and **presentation and disclosure**.

Key term

Financial statement assertions are the representations by management, explicit or otherwise, that are embodied in the financial statements, as used by the auditor to consider the different types of potential misstatements that may occur.

ISA 315 states that the auditor must use assertions for **classes of transactions** (ie income statement), **account balances** (ie statement of financial position), and **presentation and disclosures** in sufficient detail to form the basis for the assessment of risks of material misstatement and the design and performance of further audit procedures. It gives examples of assertions in these areas which are set out in the table below.

Assertions used by the auditor	
Assertions about **classes of transactions and events** for the period under audit	**Occurrence**: transactions and events that have been recorded have occurred and pertain to the entity. **Completeness**: all transactions and events that should have been recorded have been recorded. **Accuracy**: amounts and other data relating to recorded transactions and events have been recorded appropriately. **Cut-off**: transactions and events have been recorded in the correct accounting period. **Classification**: transactions and events have been recorded in the proper accounts.
Assertions about **account balances** at the period-end	**Existence**: assets, liabilities, and equity interests exist. **Rights and obligations**: the entity holds or controls the rights to assets, and liabilities are the obligations of the entity. **Completeness**: all assets, liabilities and equity interests that should have been recorded have been recorded. **Valuation and allocation**: assets, liabilities, and equity interests are included in the financial statements at appropriate amounts and any resulting valuation or allocation adjustments are appropriately recorded.
Assertions about **presentation and disclosure**	**Occurrence and rights and obligations**: disclosed events, transactions and other matters have occurred and pertain to the entity. **Completeness**: all disclosures that should have been included in the financial statements have been included. **Classification and understandability**: financial information is appropriately presented and described, and disclosures are clearly expressed. **Accuracy and valuation**: financial and other information are disclosed fairly and at appropriate amounts.

This is a key syllabus area and you **must** be very comfortable with the assertions that relate to each of the three areas, as the same assertions do not always apply to each of these areas. Exam question are very likely to test this area in the context of audit procedures to test particular assertions so it's vital that you take the time to learn, understand and test your knowledge.

Exam focus point

When designing audit plans and procedures for specific areas, you must focus on the financial statement assertions that you are trying to find evidence to support. If a question asks for audit procedures relating to a particular assertion, make sure your answer addresses only the assertion required by the question.

2.1 Audit procedures to obtain audit evidence — Pilot paper, Dec 08

FAST FORWARD

Audit evidence can be obtained by inspection, observation, inquiry and confirmation, recalculation, reperformance and analytical procedures.

The auditor obtains audit evidence by undertaking audit procedures to do the following:

- Obtain an understanding of the entity and its environment to assess the risks of material misstatement at the financial statement and assertion levels (**risk assessment procedures**)
- Test the operating effectiveness of controls in preventing, or detecting and correcting, material misstatements at the assertion level (**tests of controls**)
- Detect material misstatements at the assertion level (**substantive procedures**)

The auditor must **always** perform **risk assessment procedures** to provide a satisfactory assessment of risks.

Tests of controls are necessary to test the controls to support the risk assessment, and also when substantive procedures alone do not provide sufficient appropriate audit evidence. **Substantive**

procedures must **always** be carried out for **material** classes of transactions, account balances and disclosures.

The audit procedures described in the table below can be used as risk assessment procedures, tests of controls and substantive procedures.

Key terms

Tests of controls are performed to obtain audit evidence about the operating effectiveness of controls preventing, or detecting and correcting, material misstatements at the assertion level.

Substantive procedures are audit procedures performed to detect material misstatements at the assertion level. They are generally of two types:

- Substantive analytical procedures
- Tests of detail of classes of transactions, account balances and disclosures

Auditors obtain evidence by one or more of the following procedures.

PROCEDURES	
Inspection of tangible assets	Inspection of tangible assets that are recorded in the accounting records confirms existence, but does not necessarily confirm rights and obligations or valuation. Confirmation that assets seen are recorded in accounting records gives evidence of completeness.
Inspection of documentation or records	This is the examination of documents and records, both internal and external, in paper, electronic or other forms. This procedure provides evidence of varying reliability, depending on the nature, source and effectiveness of controls over production (if internal). Inspection can provide evidence of existence (eg a document constituting a financial instrument), but not necessarily about ownership or value.
Observation	This involves watching a procedure or process being performed (for example, post opening). It is of limited use, as it only confirms the procedure took place when the auditor was watching, and because the act of being observed could affect how the procedure or process was performed.
Inquiry	This involves seeking information from client staff or external sources. Strength of evidence depends on the knowledge and integrity of source of information. Inquiry alone does not provide sufficient audit evidence to detect a material misstatement at assertion level nor is it sufficient to test the operating effectiveness of controls.
Confirmation	This is the process of obtaining a representation of information or of an existing condition directly from a third party eg confirmation from bank of bank balances
Recalculation	This consists of checking the mathematical accuracy of documents or records and can be performed through the use of IT.
Reperformance	This is the auditor's independent execution of procedures or controls that were originally performed as part of the entity's internal control.
Analytical procedures	Evaluating and comparing financial and/or non-financial data for plausible relationships. Also include the investigation of identified fluctuations and relationships that are inconsistent with other relevant information or deviate significantly from predicted amounts.

Question

Audit evidence

(a) Discuss the quality of the following types of audit evidence, giving two examples of each form of evidence.

(i) Evidence originated by the auditors
(ii) Evidence created by third parties
(iii) Evidence created by the management of the client

(b) Describe the general considerations which auditors must bear in mind when evaluating audit evidence.

Answer

(a) **Quality of audit evidence**

(i) *Evidence originated by the auditors*

This is in general the most reliable type of audit evidence because there is little risk that it can be manipulated by management.

Examples

(1) Analytical procedures, such as the calculation of ratios and trends in order to examine unusual variations

(2) Physical inspection or observation, such as attendance at inventory counts

(3) Reperformance of calculations making up figures in the accounts, such as the computation of total inventory values

(ii) *Evidence created by third parties*

Third party evidence is more reliable than client-produced evidence to the extent that it is obtained from independent sources. Its reliability will be reduced if it is obtained from sources which are not independent, or if there is a risk that client personnel may be able to and have reason to suppress or manipulate it.

Examples

(1) Circularisation of trade receivables or payables, confirmation of bank balances.

(2) Reports produced by experts, such as property valuations, actuarial valuations, legal opinions. In evaluating such evidence, the auditors need to take into account the expert's qualifications, independence and the terms of reference for the work.

(3) Documents held by the client which were issued by third parties, such as invoices, price lists and statements. These may sometimes be manipulated by the client and so are less reliable than confirmations received directly.

(iii) *Evidence created by management*

The auditors cannot place the same degree of reliance on evidence produced by client management as on that produced outside the company. However, it will often be necessary to place some reliance on such evidence. The auditors will need to obtain audit evidence that the information supplied is complete and accurate, and apply judgement in doing so, taking into account previous experience of the client's reliability and the extent to which the client's representations appear compatible with other audit findings, as well as the materiality of the item under discussion.

Examples

(1) The company's accounting records and supporting schedules. Although these are prepared by management, the auditors have a statutory right to examine such records in full: this right enhances the quality of this information.

(2) The client's explanations of, for instance, apparently unusual fluctuations in results. Such evidence requires interpretation by the auditors and, being oral evidence, only limited reliance can be placed upon it.

(3) Information provided to the auditors about the internal control system. The auditors need to confirm that this information is accurate and up-to-date, and that it does not simply describe an idealised system which is not adhered to in practice.

(b) **General considerations in evaluating audit evidence**

Audit evidence will often not be wholly conclusive. The auditors must obtain evidence which is **sufficient and appropriate** to form the basis for their audit conclusions. The evidence gathered should also be **relevant** to those conclusions, and sufficiently **reliable** to form the basis for the audit opinion. The auditors must exercise skill and judgement to ensure that evidence is correctly interpreted and that only valid inferences are drawn from it.

Certain general principles can be stated. **Written evidence** is preferable to oral evidence; **independent evidence** obtained from outside the organisation is more reliable than that obtained internally; and **evidence generated by the auditors** is more reliable than that obtained from others.

Chapter Roundup

- Auditors must design and perform audit procedures to obtain **sufficient appropriate** audit evidence.
- Audit tests are designed to obtain evidence about the **financial statement assertions**. Assertions relate to **classes of transactions and events**, **account balances** at the period-end, and **presentation and disclosure**.
- Audit evidence can be obtained by inspection, observation, inquiry and confirmation, recalculation, reperformance and analytical procedures.

Quick Quiz

1 Define sufficiency and appropriateness as they relate to audit evidence.

2 State the financial statement assertions.

3 Fill in the blanks.

Audit evidence from external sources is .... than that obtained from the entity's records.

4 State five procedures which auditors can use to obtain audit evidence.

5 Explain what 'reperformance' is.

Answers to Quick Quiz

1. Sufficiency is the measure of the quantity of audit evidence.

   Appropriateness is the measure of the quality/reliability of audit evidence.

2. Existence, rights and obligations, occurrence, completeness, valuation, accuracy, classification and understandability, cut-off, allocation.

3. More reliable

4. Any five from:

   Inspection
   Observation
   Inquiry
   Confirmation
   Recalculation
   Reperformance
   Analytical procedures

5. 'Reperformance' is the auditor's independent execution of procedures or controls that were originally performed as part of the entity's internal control.

Now try the question below from the Exam Question Bank

Number	Level	Marks	Time
Q10	Examination	10	18 mins

PART D

Internal control

Internal control

Topic list	Syllabus reference
1 Internal control systems	D1, D5, E2
2 The use of internal control systems by auditors	D1, D2
3 The evaluation of internal control components	D5, D6
4 Internal controls in a computerised environment	D3, D4

Introduction

The auditor generally seeks to rely on the internal controls within the entity in order to reduce the amount of testing of final balances.

The initial evaluation of a client's system is essential as the auditor gains an understanding of the entity, as we outlined in Chapter 6. In this chapter, we shall look at some of the detailed requirements of ISA 315 with regard to internal controls, and shall also set out control issues the auditor may come across.

The auditor will assess the risks of material misstatement arising and, as we discussed in Chapter 6, may respond to those risks by carrying out tests of controls. If he concludes that he can rely on the controls in place, the level of substantive audit testing required can be reduced.

In this chapter we also look at the ways in which auditors can document the internal control systems using narrative notes, flowcharts, questionnaires and checklists, focusing particularly on the use of questionnaires.

We shall examine the detailed controls that businesses operate in Chapter 10 and the tests that the auditors may carry out in specific areas. You should bear in mind the principles discussed in this chapter when considering the controls needed over specific accounting areas.

Study guide

		Intellectual level
D1	**Internal control systems**	
(a)	Explain why an auditor needs to obtain an understanding of internal control activities relevant to the audit	1
(b)	Describe and explain the key components of an internal control system	1
(c)	Identify and describe the important elements of internal control including the control environment and management control activities	1
(d)	Discuss the difference between tests of control and substantive procedures	2
D2	**The use of internal control systems by auditors**	
(a)	Explain the importance of internal control to auditors	1
(b)	Explain how auditors identify weaknesses in internal control systems and how those weaknesses limit the extent of auditors' reliance on those systems	2
D3	**Transaction cycles**	
(b)	Provide examples of computer system controls	2
D4	**Tests of controls**	
(b)	List examples of application controls and general IT controls	2
D5	**The evaluation of internal control components**	
(a)	Analyse the limitations of internal control components in the context of fraud and error	
(b)	Explain the need to modify the audit strategy and audit plan following the results of tests of control	1
(c)	Identify and explain management's risk assessment process with reference to internal control components	1
D6	**Communication on internal control**	
(a)	Discuss and provide examples of how the reporting of internal control weaknesses and recommendations to overcome those weaknesses are provided to management	2
E2	**Audit procedures**	
(d)	Describe why smaller entities may have different control environments and describe the types of evidence likely to be available in smaller entities	1

Exam guide

Questions on internal control are highly likely to come up in a scenario-based setting focusing on control procedures in a given system or asking you to describe weaknesses in the system of internal control, together with recommendations of internal controls to mitigate those weaknesses. The pilot paper had five marks on control procedures relating to trade payables in question 1, and 16 marks on weaknesses in internal control over a wages system and recommendations in question 4. The December 2007 paper had similar style questions for 12 marks.

The June 2008 paper had a four mark part relating to internal control questionnaires and 12 marks in the same question on tests of control. Question 2 of this paper had three marks relating to tests of control and the impact of results on the audit opinion.

Question 1 of the December 2008 paper had 16 marks relating to controls in a wages system. There were also four marks on the control environment in a charity in question 4 of the same paper.

1 Internal control systems **Dec 08**

FAST FORWARD

The auditors must **understand** the **accounting system** and **control environment** in order to determine their audit approach.

Key term

Internal control is the process designed and effected by those charged with governance, management, and other personnel to provide reasonable assurance about the achievement of the entity's objectives with regard to reliability of financial reporting, effectiveness and efficiency of operations and compliance with applicable laws and regulations.

ISA 315 *Identifying and assessing the risks of material misstatement through understanding the entity and its environment* deals with the whole area of controls.

Internal control has five elements:

- The control environment
- The entity's risk assessment process
- The information system relevant to financial reporting
- Control activities
- Monitoring of controls

In obtaining an understanding of internal control, the auditor must understand the **design** of the internal control and the **implementation** of that control. In the following sub-sections, we look at each of the elements of internal control in turn.

1.1 Control environment

The control environment is the framework within which controls operate. The control environment is very much determined by the management of a business.

Key term

Control environment includes the governance and management functions and the attitudes, awareness and actions of those charged with governance and management concerning the entity's internal control and its importance in the entity.

A strong control environment does not, by itself, ensure the effectiveness of the overall internal control system, but can be a positive factor when assessing the risks of material misstatement. A weak control environment can undermine the effectiveness of controls.

Aspects of the control environment (such as management attitudes towards control) will nevertheless be a significant factor in determining how controls operate. Controls are more likely to operate well in an environment where they are treated as being important. In addition consideration of the control environment will mean determining whether certain controls (internal auditors, budgets) actually exist.

ISA 315 states that auditors shall have an understanding of the control environment. As part of this understanding, the auditor shall evaluate whether:

- Management has created and maintained a culture of honesty and ethical behaviour
- The strengths in the control environment provide an appropriate foundation for the other components of internal control and whether those components are not undermined by deficiencies in the control environment

The following table illustrates the elements of the control environment that may be relevant when obtaining an understanding of the control environment.

CONTROL ENVIRONMENT	
Communication and enforcement of integrity and ethical values	Essential elements which influence the effectiveness of the design, administration and monitoring of controls
Commitment to competence	Management's consideration of the competence levels for particular jobs and how those levels translate into requisite skills and knowledge
Participation by those charged with governance	• Independence from management • Experience and stature • Extent of involvement and scrutiny of activities • Appropriateness of actions and interaction with internal and external auditors
Management's philosophy and operating style	• Approach to taking and managing business risks • Attitudes and actions towards financial reporting • Attitudes towards information processing and accounting functions and personnel
Organisational structure	The framework within which an entity's activities for achieving its objectives are planned, executed, controlled and reviewed
Assignment of authority and responsibility	How authority and responsibility for operating activities are assigned and how reporting relationships and authorisation hierarchies are established
Human resource policies and practices	Recruitment, orientation, training, evaluating, counselling, promoting, compensation and remedial actions

The auditor shall assess whether these elements of the control environment have been implemented using a combination of **inquiries of management** and **observation** and **inspection**.

1.2 Entity's risk assessment process

ISA 315 says the auditor shall obtain an understanding of whether the entity has a process for:

- Identifying business risks relevant to financial reporting objectives
- Estimating the significance of the risks
- Assessing the likelihood of their occurrence
- Deciding upon actions to address those risks

If the entity has established such a process, the auditor shall obtain an understanding of it. If there is not a process, the auditor shall discuss with management whether relevant business risks have been identified and how they have been addressed.

1.3 Information system relevant to financial reporting

Key term

The **information system relevant to financial reporting** is a component of internal control that includes the financial reporting system, and consists of the procedures and records established to initiate, record, process and report entity transactions and to maintain accountability for the related assets, liabilities and equity.

The auditor shall obtain an understanding of the information system relevant to financial reporting objectives, including the following areas:

- The classes of transactions in the entity's operations that are significant to the financial statements
- The procedures, within both IT and manual systems, by which those transactions are initiated, recorded, processed, corrected, transferred to the general ledger and reported in the financial statements

- The related accounting records, supporting information, and specific accounts in the financial statements, in respect of initiating, recording, processing and reporting transactions
- How the information system captures events and conditions, other than transactions, that are significant to the financial statements
- The financial reporting process used to prepare the entity's financial statements, including significant accounting estimates and disclosures
- Controls surrounding journal entries, including non-standard journal entries used to record non-recurring, unusual transactions or adjustments

The auditor shall obtain an understanding of how the entity **communicates** financial reporting roles and responsibilities and significant matters relating to financial reporting.

1.4 Control activities

Key term

Control activities are those policies and procedures that help ensure that management directives are carried out.

ISA 315 states that the auditor shall obtain an understanding of control activities relevant to the audit and how the entity has responded to risks arising from IT.

Control activities include those activities designed to **prevent** or to **detect** and **correct errors**. Examples include activities relating to authorisation, performance reviews, information processing, physical controls and segregation of duties.

Examples of control activities	
Approval and control of documents	Transactions should be approved by an appropriate person. For example, overtime should be approved by departmental managers.
Controls over computerised applications	We shall look at computer controls later in this chapter.
Checking the arithmetical accuracy of records	For example, checking to see if individual invoices have been added up correctly.
Maintaining and reviewing control accounts and trial balances	Control accounts bring together transactions in individual ledgers. Trial balances bring together unusual transactions for the organisation as a whole. Preparing these can highlight unusual transactions or accounts.
Reconciliations	Reconciliations involve comparison of a specific balance in the accounting records with what another source says the balance should be, for example, a bank reconciliation. Differences between the two figures should only be reconciling items.
Comparing the results of cash, security and inventory counts with accounting records	For example, in a physical count of petty cash, the balance shown in the cash book should be the same as the amount held.
Comparing internal data with external sources of information	For example, comparing records of goods despatched to customers with customers' acknowledgement of goods that have been received.
Limiting physical access to assets and records	Only authorised personnel should have access to certain assets (particularly valuable or portable ones). For example, ensuring that the inventory store is only open when store personnel are there and is otherwise locked.

1.4.1 Segregation of duties

Segregation implies a **number of people** being involved in the accounting process. This makes it more difficult for fraudulent transactions to be processed (since a number of people would have to collude in the fraud), and it is also more difficult for accidental errors to be processed (since the more people are involved, the more checking there can be). Segregation should take place in various ways:

(a) **Segregation of function.** The key functions that should be segregated are the **carrying out** of a transaction, **recording** that transaction in the accounting records and **maintaining custody** of assets that arise from the transaction.

(b) The various **steps** in carrying out the transaction should also be segregated. We shall see how this works in practice when we look at the major transaction cycles in Chapter 10.

(c) The **carrying out** of various **accounting operations** should be segregated. For example the same staff should not record transactions and carry out the reconciliations at the period-end.

1.5 Monitoring of controls

Key term

Monitoring of controls is a process to assess the effectiveness of internal control performance over time. It includes assessing the design and operation of controls on a timely basis and taking necessary corrective actions modified for changes in conditions.

The auditor shall obtain an understanding of the major activities that the entity uses to monitor internal control over financial reporting, including those related to those control activities relevant to the audit, and how the entity initiates corrective actions to deficiencies in its controls.

If the entity has an **internal audit function**, the auditor shall obtain an understanding of the **nature of its responsibilities** and how it **fits** in the organisational structure, and the **activities** performed/to be performed.

The auditor shall also obtain an understanding of the **sources of the information** used in the monitoring activities and the **basis** on which management considers it reliable.

1.6 Small companies – the problem of control

Many of the controls which would be relevant to a large entity are neither practical nor appropriate for a small company. For a small company the most important form of internal control is generally the **close involvement** of the **directors or proprietors**. However, that very involvement will enable them to **override controls** and, if they wish, to **exclude transactions** from the records.

Auditors can have difficulties not because there is a general lack of controls but because the **evidence** available as to their operation and the completeness of the records is **insufficient**.

Segregation of duties will often appear inadequate in enterprises having a small number of staff. Similarly, because of the scale of the operation, organisation and management controls are likely to be rudimentary at best.

The onus is on the proprietor, by virtue of his day-to-day involvement, to compensate for this lack. This involvement should encompass physical, authorisation, arithmetical and accounting controls as well as supervision.

However it is important to stress that in a well run small company there will be a system of internal control. In any case, all companies must comply with any relevant legislation concerning the maintenance of a proper accounting system.

Where the manager of a small business is not himself the owner, he may not possess the same degree of commitment to the running of it as an owner-manager would. In such cases, the auditors will have to consider the adequacy of controls exercised by the shareholders over the manager in assessing internal control.

1.7 Limitations of accounting and control systems

Any internal control system can only provide the directors with **reasonable assurance** that their objectives are reached, because of **inherent limitations**. These include:

- The **costs** of control **not outweighing** their **benefits**
- The potential for **human error**
- **Collusion** between employees
- The possibility of **controls** being **by-passed** or **overridden** by management
- Controls being **designed to cope** with **routine** and **not non-routine transactions**

These factors demonstrate why auditors cannot obtain all their evidence from tests of the systems of internal control. The key factors in the limitations of controls system are **human error** and **potential for fraud**.

The safeguard of segregation of duties can help deter fraud. However, if employees decide to perpetrate frauds by collusion, or management commit fraud by overriding systems, the accounting system will not be able to prevent such frauds.

This is one of the reasons that auditors always need to be alert to the possibility of fraud, the subject of ISA 240, which was discussed in Chapter 6.

Question — Internal control systems

An internal control system has been described as comprising 'the control environment and control activities. It includes all the policies and procedures (internal controls) adopted by the directors and management of an entity to assist in achieving their objective of ensuring, as far as practicable, the orderly and efficient conduct of its business, including adherence to internal policies, the safeguarding of assets, the prevention and detection of fraud and error, the accuracy and completeness of the accounting records, and the timely preparation of reliable financial information'.

Explain the meaning and relevance to the auditors giving an opinion on financial statements of each of the management objectives above.

Answer

The auditors' objective in evaluating and testing internal controls is to determine the degree of reliance which they may place on the information contained in the accounting records. If they obtain reasonable assurance by means of tests of controls that the internal control system is effective in ensuring the completeness and accuracy of the accounting records, they may limit their substantive procedures.

(a) *'The orderly and efficient conduct of its business'*

An organisation which is efficient and conducts its affairs in an orderly manner is much more likely to be able to supply the auditors with sufficient appropriate audit evidence on which to base their audit opinion. More importantly, the level of inherent and control risk will be lower, giving extra assurance that the financial statements do not contain material errors.

(b) *'Adherence to internal policies'*

Management is responsible for setting up an effective system of internal control and management policy provides the broad framework within which internal controls have to operate. Unless management does have a pre-determined set of policies, then it is very difficult to imagine how the company could be expected to operate efficiently. Management policy will cover all aspects of the company's activities, ranging from broad corporate objectives to specific areas such as wage rates.

Given that the auditors must have a sound understanding of the company's affairs generally, and of specific areas of control in particular, then the fact that management policies are followed will make the task of the auditors easier in that they will be able to rely more readily on the information produced by the systems established by management.

(c) *'Safeguarding of assets'*

This objective may relate to the physical protection of assets (for example locking cash in a safe at night) or to less direct safeguarding (for example ensuring that there is adequate insurance cover for all assets). It can also be seen as relating to the maintenance of proper records in respect of all assets.

The auditors will be concerned to ensure that the company has properly safeguarded its assets so that they can form an opinion on the existence of specific assets and whether the company's records can be taken as a reliable basis for the preparation of financial statements. Reliance on the underlying records will be particularly significant where the figures in the financial statements are derived from such records rather than as the result of physical inspection.

(d) *'Prevention and detection of fraud and error'*

The directors are responsible for taking reasonable steps to prevent and detect fraud. They are also responsible for preparing financial statements which give a true and fair view of the entity's affairs. However, the auditors must plan and perform their audit procedures and evaluate and report the results of these, recognising that fraud or error may materially affect the financial statements. A strong system of internal control will give the auditors some assurance that frauds and errors are not occurring, unless management are colluding to overcome that system.

(e) *'Accuracy and completeness of the accounting records'/'timely preparation of reliable financial information'*

This objective is most clearly related to statutory requirements relating to both management and auditors. The company generally has legal obligations to maintain proper accounting records. The auditors must form an opinion on whether the company has fulfilled these obligations and also conclude whether the financial statements agree with the underlying records.

2 The use of internal control systems by auditors June 08

FAST FORWARD

The auditors shall assess the **adequacy** of the systems as a basis for the financial statements and shall identify **risks** of material misstatements to provide a basis for designing and performing further audit procedures.

Auditors are only concerned with assessing policies and procedures which are relevant to the financial statements. Auditors shall:

- **Assess the adequacy** of the accounting system as a basis for preparing the accounts
- **Identify** the types of **potential misstatements** that could occur in the accounts
- **Consider factors** that affect the **risk of misstatements**
- **Design appropriate audit procedures**

We have discussed the process of assessing the risks of material misstatement in Chapter 6. The assessment of the controls of an entity will have an impact on that risk assessment.

Risks arising from **poor control environments** are unlikely to be confined to particular assertions in the financial statements, and, if severe, may even raise questions about whether the financial statements are capable of being audited, that is, if control risk is so high that audit risk cannot be reduced to an acceptable level.

On the other hand, some **control procedures** may be closely connected to an assertion in financial statements, for example, controls over the inventory count are closely connected with the existence and completeness of inventory in the financial statements.

There may be occasions where substantive procedures alone are not sufficient to address the risks arising. Where such risks exist, auditors shall **evaluate the design** and **determine the implementation** of

the controls, that is by **controls testing**. This is most likely to be the case in a system which is highly computerised and which does not require much manual intervention.

2.1 Recording accounting and control systems

FAST FORWARD

The auditors must keep a record of the client's systems which must be updated each year. This can be done through the use of narrative notes, flowcharts, questionnaires or checklists.

There are several techniques for recording the assessment of control risk, that is, the system. One or more of the following may be used depending on the complexity of the system.

- Narrative notes
- Flowcharts
- Questionnaires
- Checklists

Whatever method of recording is used, the record will usually be retained on the permanent file and updated each year. We will look at the use of questionnaires in a little more detail here. There are two types, each with a different purpose.

- **Internal Control Questionnaires (ICQs)** are used to ask whether controls exist which meet specific control objectives.
- **Internal Control Evaluation Questionnaires (ICEQs)** are used to determine whether there are controls which prevent or detect specified errors or omissions.

The specific controls for each major transaction system (sales, purchases, inventory, cash, payroll, revenue and capital expenditure) are examined in Chapter 10.

3 The evaluation of internal control components

FAST FORWARD

If the auditors believe the system of controls is strong, they may choose to test controls to assess whether they can rely on the controls having operated effectively.

3.1 Confirming understanding

In order to confirm their understanding of the control systems, auditors will often carry out **walk-through tests**. This is where they pick up a transaction and follow it through the system to see whether all the controls they anticipate should be in existence were in operation with regard to that transaction.

3.2 Tests of control

Remember

Tests of control are tests performed to obtain audit evidence about the effectiveness of the:

- Design of the accounting and internal control systems, ie whether they are suitably designed to prevent, or detect and correct, material misstatement at the assertion level; and
- Operation of the internal controls throughout the period.

Tests of control are distinguished from substantive tests which are designed to detect material misstatements in the financial statements.

Tests of control may include the following.

(a) **Inspection of documents** supporting controls or events to gain audit evidence that internal controls have operated properly, eg verifying that a transaction has been authorised

(b) **Inquiries about internal controls** which leave no audit trail, eg determining who actually performs each function not merely who is supposed to perform it

(c) **Reperformance of control procedures**, eg reconciliation of bank accounts, to ensure they were correctly performed by the entity

(d) **Examination of evidence of management views**, eg minutes of management meetings

(e) Testing of internal controls operating on **computerised systems** or over the overall IT function, eg access controls

(f) **Observation of controls** to consider the manner in which the control is being operated

Auditors should consider:

- **How** controls were applied
- The **consistency** with which they were applied during the period
- **By whom** they were applied

Deviations in the operation of controls (caused by change of staff etc) may increase control risk and tests of control may need to be modified to confirm effective operation during and after any change.

The use of **computer-assisted audit techniques** (CAATs) may be appropriate and these are discussed in detail in Chapter 11.

In a continuing engagement, the auditor will be aware of the accounting and internal control systems through work carried out previously but will need to update the knowledge gained and consider the need to obtain further audit evidence of any changes in control.

3.3 Revision of risk assessment

The auditors may find that the evidence they obtain from controls testing indicates that controls did not operate as well as they expected. If the evidence contradicts the original risk assessment, the auditors will have to amend the further procedures they have planned to carry out.

In particular, if controls testing reveals that controls have not operated effectively throughout the year, the auditor may have to extend substantive testing.

3.4 Communication of deficiencies in internal control

Significant deficiencies in internal controls shall be communicated in writing to those charged with governance in a **report to management** in accordance with ISA 265 *Communicating deficiencies in internal control to those charged with governance and management* which states that the objective of the auditor is to communicate appropriately to those charged with governance and management deficiencies in internal control identified during the audit which the auditor considers are of sufficient importance to warrant their attention.

We will look at an example report to management in more detail in Chapter 19, but in this section we will discuss the requirements of ISA 265.

Key terms

A **deficiency in internal control** exists when a control is designed, implemented or operated in such a way that it is unable to prevent, or detect and correct, misstatements in the financial statements on a timely basis, or a control necessary to prevent, or detect and correct, misstatements in the financial statements on a timely basis is missing.

A **significant deficiency in internal control** is a deficiency or combination of deficiencies in internal control that, in the auditor's professional judgement, is of sufficient importance to merit the attention of those charged with governance.

ISA 265 requires the auditor to determine whether one or more deficiencies in internal control have been identified and if so, whether these constitute significant deficiencies in internal control. The significance of a deficiency depends on whether a misstatement has occurred and also on the likelihood of a misstatement occurring and its potential magnitude, ISA 265 includes examples of matters to consider when determining whether a deficiency in internal control is a significant deficiency:

- The **likelihood** of the deficiencies resulting in material misstatements in the financial statements in the future
- The **susceptibility to loss or fraud** of the related asset or liability

- The **subjectivity and complexity** of determining estimated amounts
- The **amounts** exposed to the deficiencies
- The **volume of activity** that has occurred or could occur
- The **importance of the controls** to the financial reporting process
- The **cause and frequency** of the exceptions identified as a result of the deficiencies
- The **interaction** of the deficiency with other deficiencies in internal control

The ISA also lists examples of indicators of significant deficiencies in internal control, which include the following:

- Evidence of **ineffective aspects** of the control environment
- Absence of a **risk assessment process**
- Evidence of an **ineffective entity risk assessment process**
- Evidence of an **ineffective response to identified significant risks**
- **Misstatements** detected by the auditor's procedures that were not prevented, or detected and corrected, by the entity's internal control
- **Restatement** of previously issued financial statements that were corrected for a material misstatement due to fraud or error

Evidence of **management's inability to oversee** the preparation of the financial statements

The auditor shall communicate any significant deficiencies in internal control to **those charged with governance** on a timely basis. The auditor shall also communicate in writing to **management** on a timely basis significant deficiencies in internal control that the auditor has communicated or intends to communicate to those charged with governance and other deficiencies in internal control that have not been communicated to management by other parties and that the auditor considers are of sufficient importance to warrant management's attention. The communication to management of other deficiencies in internal control can be done orally.

The auditor shall include the following in the written communication:

- A **description** of the deficiencies and an explanation of their **potential effects** (but there is no need to quantify the effects).
- **Sufficient information** to enable those charged with governance and management to understand the context of the communication, in particular that:
  - The purpose of the audit was for the auditor to express an opinion on the financial statements.
  - The audit included consideration of internal control relevant to the preparation of the financial statements in order to design audit procedures appropriate in the circumstances, but not to express an opinion on the effectiveness of internal control.
  - The matters being reported are limited to those deficiencies identified during the audit and which the auditor has concluded are sufficiently important to merit being reported to those charged with governance.

The auditor may also include suggestions for remedial action on the deficiencies, management's actual or proposed responses and a statement as to whether or not the auditor has undertaken any steps to verify whether management's responses have been implemented. In addition, the auditor may also include the following additional information:

- A statement that if the auditor had undertaken more extensive procedures on internal control, more deficiencies might have been identified or some of the reported deficiencies need not have been reported.
- The written communication is for the purpose of those charged with governance and may not be suitable for other purposes.

4 Internal controls in a computerised environment

There are special considerations for auditors when a system is computerised. IT controls comprise **general** and **application** controls.

The internal controls in a computerised environment include both manual procedures and procedures designed into computer programs. Such control procedures comprise two types of control, **general controls** and **application controls**.

Key term

General IT controls are policies and procedures that relate to many applications and support the effective functioning of application controls by helping to ensure the continued proper operation of information systems. They commonly include controls over data centre and network operations, system software acquisition, change and maintenance, access security, and application system acquisition, development and maintenance.

Application controls are manual or automated procedures that typically operate at a business process level. They can be preventative or detective in nature and are designed to ensure the integrity of the accounting records. Accordingly, they relate to procedures used to initiate, record, process and report transactions or other financial data.

4.1 General controls

GENERAL CONTROLS	EXAMPLES
Development of computer applications	**Standards** over systems design, programming and documentation Full **testing procedures** using test data **Approval** by computer users and management **Segregation of duties** so that those responsible for design are not responsible for testing **Installation procedures** so that data is not corrupted in transition **Training** of staff in new procedures and availability of adequate **documentation**
Prevention or detection of unauthorised changes to programs	**Segregation of duties** **Full records** of program changes **Password protection** of programs so that access is limited to computer operations staff. **Restricted access** to central computer by locked doors, keypads Maintenance of **programs logs** **Virus checks** on software: use of anti-virus software and policy prohibiting use of non-authorised programs or files **Back-up copies** of programs being taken and stored in other locations **Control copies** of programs being preserved and regularly compared with actual programs **Stricter controls** over certain programs (utility programs) by use of **read-only memory**
Testing and documentation of program changes	Complete **testing procedures** **Documentation standards** **Approval** of changes by computer users and management **Training** of staff using programs

GENERAL CONTROLS	EXAMPLES
Controls to prevent wrong programs or files being used	**Operation controls** over programs **Libraries** of programs **Proper job scheduling**
Controls to prevent unauthorised amendments to data files	**Password protection** **Restricted access** to authorised users only
Controls to ensure continuity of operation	Storing **extra copies** of programs and data files off-site **Protection of equipment** against fire and other hazards **Back-up power sources** **Disaster recovery procedures** eg availability of back-up computer facilities. **Maintenance agreements** and **insurance**

The auditors will wish to test some or all of the above general IT controls, having considered how they affect the computer applications significant to the audit.

General IT controls that relate to some or all applications are usually interdependent controls, ie their operation is often essential to the effectiveness of application controls. As application controls may be useless when general controls are ineffective, it will be more efficient to review the design of general IT controls first, before reviewing the application controls.

4.2 Application controls

The purpose of application controls is to establish **specific control procedures** over the accounting applications in order to provide reasonable assurance that all transactions are authorised and recorded, and are processed completely, accurately and on a timely basis. Application controls include the following.

APPLICATION CONTROLS	EXAMPLES
Controls over **input: completeness**	Manual or programmed agreement of **control totals** **Document counts** **One-for-one checking** of processed output to source documents **Programmed matching** of input to an expected input control file **Procedures** over resubmission of rejected controls
Controls over **input: accuracy**	**Programmes to check data** fields (for example value, reference number, date) on input transactions for plausibility: • Digit verification (eg reference numbers are as expected) • Reasonableness test (eg sales tax to total value) • Existence checks (eg customer name) • Character checks (no unexpected characters used in reference) • Necessary information (no transaction passed with gaps) • Permitted range (no transaction processed over a certain value) **Manual scrutiny** of output and reconciliation to source Agreement of **control totals** (manual/programmed)
Controls over **input authorisation:**	**Manual checks** to ensure information input was: • Authorised • Input by authorised personnel
Controls over **processing**	Similar controls to input must be in place when input is completed, for example, **batch reconciliations**. **Screen warnings** can prevent people logging out before processing is complete

APPLICATION CONTROLS	EXAMPLES
Controls over **master files and standing data**	**One-to-one checking** **Cyclical reviews** of all master files and standing data **Record counts** (number of documents processed) and **hash totals** (for example, the total of all the payroll numbers) used when master files are used to ensure no deletions **Controls** over the deletion of accounts that have no current balance

Controls over input, processing, data files and output may be carried out by IT personnel, users of the system, a separate control group and may be programmed into application software. The auditors may wish to test the following application controls.

TESTING OF APPLICATION CONTROLS	
Manual controls exercised by the user	If manual controls exercised by the user of the application system are capable of providing reasonable assurance that the system's output is complete, accurate and authorised, the auditors may decide to limit tests of control to these manual controls.
TESTING OF APPLICATION CONTROLS	
Controls over system output	If, in addition to manual controls exercised by the user, the controls to be tested use information produced by the computer or are contained within computer programs, such controls may be tested by examining the system's output using either manual procedures or computers. Such output may be in the form of magnetic media, microfilm or printouts. Alternatively, the auditor may test the control by performing it with the use of computers.
Programmed control procedures	In the case of certain computer systems, the auditor may find that it is not possible or, in some cases, not practical to test controls by examining only user controls or the system's output. The auditor may consider performing tests of control by using computers, reprocessing transaction data or, in unusual situations, examining the coding of the application program.

As we have already noted, general IT controls may have a pervasive effect on the processing of transactions in application systems. If these general controls are not effective, there may be a risk that misstatements occur and go undetected in the application systems. Although weaknesses in general IT controls may preclude testing certain IT application controls, it is possible that manual procedures exercised by users may provide effective control at the **application level**.

Exam focus point

The examiner expects you to be comfortable with a computerised scenario so it's important that you understand the use of IT controls within an organisation. The August 2009 edition of *Student Accountant* contains a very useful article on auditing in a computerised environment. You can also access this article on the ACCA's website in the students' area.

Chapter Roundup

- The auditors must **understand** the **accounting system** and **control environment** in order to determine their audit approach.
- The auditors shall assess the **adequacy** of the systems as a basis for the financial statements and shall identify **risks** of material misstatements to provide a basis for designing and performing further audit procedures.
- The auditors must keep a record of the client's systems which must be updated each year. This can be done through the use of narrative notes, flowcharts, questionnaires or checklists.
- If the auditors believe the system of controls is strong, they may choose to test controls to assess whether they can rely on the controls having operated effectively.
- There are special considerations for auditors when a system is computerised. IT controls comprise **general** and **application** controls.

Quick Quiz

1 Complete the definition taking the words given below.

The .... includes the governance and management functions and the................., ... and .... of those charged with .... and management concerning the entity's internal .... and its .... in the entity.

attitudes	importance	control	environment	awareness	governance	actions	control

2 Name two **key** inherent limitations of an internal control system

1 ....

2 ....

3 Put the controls below in the correct category

Application controls	General controls

One-to-one checking	Virus checks	Hash totals
Segregation of duties	Passwords	Program libraries
Review of master files	Training	Controls over account deletions
Back-up copies	Record counts	Back-up power source

4 Which of the following is not a test of control?

A Inspection of documents
B Reperformance of control procedures
C Observation of controls
D Verification of value to invoice

5 After the controls have been assessed, the audit plan may be modified.

True ☐

False ☐

Answers to Quick Quiz

1 control environment, attitudes, awareness, actions, governance, control, importance

2 Human error

Possibility of staff colluding in fraud

3

Application controls	General controls
One-to-one checking	Virus checks
Hash totals	Program libraries
Review of master files	Segregation of duties
Record counts	Passwords
	Controls over account deletion
	Training
	Back-up power source
	Back-up copies

4 D

5 True

Now try the question below from the Exam Question Bank

Number	Level	Marks	Time
Q11	Examination	30	54 mins

10

Tests of controls

Topic list	Syllabus reference
1 The sales system	D3, D4
2 The purchases system	D3, D4
3 The inventory system	D3, D4
4 The cash system	D3, D4
5 The payroll system	D3, D4
6 Revenue and capital expenditure	D3, D4

Introduction

We discussed tests of controls in the last chapter. In this chapter we will look at how tests of controls might be applied in practice. We will examine each major component of a typical accounting system.

We have already stated that the auditors must establish what the accounting system and the system of internal control consist of. The auditors will then decide which controls, if any, they wish to rely on and plan tests of controls to obtain the audit evidence as to whether such reliance can be warranted. For each of the major transaction systems we will look at the system objectives the auditors will bear in mind while assessing the internal controls and give examples of common controls. We shall then go on to look at a 'standard' programme of tests of controls.

Study guide

		Intellectual level
D3	**Transaction cycles**	
(a)	Explain, analyse and provide examples of internal control procedures and control activities	2
D4	**Tests of control**	
(a)	Explain and tabulate tests of control suitable for inclusion in audit working papers	2

Exam guide

Questions on tests of control are likely to come up in scenario-based situations. You might be asked to describe controls that should be in place over a particular system or explain the control objectives for a given system.

For example, a question in the pilot paper asked for control weaknesses in a wages system together with recommendations to overcome the weaknesses identified, in the style of a report to management. The December 2007 paper asked for the weaknesses in a company's control system for counting inventory and recommendations to mitigate them. There was also a similar requirement in this paper in relation to a company's petty cash system, worth 20 marks. The June 2008 paper had a 12 mark part on tests of control on a sales system. The December 2008 paper had 16 marks on a wages system. This type of question is therefore very common and highly likely to come up. You need to be familiar with the major transaction cycles so that you can answer such questions competently. The June 2009 paper had a question on the cash sales system of an entity (question 1).

1 The sales system

June 08, June 09

FAST FORWARD

The tests of controls in the **sales system** will be based around:

- **Selling** (authorisation)
- **Goods outwards** (custody)
- **Accounting** (recording)

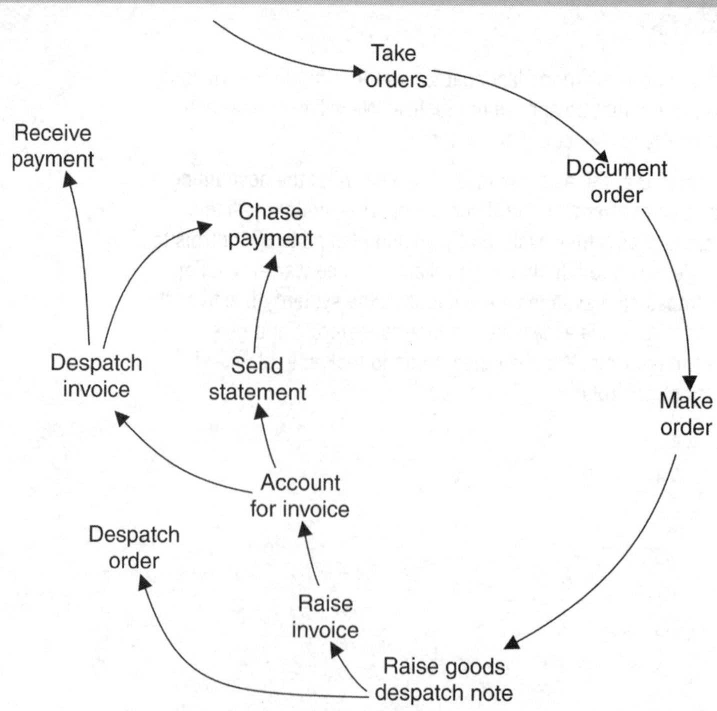

1.1 Sales system: Control objectives, controls and tests of controls

Assertion	Control objectives	Controls	Tests of controls
Occurrence and existence	• One person is not responsible for taking orders, recording sales and receiving payment.	• Segregation of duties	• Observe and evaluate whether proper segregation of duties is operating.
	• Recorded sales transactions represent goods shipped.	• Sales recorded only with approved sales order form and shipping documentation.	• Test a sample of sales invoices for authorised sales order form and shipping documentation. • Examine application controls for authorisation.
		• Accounting for numerical sequences of invoices.	• Review and test entity's procedures for accounting for numerical sequences of invoices.
		• Monthly customer statements sent out and customer queries and complaints handled independently.	• Review entity's procedures for sending out monthly statements and dealing with customer queries and complaints.
	• Goods and services are only supplied to customers with good credit ratings.	• Authorisation of credit terms to customers (senior staff authorisation, references/credit checks for new customers, regular review of credit limits)	• Review entity's procedures for granting credit to customers.
		• Authorisation by senior staff required for changes in other customer data such as address etc.	• Examine a sample of sales orders for evidence of proper credit approval by the appropriate senior staff member.
		• Orders not accepted unless credit limits reviewed first.	• Examine application controls for credit limits.

Assertion	Control objectives	Controls	Tests of controls
			• Review all new customer files to ensure satisfactory credit references have been obtained.
	• Goods and services are provided at authorised prices and on authorised terms. • Customers are encouraged to pay promptly.	• Authorised price lists and specified terms of trade in place.	• Compare prices and terms on a sample of sales invoices to the authorised price list and terms of trade. • Examine application controls for authorised prices and terms.
Completeness	• All revenue relating to goods dispatched is recorded.	• Accounting for numerical sequences of invoices.	• Review and test entity's procedures for accounting for numerical sequences of invoices.
	• All goods and services sold are correctly invoiced.	• Shipping documentation is matched to sales invoices. • Sales invoices are reconciled to the daily sales report. • An open-order file is maintained and reviewed regularly.	• Trace a sample of shipping documents to the sales invoices and ledger. • Review a sample of reconciliations performed. • Inspect the open-order file for unfilled orders.
Accuracy	• All sales and adjustments are correctly journalised, summarised and posted to the correct accounts.	• Sales invoices and matching documents required for all entries.	• Vouch recorded sales to supporting documents.
Cut-off	• Transactions have been recorded in the correct period.	• All shipping documentation is forwarded to the invoicing section on a daily basis.	• Compare dates on sales invoices with dates of corresponding shipping documentation.
		• Daily invoicing of goods shipped.	• Compare dates on sales invoices with dates recorded in the sales ledger.

Assertion	Control objectives	Controls	Tests of controls
Classification	• All transactions are properly classified in accounts.	• Chart of accounts in place. • Codes in place for different types of products or services.	• Review sales ledger for proper classification. • Examine a sample of sales invoices for proper classification. • Test application controls for proper codes.

Question

Sales system

You are the auditor of Arcidiacono Stationery, and you have been asked to suggest how audit work should be carried out on the sales system.

Arcidiacono Stationery Ltd sells stationery to shops. Most sales are to small customers who do not have a sales ledger account. They can collect their purchases and pay by cash. For cash sales:

(a) The customer orders the stationery from the sales department, which raises a pre-numbered multi-copy order form.

(b) The dispatch department make up the order and give it to the customer with a copy of the order form.

(c) The customer gives the order form to the cashier who prepares a hand-written sales invoice.

(d) The customer pays the cashier for the goods by cheque or in cash.

(e) The cashier records and banks the cash.

Required

(a) State the deficiencies in the cash sales system.
(b) Describe the systems-based tests you would carry out to audit the controls over the system.

Answer

(a) **Deficiencies in the cash sales system**

(i) The physical location of the dispatch department and the cashier are not mentioned here, but there is a risk of the customer taking the goods without paying. The customer should pay the cashier on the advice note and return for the goods, which should only be released on sight of the paid invoice.

(ii) There is a failure in segregation of duties in allowing the cashier to both complete the sales invoice and receive the cash as he could perpetrate a fraud by replacing the original invoice with one of lower value and keeping the difference.

(iii) No-one checks the invoices to make sure that the cashier has completed them correctly, for example by using the correct prices and performing calculations correctly.

(iv) The completeness of the sequence of sales invoices cannot be checked unless they are pre-numbered sequentially and the presence of all the invoices is checked by another person. The order forms should also be pre-numbered sequentially.

(v) There is no check that the cashier banks all cash received, and this is a further failure of segregation of duties.

If the sales department prepared and posted the invoices and also posted the cash for cash sales to a sundry sales account, this would solve some of the internal control problems mentioned above. In addition, the sales department could run a weekly check on the account to look for invoices for which no cash had been received. These could then be investigated.

All of these deficiences, and possible remedies, should be reported to management.

(b) **Tests**

(i) Select a sample of order forms issued to customers during the year. Trace the related sales invoice and check that the details correlate (date, unit amounts etc). The customer should have signed for the goods and this copy should be retained by the dispatch department.

(ii) For the sales invoices discovered in the above test, I would check that the correct order form number is recorded on the invoice, that the prices used are correct (by reference to the prevailing price list) and that the castings and cross-castings are correct.

(iii) I would then trace the value of the sales invoices to the cash book and from the cash book that the total receipts for the day have been banked and appear promptly on the bank statement.

(iv) I would check that the sales invoices have been correctly posted to a cash or sundry sales account. For any sales invoices missing from this account (assuming they are sequentially numbered), I would trace the cancelled invoice and check that the cancelled invoice was initialled by the customer and replaced by the next invoice in sequence.

(v) Because of the weaknesses in the system I would carry out the following sequence checks on large blocks of order forms/invoices, eg four blocks of 100 order forms/invoices.

(1) Inspect all order forms to ensure all present; investigate those missing

(2) Match sales invoices to order forms

(3) Check all sales invoices in a sequence have been used; investigate any missing

(4) Cash for each sales invoice has been entered into the cash book

Using the results of the above tests I would decide whether the system for cash sales has operated without material fraud or error. If I am not satisfied that it has then this may impact on the audit report.

2 The purchases system **Pilot paper**

FAST FORWARD

The tests of controls in the **purchases system** will be based around:

- **Buying** (authorisation)
- **Goods** inwards (custody)
- **Accounting** (recording)

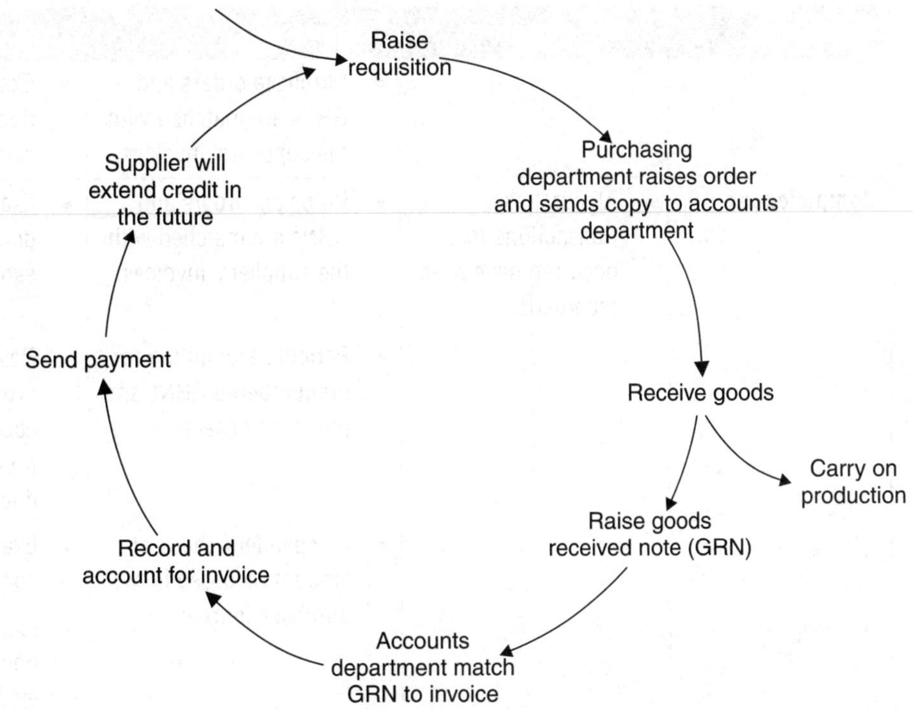

2.1 Control objectives, controls and tests of controls

Assertion	Control objectives	Controls	Tests of controls
Occurrence and existence	• Recorded purchases represent goods and services received.	• Authorisation procedures and policies in place for ordering goods and services. • Segregation of duties. • Purchase orders raised for each purchase and authorised by appropriate senior personnel. • Approved purchase order for each receipt of goods. • Staff receiving goods check them to the purchase order. • Stores clerks sign for goods received.	• Inspect policies and procedures and inquire about them. • Observe and evaluate segregation of duties. • Examine a sample of purchase orders to ensure they have been appropriately authorised. • Review the delegated list of authority for purchases. • For a sample of orders, examine the goods received note (GRN) and match it to the order. • Observe receipt of goods by staff to confirm whether the check is done. • Inspect a sample to confirm whether stores staff undertake this check.

Assertion	Control objectives	Controls	Tests of controls
		• Purchase orders and GRNs are matched with the suppliers' invoices.	• Examine supporting documentation for a sample of invoices.
Completeness	• All purchase transactions that occurred have been recorded.	• Purchase orders and GRNs are matched with the suppliers' invoices. • Periodic accounting for prenumbered GRNs and purchase orders. • Independent check of amount recorded in the purchase journal.	• Examine supporting documentation for a sample of invoices. • Review entity's procedures for accounting for prenumbered documents. • Examine application controls. • Examine documentation for evidence of this check.
Rights and obligations	• Recorded purchases represent the liabilities of the entity.	• Purchase orders and GRNs are matched with the suppliers' invoices.	• Examine supporting documentation for a sample of invoices.
Accuracy, classification and valuation	• Purchase transactions are correctly recorded in the accounting system.	• Purchase orders and GRNs are matched with the suppliers' invoices. • Mathematical accuracy of the supplier's invoice is verified. • Amount posted to general ledger is reconciled to the purchases ledger. • Chart of accounts in place.	• Examine supporting documentation for a sample of invoices. • Recalculate the mathematical accuracy of a sample of suppliers' invoices. • Review reconciliations for evidence of this check. • Review purchases journal and general ledger for reasonableness.
Cut-off	• Purchase transactions are recorded in the correct accounting period.	• All goods received reports forwarded to accounts payable department daily. • Procedures in place that require recording of purchases as soon as possible after goods/services received.	• Compare dates on reports to dates on relevant vouchers. • Compare dates on vouchers with dates they were recorded in the purchases journal.

Purchase controls

Derek, a limited liability company, operates a computerised purchase system. Invoices and credit notes are posted to the purchases ledger by the purchases ledger department. The computer subsequently raises a cheque when the invoice has to be paid.

Required

List the controls that should be in operation:

(a) Over the addition, amendment and deletion of suppliers, ensuring that the standing data only includes suppliers from the company's list of authorised suppliers

(b) Over purchase invoices and credit notes, to ensure only authorised purchase invoices and credit notes are posted to the purchase ledger

Answer

(a) Controls over the standing data file containing suppliers' details will include the following.

  (i) All amendments/additions/deletions to the data should be authorised by a responsible official. A standard form should be used for such changes.

  (ii) The amendment forms should be input in batches (with different types of change in different batches), sequentially numbered and recorded in a batch control book so that any gaps in the batch numbers can be investigated. The output produced by the computer should be checked to the input.

  (iii) A listing of all such adjustments should automatically be produced by the computer and reviewed by a responsible official, who should also check authorisation.

  (iv) A listing of suppliers' accounts on which there has been no movement for a specified period should be produced to allow decisions to be made about possible deletions, thus ensuring that the standing data is current. The buying department manager might also recommend account closures on a periodic basis.

  (v) Users should be controlled by use of passwords. This can also be used as a method of controlling those who can amend data.

  (vi) Periodic listings of standing data should be produced in order to verify details (for example addresses) with suppliers' documents (invoices/ statements).

(b) The input of authorised purchase invoices and credit notes should be controlled in the following ways.

  (i) Authorisation should be evidenced by the signature of the responsible official such as the Chief Accountant. In addition, the invoice or credit note should show initials to demonstrate that the details have been agreed: to a signed GRN; to a purchase order; to a price list; for additions and extensions.

  (ii) There should be adequate segregation of responsibilities between the posting function, inventory custody and receipt, payment of suppliers and changes to standing data.

  (iii) Input should be restricted by use of passwords linked to the relevant site number.

  (iv) A batch control book should be maintained, recording batches in number sequence. Invoices should be input in batches using pre-numbered batch control sheets. The manually produced invoice total on the batch control sheet should be agreed to the computer generated total. Credit notes and invoices should be input in separate batches to avoid one being posted as the other.

  (v) A program should check calculation of sales tax at standard rate and total of invoice. Non-standard sales tax rates should be highlighted.

(vi) The input of the supplier code should bring up the supplier name for checking by the operator against the invoice.

(vii) Invoices for suppliers which do not have an account should be prevented from being input. Any sundry suppliers account should be very tightly controlled and all entries reviewed in full each month.

(viii) An exception report showing unusual expense allocation (by size or account) should be produced and reviewed by a responsible official. Expenses should be compared to budget and previous years.

(ix) There should be monthly reconciliations of purchase ledger balances to suppliers' statements by someone outside the purchasing (accounting) function.

3 The inventory system Dec 07

FAST FORWARD

Inventory controls are designed to ensure safe custody. Such controls include restriction of access, documentation and authorisation of movements, regular **independent inventory counting** and **review of inventory condition**.

3.1 Introduction

The inventory system can be very important in an audit because of the high value of inventory or the complexity of its audit. It is closely connected with the sales and purchases systems covered in the previous sections.

There are three possible approaches to the audit of inventory and the approach chosen depends on the control in system in place over inventory.

(a) If the entity has a perpetual inventory system in place where inventory is counted continuously throughout the year, and therefore a year-end count is not undertaken, a controls-based approach can be taken if control risk has been assessed as low.

(b) If an inventory count is to be undertaken near the year-end and adjusted by perpetual inventory records for the year-end value, this approach also requires control risk to be assessed as low.

(c) If inventory quantities will be determined by an inventory count at the year-end date, a substantive approach is taken and no reliance is placed on controls. This substantive approach is covered in Chapter 13.

3.2 Control objectives, controls and tests of controls

Most of the controls testing relating to inventory has been covered in the purchase and sales testing outlined in sections 1 and 2. Auditors will primarily be concerned at this stage with ensuring that the business keeps track of inventory. To confirm this, tests must be undertaken on how inventory **movements** are **recorded** and how **inventory** is **secured**. Auditors will carry out extensive tests on the **valuation** of inventory at the substantive testing stage (see Chapter 13).

Assertion	Control objectives	Controls	Tests of controls
Occurrence and existence	• All inventory movements are authorised and recorded.	• Prenumbered documentation such as GDNs and GRNs in use. • Reconciliations of inventory records with general ledger. • Segregation of duties	• Review documentation in use. • Review a sample of reconciliations to confirm they are performed and then reviewed by an independent person. • Observe and evaluate proper segregation of duties.
	• Inventory included on the statement of financial position physically exists.	• Physical safeguards in place to ensure inventory is not stolen. • Separate responsibilities for maintenance of records and custodianship. • Inventory counted regularly.	• Review security systems in place (eg locked warehouses, CCTV etc). • Review policies and procedures in place; discuss procedures with relevant staff. • Review procedures for counting inventory. • Attend inventory count.
Completeness	• All purchases and sales of inventory have been recorded in the accounting system.	• Procedures in place to include inventory held at third parties and exclude inventory held on consignment for third parties. • Reconciliations of accounting records with physical inventory.	• Review entity's procedures relating to consignment inventory. • Review reconciliations performed and whether reviewed by independent person.
Rights and obligations	• Inventory records only include items that belong to the entity.	• Procedures in place to include inventory held at third parties and exclude inventory held on consignment for third parties.	• Review entity's procedures relating to consignment inventory.
Accuracy, classification and valuation	• Inventory quantities have been accurately determined.	• Periodic or annual comparison of inventory with amounts shown in continuous (perpetual) inventory records.	• Review and test entity's procedures for taking physical inventory.

Assertion	Control objectives	Controls	Tests of controls
		• Standard costs reviewed by management. • Review of cost accumulation and variance reports.	• Review and test entity's procedures for developing standard costs. • Inspect variance reports produced.
	• Inventory is properly stated at the lower of cost and net realisable value.	• Inventory managers review inventory regularly to identify slow-moving, obsolete and excess inventory.	• Discuss with inventory managers how this is done. • Observe the procedure being performed.
Cut-off	• All purchases and sales of inventory are recorded in the correct accounting period.	• All dispatch documents processed daily to record the dispatch of finished goods. • All goods inwards reports processed daily to record the receipt of inventory. • Reconciliations of inventory records with general ledger.	• Inspect documentation to confirm daily processing. • Inspect documentation to confirm daily processing. • Review reconciliations performed.
Presentation and disclosure assertions	• Inventory transactions and balances are properly identified and classified in the financial statements.	• Orders for materials and production data forms used to process goods through manufacturing.	• Review entity's procedures and documentation used to classify inventory.
	• Disclosures relating to classification and valuation are sufficient.	• Approval by Finance Director	• Review entity's working papers for evidence of review.

4 The cash system

Dec 07

FAST FORWARD

Controls over cash receipts and payments should prevent fraud or theft.

4.1 Control objectives, controls and tests of controls

The following table sets out the control objectives, controls and possible tests of controls over **cash payments**.

Assertion	Control objectives	Controls	Tests of controls
Occurrence	• Only valid cash payments are made.	• Segregation of duties	• Observe and evaluate proper segregation of duties.
		• Supplier statements independently reviewed and reconciled to trade payable records.	• Review procedures for reconciling supplier statements.
		• Monthly bank reconciliations prepared and reviewed.	• Review reconciliations to confirm whether undertaken and reviewed.
		• Only authorised staff can make electronic cash payments and issue cheques.	• Review delegated list of authority for cash payments.
		• Electronic cash payments and cheques prepared only after all source documents have been independently approved.	• Inspect relevant documentation for evidence of approval by senior personnel.
Completeness	• All cash payments that occurred are recorded.	• Segregation of duties	• Observe and evaluate proper segregation of duties.
		• Supplier statements independently reviewed and reconciled to trade payable records.	• Review procedures for reconciling supplier statements.
		• Monthly bank reconciliations prepared and reviewed.	• Review reconciliations to confirm whether undertaken and independently reviewed.
		• Review of cash payments by manager before release.	• Inspect sample of listings for evidence of senior review.
		• Daily cash payments reconciled to posting to payable accounts.	• Review a sample of reconciliations for evidence that they have been done.
		• Use of prenumbered cheques.	• Examine evidence of use of prenumbered cheques.

Assertion	Control objectives	Controls	Tests of controls
Accuracy, classification and valuation	• Cash payments recorded correctly in the ledger.	• Reconciliation of daily payments report to electronic cash payment transfers and cheques issued. • Supplier statements reconciled to payable accounts regularly. • Monthly bank reconciliations of bank statements to ledger account.	• Review reconciliation, to ensure performed, reviewed and any discrepancies followed up on a timely basis. • Review reconciliations for a sample of accounts. • Review bank reconciliation for evidence it was done and independently reviewed.
	• Cash payments posted to correct payable accounts and to the general ledger.	• Supplier statements reconciled to payable accounts regularly. • Agreement of monthly cash payments journal to general ledger posting. • Payable accounts reconciled to general ledger control account.	• Review reconciliations for a sample of accounts. • Review postings from journal to general ledger. • Review reconciliation, to ensure performed, reviewed and any discrepancies followed up on a timely basis.
Cut-off	• Cash payments are recorded in the correct accounting period.	• Reconciliation of electronic funds transfers and cheques issued with postings to cash payments journal and payable accounts.	• Review reconciliation and check it is carried out regularly.
Presentation and disclosure assertions	• Cash payments are charged to the correct accounts.	• Chart of accounts • Independent approval and review of general ledger account assignment.	• Review cash payments journal to assess reasonableness of charging of accounts. • Review assignment of general ledger account.

The following table sets out the control objectives, controls and possible tests of controls over **cash receipts**.

Assertion	Control objectives	Controls	Tests of controls
Occurrence	• All valid cash receipts are received and deposited.	• Segregation of duties	• Observe and evaluate proper segregation of duties.
		• Use of electronic cash receipts transfer not received or deposited.	• Examine application controls for electronic cash receipts transfer.
		• Monthly bank reconciliations performed and independently reviewed.	• Review monthly bank reconciliations to confirm performed and reviewed.
		• Use of cash registers or point-of-sale devices.	• Observe cash sales procedures.
		• Periodic inspections of cash sales procedures.	• Inquire of managers about results of inspections.
		• Restrictive endorsement of cheques immediately on receipt.	• Observe mail opening, including endorsement of cheques.
		• Mail opened by two staff members.	• Observe mail opening procedures.
		• Immediate preparation of cash book or list of mail receipts.	• Observe preparation of cash receipts' records.
		• Independent check of agreement of cash/cheques to be deposited at bank with register totals and receipts listing.	• Review documentation for evidence of independent check.
		• Independent check of agreement of bank deposit slip with daily cash summary.	• Review documentation for evidence of independent check.

Assertion	Control objectives	Controls	Tests of controls
Completeness	• All cash receipts are recorded.	• Segregation of duties	• Observe and evaluate proper segregation of duties.
		• Use of electronic cash receipts transfer not received or deposited.	• Examine application controls for electronic cash receipts transfer.
		• Monthly bank reconciliations performed and independently reviewed.	• Review monthly bank reconciliations to confirm performed and reviewed.
		• Daily cash receipts listing reconciled with posting to customer accounts.	• Review reconciliation.
		• Customer statements prepared and sent out on a regular basis.	• Inquire of management about handling of customer statements. • Examine a sample of customers and note frequency of statements.
Accuracy, classification and valuation	• Cash receipts recorded at correct amounts.	• Daily remittance report reconciled to control listing of remittance advices.	• Review reconciliations.
		• Monthly bank statement performed and reviewed independently.	• Review reconciliations for evidence they were performed and independently reviewed.
	• Cash receipts posted to correct receivables accounts and to the general ledger.	• Daily remittance report reconciled daily with postings to cash receipts journal and customer accounts.	• Review reconciliations.
		• Monthly customer statements sent out.	• Review entity's procedures for sending out customer statements.
		• Monthly cash receipts journal agreed to general ledger posting.	• Review journal and posting to general ledger.

Assertion	Control objectives	Controls	Tests of controls
		• Receivables' ledger reconciled to control account.	• Review reconciliations.
Cut-off	• Cash receipts are recorded in the correct accounting period.	• Bank reconciliation at period-end.	• Review and test reconciliation.
Presentation and disclosure assertions	• Cash receipts are charged to the correct accounts.	• Chart of accounts.	• Review cash receipts journal for unusual items. • Trace cash receipts from listing to cash receipts journal for proper classification.

5 The payroll system

Pilot paper, Dec 08

FAST FORWARD

Key controls over **payroll** cover:

- **Documentation** and **authorisation** of staff changes
- **Calculation** of wages and salaries
- **Payment** of wages
- **Authorisation** of **deductions**

5.1 Control objectives, controls and tests of controls

Assertion	Control objectives	Controls	Tests of controls
Occurrence and existence	• Payment is made only to bona fide employees of the entity.	• Segregation of duties between HR and payroll functions • Personnel files held for all employees. • Authorisation procedures for hiring, terminating, time worked, wage rates, overtime, benefits etc. • Any changes in employment status of employees (eg maternity, special leave etc) informed to Human Resources department. • Use of time clocks to record time worked. • Clock cards approved by supervisor. • Only employees with valid employee numbers are paid. • Payroll budgets in place and reviewed by management.	• Observe and evaluate proper segregation of duties. • Review a sample of starters and leavers in the year to ensure correct documentation is in place. • Review and test authorisation procedures in place. • Review policies and procedures in place for changing status and consider whether adequate. • Review personnel files for a sample of employees whose status changed in the year. • Observe employees' use of time clocks. • Inspect a sample of clock cards for evidence of approval by appropriate level of management. • Review and test procedures for entering and removing employee numbers from the payroll master file. • Review budgeting procedures.

Assertion	Control objectives	Controls	Tests of controls
Completeness	• All payroll costs are recorded for work done by employees.	• Prenumbered clock cards in use. • Segregation of duties • Authorisation of wage cheque cashed • Custody of cash – Encashment of cheque – Security of pay packets – Security of transit – Security and prompt banking of unclaimed wages • Verification of identity • Recording of distributions • Preparation and authorisation of cheques and bank transfer lists • Comparison of cheques and bank transfer list with payroll • Maintenance and reconciliation of wages and salaries bank account • Preparation and authorisation of cheques and bank transfer lists • Comparison of cheques and bank transfer list with payroll • Maintenance and reconciliation of wages and salaries bank account	• Review numerical sequence of clock cards. • Observe and evaluate proper segregation of duties. *If wages are paid in cash* • Attend the pay-out of wages to confirm that the official procedures are being followed. • Before the wages are paid compare payroll with wage packets to ensure all employees have a wage packet. • Examine receipts given by employees; check unclaimed wages are recorded in unclaimed wages book. • Observe whether any employee receives more than one wage packet. • Inspect the unclaimed wages book entries with the entries on the payroll to ensure they agree. • Check that unclaimed wages are banked regularly by inspection of bank statements and supporting documentation. • Inspect that unclaimed wages books to check it shows reasons why wages are unclaimed.

Assertion	Control objectives	Controls	Tests of controls
			• Review pattern of unclaimed wages in unclaimed wages book; variations may indicate failure to record. *Holiday pay* • Verify a sample of payments with the underlying records and check the calculation of the amounts paid by recalculation. • For salaries, review whether comparisons are being made between payment records. • Examine paid cheques or a certified copy of the bank list for employees paid by cheque or bank transfer.
Accuracy, classification and valuation	• All benefits and deductions (tax, pension etc) are computed correctly.	• Verification of payroll amounts and benefit calculations. • Payroll budgets in place and reviewed by management. • Agreement of gross earnings and total tax deducted with taxation returns.	• Recalculate benefits and deductions for a sample of employees. • Review budgeting procedures. • Inspect documentation for evidence of management's review.
	• Payroll transactions correctly recorded in the accounting system.	• Changes to master payroll file verified through 'before and after' reports. • Payroll master file reconciled to general ledger.	• Review reconciliation 'before and after' reports to payroll master file. • Review reconciliation payroll master file to general ledger. Confirm whether discrepancies are followed-up promptly and resolved.

Assertion	Control objectives	Controls	Tests of controls
Cut-off	• Payroll transactions are recorded in the correct accounting period.	• All starters, leavers, changes to salaries and deductions are reported promptly to payroll department and changes are updated to the payroll master file promptly.	• Review entity's procedures for reporting changes to the payroll department. • Check sample of starters and leavers.
Presentation and disclosure assertions	• Payroll transactions are properly classified in the financial statements.	• Chart of accounts • Independent approval and review of accounts charged to payroll. • Payroll budgets in place and reviewed by management.	• Review chart of accounts. • Review procedures for classifying payroll costs. • Review budgeting procedures.

6 Revenue and capital expenditure

FAST FORWARD

Most of the key controls over capital and revenue expenditure are the general purchase controls.

The nature of a statement of financial position and statement of comprehensive income means that it is important to classify capital and revenue expenditure correctly, or profit will be over or understated. You should know the distinction between them from your financial reporting knowledge.

The controls and tests outlined below are often considered and performed during the audit of non-current assets (see Chapter 12) as this is where the main issue of capitalisation occurs.

6.1 Control objectives and objectives

Assertion	Controls	Tests of control
Authorisation	• All expenditure is authorised. • Orders for capital items should be authorised by appropriate levels of management. • Order should be requisitioned on appropriate (different to revenue) documentation. • Invoices should be approved by the person who authorised the order. • Invoices should be marked with the appropriate general ledger code.	• Review policies and procedures in place. • Examine a sample of orders for appropriate authorisation.
Classification	• All expenditure is classified correctly in the financial statements as capital or revenue expenditure. • All the standard controls over purchases are relevant here (see Section 2).	• See section 2

Assertion	Controls	Tests of control
Completeness	• All non-current assets are correctly recorded in the accounting system. • Capital items should be written up in the non-current asset register. • The non-current asset register should be reconciled regularly to the general ledger and any differences investigated and resolved promptly.	• Review reconciliation to ensure it is regularly carried out, reviewed by a more senior person, and that all discrepancies are followed up and resolved on a timely basis.

6.2 Tests of controls

If the ordering documentation is different for capital purchases, all the standard purchase control tests should be carried out. If the documentation is not different, the auditor should also enquire as to the client's system for recording and filing capital invoices.

It is likely that the number of capital purchases in the year will be less than the number of standard purchases in the year and if the invoices are not segregated it may not be cost-efficient to test the controls over this area in which case substantive testing would have to be undertaken.

These substantive tests are often carried out as part of the substantive audit of non-current assets, which is covered in Chapter 12.

The auditor should be aware of the risks attaching to the audit of this area. As tests of controls might not be cost-effective, control risk in this area is higher than it would have been if they were tested.

Inherent risk can also be high in this area. Capital and revenue expenditure is treated differently for the purposes of tax, and if the client is sensitive to the tax bill, there may be an incentive to account creatively.

Question — System control weaknesses

Jonathan is the sole shareholder of Furry Lion Stores, a company which owns five stores in the west of England. The stores sell mainly food and groceries.

Each store is run by a full-time manager and three or four part-time assistants. Jonathan spends on average ½ a day a week at each store, and spends the rest of his time at home, dealing with his other business interests.

All sales are for cash and are recorded on till rolls which the manager retains. Shop managers' wages are paid monthly by cheque by Jonathan. Wages of shop assistants are paid in cash out of the takings.

Most purchases are made from local wholesalers and are paid for in cash out of the takings. Large purchases (over $250) must be made by cheques signed by the shop manager and countersigned by Jonathan.

Shop managers bank surplus cash once a week, apart from a float in the till.

All accounting records including the cash book, wages and sales tax records are maintained by the manager. Jonathan reviews the weekly bank statements when he visits the shops. He also has a look at inventory to see if inventory levels appear to be about right. All invoices are also kept in a drawer by a manager and marked with a cash book reference, and where appropriate a cheque number when paid.

Required

Discuss the deficiencies in the control systems of Furry Lion Stores, and how the weaknesses can be remedied.

Answer

Deficiencies in the system, and their remedies, are as follows.

Inventory

The shops do not appear to have any inventory movement records. Jonathan has also only a very approximate indication of inventory levels. Hence it will be difficult to detect whether inventory levels are too high, or too low with a risk of running out of inventory. Theft of inventory would also be difficult to detect. The company should therefore introduce inventory movement records, detailing values and volumes.

In addition regular inventory counts should be made either by Jonathan or by staff from another shop. Discrepancies between the inventory records and the actual inventory counted should be investigated.

Cash controls

Too much cash appears to be held on site. In addition the fact that most payments appear to be for cash may mean inadequate documentation is kept. The level of cash on site can be decreased by daily rather than weekly bankings. In addition the need for cash on site can be decreased by paying wages by cheque, and by paying all but the smallest payments by cheque.

The cash book should obviously still be maintained but cheque stubs should also show details of amounts paid. The cash book should be supported by invoices and other supporting documentation, and should be cross-referenced to the general ledger (see below).

Cash reconciliations

There is no indication of the till-rolls that are kept being reconciled to cash takings.

There should be a daily reconciliation of cash takings and till rolls; this should be reviewed if not performed by the shop manager.

Bank reconciliations

There is no mention of bank reconciliations taking place.

Bank reconciliations should be carried out at least monthly by the shop manager, and reviewed by the owner.

Purchases

There is no formal system for recording purchases. Invoices do not appear to be filed in any particular way. It would be difficult to see whether accounting records were complete, and hence it would be difficult to prepare a set of accounts from the accounting records available.

In addition the way records are maintained means that accounts would have to be prepared on a cash basis, and not on an accruals basis.

A purchase day book should be introduced. Invoices should be recorded in the purchase day book, and filed in a logical order, either by date received or by supplier.

General ledger

There is no general ledger, and again this means that annual accounts cannot easily be prepared (and also management accounts).

A general ledger should be maintained with entries made from the cash book, wages records and purchase day book. This will enable accounts to be prepared on an accruals basis.

Supervision

Jonathan does not take a very active part in the business, only signing cheques over $250, and visiting the shops only half a day each week. This may mean that assets can easily go missing, and Jonathan cannot readily see whether the business is performing as he would wish.

Jonathan should review wage/sales tax/cash book reconciliations. Management accounts should also be prepared by shop managers for Jonathan.

Tutorial note. This question deals with controls that are possible given the circumstances of the business. Greater segregation of duties does not appear to be possible as the shops are small, and Jonathan cannot spend more time at the shops (although he can use his time more productively by reviewing reconciliations).

Exam focus point

In the exam you may be asked for deficiencies in a system, and the consequences of those deficiencies, or you could be asked for tests of controls.

If you are asked about appropriate controls or deficiencies, remember the **control objectives** for the accounting area. Controls should be in place to **fulfil** the **objectives** given, deficiencies will mean that the objectives are not fulfilled. You should give enough detail about the controls you suggest to enable a non-accountant to implement the controls.

You should use a similar thought process when deciding how to test the controls. Think of the **objectives** of the system; assess how the controls given **fulfil** those **objectives**; and set out tests which demonstrate whether the controls are working. Remember that different types of test can be used to test different controls. For example, inspection can be used to test whether different documents are being compared or documents are being properly authorised. Recalculation and reperformance can be used to test that invoices have been properly completed or reconciliations correctly performed.

Chapter Roundup

- The tests of controls in the **sales system** will be based around:
  - **Selling** (authorisation)
  - **Goods outwards** (custody)
  - **Accounting** (recording)
- The tests of controls in the **purchases system** will be based around:
  - **Buying** (authorisation)
  - **Goods inwards** (custody)
  - **Accounting** (recording)
- **Inventory controls** are designed to ensure safe custody. Such controls include restriction of access, documentation and authorisation of movements, regular **independent inventory counting** and **review of inventory condition**.
- Controls over cash receipts and payments should prevent fraud or theft.
- Key controls over **payroll** cover:
  - **Documentation** and **authorisation** of staff changes
  - **Calculation** of wages and salaries
  - **Payment** of wages
  - **Authorisation** of **deductions**
- Most of the key controls over capital and revenue expenditure are the general purchase controls.

Quick Quiz

1 Complete the table, putting the sales system control considerations under the correct headings.

Ordering/credit approval	Dispatch/invoicing	Recording/accounting

(a) All sales that have been invoiced have been put in the general ledger
(b) Orders are fulfilled
(c) Cut-off is correct
(d) Goods are only supplied to good credit risks
(e) Goods are correctly invoiced
(f) Customers are encouraged to pay promptly

2 State five controls relating to the ordering and granting of credit process.

1 ....

2 ....

3 ....

4 ....

5 ....

3 Complete the table, putting the purchase system control considerations under the correct headings.

Ordering	Receipts/invoices	Accounting

(a) Orders are only made to authorised suppliers
(b) Liabilities are recognised for all goods and services received
(c) Orders are made at competitive prices
(d) All expenditure is authorised
(e) Cut-off is correctly applied
(f) Goods and services are only accepted if there is an authorised order

4 (a) State four examples of purchase documentation on which numerical sequence should be checked.

1 ....

2 ....

3 ....

4 ....

(b) Why is numerical sequence checked?

5 State five control objectives relating to inventory.

1 ....

2 ....

3 ....

4 ....

5 ....

6 List the five key aims of controls in the cash system.

1 ....

2 ....

3 ....

4 ....

5 ....

7 Give five examples of tests to be performed on the cash payments book.

1 ....

2 ....

3 ....

4 ....

5 ....

8 Describe six procedures auditors should carry out if wages are paid in cash.

1 ....

2 ....

3 ....

4 ....

5 ....

6 ....

Answers to Quick Quiz

1

Ordering/credit approval	Dispatch/invoicing	Recording/accounting
(b) (d) (f)	(e)	(a) (c)

2
- Segregation of duties; credit control, invoicing and inventory dispatch
- Authorisation of credit terms to customers
  - References/credit checks obtained
  - Authorisation by senior staff
  - Regular review
- Authorisation for changes in other customer data
  - Change of address supported by letterhead
  - Deletion requests supported by evidence balances cleared/customer in liquidation
- Orders only accepted from customers who have no credit problems
- Sequential numbering of blank pre-printed order documents
- Correct prices quoted to customers
- Matching of customer orders with production orders and dispatch notes and querying of orders not matched
- Dealing with customer queries

3

Ordering	Receipts/invoices	Accounting
(a) (c)	(b) (f)	(d) (e)

4 (a) (1) purchase requisitions, (2) purchase orders, (3) goods received notes, (4) goods returned notes, (5) suppliers invoices

(b) Sequence provides a control that sales are complete. Missing documents should be explained, or cancelled copies available.

5
- To ensure that all inventory movements are authorised and recorded
- To ensure that inventory records only include items that belong to the client
- To ensure that inventory records include inventory that exists and is held by the client
- To ensure that inventory quantities have been recorded correctly
- To ensure that cut-off procedures are properly applied to inventory
- To ensure that inventory is safeguarded against loss, pilferage or damage
- To ensure that the costing system values inventory correctly
- To ensure that allowance is made for slow-moving, obsolete or damaged inventory
- To ensure that levels of inventory held are reasonable

6
- All monies received are recorded.
- All monies received are banked.
- Cash and cheques are safeguarded against loss or theft.
- All payments are authorised, made to the correct payees and recorded.
- Payments are not made twice for the same liability.

7 For a sample of payments:

- Compare with paid cheques to ensure payee agrees.
- Observe whether cheques are signed by the persons authorised to do so within their authority limits.
- Match to suppliers' invoices for goods and services. Verify that supporting documents are signed as having been checked and passed for payment and have been stamped 'paid'.
- Match to suppliers' statements.
- Agree to other documentary evidence, as appropriate (agreements, authorised expense vouchers, wages/salaries records, petty cash books etc).

8

- Arrange to attend the pay-out of wages to confirm that the official procedures are being followed.
- Before the wages are paid compare payroll with wage packets to ensure all employees have a wage packet.
- Examine receipts given by employees; confirm that unclaimed wages are recorded by inspecting the unclaimed wages book.
- Confirm that no employee receives more than one wage packet by attending the pay-out.
- Agree entries in the unclaimed wages book with the entries on the payroll.
- Confirm that unclaimed wages are banked regularly by scrutinising bank statements and matching to amounts in the unclaimed wages book.
- Confirm that unclaimed wages books shows reasons why wages are unclaimed by reviewing it.
- Review the pattern of unclaimed wages in unclaimed wages book; variations may indicate failure to record.
- Verify a sample of holiday pay payments with the underlying records and confirm the accuracy of the calculation of the amounts paid by recalculation.

Now try the questions below from the Exam Question Bank

Number	Level	Marks	Time
Q12	Examination	30	54 mins
Q13	Examination	20	36 mins

PART E

Audit evidence

11

Audit procedures and sampling

Topic list	Syllabus reference
1 Substantive procedures	E2
2 Accounting estimates	E2
3 Audit sampling	E4
4 Computer-assisted audit techniques	E5
5 Using the work of others	C7

Introduction

In this chapter we look at various audit procedures and the use of audit sampling.

Firstly we consider substantive testing which encompasses tests of detail and the use of analytical procedures as substantive tests. These methods form the basis for the next five chapters which examine the detailed testing for various financial statement account areas such as cash and inventory.

We also examine the audit of accounting estimates. We have mentioned in previous chapters that judgement has to be used in accounting for some of the figures in the accounts. Examples of accounting estimates include depreciation and provisions.

We will look in detail at audit sampling, which is an important aspect of the audit. We consider different types of audit sampling and the evaluation of errors.

Computer-assisted audit techniques (CAATs) are an important tool in the audit and we examine the two main types of CAATs, audit software and test data.

Finally in this chapter we will look at how the auditor can make use of the work of others as a source of audit evidence. We consider the use of auditor's experts, the work of internal audit and the use of service organisations in this regard.

Study guide

		Intellectual level
E2	**Audit procedures**	
(b)	Discuss and provide examples of how analytical procedures are used as substantive procedures	2
(c)	Discuss the problems associated with the audit and review of accounting estimates	2
E4	**Audit sampling and other means of testing**	
(a)	Define audit sampling and explain the need for sampling	1
(b)	Identify and discuss the differences between statistical and non-statistical sampling	2
(c)	Discuss and provide relevant examples of the application of the basic principles of statistical sampling and other selective testing procedures	2
(d)	Discuss the results of statistical sampling, including consideration of whether additional testing is required	2
E5	**Computer-assisted audit techniques**	
(a)	Explain the use of computer-assisted audit techniques in the context of an audit	1
(b)	Discuss and provide relevant examples of the use of test data and audit software for the transaction cycles and balances mentioned in sub-capability 3	2
(c)	Discuss the use of computers in relation to the administration of the audit	2
C7	**The work of others**	
(a)	Discuss the extent to which auditors are able to rely on the work of experts	2
(b)	Discuss the extent to which external auditors are able to rely on the work of internal audit	2
(c)	Discuss the audit considerations relating to entities using service organisations	2
(d)	Discuss why auditors rely on the work of others	2
(e)	Explain the extent to which reference to the work of others can be made in audit reports	1

Exam guide

This chapter forms a basis for the next five chapters in terms of substantive audit procedures to carry out during an audit. It also covers analytical procedures, sampling and the use of computer-assisted audit techniques (CAATs) which could come up in the knowledge-based section of a question. The extent to which external auditors can place reliance on the work done by internal auditors could come up in a question on audit evidence or in one on internal audit.

CAATs were tested in both the pilot paper and December 2007. The pilot paper also had a six mark part on the factors to consider when appointing an external consultant. The June 2008 paper had an eight mark knowledge-based question on analytical procedures in question 3. The December 2008 paper had a six mark part in question 1 on substantive analytical procedures in a scenario context. Question 2 of this paper had a three mark part on the use of an expert.

The June 2009 paper had 12 marks (question 1) on substantive analytical procedures relating to income. There were four marks in question 2 of this paper for explaining sampling methods. The same paper had a question on the use of audit software.

1 Substantive procedures

June 08, Dec 08, June 09

FAST FORWARD

Auditors need to obtain **sufficient appropriate audit evidence** to support the financial statement assertions. Substantive procedures can be used to obtain that evidence.

1.1 Types of audit tests

To recap, **substantive procedures** are tests to obtain audit evidence to detect material misstatements in the financial statements. They are generally of two types:

- Analytical procedures
- Tests of detail of transactions, account balances and disclosures

The types of substantive tests carried out to obtain evidence about various financial statement assertions are outlined in the table below.

Audit assertion	Type of assertion	Typical audit tests
Completeness	Classes of transactions Account balances Presentation and disclosure	(a) Review of post year-end items (b) Cut-off testing (c) Analytical review (d) Confirmations (e) Reconciliations to control accounts
Rights and obligations	Account balances Presentation and disclosure	(a) Reviewing invoices for proof that item belongs to the company (b) Confirmations with third parties
Valuation and allocation	Account balances Presentation and disclosure	(a) Matching amounts to invoices (b) Recalculation (c) Confirming accounting policy consistent and reasonable (d) Review of post year-end payments and invoices (e) Expert valuation
Existence	Account balances	(a) Physical verification (b) Third party confirmations (c) Cut-off testing
Occurrence	Classes of transactions Presentation and disclosure	(a) Inspection of supporting documentation (b) Confirmation from directors that transactions relate to business (c) Inspection of items purchased
Accuracy	Classes of transactions Presentation and disclosure	(a) Recalculation of correct amounts (b) Third party confirmation (c) Analytical review
Classification and understandability	Classes of transactions Presentation and disclosure	(a) Confirming compliance with law and accounting standards (b) Reviewing notes for understandability
Cut-off	Classes of transactions	(a) Cut-off testing (b) Analytical review

Use the following model for drawing up an audit plan:

- **Agree opening balances** with **previous year's working papers**
- **Review general ledger** for unusual records
- **Agree client schedules to/from accounting records** to ensure completeness

- Carry out **analytical review**
- **Test transactions in detail**
- **Test balances in detail**
- **Review presentation** and **disclosure** in accounts

Exam focus point

Auditing exams require a good knowledge of how the **financial statement assertions** determine audit objectives, and the procedures for obtaining audit evidence. Students should be aiming to produce a description of procedures that could be followed by an inexperienced staff member.

1.2 Directional testing

FAST FORWARD

Substantive tests are designed to discover errors or omissions.

Broadly speaking, substantive procedures can be said to fall into two categories:

- Tests to discover **errors** (resulting in over or understatement)
- Tests to discover **omissions** (resulting in understatement)

1.2.1 Tests designed to discover errors

These tests will start with the **accounting records** in which the transactions are recorded to supporting documents or other evidence. Such tests should detect any overstatement and also any understatement through causes other than omission. For example, if a test is designed to ensure that sales are priced correctly, it would begin with a sales invoice selected from the sales ledger. Prices would then be checked to the official price list.

1.2.2 Tests designed to discover omissions

These tests must start from **outside the accounting records** and then matched back to those records. Understatements through omission will never be revealed by starting with the account itself as there is clearly no chance of selecting items that have been omitted from the account. For example, if a test is designed to discover whether all raw material purchases have been properly processed, it would start with goods received notes to be agreed to the inventory records or purchase ledger.

1.2.3 Directional testing

For most systems auditors would include tests designed to discover both errors and omissions. The type of test, and direction of the test, should be recognised before selecting the test sample. If the sample which tested the accuracy and validity of the sales ledger were chosen from a file of sales invoices then it would not substantiate the fact that there were no errors in the sales ledger.

Directional testing is particularly appropriate when testing the financial statement assertions of existence, completeness, rights and obligations, and valuation.

The concept of directional testing derives from the principle of double-entry bookkeeping, in that for every **debit** there should be a **corresponding credit**. Therefore, any **misstatement** of a **debit entry** will result in either a corresponding **misstatement** of a **credit entry** or a **misstatement** in the opposite direction, of **another debit entry**.

By designing audit tests carefully the auditors are able to use this principle in drawing audit conclusions, not only about the debit or credit entries that they have directly tested, but also about the corresponding credit or debit entries that are necessary to balance the books.

Tests are therefore designed in the following way.

Test item	Example
Test **debit items** (expenditure or assets) for overstatement by selecting debit entries recorded in the nominal ledger and checking value, existence and ownership	If a non-current asset entry in the nominal ledger of $1,000 is selected, it would be overstated if it should have been recorded at anything less than $1,000 or if the company did not own it, or indeed if it did not exist (eg it had been sold or the amount of $1,000 in fact represented a revenue expense).
Test **credit items** (income or liabilities) for understatement by selecting items from appropriate sources independent of the nominal ledger and ensuring that they result in the correct nominal ledger entry	Select a goods dispatched note and agree that the resultant sale has been recorded in the nominal ledger sales account. Sales would be understated if the nominal ledger did not reflect the transaction at all (completeness) or reflected it at less than full value (say if goods valued at $1,000 were recorded in the sales account at $900, there would be an understatement of $100).

A test for the overstatement of an asset simultaneously gives comfort on understatement of other assets, overstatement of liabilities, overstatement of income and understatement of expenses.

So, by performing the primary tests, the auditors obtain audit assurance in other audit areas. Successful completion of the primary tests will therefore result in them having tested all account areas both for overstatement and understatement.

1.3 Analytical procedures

FAST FORWARD

Analytical procedures are used at all stages of the audit, including as substantive procedures. When using analytical procedures as **substantive tests**, auditors must consider the information available, assessing its **availability, relevance** and **comparability**.

We introduced analytical procedures in Chapter 6 where they were used at the planning stage of an audit. They can also be used as substantive procedures to obtain audit evidence directly.

ISA 520 *Analytical procedures* provides guidance to auditors on the use of analytical procedures as substantive procedures. Remember from chapter 6 that analytical procedures include:

(a) The consideration of comparisons with:

- **Comparable information** for prior periods
- **Anticipated results** of the entity, from budgets or forecasts
- **Expectations** prepared by the auditors (e.g. estimation of depreciation)
- **Industry information**

(b) Those between elements of financial information that are expected to conform to a predicted pattern based on the entity's experience, such as the relationship of gross profit to sales

(c) Those between financial information and relevant non-financial information, such as the relationship of payroll costs to number of employees

ISA 520 states that when using analytical procedures as substantive tests, the auditor must:

- Determine the **suitability** of particular analytical procedures for given assertions.
- Evaluate the **reliability of data** from which the auditor's expectation of recorded amounts or ratios is developed.
- **Develop an expectation** of recorded amounts or ratios and evaluate whether this is **sufficiently precise** to identify a misstatement that may cause the financial statements to be materially misstated.
- Determine the amount of any difference that is **acceptable** without further investigation.

1.3.1 Suitability of analytical procedures

Substantive analytical procedures are usually more applicable to large volumes of transactions that tend to be predictable over time. The suitability of a particular analytical procedure will depend on the auditor's assessment of how effective it will be in detecting material misstatements. Determining the suitability will be influenced by the nature of the assertion and the auditor's assessment of the risk of material misstatement.

1.3.2 Reliability of data

The ISA sets out factors which influence the reliability of data which are set out in the following table, with examples.

Reliability factors	Example
Source of the information	Information may be more reliable when obtained from independent sources outside the entity.
Comparability of information available	Broad industry data may need to be supplemented so it is comparable to that of an entity that produces and sells specialised products.
Nature and relevance of the information available	Whether budgets have been set up as results to be expected rather than goals to be achieved
Controls over the preparation of the information to ensure its **completeness, accuracy and validity**	Controls over the preparation, review and maintenance of budgets

The auditor will need to consider testing the controls, if any, over the **preparation** of **information** used in applying analytical procedures. When such controls are effective, the auditor will have greater confidence in the reliability of the information, and therefore in the results of analytical procedures.

The **controls** over **non-financial information** can often be tested in conjunction with tests of **accounting-related controls**. For example, in establishing controls over the processing of sales invoices, a business may include controls over unit sales recording. The auditor could therefore test the controls over the recording of unit sales in conjunction with tests of controls over the processing of sales invoices.

Alternatively the auditor may consider whether the information was subjected to audit testing. ISA 500 contains guidance in determining the audit procedures to be performed on information to be used for substantive analytical procedures.

1.3.3 Evaluation of whether the expectation is sufficiently precise

The factors to consider when evaluating whether the expectation can be developed sufficiently precisely to identify a misstatement that may cause the financial statements to be materially misstated are set out in the following table.

Factors to consider	Example
The **accuracy** with which the expected results of analytical procedures can be predicted	The auditor may expect greater consistency in comparing the relationship of gross profit to sales from one period to another than in comparing discretionary expenses, such as research or advertising.
The **degree to which information can be disaggregated**	Analytical procedures may be more effective when applied to financial information on individual sections of an operation or to the financial statements of components of a diversified entity than when applied to the financial statements as a whole.
The **availability** of the information	The auditor may consider whether financial information (e.g. budgets or forecasts) and non-financial information (e.g. number of units produced or sold) is available.

1.3.4 Acceptable differences

The amount of the difference of recorded amounts from the expected value that is acceptable depends on **materiality** and **consistency with the desired level of assurance**, having taken into account that a misstatement may cause the financial statements to be materially misstated. Therefore as the **assessed risk increases**, the **amount of the difference that is acceptable** without further investigation **decreases**.

1.3.5 Practical techniques

Analytical procedures can be performed using various techniques, ranging from simple comparisons to complex analyses using advanced statistical techniques. In this section we look at some of the techniques that can be used to carry out analytical procedures.

Ratio analysis can be a useful technique. However ratios mean very little when used in isolation. They should be calculated for previous periods and for comparable companies. This may involve a certain amount of initial research, but subsequently it is just a matter of adding new statistics to the existing information each year. The permanent file should contain a section with summarised accounts and the chosen ratios for prior years.

In addition to looking at the more usual ratios the auditors should consider examining other ratios that may be relevant to the particular clients' business.

Other analytical techniques include:

(a) **Examining related accounts** in conjunction with each other. Often revenue and expense accounts are related to accounts in the statement of financial position and comparisons should be made to ensure relationships are reasonable.

(b) **Trend analysis.** Sophisticated statistical techniques can be used to compare this period with previous periods.

(c) **Reasonableness test**. This involves calculating the **expected value** of an item and comparing it with its actual value, for example, for straight-line depreciation.

(Cost + Additions – Disposals) × Depreciation % = Charge in statement of comprehensive income

Important accounting ratios	• Gross profit margins, in total and by product, area and months/quarter (if possible) • Receivables' ratio (average collection period) • Inventory revenue ratio (revenue divided into cost of sales) • Current ratio (current assets to current liabilities) • Quick or acid test ratio (liquid assets to current liabilities) • Gearing ratio (debt capital to equity capital) • Return on capital employed (profit before tax to total assets less current liabilities)
Related items	• Payables and purchases • Inventories and cost of sales • Non-current assets and depreciation, repairs and maintenance expense • Intangible assets and amortisation • Loans and interest expense • Investments and investment income • Receivables and bad debt expense • Receivables and sales

Other areas for consideration
• **Examine changes** in **products, customers and levels** of **returns**
• **Assess** the effect of **price and mix changes** on the cost of sales
• **Consider** the effect of **inflation, industrial disputes, changes in production methods** and **changes in activity** on the charge for wages

Other areas for consideration
• **Obtain explanations** for all **major variances** analysed using a standard costing system. Particular attention should be paid to those relating to the over or under absorption of overheads since these may, inter alia, affect inventory valuations
• **Compare trends in production and sales** and assess the effect on any provisions for obsolete inventory
• **Ensure** that **changes in the percentage labour or overhead content** of production costs are also reflected in the inventory valuation
• **Review other expenditure**, comparing: – Rent with annual rent per rental agreement – Rates with previous year and known rates increases – Interest payable on loans with outstanding balance and interest rate per loan agreement – Hire or leasing charges with annual rate per agreements – Vehicle running expenses to vehicles – Other items related to activity level with general price increase and change in relevant level of activity (for example telephone expenditure will increase disproportionately if export or import business increases) – Other items not related to activity level with general price increases (or specific increases if known)
• **Review** statement of comprehensive income for **items** which may have been **omitted** (eg scrap sales, training levy, special contributions to pension fund, provisions for dilapidation etc)
• **Ensure expected variations** arising from the following have occurred: – Industry or local trends – Known disturbances of the trading pattern (for example strikes, depot closures, failure of suppliers)

Some comparisons and ratios measuring liquidity and longer-term capital structure will assist in evaluating whether the company is a going concern, in addition to contributing to the overall view of the accounts. We shall see in Chapter 18 however, that there are factors other than declining ratios that may indicate going concern problems.

The working papers must contain the completed results of analytical procedures. They should include:

- The outline **programme** of the work
- The summary of **significant figures** and relationships for the period
- A summary of **comparisons** made with budgets and with previous years
- Details of all **significant fluctuations** or **unexpected relationships** considered
- Details of the **results of investigations** into such fluctuations/relationships
- The audit **conclusions** reached
- **Information considered** necessary for assisting in the **planning** of subsequent audits

1.3.6 Investigating the results of analytical procedures

ISA 520 states that where analytical procedures identify fluctuations or relationships that are inconsistent with other relevant information or that differ significantly from the expected results, the auditor shall investigate by:

- **Inquiries of management** and obtaining appropriate audit evidence relevant to **management's responses**
- Performing **other audit procedures** if necessary (e.g. if management cannot provide an explanation or the explanation is not adequate)

Question

You are part of the audit team auditing the financial statements of Sweep Co, a small office supplies business, for the year ended 31 March 20X9. The company employed the following staff at the start of the financial year: 7 office and warehouse managers, 20 warehouse staff and 25 office staff.

The pay ranges for each category of staff is shown below:

Office and warehouse managers:	$35-$50k per year
Warehouse and office staff:	$18-$25k per year

You have been asked to audit the wages and salaries expense for the year. All staff were given a 4% pay rise in the year, backdated to the start of the year. One of the office managers left the company part-way through the year. There were two new members of warehouse staff and three new members of office staff.

The expense for the year is shown in the draft income statement as $1,249,450.

Required

Using analytical procedures, perform a proof in total on the wages and salaries expense for the year.

Answer

An expectation of the charge for the year can be developed using the information provided and compared to the charge in the draft income statement to assess its reasonableness.

Managers	
Based on salary range, average annual salary:	$42,500
Applying the 4% rise:	$44,200
Total average salary for year (i.e. × 7):	$309,400
Assume leaver left half-way through year:	($22,100)
Total for managers:	**$287,300**
Office and warehouse staff	
Based on salary range, average annual salary:	$21,500
Applying the 4% rise:	$22,360
Total average salary for year (i.e. × 40, exclude starters):	$1,006,200
Assume starters started half-way through year:	$55,900
Total for office and warehouse staff:	**$1,062,100**
Expected total expense for wages and salaries:	**$1,349,400**
Expense per draft income statement:	**$1,249,450**
Difference:	**8%**

The difference between the expected total and the expense in the draft income statement is 8%. The auditor needs to consider whether this is acceptable in light of materiality for the financial statements as a whole and performance materiality and the risk of material misstatement and whether further explanations from management may be necessary.

Exam focus point

Mention of analytical procedures will generally be worth a couple of marks in any question on substantive testing. However you will not get any marks just for saying 'perform analytical procedures' – you will need to give details of the specific procedures that should be performed.

2 Accounting estimates

FAST FORWARD

When auditing **accounting estimates** auditors must:

- Test the management process
- Use an independent estimate
- Review subsequent events

in order to assess whether the estimates are reasonable.

2.1 The nature of accounting estimates

ISA 540 *Auditing accounting estimates, including fair value accounting estimates, and related disclosures* provides guidance on the audit of accounting estimates contained in financial statements. The auditor's objective is to obtain sufficient appropriate audit evidence about whether accounting estimates are reasonable and related disclosures are adequate.

Key terms

An **accounting estimate** is an approximation of a monetary amount in the absence of a precise means of measurement.

Estimation uncertainty is the susceptibility of an accounting estimate and related disclosures to an inherent lack of precision in its measurement.

Management's point estimate is the amount selected by management for recognition or disclosure in the financial statements as an accounting estimate.

Auditor's point estimate or **auditor's range** is the amount, or range of amounts, respectively, derived from audit evidence for use in evaluating management's point estimate.

Examples of accounting estimates include:

- Allowance for doubtful accounts
- Inventory obsolescence
- Warranty obligations
- Depreciation method or asset useful life
- Outcome of long-term contracts
- Costs arising from litigation settlements and judgements
- Provision against the carrying amount of an investment where there is uncertainty regarding its recoverability

Some financial statement items cannot be measured precisely, only estimated. The **nature and reliability** of information available to management to support accounting estimates can vary enormously and this therefore affects the **degree of uncertainty** associated with accounting estimates, which in turn affects the **risk of material misstatement** of accounting estimates.

2.2 Risk assessment procedures

ISA 540 states that the auditor shall obtain an understanding of the following to provide a basis for the identification and assessment of the risks of material misstatement for accounting estimates:

- The requirements of the applicable financial reporting framework
- How management identifies those transactions, events and conditions that may give rise to the need for accounting estimates
- How management makes the accounting estimates and an understanding of the data on which they are based including:
  - Method
  - Relevant controls
  - Assumptions

- Whether change from prior period in method used
- Whether management has assessed the effect of estimation uncertainty

The ISA also states that the auditor shall review the **outcome** of accounting estimates included in the **prior period**.

2.3 Risk identification and assessment

The auditor shall also evaluate the degree of **estimation uncertainty** associated with an accounting estimate. Where estimation uncertainty is assessed as high, the auditor shall determine whether these give rise to **significant risks**.

2.4 Responding to the assessed risks

The ISA requires the auditor to perform one or more of the following:

- Determine whether events occurring up to the date of the auditor's report provide audit evidence regarding the accounting estimate.
- Test how management made the accounting estimate and the data on which it is based.
- Test the operating effectiveness of controls over how the accounting estimate was made.
- Develop a point estimate or a range to evaluate management's point estimate.

2.5 Substantive procedures in response to significant risks

Where the auditor judges that the accounting estimate gives rise to a significant risk, he shall evaluate the following in accordance with ISA 540:

- How management has considered alternative assumptions and why these have been rejected
- Whether the assumptions used are reasonable
- Management's intent to carry out specific courses of action and its ability to do so

If the auditor considers that management has not adequately addressed the effects of estimation uncertainty on accounting estimates that give rise to significant risks, he shall, if necessary, develop a **range** with which to evaluate the reasonableness of the accounting estimate.

2.6 Other audit procedures

ISA 540 requires the auditor to do the following:

- Evaluate whether the accounting estimates are either **reasonable or misstated**.
- Obtain sufficient appropriate audit evidence about whether **disclosures** are correct.
- For accounting estimates that give rise to significant risks, evaluate the adequacy of **disclosure of their estimation uncertainty**.
- Review the judgements and decisions of management in making the accounting estimates to identify if there are indications of **possible management bias**.
- Obtain **written representations** from management whether management believes significant assumptions used are reasonable.

3 Audit sampling

June 09

Auditors usually seek evidence from less than 100% of items of the balance or transaction being tested by using **sampling techniques**.

3.1 Introduction to audit sampling

Key terms

Audit sampling is the application of audit procedures to less than 100% of items within a population of audit relevance such that all sampling units have a chance of selection. This will enable the auditor to obtain and evaluate audit evidence about some characteristic of the items selected in order to provide the auditor with a reasonable basis on which to draw conclusions about the entire population. Audit sampling can be applied using either statistical or non-statistical approaches.

The **population** is the entire set of data from which a sample is selected and about which the auditor wishes to draw conclusions.

Auditors do not normally examine all the information available to them as it would be impractical to do so and using audit sampling will produce valid conclusions. ISA 530 *Audit sampling provides guidance to auditors.*

Some testing procedures do **not** involve sampling, such as:

- **Testing 100%** of items in a population
- Testing all items with a **certain characteristic** as selection is not representative

Auditors are unlikely to test 100% of items when carrying out tests of controls, but 100% testing may be appropriate for certain substantive procedures. For example, if the population is made up of a small number of high value items, there is a high risk of material misstatement and other means do not provide sufficient appropriate audit evidence, then 100% examination may be appropriate.

Audit sampling can be done using either **statistical sampling** or **non-statistical sampling** methods.

Key terms

Statistical sampling is an approach to sampling that involves random selection of the sample items, and the use of probability theory to evaluate sample results, including measurement of sampling risk.

Non-statistical sampling is a sampling approach that does not have these characteristics.

The auditor may alternatively select certain items from a population because of specific characteristics they possess. The results of items selected in this way cannot be projected onto the whole population but may be used in conjunction with other audit evidence concerning the rest of the population.

- **High value or key items.** The auditor may select high value items or items that are suspicious, unusual or prone to error.
- **All items over a certain amount**. Selecting items this way may mean a large proportion of the population can be verified by testing a few items.
- **Items to obtain information** about the client's business, the nature of transactions, or the client's accounting and control systems.
- **Items to test procedures,** to see whether particular procedures are being performed.

3.2 Design of the sample

Key terms

Sampling risk arises from the possibility that the auditor's conclusion, based on a sample of a certain size, may be different from the conclusion that would be reached if the entire population were subjected to the same audit procedure.

Non-sampling risk arises from factors that cause the auditor to reach an erroneous conclusion for any reason not related to the size of the sample. For example, the use of inappropriate audit procedures, or misinterpretation of audit evidence and failure to recognise a misstatement or deviation.

Sampling unit is the individual items constituting a population. It may be a physical item (e.g. credit entries on bank statements, sales invoices, receivables' balances) or a monetary unit.

Stratification is the process of dividing a population into sub-populations, each of which is a group of sampling units which have similar characteristics, often monetary value.

The auditor must consider the **purpose** of the audit procedure when designing an audit sample. The auditor must also consider the **characteristics of the population**. When considering the characteristics of the population, the auditor might determine that **stratification** or **value-weighted selection** is appropriate.

The auditor must design a sample size sufficient to reduce sampling risk to an **acceptably low level**. Sampling risk can lead to two types of erroneous conclusions: for tests of controls, that they are more effective that they actually are or for tests of details, that a material misstatement does not exist when it actually does; and for tests of controls, that controls are less effective than they actually are or for tests of details, that a material misstatement exists when it actually does not. The lower the risk the auditor is willing to accept, the greater the sample size will need to be. Sample size can be determined using a statistically-based formula or through the use of judgement.

ISA 530 also requires the auditor to select items for the sample in such a way that each sampling unit in the population has a chance of selection. When statistical sampling is used, each sampling unit has a **known probability** of being selected. When non-statistical sampling is used, judgement is applied. However, it is important that the auditor selects a **representative sample**, free from bias, by choosing sample items that have **characteristics typical** of the population. The main methods of selecting samples are **random selection, systematic selection** and **haphazard selection**. We discuss these and other methods below.

(a) **Random selection** ensures that all items in the population have an equal chance of selection, eg by use of random number tables or random number generators.

(b) **Systematic selection** involves selecting items using a constant interval between selections, the first interval having a random start. When using systematic selection auditors must ensure that the population is not structured in such a manner that the sampling interval corresponds with a particular pattern in the population.

(c) **Haphazard selection** may be an alternative to random selection provided auditors are satisfied that the sample is representative of the entire population. This method requires care to guard against making a selection which is biased, for example towards items which are easily located, as they may not be representative. It should not be used if auditors are carrying out statistical sampling.

(d) **Block selection** may be used to check whether certain items have particular characteristics. For example an auditor may use a sample of 50 consecutive cheques to test whether cheques are signed by authorised signatories rather than picking 50 single cheques throughout the year. Block sampling may however produce samples that are not representative of the population as a whole, particularly if errors only occurred during a certain part of the period, and hence the errors found cannot be projected onto the rest of the population.

(e) **Monetary Unit Sampling** is a type of value-weighted selection in which sample size, selection and evaluation results in a conclusion in monetary amounts.

3.3 Performing audit procedures

Once the sample has been selected, the auditor must perform **appropriate audit procedures** on each item in the sample. If the audit procedure is not applicable to the selected item, the test must be performed on a **replacement item**. This could happen if, for example, a voided check is selected when testing for evidence of authorisation of payment.

If the auditor cannot apply the designed audit procedures (e.g. if documentation relating to the item has been lost), or suitable alternative audit procedures, to the selected item, that item must be treated as a **deviation** from the prescribed control (for tests of controls) or a **misstatement** (for tests of details).

3.4 Deviations and misstatements

Key term

An **anomaly** is a misstatement or deviation that is demonstrably not representative of misstatements or deviations in a population.

Once the sample has been tested, the auditor must investigate the nature and cause of any deviations or misstatements found and evaluate their possible effect on the purpose of the audit procedure and on other areas of the audit.

In rare cases, a deviation or misstatement may be considered an **anomaly**, in which case the auditor must obtain a high degree of certainty that this is not representative of the population, by carrying out additional audit procedures.

3.5 Projection of misstatements

For **tests of details**, the auditor shall **project** misstatements found in the sample to the population to obtain a broad view of the scale of the misstatement but this may not be enough to determine an amount to be recorded.

Misstatements established as **anomalies** can be excluded when projecting sample errors to the population. However, note that the effect of any uncorrected anomalies still needs to be considered. Projected errors and anomalies are combined together when considering the possible effect of errors on the total class of transactions or account balance. Where the audited entity has corrected specific errors found in the sample, the projected error may be reduced by the amount of these corrections.

ISA 530 states that for **tests of controls**, no explicit projection of errors is necessary because the sample deviation rate is also the projected deviation rate for the population as a whole. So for example, if in sample of 75, four errors are discovered, the projected deviation rate is 4/75, i.e. 5%.

3.6 Evaluating the results

Key terms

Tolerable misstatement is a monetary amount set by the auditor in respect of which the auditor seeks to obtain an appropriate level of assurance that the monetary amount set by the auditor is not exceeded by the actual misstatement in the population.

Tolerable rate of deviation is a rate of deviation from prescribed internal control procedures set by the auditor in respect of which the auditor seeks to obtain an appropriate level of assurance that the rate of deviation set by the auditor is not exceeded by the actual rate of deviation in the population.

ISA 530 requires the auditor to evaluate the results of the sample.

For tests of controls, an unexpectedly high deviation rate in the sample may result in an increase in the assessed risk of material misstatement, unless further audit evidence to substantiate the initial assessment of risk is obtained.

For tests of details, an unexpectedly high misstatement amount in the sample may lead the auditor to conclude that a class of transactions or account balance is materially misstated, in the absence of further audit evidence that no misstatement exists.

For tests of details, the total of the projected misstatement and anomalous misstatement is the auditor's best estimate of misstatement in the population. If the total exceeds tolerable misstatement, the sample does not provide a reasonable basis for conclusions about the population. The closer the total figure is to tolerable misstatement, the more likely it is that actual misstatement in the population could exceed tolerable misstatement. The auditor must therefore also consider the results of other audit procedures to assist in determining the risk that actual misstatement in the population exceeds tolerable misstatement. The risk may be reduced if additional audit evidence is obtained.

The auditor must also evaluate whether the use of sampling has provided a reasonable basis for conclusions about the population from which the sample was drawn. If the conclusion is that sampling has not provided this, the auditor may request management to investigate misstatements that have been identified and make any necessary adjustments, or tailor the nature, timing and extent of further audit procedures to best achieve the assurance required.

3.7 Summary

Key stages in the sampling process are as follows.

- Determining **objectives and characteristics of the population**
- Determining **sample size**
- Choosing method of **sample selection**
- **Projecting errors** and **evaluating** the **results**

Being able to apply the techniques of audit sampling discussed in this section will assist you in achieving PER objective 17 on preparing for and collecting evidence for audit.

4 Computer-assisted audit techniques Pilot paper, Dec 07, June 09

AST FORWARD

CAATs are the use of computers for audit work. The two most commonly used CAATs are **audit software** and **test data**.

ey term

Computer-assisted audit techniques (CAATs) are the applications of auditing procedures using the computer as an audit tool.

The overall objectives and scope of an audit do not change when an audit is conducted in a computerised environment. However, the application of auditing procedures may require auditors to consider techniques that use the computer as an audit tool. These uses of the computer for audit work are known as **computer-assisted audit techniques** (CAATs).

CAATs may be used in performing various auditing procedures, including the following.

- **Tests of details** of transactions and balances
- **Analytical review procedures**
- **Tests of computer information system controls**

The advantages of using CAATs are:

- Auditors can test programme controls as well as general internal controls associated with computers.
- Auditors can test a greater number of items more quickly and accurately than would be the case otherwise.
- Auditors can test transactions rather than paper records of transactions that could be incorrect.
- CAATs are cost-effective in the long-term if the client does not change its systems.
- Results from CAATs can be compared with results from traditional testing – if the results correlate, overall confidence is increased.

The major steps to be undertaken by the auditors in the application of a CAAT are as follows.

- **Set the objective** of the CAAT application
- **Determine** the **content** and **accessibility** of the entity's files
- **Define** the **transaction types** to be tested
- **Define** the **procedures** to be performed on the data
- **Define** the **output requirements**
- **Identify** the audit and computer **personnel** who may participate in the design and application of the CAAT
- **Refine** the estimates of **costs** and **benefits**
- Ensure that the **use of the CAAT is properly controlled** and **documented**
- Arrange the **administrative activities**, including the necessary skills and computer facilities
- Execute the **CAAT application**
- **Evaluate the results**

There are two particularly common types of CAAT, **audit software** and **test data**.

Exam focus point

Use of computers on audits is common practice. The examiner expects you to consider the computer aspects of auditing as a matter of course. Therefore in answering questions on obtaining evidence, remember to include reference to CAATs if they seem relevant. There is a very useful article on auditing in a computerised environment in the August 2009 edition of *Student Accountant* which you should read (it is also accessible on the ACCA's website).

4.1 Audit software

Key term

Audit software consists of computer programs used by the auditors, as part of their auditing procedures, to process data of audit significance from the entity's accounting system. It may consist of generalised audit software or custom audit software. Audit software is used for substantive procedures.

Generalised audit software allows auditors to perform tests on computer files and databases, such as reading and extracting data from a client's systems for further testing, selecting data that meets certain criteria, performing arithmetic calculations on data, facilitating audit sampling and producing documents and reports. Examples of generalised audit software are ACT and IDEA.

Custom audit software is written by auditors for specific tasks when generalised audit software cannot be used.

The following table provides some examples of the use of audit software in the course of an audit.

Audit software: examples of use
• Perform calculations and comparisons in analytical procedures
• Sampling programs to extract data for audit testing, e.g. select a sample of receivables for confirmation
• Scan a file to ensure that all documents in a series have been accounted for or to search for large and unusual items
• Compare data elements in different files for agreement (e.g. prices on sales invoices to authorised prices in master file)
• Reperform calculations e.g. totalling sales ledger
• Prepare documents and reports e.g. produce receivables' confirmation letters and monthly statements

4.2 Test data

Key term

Test data techniques are used in conducting audit procedures by entering data (eg a sample of transactions) into an entity's computer system, and comparing the results obtained with pre-determined results. Test data is used for tests of controls.

Examples include:

(a) Test data used to test **specific controls** in computer programs such as on-line password and data access controls.

(b) Test transactions selected from previously processed transactions or created by the auditors to test **specific processing characteristics** of an entity's computer system. Such transactions are generally processed separately from the entity's normal processing. Test data can for example be used to check the controls that prevent the processing of **invalid data** by entering data with say a non-existent customer code or worth an unreasonable amount, or a transaction which may if processed break customer credit limits.

(c) Test transactions used in an **integrated test facility**. This is where a 'dummy' unit (eg a department or employee) is established, and to which test transactions are posted during the normal processing cycle.

A significant problem with test data is that any resulting corruption of data files has to be corrected. This is difficult with modern real-time systems, which often have built-in (and highly desirable) controls to ensure that data entered **cannot** be easily removed without leaving a mark.

Other problems with **test data** are that it only tests the operation of the system at a **single point of time**, and auditors are only testing controls in the programs being run and controls which they know about. The problems involved mean that test data is being used less as a CAAT.

One of the PER performance objectives is to use information and communications technology (objective 6). The use of CAATs by you during an audit assignment will help to achieve this objective.

5 Using the work of others **Pilot paper, Dec 08**

External auditors may make use of the work of an **auditor's expert**, **internal auditors** and **service organisations** and their auditors when carrying out audit procedures.

5.1 Using the work of an expert

Key terms

An **auditor's expert** is an individual or organisation who has expertise in a field other than auditing or accounting, whose work in that field is used by the auditor to assist the auditor in obtaining sufficient appropriate audit evidence. An auditor's expert may be an auditor's internal expert (partner or staff, including temporary staff, of the auditor's firm or network firm) or an auditor's external expert.

Management's expert is an individual or organisation having expertise in a field other than auditing or accounting, whose work in that field is used by the entity to assist the entity in preparing the financial statements.

Professional audit staff are highly trained and educated, but their experience and training is limited to accountancy and audit matters. In certain situations it will therefore be necessary to employ an **auditor's expert**. Guidance on this area is provided by ISA 620 *Using the work of an auditor's expert*. An auditor's expert could be employed by the auditor to assist in the following areas:

- Obtaining an understanding of the entity and its environment, including its internal control
- Identifying and assessing the risks of material misstatement
- Determining and implementing overall responses to assessed risks at the financial statement level
- Designing and performing further audit procedures to respond to assessed risks at the assertion level
- Evaluating the sufficiency and appropriateness of audit evidence obtained in forming an opinion on the financial statements

5.1.1 Competence, capabilities and objectivity of the auditor's expert

ISA 620 requires the auditor to evaluate whether the auditor's expert has the necessary competence, capabilities and objectivity. Where the auditor's expert is external, the evaluation of objectivity will include inquiry of interests and relationships that could create a threat to objectivity.

Information on these areas may come from the following sources:

- **Personal experience** with previous work done by the expert
- **Discussions with the expert**
- **Discussions with other people** who are familiar with the expert's work
- Knowledge of the expert's **qualifications, membership of a professional body or industry association, licence to practise** etc
- **Published papers or books** by the expert
- The auditor's firm's **quality control policies and procedures**

5.1.2 Obtaining an understanding of the field of expertise

The auditor shall obtain a sufficient understanding of the auditor's expert's field of expertise to allow the auditor to determine the nature, scope and objectives of the work and to evaluate the adequacy of the work done.

5.1.3 Agreement

ISA 620 requires the auditor to agree in writing the following with the auditor's expert:

- **Nature, scope and objectives** of the work
- Respective **roles and responsibilities** of the auditor and the auditor's expert
- **Nature, timing and extent of communication** between auditor and auditor's expert, including the **form of any report**
- **Confidentiality requirements**

The agreement between the auditor and the auditor's expert is often in the form of an engagement letter. The Appendix to ISA 620 lists matters to consider for inclusion in the engagement letter

5.1.4 Evaluating the work of the auditor's expert

The auditor shall evaluate the adequacy of the auditor's expert's work, which will include the following:

- The **relevance and reasonableness** of the expert's work and **consistency** with other audit evidence
- The relevance and reasonableness of any **assumptions and methods** used
- The relevance, completeness and accuracy of any **source data** used

If the auditor's evaluation results in a conclusion that the expert's work is not adequate, the auditor must agree on the nature and extent of further work to be done by the expert, and perform additional audit procedures that may be necessary in the circumstances.

5.1.5 Reference to the auditor's expert in the auditor's report

The auditor must not refer to the work of an auditor's expert in the auditor's report containing an unmodified opinion (unless required by law or regulation). If the auditor makes reference to the work of an auditor's expert in the auditor's report because it is relevant to understanding a modification to the opinion, the auditor must state in the auditor's report that this reference does not reduce the auditor's responsibility for the opinion.

5.2 Using the work of internal audit

ISA 610 *Using the work of internal auditors* provides guidance to the external auditor when the external auditor has determined that the internal audit function is likely to be relevant to the audit. The objectives of the auditor are to determine whether and to what extent the work of internal auditors can be used, and if so, whether the work is adequate for the audit. Although the work of internal audit may be used for the purposes of the external audit, it is important to note that the external auditor has sole responsibility for the audit opinion expressed on the financial statements.

5.2.1 Scope and objectives of internal auditing

As we discussed in Chapter 5, the scope and objectives of internal auditing vary widely. Normally however, internal audit operates in one or more of the following broad areas.

- Monitoring of internal control
- Examination of financial and operating information
- Review of operating activities
- Review of compliance with laws and regulations
- Risk management
- Governance

5.2.2 Understanding and preliminary assessment of the role and scope of internal audit

An effective internal audit function may reduce, modify or alter the timing of external audit procedures, but it can **never** eliminate them entirely. Even where the internal audit function is deemed ineffective, it may still be useful to be aware of the conclusions formed. The effectiveness of internal audit will have a great impact on how the external auditors assess the whole control system and the assessment of audit risk.

The external auditor shall determine whether the work of internal auditors is likely to be **adequate** for the audit and if so, the **planned effect** of this work on the nature, timing or extent of the external auditor's procedures.

The following important criteria will be considered by the external auditors when determining if the work of internal auditors is likely to be adequate.

ASSESSMENT OF INTERNAL AUDIT	
Objectivity of function	Consider the **status** of the internal audit function, to whom it **reports**, any **conflicting responsibilities**, any **constraints or restrictions**, whether those charged with governance oversee **employment decisions** regarding internal auditors, whether management acts on **recommendations** made
Technical competence	Consider whether internal auditors are **members of relevant professional bodies**, have adequate **technical training and proficiency**, whether there are **established policies for hiring and training**
Due professional care	Consider whether internal audit activities are **properly planned, supervised, reviewed and documented**, the **existence of audit manuals, work programs** and **internal audit documentation**
Effective communication	Communication will be most effective when internal auditors are **free to communicate openly** with external auditors and **meetings are held regularly**, the external auditor has **access** to relevant internal audit reports and is informed of any **significant matters**, and the external auditor informs the internal auditors of any **significant matters**.

When determining the planned effect of the work of the internal auditors on the nature, timing or extent of the external auditor's procedures, the external auditor must consider the following:

- **Nature and scope** of specific work performed or to be performed
- **Assessed risks** of material misstatement at assertion level
- **Degree of subjectivity** involved in evaluation of audit evidence gathered by internal auditors

5.2.3 Using the work of internal audit

The external auditors need to **evaluate** and **perform audit procedures** on the work done by internal auditors that they might be able to use, in order to determine its adequacy.

The evaluation includes the following:

- Whether the work was done by internal auditors having **adequate technical training and proficiency**
- Whether the work was **properly supervised, reviewed and documented**
- Whether **adequate audit evidence** was obtained to allow the internal auditors to draw reasonable conclusions
- Whether the **conclusions** reached are **appropriate** and any reports are **consistent** with the results of the work done
- Whether any **exceptions or unusual matters** disclosed are **properly resolved**

The nature, timing and extent of the audit procedures performed on specific work of the internal auditors will depend upon the external auditor's assessment of the risk of material misstatement of the area concerned, the evaluation of internal audit and the evaluation of the specific work of the internal auditors. Audit procedures might include:

- Examination of items **already examined** by the internal auditors
- Examination of **other similar items**
- **Observation of procedures** performed by the internal auditors

5.2.4 Documentation of work

ISA 610 requires the external auditors to document conclusions about the evaluation of the adequacy of the work of the internal auditors and any audit procedures performed by the external auditors on that work.

5.3 Service organisations

FAST FORWARD

A **service organisation** provides services to user entities. There may be special considerations for the auditor of a user entity when that entity makes use of a service organisation.

Key terms

A **service organisation** is a third party organisation that provides services to user entities that are part of those entities' information systems relevant to financial reporting.

A **user entity** is an entity that uses a service organisation and whose financial statements are being audited.

A **user auditor** is an auditor who audits and reports on the financial statements of a user entity.

A **service auditor** is an auditor who, at the request of the service organisation, provides an assurance report on the controls of a service organisation.

ISA 402 *Audit considerations relating to an entity using a service organisation* provides guidance to auditors whose clients uses such an organisation. It expands on how the user auditor obtains an understanding of the user entity, including internal control sufficient to identify and assess the risks of material misstatement and in designing and performing further audit procedures responsive to those risks.

A client may use a service organisation such as one that executes transactions and maintains related accountability or records transactions and processes related data. Many companies now outsource some aspects of their business activities to external service organisations. Examples relevant to the independent auditors include:

- Payroll processing
- Maintenance of accounting records

5.3.1 Understanding the services provided

User auditors must obtain an understanding of the services provided by the service organisation in accordance with ISA 315. This understanding must include the following:

- Nature of services provided and the significance of these to the user entity, including effect on user entity's internal control
- Nature and materiality of transactions processed or financial reporting processes affected
- Degree of interaction
- Nature of relationship including contractual terms

When obtaining an understanding of the internal control relevant to the audit, the user auditor must evaluate the design and implementation of relevant controls at the user entity that relate to the services provided by the service organisation.

The user auditor needs to determine whether a sufficient understanding of the nature and significance of the services provided and their effect on internal control has been obtained to allow for the identification and assessment of risks of material misstatement in the financial statements.

If the user auditor cannot get this understanding from the user entity, the understanding needs to be obtained from one or more of the following procedures:

- Obtaining a type 1 report (report on description and design of controls at a service organisation) or type 2 report (report on the description, design and operating effectiveness of controls at a service organisation) from a service auditor, if available
- Contacting the service organisation through the user entity
- Visiting the service organisation and performing necessary procedures
- Using another auditor to perform necessary procedures

If the user auditor uses a type 1 or type 2 report to obtain an understanding of the services, the auditor must be satisfied as to the service auditor's professional competence and independence, and the adequacy of standards used.

5.3.2 Responding to the assessed risks of material misstatement

In responding to the assessed risks in accordance with ISA 330, the user auditor must:

(a) Determine whether **sufficient appropriate audit evidence** concerning the relevant financial statement assertions is available from records held at the user entity; and if not

(b) Perform further audit procedures to obtain sufficient appropriate audit evidence or use another auditor to perform those procedures at the service organisation on the user auditor's behalf.

5.3.3 Reporting by the user auditor

The user auditor is always **solely responsible** for the auditor's opinion. He must be assured that he has gained sufficient appropriate audit evidence to form an opinion on the financial statements and he must then express his opinion in the auditor's report. The user auditor must therefore not refer to the work of a service auditor in the user auditor's report if it contains an unmodified opinion (unless required by law or regulation). If the user auditor makes reference to the work of a service auditor in the user auditor's report because it is relevant to understanding a modification to the opinion, the user auditor must state in the user auditor's report that this reference does not reduce the user auditor's responsibility for the opinion.

Chapter Roundup

- Auditors need to obtain **sufficient appropriate audit evidence** to support the financial statement assertions. Substantive procedures aim to obtain that evidence.
- Substantive tests are designed to discover errors or omissions.
- Analytical procedures are used at all stages of the audit, including as substantive procedures. When using analytical procedures as **substantive tests**, auditors must consider the information available, assessing its **availability, relevance** and **comparability.**
- When auditing **accounting estimates** auditors must:
  - Test the management process
  - Use an independent estimate
  - Review subsequent events

  in order to assess whether the estimates are reasonable.
- Auditors usually seek evidence from less than 100% of items of the balance or transaction being tested by using **sampling techniques**.
- CAATs are the use of computers for audit work. The two most commonly used CAATs are **audit software** and **test data**.
- External auditors may make use of the work of an **auditor's expert**, **internal auditors** and **service organisations** and their auditors when carrying out audit procedures.
- A **service organisation** provides services to user entities. There may be special considerations for the auditor of a user entity when that entity makes use of a service organisation.

Quick Quiz

1 Link the type of account with the purpose of the primary test in directional testing.

(a)	Assets	(i)	Overstatement
(b)	Liabilities	(ii)	Overstatement
(c)	Income	(iii)	Understatement
(d)	Expense	(iv)	Understatement

2 Identify the significant relationships in the list of items below.

(a)	payables	(b)	interest	(c)	purchases	(d)	sales
(e)	amortisation	(f)	loans	(g)	receivables	(h)	intangibles

3 Complete the definition.

An accounting estimate is an .... of the .... of an item in the absence of a .... of measurement.

4 Give three examples of sample selection methods that can be used in audit sampling.

(1) ....

(2) ....

(3) ....

5 Name two types of CAAT that are commonly used.

(1) ....

(2) ....

6 There are four criteria for evaluating the internal audit function. State these criteria.

(1) ....

(2) ....

(3) ....

(4) ....

7 If the auditor relies on the work of an auditor's expert or service organisation, he may refer to that individual or organisation in the auditor's report and share responsibility with them.

True ☐

False ☐

Answers to Quick Quiz

1 (a) (i)
(b) (iii)
(c) (ii)
(d) (iv)

2 (a) (c)
(b) (f)
(d) (g)
(e) (h)

3 approximation, amount, precise means

4 From:

- Random
- Systematic
- Haphazard
- Block
- Monetary unit sampling

5 (1) Audit software

(2) Test data

6 (1) Objectivity of function
(2) Technical competence
(3) Due professional care
(4) Effective communication

7 False

Now try the questions below from the Exam Question Bank

Number	Level	Marks	Time
Q14	Examination	20	36 mins
Q15	Examination	20	36 mins

12 Non-current assets

Topic list	Syllabus reference
1 Tangible non-current assets	E3
2 Intangible non-current assets	E3

Introduction

This chapter covers the audit of non-current assets, a key area of the statement of financial position.

It highlights the key objectives for each major component of non-current assets. You must understand what objectives the various audit tests are designed to achieve in relation to the financial statement assertions. Objectives of particular significance for tangible non-current assets are rights and obligations (ownership), existence and valuation.

Valuation is the other important assertion. The auditors will concentrate on testing any external valuations made during the year, and also whether other values appear reasonable given asset usage and condition. A very important aspect of testing valuation is reviewing depreciation rates. A topic we covered in chapter 11, using the work of an expert, may well be important in the audit of non-current assets in respect of valuation.

Study guide

		Intellectual level
E3	**The audit of specific items: (e) non-current assets** (i) Evidence in relation to non-current assets, and (iii) The related income statement entries	
•	Explain the purpose of substantive procedures in relation to financial statement assertions	2
•	Explain the substantive procedures used in auditing each balance	2
•	Tabulate those substantive procedures in a work program	2

Exam guide

In the audit of non-current assets you may be asked to list and explain audit procedures you would perform to confirm specific assertions set out in the question. When doing so, you must explain why you are carrying out that procedure.

The December 2008 paper had a four mark part in question 2 on four assertions relevant to the audit of tangible non-current assets and an audit procedure for each assertion listed.

1 Tangible non-current assets

Dec 08

FAST FORWARD

Key areas when testing **tangible non-current assets** are:

- **Confirmation** of ownership
- **Inspection** of non-current assets
- **Valuation** by third parties
- **Adequacy** of **depreciation** rates

1.1 Audit objectives for tangible non-current assets

Financial statement assertion	Audit objective
Existence and occurrence	– Additions represent assets acquired in the year and disposal represent assets sold o scrapped in the year – Recorded assets represent those in use at the year-end
Completeness	– All additions and disposals that occurred in the year have been recorded – Balances represent assets in use at the year-end
Rights and obligations	– The entity has rights to the assets purchased and those recorded at the year-end
Accuracy, classification and valuation	– Non-current assets are correctly stated at cost less accumulated depreciation – Additions and disposals are correctly recorded
Assertions relating to presentation and disclosure (occurrence and rights and obligations, completeness, classification and understandability, accuracy and valuation)	– Disclosures relating to cost, additions and disposals, depreciation policies, useful lives and assets held under finance leases are adequate and in accordance with accounting standards

1.2 Internal control considerations

The **non-current asset register** is a very important aspect of the internal control system. It enables assets to be identified, and comparisons between the general ledger, non-current asset register and the assets themselves provide **evidence** that the assets are **completely recorded**.

Another significant control is procedures over acquisitions and disposals, that acquisitions are properly **authorised**, **disposals** are **authorised** and **proceeds accounted for**.

Other significant aspects are whether:

- **Security arrangements** over non-current assets are **sufficient**.
- **Non-current assets** are **maintained properly**.
- **Depreciation** is **reviewed every year**.
- **All income** is **collected** from **income-yielding assets**.

1.3 Audit procedures for tangible non-current assets

AUDIT PLAN: TANGIBLE NON-CURRENT ASSETS	
COMPLETENESS	• **Obtain** or **prepare** a **summary** of tangible non-current assets showing how: – **Gross book value** – **Accumulated depreciation** – **Net book value** **reconcile** with the **opening position**. • **Compare non-current assets** in the general ledger with the **non-current assets register** and **obtain explanations** for **differences**. • For a sample of assets which physically exist agree that they are **recorded** in the **non-current asset register**. • If a non-current asset register is not kept, **obtain** a **schedule** showing the original costs and present depreciated value of major non-current assets. • **Reconcile** the **schedule** of non-current assets with the **general ledger**.
EXISTENCE	• **Confirm** that the **company physically inspects** all items in the non-current asset register each year. • **Inspect assets**, concentrating on high value items and additions in-year. Confirm that items inspected: – Exist – Are in use – Are in good condition – Have correct serial numbers • **Review records** of **income-yielding assets**. • **Reconcile** opening and closing **vehicles** by numbers as well as amounts.
VALUATION	• **Verify valuation** to valuation certificate. • **Consider reasonableness** of **valuation**, reviewing: – Experience of valuer – Scope of work – Methods and assumptions used – Valuation bases are in line with accounting standards • **Reperform** calculation of revaluation surplus.

AUDIT PLAN: TANGIBLE NON-CURRENT ASSETS	
	• Confirm whether valuations of all assets that have been revalued have been **updated regularly** (full valuation every five years and an interim valuation in year three generally) by inquiries of Finance Director and inspection of previous financial statements. • **Inspect** draft accounts to check that client has **recognised** in the **statement of comprehensive income** revaluation losses unless there is a credit balance in respect of that asset in equity, in which case it should be debited to equity to cancel the credit. All revaluation gains should be credited to equity. • **Review depreciation** rates applied in relation to: – Asset lives – Residual values – Replacement policy – Past experience of gains and losses on disposal – Consistency with prior years and accounting policy – Possible obsolescence • **Review** non-current assets register to ensure that **depreciation** has been **charged on all assets** with a limited useful life. • For **revalued assets**, ensure that the charge for **depreciation** is based on the revalued amount by recalculating it for a sample of revalued assets. • **Reperform calculation** of depreciation rates to ensure it is correct. • **Compare ratios** of depreciation to non-current assets (by category) with: – Previous years – Depreciation policy rates • **Scrutinise** draft accounts to ensure that **depreciation policies** and rates are **disclosed** in the accounts. • **Review insurance policies** in force for all categories of tangible non-current assets and consider the adequacy of their insured values and check expiry dates.
RIGHTS AND OBLIGATIONS	• **Verify title** to land and buildings by inspection of: – Title deeds – Land registry certificates – Leases • Obtain a certificate from solicitors/bankers: – **Stating purpose** for which the deeds are being held (custody only) – **Stating deeds** are **free** from **mortgage** or **lien**. • **Inspect registration documents** for vehicles held, confirming that they are in client's name. • **Confirm** all vehicles are used for the **client's business**. • **Examine documents** of **title** for other assets (including purchase invoices, architects' certificates, contracts, hire purchase or lease agreements). • **Review for evidence** of charges in statutory books and by company search. • **Review leases** of leasehold properties to ensure that company has fulfilled covenants therein. • **Examine invoices received after year-end, orders** and **minutes** for evidence of capital commitments.

AUDIT PLAN: TANGIBLE NON-CURRENT ASSETS	
ADDITIONS	These tests are to confirm **rights and obligations**, **valuation** and **completeness**. • Verify additions by inspection of architects' certificates, solicitors' completion statements, suppliers' invoices etc. • **Review** capitalisation of expenditure by examining for non-current assets additions and items in relevant expense categories (repairs, motor expenses, sundry expenses) to ensure that: – Capital/revenue distinction is correctly drawn – Capitalisation is in line with consistently applied company policy • **Inspect** non-current asset accounts for a sample of purchases to ensure they have been **properly allocated**. • Check purchases have been **authorised** by directors/senior management by **reviewing board minutes**. • Ensure that appropriate **claims** have been made for **grants**, and grants received and receivable have been received, by **inspecting** claims documentations and bank statements. • Check **additions** have been **recorded** by **scrutinising** the non-current asset register and general ledger.
SELF-CONSTRUCTED ASSETS	These tests are to confirm **valuation** and **completeness**. • **Verify material** and **labour** costs and **overheads** to invoices, wage records etc. • Ensure expenditure has been **analysed correctly** and **properly charged** to capital. • Expenditure should be capitalised if it: – **Enhances** the **economic benefits** of the asset in excess of its previously assessed standard of performance – **Replaces or restores a component** of the asset that has been treated separately for depreciation purposes, and depreciated over its useful economic life – Relates to a **major inspection** or **overhaul** that restores the economic benefits of the asset that have been consumed by the entity, and have already been reflected in depreciation • **Review** costs to ensure that no profit element has been included. • **Review** accounts to ensure that **finance costs** have been **capitalised** or not capitalised on a consistent basis, and costs capitalised in period do not exceed total finance costs for period.
DISPOSALS	These tests are to confirm **rights and obligations**, **completeness**, **occurrence** and **accuracy**. • **Verify disposals** with supporting documentation, checking transfer of title, sales price and dates of completion and payment. • **Recalculate** profit or loss on disposal. • Check that **disposals** have been **authorised** by reviewing boards minutes. • **Consider** whether **proceeds** are **reasonable**. • If the asset was **used as security**, ensure **release from security** has been correctly made.
CLASSIFICATION AND UNDERSTAND-ABILITY	• **Review** non-current asset disclosures in the financial statements to ensure they meet IAS 16 criteria. • For a sample of **fully depreciated assets**, inspect the register to ensure no further depreciation is charged. • **Inspect** draft accounts to ensure that **depreciation policies and rates** are correctly **disclosed**.

Question

You are the manager in charge of the audit of Puppy, a building and construction company, and you are reviewing the non-current asset section of the current audit file for the year ended 30 September 20X5. You find the following five matters which the audit senior has identified as problem areas. He is reviewing the company's proposed treatment of the five transactions in the accounts and is not sure that he has yet carried out sufficient audit work.

(a) During the year Puppy built a new canteen for its own staff at a cost of $450,000. This amount has been included in buildings as at 30 September 20X5.

(b) Loose tools included in the financial statements at a total cost of $166,000 are tools used on two of the construction sites on which Puppy operates. They are classified as non-current assets and depreciated over two years.

(c) A dumper truck, previously written-off in the company's accounting records has been refurbished at a cost of $46,000 and this amount included in plant and machinery as at 30 September 20X5.

(d) The company's main office block has been revalued from $216,000 to $266,000 and this amount included in the statement of financial position as at 30 September 20X5.

(e) A deposit of $20,000 for new equipment has been included under the heading 'plant and machinery' although the final instalment of $35,000 was not paid over until 31 October 20X5, which was the date of delivery of the plant.

You are required, for each of the above matters, to:

(a) Comment on the acceptability of the accounting treatment and disclosure as indicated above.
(b) Outline the audit work and evidence required to substantiate the assets.

Answer

(a) *Acceptability of accounting treatment and disclosure*

(i) *New staff canteen.* The costs of building a new staff canteen can quite properly be capitalised and treated as part of buildings in the balance sheet as work has produced future economic benefits (IAS 16). The company's normal depreciation policy should be applied, subject only to the canteen being completed and in use at the year-end.

(ii) *Loose tools.* Loose tools tend to have a very limited life and to be immaterial in value individually. For these reasons any capitalisation policy must be extremely prudent. The acceptability of this accounting treatment would depend on the policy in previous years and normal practice within the industry.

(iii) *Dumper truck.* The refurbishment costs have obviously extended the useful life of this asset and it therefore seems reasonable to capitalise the expenditure. Depreciation should be charged on the refurbishment costs over the estimated remaining useful life.

(iv) *Revaluation of office block.* The revaluation of property is acceptable, but the auditors will need to ensure that the company complies with a number of disclosure requirements. A note to the accounts should give details of the revaluation and the name of the valuer. The surplus on revaluation should be transferred to a separate non-distributable reserve in the statement of financial position as part of shareholders' funds. Furthermore, any other assets of a similar nature to this should also be revalued.

(v) *Deposit for new equipment.* As the equipment was not actually in the company's possession and use at the year-end, the deposit should not have been shown as plant and machinery, but rather as a payment on account. If the amount was considered to be material a note to the accounts should give details of this prepayment.

(b) The audit work and evidence required to substantiate each of the assets referred to in (a) above would be as follows.

(i) *New staff canteen*

(1) Physically confirm existence of the asset.

(2) Confirm title to building by reference to central registry certificate.

(3) Ascertain and confirm the details of any security granted over the asset, ensuring that this is properly recorded and disclosed.

(4) Review the detailed costings of the building and obtain explanations for any material variances from the original budget. Particular care should be taken in assessing the reasonableness of any overheads included as an element of cost.

(5) Review the depreciation policy for adequacy and consistency.

(ii) *Loose tools*

(1) Visit the two sites where the loose tools are used to confirm the existence and condition of a sample of them.

(2) Vouch the cost and ownership of the loose tools to purchase invoices and the company's asset register.

(3) Confirm the company's estimate of a two year life for these assets.

(4) Review control procedures for safe custody of the loose tools.

(5) Review the company's policy with regard to scrapping and/or sale of tools no longer required to ensure that any proceeds are properly recorded and the assets register appropriately updated and tools are completely recorded.

(iii) *Dumper truck*

(1) Inspect the truck to confirm its existence and to gain evidence of its valuation by reviewing its condition and the fact that it is still being used.

(2) If the vehicle is used at all on public roads then the vehicle registration document should be inspected as some evidence of title.

(3) Inspect the insurance policy for the truck as evidence of valuation.

(4) Vouch the expenditure on refurbishment to suppliers' invoices or company's payroll records where any of the work has been done by the client's own staff.

(5) Review the depreciation policy and assess for reasonableness by discussion with management and past experience of similar vehicles.

(iv) *Revaluation of office block*

(1) Inspect the building to confirm its existence and state of repair.

(2) Examine documents of title to confirm ownership.

(3) Enquire about any charges on the building and confirm that these have been properly recorded and disclosed.

(4) Review the valuer's certificate and agree to the amount used in the financial statements, with consideration also being given to his qualifications, experience and reputation.

(5) Assess the reasonableness of the valuation by comparison with any similar properties which may have recently changed hands on the open market.

(v) *Deposit for new equipment*

(1) Agree the payment of the deposit to the contract for purchase of the equipment.

(2) Confirm the existence of the plant following its delivery on 31 October 20X5 as it is unlikely that the audit work will have been completed by that date.

Exam focus point

Note that inspection of a building's title deeds does **not** give audit evidence about **existence** and if there is doubt that a building actually exists, the auditors should physically inspect it.

2 Intangible non-current assets

FAST FORWARD

Key assertions for intangible non-current assets are **existence** and **valuation**.

The key assertions relating to intangibles are **existence** (not so much 'do they exist?', but 'are they genuinely assets?') and **valuation**. They will therefore be audited with reference to criteria laid down in the financial reporting standards. As only purchased goodwill or intangibles with a readily ascertainable market value can be capitalised, **audit evidence should be available** (purchase invoices or specialist valuations). The audit of **amortisation** will be similar to the audit of depreciation.

AUDIT PLAN: OTHER NON-CURRENT ASSETS	
Goodwill	• Agree the consideration to sales agreement by **inspection**. • Consider whether asset valuation is reasonable. • Agree that the calculation is correct by **recalculation**. • **Review** the impairment review and **discuss** with management. • Ensure valuation of goodwill is reasonable/there has been no impairment not adjusted through **discussion** with management.
Research and development costs	• Confirm that capitalised development costs conform to IAS 38 criteria by **inspecting** details of projects and **discussions** with technical managers. • Confirm feasibility and viability by **inspection** of budgets. • **Recalculate** amortisation calculation, to ensure it commences with production/is reasonable. • **Inspect** invoices to verify expenditure incurred on R&D projects.
Other intangibles	• Agree purchased intangibles to purchase documentation agreement by **inspection**. • **Inspect** specialist valuation of intangibles and ensure it is reasonable. • Review amortisation calculations and ensure they are correct by **recalculation**.

Chapter Roundup

- Key areas when testing **tangible non-current assets** are:
  - **Confirmation** of ownership
  - **Inspection** of non-current assets
  - **Valuation** by third parties
  - **Adequacy** of **depreciation** rates
- Key assertions for intangible non-current assets are **existence** and **valuation**.

Quick Quiz

1 State the key financial statement assertions for tangible non-current assets.

2 Complete the table, showing which tests are designed to provide evidence over which financial statement assertion.

Completeness	**Existence**
Valuation	**Rights and obligations**

(a) Inspect assets.

(b) Verify to valuation certificate.

(c) Inspect title deeds.

(d) Compare assets in ledger to non-current asset register.

(e) Review depreciation rates.

(f) Verify material on self-constructed asset to invoices.

(g) Examine invoices after the year-end.

(h) Review repairs in general ledger.

3 Which of the following tests would provide audit evidence as to the existence of a tangible non-current asset?

(a) Inspecting board minutes approving authorisation of the asset
(b) Physically inspecting the asset
(c) Reviewing the non-current asset register for inclusion of the asset
(d) Inspecting the invoice and purchase order documentation of the asset

4 Inspecting the title deeds of a building provides audit evidence concerning which one of the following financial statement assertions?

(a) Existence
(b) Valuation
(c) Rights and obligations
(d) Completeness

5 What are the key financial statement assertions for other non-current assets?

Answers to Quick Quiz

1 Rights and obligations, existence, valuation, completeness

2

Completeness	Existence
(d) Compare assets in ledger to register. (h) Review repairs in general ledger.	(a) Inspect assets.
Valuation	**Rights and obligations**
(b) Verify to valuation certificate. (e) Review valuation rates. (f) Verify material on self-constructed assets to invoice.	(c) Inspect title deeds. (g) Examine invoices after the year-end.

3 (b) Physically inspecting the asset

4 (c) Rights and obligations

5 Existence, valuation

Now try the question below from the Exam Question Bank

Number	Level	Marks	Time
Q16	Examination	20	36 mins

13

Inventory

Topic list	Syllabus reference
1 Introduction to auditing inventory	E3
2 Accounting for inventory	E3
3 Audit procedures for inventory	E3
4 The physical inventory count	E3
5 Cut-off	E3
6 Valuation	E3

Introduction

No area of the statement of financial position creates more potential problems for the auditors than that of inventory.

Closing inventory does not normally form an integrated part of the double entry bookkeeping system and hence a misstatement (under or overstatement) may not be detected from tests in other audit areas.

The four main assertions relating to the substantive audit of inventory (completeness, existence, rights and obligations, and valuation) require careful consideration.

The auditor's attendance at the inventory count is a particularly important part of the audit of inventory. This is because the inventory count gives evidence about the existence and completeness of inventory, and a review of the condition of the inventory is an important part of assessing whether it has been correctly valued.

Study guide

		Intellectual level
E3	**The audit of specific items: (b) inventory** (i) Inventory counting procedures in relation to year-end and continuous inventory systems (ii) Cut-off (iii) Auditor's attendance at inventory counting (iv) Direct confirmation of inventory held by third parties (v) Other evidence in relation to inventory	
•	Explain the purpose of substantive procedures in relation to financial statement assertions	2
•	Explain the substantive procedures used in auditing each balance	2
•	Tabulate those substantive procedures in a work program	2

Exam guide

You may be asked to list and explain audit procedures you would perform to confirm specific assertions relating to inventory. As inventory is often the most difficult area in practice for auditors it is also very important in the syllabus. The December 2007 paper had two marks in question 1 on audit procedures to perform before attending the inventory count and two marks for stating a substantive audit procedure at the inventory count.

1 Introduction to auditing inventory

FAST FORWARD

The key assertions relating to inventory are:

- **Existence**
- **Completeness**
- **Rights and obligations**
- **Valuation**
- **Cut-off**

The audit of inventory can pose problems for auditors as a result of its nature and potential material value on the statement of financial position. The audit approach taken depends on the auditor's assessment of the controls in place. In this chapter we focus on the **substantive** audit of inventory.

The following table demonstrates the audit objectives for inventory and the related financial statement assertions. The audit procedures described in the remainder of this chapter are undertaken to provide audit evidence to support these assertions.

Financial statement assertion	Audit objective
Existence and occurrence	– Recorded purchases and sales represent inventories bought and sold. – Inventory on the statement of financial position physically exists.
Completeness	– All purchases and sales are recorded. – All inventory at year-end is included on the statement of financial position.
Rights and obligations	– The entity has rights to inventory recorded in the period and at the year-end.

Financial statement assertion	Audit objective
Accuracy, classification and valuation	– Costs are accurately determined in accordance with accounting standards. – Inventory is recorded at year-end at the lower of cost and net realisable value.
Cut-off	– All purchases and sales of inventories are recorded in the correct period.
Assertions relating to presentation and disclosure (classification and understandability, completeness, accuracy and valuation)	– Inventory is properly classified in the accounts. – Disclosures relating to classification and valuation are adequate and in accordance with accounting standards.

2 Accounting for inventory

FAST FORWARD

The **valuation** and **disclosure** rules for inventory are laid down in IAS 2 *Inventories*. Inventory should be valued at the **lower** of cost and net realisable value.

Key terms

Cost is defined by IAS 2 as comprising all costs of purchase and other costs incurred in bringing inventory to its present location and condition.

Net realisable value is the estimated selling price in the ordinary course of business, less the estimated costs of completion and the estimated costs necessary to make the sale.

Production costs (costs of conversion) include:

(a) Costs specifically attributable to units of production
(b) Production overheads
(c) Other overheads attributable to bringing the product or service to its present location and condition

3 Audit procedures for inventory

The following table sets out audit procedures to test year-end inventory. The physical inventory count is discussed in detail in section 4 of this chapter, and cut-off and valuation are expanded upon in sections 5 and 6.

AUDIT PLAN: INVENTORY	
COMPLETENESS	• Complete the **disclosure checklist** to ensure that all the disclosures relevant to inventory have been made. • **Trace** test counts to the detailed inventory listing. • Where inventory is held in **third party locations**, **physically inspect** this inventory or **review confirmations** received from the third party and match to the general ledger. • **Compare** the gross profit % to the previous year or industry data.
EXISTENCE	• Observe the **physical inventory count** (see section 4 for details of attendance at the inventory count).
RIGHTS AND OBLIGATIONS	• Verify that any **inventory held for third parties** is not included in the year-end inventory figure by being appropriately segregated during the inventory count. • For any **'bill-and-hold' inventory** (i.e. where the inventory has been sold but is being held by the entity until the customer requires it), identify such inventory and ensure that it is segregated during the inventory count so that it is not included in the year-end inventory figure.

AUDIT PLAN: INVENTORY	
	• Confirm that any inventory held at **third party locations** is included in the year-end inventory figure by reviewing the inventory listing.
VALUATION AND ALLOCATION	• Obtain a copy of the inventory listing and **agree** the totals to the general ledger. • **Cast** the inventory listing to ensure it is mathematically correct. • **Vouch** a sample of inventory items to suppliers' invoices to ensure it is correctly valued. • Where **standard costing** is used, test a sample of inventory to ensure it is correctly valued. • For **materials**, agree the valuation of raw materials to invoices and price lists. • Confirm that an appropriate **basis of valuation** (eg FIFO) is being used by discussing with management. • For **labour** costs, agree costs to wage records. • **Review** standard labour costs in the light of actual costs and production. • **Reconcile** labour hours to time summaries. • Make **inquiries of management** to ascertain any slow-moving or obsolete inventory that should be written down. • **Examine prices** at which finished goods have been sold after the year-end to ascertain whether any finished goods need to be written down. • If significant levels of finished goods remain unsold for an unusual period of time, **discuss** with management and consider the need to make allowance. • **Compare** the gross profit % to the previous year or industry data. • **Compare** raw material, finished goods and total inventory turnover to the previous year and industry averages. • **Compare** inventory days to the previous year and industry average. • **Compare** the current year standard costs to the previous year after considering current conditions. • **Compare** actual manufacturing overhead costs with budgeted or standard manufacturing overhead costs.
CUT-OFF	• Note the numbers of the **last GDNs and GRNs** before the year-end and the **first GDNs and GRNs** after the year-end and check that these have been included in the correct financial year.
ACCURACY	• Obtain a copy of the inventory listing and **cast** it, and test the mathematical extensions of quantity multiplied by price. • **Trace** test counts back to the inventory listing. • If the entity has adjusted the general ledger to agree with the physical inventory count amounts, **agree** the two amounts. • Where a **continuous (perpetual) inventory system** is maintained, agree the total on the inventory listing to the continuous inventory records, using CAATs.
OCCURRENCE AND RIGHTS AND OBLIGATIONS	• **Inquire** of management and **review** any loan agreements and board minutes for evidence that inventory has been pledged or assigned. • Inquire of management about warranty obligation issues.

CLASSIFICATION AND UNDERSTANDABILITY	• **Review** the inventory listing to ensure that inventory has been properly classified between raw materials, work-in-progress and finished goods. • **Read** the notes to the accounts relating to inventory to ensure they are understandable.
ACCURACY AND VALUATION	• **Review** the financial statements to confirm whether the cost method used to value inventory is accurately disclosed. • **Read** the notes to the accounts to ensure that the information is accurate and properly presented at the appropriate amounts.

4 The physical inventory count   Dec 07

Physical inventory count procedures are vital as they provide evidence which cannot be obtained elsewhere or at any other time about the quantities and conditions of inventories and work-in-progress.

ISA 501 *Audit evidence – specific considerations for selected items* provides guidance to auditors on attending the physical inventory count to obtain evidence regarding the existence and condition of inventory.

It states that where inventory is **material**, auditors shall obtain sufficient appropriate audit evidence regarding its **existence** and **condition** by attending the physical inventory count (unless this is impracticable) to do the following:

- Evaluate management's instructions and procedures for recording and controlling the result of the physical inventory count.
- Observe the performance of the count procedures.
- Inspect the inventory.
- Perform test counts.

The auditor shall also perform audit procedures over the entity's final inventory records to determine whether they accurately reflect the count results.

Attendance at the inventory count can serve as either substantive procedures or tests of controls, depending on the auditor's risk assessment, planned approach and specific procedures carried out.

Factors to consider when planning attendance at the inventory count include the following:

- The **risks of material misstatement** of inventory
- **Internal controls** related to inventory
- Whether **adequate procedures** are expected to be established and **proper instructions** issued for counting
- The **timing** of the count
- Whether the entity maintains a **perpetual inventory system**
- **Locations** at which inventory is held (including materiality at different locations)
- Whether the assistance of an **auditor's expert** is required

4.1 The inventory count

A business may count inventory by one or a combination of the following methods.

(a) **Physical inventory counts** at the **year-end**

From the viewpoint of the auditor this is often the best method.

(b) **Physical inventory counts before** or **after** the **year-end**

This will provide audit evidence of varying reliability depending on:

(i) The **length of time** between the physical inventory count and the year-end (the greater the time period, the less the value of audit evidence)

(ii) The **business's system** of **internal controls**

(iii) The **quality of records** of **inventory movements** in the period between the physical inventory count and the year-end

(c) **Perpetual** (or **continuous**) **inventory** where management has a programme of inventory-counting throughout the year

If **perpetual** inventory counting is used, auditors will verify that management:

(a) Ensures that all inventory lines are counted at least once a year

(b) Maintains **adequate inventory records** that are kept up-to-date. Auditors may compare sales and purchase transactions with inventory movements, and carry out other tests on the inventory records, for example, checking casts and classification of inventory.

(c) Has **satisfactory procedures** for **inventory counts** and **test-counting**. Auditors should confirm the inventory count arrangements and instructions are as rigorous as those for a year-end inventory count by reviewing instructions and observing counts. Auditors will be particularly concerned with **cut-off**, that there are no inventory movements whilst the count is taking place, and inventory records are updated up until the time of the inventory count.

(d) **Investigates** and **corrects** all **material differences**. Reasons for differences should be recorded and any necessary corrective action taken. All corrections to inventory movements should be **authorised** by a manager who has not been involved in the detailed work. These procedures are necessary to guard against the possibility that inventory records may be adjusted to conceal shortages. Auditors should check that the procedures are being operated.

AUDIT PLAN: PERPETUAL INVENTORY COUNT

- **Attend** one of the inventory counts (to observe and confirm that instructions are being adhered to).
- **Follow-up** the **inventory counts attended** to compare quantities counted by the auditors with the inventory records, obtaining and verifying explanations for any differences, and checking that the client has reconciled count records with book inventory records.
- **Review** the **year's inventory counts** to confirm the extent of counting, the treatment of discrepancies and the overall accuracy of records (if matters are not satisfactory, auditors will only be able to gain sufficient assurance by a full count at the year-end).
- Assuming a full count is not necessary at the year-end, **compare** the **listing of inventory with the detailed inventory records**, and carry out other procedures (**cut-off, analytical review**) to gain further comfort.

The audit work when perpetual inventory counting is used focuses on tests of controls rather than substantive audit work. Nevertheless, the auditor will also need to do some further substantive audit work on completeness and existence at the year-end.

Attendance at an inventory count gives evidence of the **existence** and apparent **ownership** of inventory. It also gives evidence of the **completeness** of inventory, as do the follow-up tests to ensure all inventory sheets were included in the final count.

4.2 Planning attendance at inventory count

Before the physical inventory count the auditors should ensure audit **coverage** of the **count** is **appropriate**, and that the client's **count instructions** have been reviewed.

AUDIT PLAN: PLANNING INVENTORY COUNT	
Gain knowledge	• **Review** previous year's **arrangements**. • **Discuss with management** inventory count arrangements and significant changes.
Assess key factors	• The **nature** and **volume** of the **inventory** • **Risks** relating to inventory • **Identification** of **high value items** • **Method of accounting for inventory** • **Location** of inventory and how it affects inventory control and recording • **Internal control** and **accounting systems** to identify potential areas of difficulty
Plan procedures	• **Ensure** a **representative selection** of **locations**, **inventory** and **procedures** are covered. • Ensure sufficient attention is given to **high value items**. • **Arrange to obtain** from any **third parties' confirmation** of inventory they hold. • Consider the need for **expert help**.
REVIEW OF INVENTORY COUNT INSTRUCTIONS	
Organisation of count	• **Supervision** by senior staff including senior staff not normally involved with inventory • **Tidying** and **marking** inventory to help counting • **Restriction** and **control** of the production process and inventory movements during the count • **Identification of damaged, obsolete, slow-moving, third party** and **returnable** inventory
Counting	• **Systematic counting** to ensure all inventory is counted • Teams of **two counters,** with one counting and the other checking or **two independent counts**
Recording	• **Serial numbering, control** and **return** of all inventory sheets • Inventory sheets being **completed** in **ink** and **signed** • **Information** to be recorded on the **count records** (location and identity, count units, quantity counted, conditions of items, stage reached in production process) • Recording of **quantity, conditions** and **stage of production** of **work-in-progress** • Recording of last numbers of **goods inwards** and **outwards** records and of internal transfer records • **Reconciliation** with **inventory records** and **investigation** and correction of any **differences**

4.3 Attendance at inventory count

During the count the auditors should **observe** whether the count is being carried out according to instructions, carry out **test counts**, and watch out for **third party inventory** and **slow moving inventory** and **cut-off problems.**

AUDIT PLAN: ATTENDANCE AT INVENTORY COUNT
• **Observe** whether the **client's staff** are following instructions as this will help to ensure the count is complete and accurate. • **Perform test counts** to ensure procedures and internal controls are working properly. • **Ensure** that the **procedures** for **identifying damaged, obsolete** and **slow-moving** inventory operate properly; the auditors should obtain information about the inventory's condition, age, usage and in the case of work-in-progress, its stage of completion to ensure that it is later valued appropriately. • **Confirm** that **inventory held** on behalf of **third parties** is separately identified and accounted for so that inventory is not overstated. • **Conclude** whether the **count** has been **properly carried out** and is sufficiently reliable as a basis for determining the existence of inventories. • **Consider** whether any **amendment** is necessary to subsequent **audit procedures**. • **Gain** an **overall impression** of the levels and values of inventories held so that the auditors may, in due course, judge whether the figure for inventory appearing in the financial statements is reasonable.

When carrying out test counts the auditors should select items from the count records and from the physical inventory and check one to the other, to confirm the accuracy of the count records. These two-way tests provide evidence for completeness and existence. The auditors should concentrate on high value inventory. If the results of the test counts are not satisfactory, the auditors may request that inventory is recounted.

The auditors' working papers should include:

- Details of their **observations** and **tests**
- The manner in which **points** that are **relevant** and **material** to the inventory being counted or measured have been dealt with by the client
- Instances where the **client's procedures** have **not been satisfactorily carried out**
- **Items for subsequent testing**, such as photocopies of (or extracts from) rough inventory sheets
- **Details** of the **sequence** of **inventory sheets**
- The **auditors' conclusions**

4.4 After the inventory count

After the count the auditors should check that **final inventory sheets** have been **properly compiled** from count records and that **book inventory** has been **appropriately adjusted**.

After the count, the matters recorded in the auditors' working papers at the time of the count or measurement should be followed up. Key tests include the following.

AUDIT PLAN: FOLLOWING UP THE INVENTORY COUNT
• **Trace items** that were **test counted** to final inventory sheets.
• **Observe whether all count** records have been **included** in final inventory sheets.
• **Inspect final inventory sheets** to ensure they are **supported by** count records.
• **Ensure** that **continuous inventory records** have been **adjusted** to the amounts physically counted or measured, and that differences have been investigated.
• **Confirm cut-off** by using details of the last serial number of goods inwards and outwards notes and of movements during the count.
• **Review replies** from **third parties** about inventory held by or for them.
• **Confirm** the client's final **valuation** of inventory has been calculated correctly.
• **Follow up queries** and **notify problems** to management.

4.5 Inventory held by third parties

Where the entity has inventory that is held by third parties and which is material to the financial statements, the auditor shall obtain sufficient appropriate audit evidence by performing one or both of the following:

- **Direct confirmation** from the third party regarding quantities and condition (in accordance with ISA 505 *External confirmations*)
- **Inspection** or other **appropriate audit procedures** (if third party's integrity and objectivity are doubtful, for example)

The other appropriate audit procedures referred to above could include the following:

- Attending, or arranging for another auditor to attend, the third party's inventory count
- Obtaining another auditor's report on the adequacy of the third party's internal control for ensuring that inventory is properly counted and adequately safeguarded
- Inspecting documentation in respect of third party inventory (e.g. warehouse receipts)
- Requesting confirmation from other parties when inventory has been pledged as collateral

Question

In connection with your examination of the financial statements of Camry Products Co, a limited liability company, for the year ended 31 March 20X9, you are reviewing the plans for a physical inventory count at the company's warehouse on 31 March 20X9. The company assembles domestic appliances, and inventory of finished appliances, unassembled parts and sundry inventory are stored in the warehouse which is adjacent to the company's assembly plant. The plant will continue to produce goods during the inventory count until 5pm on 31 March 20X9. On 30 March 20X9, the warehouse staff will deliver the estimated quantities of unassembled parts and sundry inventory which will be required for production for 31 March 20X9; however, emergency requisitions by the factory will be filled on 31 March. During the inventory count, the warehouse staff will continue to receive parts and sundry inventory, and to dispatch finished appliances. Appliances which are completed on 31 March 20X9 will remain in the assembly plant until after the count has been completed.

Required

(a) List the principal procedures which the auditors should carry out when planning attendance at a company's physical inventory count.

(b) Describe the procedures which Camry Products should establish in order to ensure that all inventory items are counted and that no item is counted twice.

Answer

(a) In planning attendance at a physical inventory count the auditors should:

(i) Review previous year's audit working papers and discuss any developments in the year with management.

(ii) Obtain and review a copy of the company's count instructions.

(iii) Arrange attendance at count planning meetings, with the consent of management.

(iv) Gain an understanding of the nature of the inventory and of any special problems this is likely to present, for example liquid in tanks, scrap in piles.

(v) Consider whether expert involvement is likely to be required as a result of any circumstances noted in (iv) above.

(vi) Obtain a full list of all locations at which inventories are held, including an estimate of the amount and value of inventories held at different locations.

(vii) Using the results of the above steps, plan for audit attendance by appropriately experienced audit staff at all locations where material inventories are held, subject to other factors (for example rotational auditing, reliance on internal controls).

(viii) Consider the impact of internal controls upon the nature and timing of attendance at the count.

(ix) Ascertain whether inventories are held by third parties and if so make arrangements to obtain written confirmation of them or, if necessary, to attend the count.

(b) Procedures to ensure a complete count and to prevent double-counting are particularly important in this case because movements will continue throughout the count.

(i) Clear instructions should be given as to procedures, and an official, preferably not someone normally responsible for inventories, should be given responsibility for organising the count and dealing with queries.

(ii) Before the count, all locations should be tidied and inventory should be laid out in an orderly manner.

(iii) All inventory should be clearly identified and should be marked after being counted by a tag or indelible mark, so that it is evident that it has been counted.

(iv) Pre-numbered sheets should be issued to counters and should be accounted for at the end of the count.

(v) Counters should be given responsibility for specific areas of the warehouse. Each area should be subject to a recount.

(vi) A separate record should be kept of all goods received or issued during the day (for example by noting the goods received note or dispatch note numbers involved).

(vii) Goods received on the day should be physically segregated until the count has been completed.

(viii) Similarly, goods due to be dispatched on the day should be identified in advance and moved to a special area or clearly marked so that they are not inadvertently counted in inventory as well as being included in sales.

Exam focus point

You **must** have a thorough knowledge of audit procedures before, during and after the physical inventory count.

5 Cut-off

Auditors should test **cut-off** by noting the **serial numbers** of GDNs and GRNs received and dispatched just before and after the year-end, and subsequently testing that they have been included in the **correct period**.

5.1 The importance of cut-off

Cut-off is most critical to the accurate recording of transactions in a manufacturing enterprise at particular points in the accounting cycle as follows:

- The **point** of **purchase** and **receipt** of **goods** and **services**
- The **requisitioning** of **raw materials** for production
- The **transfer** of **completed work-in-progress** to finished goods
- The **sale** and **dispatch** of **finished goods**

5.2 Audit procedures

The auditors should consider whether management has implemented adequate cut-off procedures: procedures intended to ensure that movements into, within and out of inventories are properly identified and reflected in the accounting records.

Purchase invoices should be recorded as liabilities only if the goods were received prior to the count. A schedule of 'goods received not invoiced' should be prepared, and items on the list should be accrued for in the accounts.

Sales cut-off is generally more straightforward to achieve correctly than purchases cut-off. Invoices for goods dispatched after the count should not appear in the income statement for the period.

Prior to the physical inventory count, management should make arrangements for cut-off to be properly applied.

(a) Appropriate systems of recording of receipts and dispatches of goods are in place, and also a system for documenting materials requisitions. Goods received notes (GRNs) and goods dispatched notes (GDNs) should be sequentially pre-numbered.

(b) Final GRN and GDN and materials requisition numbers are noted. These numbers can then be used to check subsequently that purchases and sales have been recorded in the current period.

(c) Arrangements should be made to ensure that the cut-off arrangement for inventories held by third parties are satisfactory.

There should ideally be no movement of inventory during the count. Preferably, receipts and dispatches should be suspended for the full period of the count. It may not be practicable to suspend all deliveries, in which case any deliveries which are received during the count should be segregated from other inventory and carefully documented.

6 Valuation

FAST FORWARD

Auditing the **valuation** of inventory includes:

- Testing the **allocation of overheads** is appropriate
- Confirming inventory is carried at the **lower** of **cost** and **net realisable value**

6.1 Assessment of cost and net realisable value

Auditors must understand how the company determines the cost of an item for inventory valuation purposes. Cost should include an appropriate proportion of overheads, in accordance with IAS 2.

There are several ways of determining cost. Auditors must ensure that the company is **applying** the method **consistently** and that each year the method used gives a **fair approximation** to cost. They may need to support this by additional procedures:

- **Reviewing price** changes near the year-end
- **Ageing the inventory** held
- **Checking gross profit** margins to reliable management accounts

6.1.1 Valuation of raw materials and brought-in components

The auditors should perform work to test whether the correct prices have been used to value raw materials and brought-in components valued at actual costs by **referring** to **suppliers' invoices**. The valuation may include unrealised profit if inventory is valued at the latest invoice price. Reference to suppliers' invoice will also provide the auditors with assurance as regards ownership.

If standard costs are used, auditors should **check** the **basis** of the **standards**, **compare standard costs** with **actual costs** and **confirm** that **variances** are being **treated appropriately**.

6.1.2 Valuation of work-in-progress and finished goods

'Cost' comprises the cost of purchase plus the costs of conversion. The cost of conversion comprises:

- Costs specifically attributable to units of production
- Production overheads
- Other overheads attributable to bringing the product or service to its present location and condition

(Work-in-progress relating to construction contracts is outside the scope of the F8 syllabus.)

6.2 Audit procedures

The audit procedures will depend on the methods used by the client to value work-in-progress and finished goods, and on the adequacy of the system of internal control.

The auditors should consider what tests they can carry out to check the reasonableness of the valuation of finished goods and work-in-progress. **Analytical procedures** may assist comparisons being made with items and categories from the previous year's summaries. If the client has a computerised accounting system, the auditors may be able to request an exception report listing, for example, all items whose value has changed by more than a specified amount. A reasonableness check will also provide the auditors with assurance regarding completeness.

6.2.1 Cost

The auditors should ensure that the client includes a proportion of overheads **appropriate** to **bringing** the **inventory** to its **present location and condition**. The basis of overhead allocation should be:

- Consistent with prior years
- Calculated on the normal level of production activity

Thus, overheads arising from **reduced levels of activity**, **idle time** or **inefficient production** should be written-off to the income statement, rather than being included in inventory.

Difficulty may be experienced if the client operates a system of total overhead absorption. It will be necessary for those overheads that are of a general, non-productive nature to be identified and excluded from the valuation.

6.2.2 Cost vs NRV

Auditors should **compare cost and net realisable value** for each item of inventory. Where this is impracticable, the comparison may be done by group or category.

Net realisable value is likely to be less than cost when there has been:

- An **increase in costs** or a fall in selling price
- **Physical deterioration**
- **Obsolescence** of products
- A **marketing decision** to manufacture and sell products at a loss
- Errors in production or purchasing

For work-in-progress, the **ultimate selling price** should be **compared** with the **carrying value** at the year-end plus **costs** to be **incurred** after the year-end to bring work-in-progress to a finished state.

Question — **Cost v NRV**

Your firm is the auditor of Arnold Electrical, a limited liability company, and you have been asked to audit the valuation of the company's inventory at 31 May 20X1 in accordance with IAS 2. Arnold Electrical operates from a single store and purchases domestic electrical equipment from wholesalers and manufacturers and sells them to the general public. These products include video and audio equipment, washing machines, refrigerators and freezers. In addition, it sells small items such as electrical plugs, tapes for video recorders, records and compact discs.

A full physical inventory count was carried out at the year-end, and you are satisfied that the inventory was counted accurately and there are no cut-off errors. Because of the limited time available between the year-end and the completion of the audit, the company has valued the inventory at cost by recording the selling price and deducting the normal gross profit margin. Inventory which the company believes to be worth less than cost has been valued at net realisable value. The selling price used is that on the item in the store when it was counted.

The inventory has been divided into three categories.

(a) Video and audio equipment: televisions, video recorders, video cameras and audio equipment
(b) Domestic equipment: washing machines, refrigerators and freezers
(c) Sundry inventory: electrical plugs, magnetic tapes and compact discs

The normal gross profit margin for each of these categories has been determined and this figure has been used to calculate the cost of the inventory (by deducting the gross profit margin from the selling price). In answering the question you should assume there are no sales taxes.

Required

(a) List and describe the audit work you will carry out to check that inventory has been correctly valued at cost.

(b) List and describe the audit work you will carry out to:

  (i) Find inventory which should be valued at net realisable value
  (ii) Check that the net realisable value is correct

(c) List and describe the other work you will perform to check that the inventory value is accurate.

Note. In answering the question you are only required to check that the price per unit of the inventory is correct. You should assume that the inventory quantities are accurate and there are no purchases or sales cut-off errors.

Answer

(a) This method of valuation at cost is permitted by IAS 2, but it is usually applied to large retail concerns which inventory thousands of low value items, for example supermarket chains. This method is only permitted when it can be shown that it gives a reasonable approximation of the actual cost.

The following tests should be performed to ensure that the inventory is correctly valued at cost.

  (i) Obtain a schedule of the client's calculations of the gross profit margins. Check the mathematical accuracy and consider the reliability of all sources of information used in the calculation.

  (ii) Where the normal overall gross margin has been used, check the reasonableness of the figure by comparing it to the monthly management accounts for the year and last year's published accounts.

  (iii) Test a sample of items to make sure that gross profit does not vary too much across all items of inventory (which is unlikely for Arnold Electrical). The test will compare selling price to purchase price.

  (iv) If a weighted average gross margin has been used, check that the weighting is correct in terms of the proportion of each type of product in closing inventory.

  (v) Select a sample of high value lines and check the reasonableness of the gross profit estimate by calculating the gross profit for each of those lines. Sales price will be compared to inventory sheets and to sales prices in the shop at the year-end. Cost will be checked by examining purchase invoices. The weighted average profit margin for the selected lines can then be calculated and compared to the gross margin applied to the whole inventory.

  (vi) Overvaluation of slow moving inventory is possible when the prices of those items are affected by inflation. To check this, examine the inventory sheets for any slow moving items (or ask the management of the company or use own observation). Compare the value of the inventory at the end of the accounting period to cost according to purchase invoices. If an overvaluation has occurred it should be quantified.

  (vii) Check whether any goods were being offered for sale at reduced prices at the year-end. If the reduced price is greater than cost, the use of an average gross profit percentage will cause inventory to be undervalued. This undervaluation must be quantified. If full selling price was used in the calculation then the problem will not arise. Check a sample of inventory items to sales invoices issued around the year-end to make sure that the correct price was used in the costing calculation.

(b) (i) Inventory which may be worth less than cost will include:

- Slow moving inventory
- Obsolete or superseded inventory
- Seconds and items that have been damaged
- Inventories which are being, or are soon likely to be, sold at reduced prices
- Discontinued lines

Finished goods where the selling price is less than cost will be valued at net realisable value. This is defined as the actual or estimated selling price less costs to completion and marketing, selling and distribution expenses.

To identify inventories which may be worth less than cost the following work will be carried out.

- Examine the computerised inventory control system and list items showing an unacceptably low turnover rate. An unacceptable rate of turnover may be different for different items, but inventory representing more than six months' sales is likely to qualify.
- Review the inventory printout for items already described as seconds or recorded as damaged.
- Discuss with management the current position regarding slow moving inventories and their plans and expectations in respect of products that may be discontinued. The standard system must be carefully considered and estimates obtained of the likely selling price of existing inventories. The most likely outcome regarding the use and value of discontinued components must be decided.
- At the physical inventory count, look for inventory which is dusty, inaccessible and in general not moving and mark on the inventory sheets.
- Find out whether any lines are unreliable and therefore frequently returned for repairs as these may be unpopular.
- Review the trade press or other sources to see whether any of the equipment is out of date.

(ii) Determining the net realisable value of inventory involves management judging how much inventory can be sold and at what price, together with deciding whether to sell off raw materials and components separately or to assemble them into finished products. Each separate type of inventory item should be considered individually in deciding on the level of prudent provision.

The following tests should be carried out.

- Find the actual selling prices from the latest sales invoice. For items still selling, invoices will be very recent, but for slow moving and obsolete items the invoiced prices will be out of date and allowance will have to be made for this.
- Estimate the value of marketing, selling and distribution expenses using past figures for the types of finished goods concerned as a base. Update and review for reasonableness against the most recent accounting records.
- Discuss with management what selling prices are likely to be where there is little past evidence. Costs to completion will be questioned where these are difficult to estimate and where there are any unusual assembly, selling or distribution problems.

(c) The following procedures would also be performed to check the value of inventory at the year-end.

(i) Compare current results with prior year(s). This would include gross profit margins, sales and turnover. Marked variations from the current year's results should be investigated.

(ii) Consider the effects of new technology and new fashions. The electrical appliance business will be exposed to obsolescence problems. Quantify any necessary write-down.

(iii) Compare selling prices to those charged elsewhere. If the prices elsewhere are lower, than the distortion in selling price might affect the value of the inventory of Arnold Electrical. Alternatively, if prices elsewhere are higher, then the company's prices may occasionally fall below cost. Again, any adjustment discovered to be necessary must be quantified.

(iv) Compare the valuation of inventory this year to that at the end of last year. This will be particularly useful for lines held at both dates. If the values are comparable, taking account of inflation, then the current valuation is more likely to be correct.

(v) Sale prices should be monitored as long after the year-end as possible, to make sure that prices were not kept artificially high over the year-end and then reduced at a later date. Inventory turnover should also be examined on the same basis.

Chapter Roundup

- The key assertions relating to inventory are:
  - **Existence**
  - **Completeness**
  - **Rights and obligations**
  - **Valuation**
  - **Cut-off**
- The **valuation** and **disclosure** rules for inventory are laid down in IAS 2 *Inventories*. Inventory should be valued at the **lower** of cost and net realisable value.
- Physical inventory count procedures are vital as they provide evidence which cannot be obtained elsewhere or at any other time about the quantities and conditions of inventory and work-in-progress.
- Auditors should test **cut-off** by noting the serial numbers of GDNs and GRNs received and dispatched just before and after the year-end, and subsequently testing that they have been included in the **correct period**.
- Auditing the **valuation** of inventory includes:
  - Testing the **allocation of overheads** is appropriate
  - Confirming inventory is carried at the **lower** of **cost** and **net realisable value**

Quick Quiz

1 Complete the definition, using the words given below.

.... is defined by IAS 2 as comprising all costs of .... and other costs incurred in bringing the inventory to its .... and ....

purchase	condition	present	cost	location

2 List three methods of inventory counting

(1) ....

(2) ....

(3) ....

3 When should the following inventory counting tests take place?

(a) Observe whether client staff are following instructions.

(b) Review previous year's inventory count arrangements.

(c) Assess method of accounting for inventories.

(d) Trace counted items to final inventory sheets.

(e) Review replies from third parties about inventory held for them.

(f) Conclude as to whether inventory count has been properly carried out.

(g) Gain an overall impression of levels and values of inventory.

(h) Consider the need for expert help.

BEFORE	DURING	AFTER

4 State four points in the accounting cycle when cut-off is critical.

(1) ....

(2) ....

(3) ....

(4) ....

5 Give four occasions when the net realisable value of inventory is likely to fall below cost.

(1) ....

(2) ....

(3) ....

(4) ....

Answers to Quick Quiz

1 Cost, purchase, present location, condition

2 (1) Year-end
(2) Pre/post year-end
(3) Continuous

3 (a) DURING (b) BEFORE (c) BEFORE (d) AFTER
(e) AFTER (f) DURING (g) DURING (h) BEFORE

4 (1) The point of purchase and receipt of goods and services
(2) The requisitioning of raw materials for production
(3) The transfer of completed work-in-progress to finished goods
(4) The sale and dispatch of finished goods

5 From:

- An increase in costs or a fall in selling price
- Physical deterioration
- Obsolescence of products
- A marketing decision to manufacture and sell products at a loss
- Errors in production or purchasing

Now try the questions below from the Exam Question Bank

Number	Level	Marks	Time
Q17	Examination	20	36 mins
Q18	Examination	20	36 mins

14

Receivables

Topic list	Syllabus reference
1 Introduction	E3
2 Audit procedures for receivables	E3
3 The receivables' confirmation	E3
4 Sales	E3

Introduction

Receivables will generally be a material figure on a company's statement of financial position. You must ensure that you are fully conversant with the 'standard' procedures such as the confirmation of receivables. The receivables' confirmation is primarily designed to test the client's entitlement to receive the debt, not the customer's ability to pay.

Auditors also need to consider cut-off for receivables. Sales testing is often carried out in conjunction with the audit of receivables as the two are linked. We also briefly consider the audit of prepayments which is normally carried out using analytical procedures.

Study guide

		Intellectual level
E3	**The audit of specific items: (a) receivables** (i) Direct confirmation of accounts receivables (ii) Other evidence in relation to receivables and prepayments (iii) The related income statement entries	
•	Explain the purpose of substantive procedures in relation to financial statement assertions	2
•	Explain the substantive procedures used in auditing each balance	2
•	Tabulate those substantive procedures in a work program	2

Exam guide

You may be asked to list and explain audit procedures you would perform to confirm specific assertions relating to receivables. In June 2008, question 1 had 14 marks worth relating to the confirmation of receivables, in terms of financial statement assertions and choosing a sample for confirmation. The June 2009 paper had four marks in question 1 on audit procedures for receivables.

1 Introduction

FAST FORWARD

Receivables are usually audited using a combination of **tests of details** and **analytical procedures**.

The audit of receivables is important as this is likely to be a material area. A combination of analytical procedures and tests of details are used, with sales also being tested in conjunction with trade receivables.

The following table sets out the assertions that apply to receivables. The audit procedures in the remainder of this chapter are used to provide evidence for these assertions.

Assertions about classes of transactions	– All sales transactions recorded have occurred and relate to the entity **(occurrence)** – All sales transactions that should have been recorded have been recorded **(completeness)** – Amounts relating to transactions have been recorded appropriately **(accuracy)** – All transactions have been recorded in the correct period **(cut-off)** – All transactions are recorded properly **(classification)**
Assertions about account balances at the period-end	– Recorded receivables exist **(existence)** – The entity controls the rights to receivables and related accounts **(rights and obligations)** – All receivables that should have been recorded have been recorded **(completeness)** – Receivables are included in the accounts at the correct amounts **(valuation and allocation)**
Assertions about presentation and disclosure	– All disclosed events and transactions relating to receivables have occurred and pertain to the entity **(occurrence, rights and obligations)** – All disclosures required have been included **(completeness)** – Financial information is appropriately presented and described and disclosures clearly expressed **(classification and understandability)** – Financial and other information is disclosed fairly and at appropriate amounts **(accuracy and valuation)**

2 Audit procedures for receivables

FAST FORWARD

Existence, completeness and **valuation** are key assertions relating to the audit of receivables.

Audit procedures for receivables are set out in the table below. This covers the audit of sales and prepayments as well as trade receivables. Receivables are often tested in conjunction with sales. The key assertions for sales are occurrence, completeness and accuracy. The receivables' confirmation is used as an audit procedure in the table below and is described in more detail in section 3. Section 4 contains additional information on the audit of sales.

AUDIT PLAN: RECEIVABLES	
COMPLETENESS	• **Agree** the balance from the individual sales ledger accounts to the aged receivables' listing and vice versa. • **Match** the total of the aged receivables' listing to the sales ledger control account. • **Cast and cross-cast** the aged trial balance before selecting any samples to test. • **Trace** a sample of shipping documentation to sales invoices and into the sales and receivables' ledger. • Complete the **disclosure checklist** to ensure that all the disclosures relevant to receivables have been made. • **Compare** the gross profit % by product line with the previous year and industry data. • **Compare** the level of prepayments to the previous year to ensure the figure is materially correct and complete. • **Review detailed statement of financial position** to ensure all likely prepayments have been included.
EXISTENCE	• Perform a **receivables' circularisation** on a sample of year-end trade receivables (see section 3 for details of how to undertake the receivables' circularisation). • **Follow up** all balance disagreements and non-replies to the receivables' confirmation. • **Perform alternative procedures** for any exceptions and non-replies to the receivables' confirmation, such as: • **Review after-date cash receipts** by inspecting bank statements and cash receipts documentation. • Examine the **customer's account and customer correspondence** to assess whether the balance outstanding represents specific invoices and confirm their validity. • Examine the **underlying documentation** (purchase order, dispatch documentation, duplicate sales invoice etc). • **Inquire from management** explanations for invoices remaining unpaid after subsequent ones have been paid. • **Observe** whether the balance on the account is growing and if so, find out why by discussing with management.
RIGHTS AND OBLIGATIONS	• Review **bank confirmation** for any liens on receivables. • Make **inquiries of management, review** loan agreements and review board minutes for any evidence of receivables being sold (eg to factors).

AUDIT PLAN: RECEIVABLES		
VALUATION AND ALLOCATION	•	**Compare** receivables' turnover and receivables' days to the previous year and/or to industry data.
	•	**Compare** the aged analysis of receivables from the aged trial balance to the previous year.
	•	**Review** the adequacy of the allowance for uncollectable accounts through discussion with management.
	•	**Compare** the bad debt expense as a % of sales to the previous year and/or to industry data
	•	**Compare** the allowance for uncollectable accounts as a % of receivables or credit sales to the previous year and/or to industry data.
	•	Confirm adequacy of allowance by **reviewing correspondence** with customers and solicitors.
	•	**Examine credit notes** issued after year-end for allowances that should be made against current period balances.
	•	**Examine** large customer accounts individually and compare to the previous year's balances.
	•	For a sample of old debts on the aged trial balance, obtain further information regarding their recoverability by **discussions** with management and **review** of customer correspondence.
	•	For a sample of prepayments from the prepayments' listing, **recalculate** the amount prepaid to ensure that it has been accurately calculated.
CUT-OFF	•	For a sample of sales invoices around the year-end, **inspect the dates** and compare with the dates of dispatch and the dates recorded in the ledger for application of correct cut-off.
	•	For **sales returns**, select a sample of returns documentation around the year-end and trace to the related credit entries.
	•	Perform **analytical procedures** on sales returns, comparing the ratio of sales returns to sales.
	•	**Review material** after-date invoices, credit notes and adjustments and ensure that they are recorded correctly in the relevant financial period.
CLASSIFICATION	•	Take a sample of sales invoices and examine for proper **classification** into revenue accounts.
ACCURACY	•	For a sample of sales invoices, **compare** the prices and terms to the authorised price list and terms of trade documentation.
	•	Test whether **discounts** have been properly applied by **recalculating** them for a sample of invoices.
	•	Test the correct calculation of **tax** on a sample of invoices.
OCCURRENCE	•	For a sample of sales transactions recorded in the ledger, **vouch** the sales invoice back to customer orders and dispatch documentation.
OCCURRENCE AND RIGHTS AND OBLIGATIONS	•	Determine, through **discussion** with management, whether any receivables have been pledged, assigned or discounted and whether such items require disclosure in the financial statements.
CLASSIFICATION AND UNDERSTANDABILITY	•	**Review** the aged analysis of receivables for any large credits, non-trade receivables and long-term receivables and consider whether such items require separate disclosure.
	•	**Read** the disclosure notes relevant to receivables in the draft financial statements and review for understandability.
ACCURACY AND VALUATION	•	**Read** the disclosure notes to ensure the information is accurate and properly presented at the appropriate amounts.

3 The receivables' confirmation **June 08**

FAST FORWARD

A **confirmation of receivables** is a major procedure, usually achieved by **direct contact** with customers. There are two methods of confirmation: **positive** and **negative**.

3.1 Objectives of confirmation

Key term

External confirmations are audit evidence obtained as a direct written response to the auditor from a third party in paper form or by electronic or other medium.

ISA 505 *External confirmations* covers the confirmation of amounts by third parties, including the confirmation of amounts by receivables.

The verification of trade receivables by direct confirmation is the normal means of providing audit evidence to satisfy the objective of testing whether customers exist and owe *bona fide* amounts to the company (**existence** and **rights and obligations**).

Confirmation will produce for the current audit file a written statement from each respondent that the amount owed at the date of the confirmation is correct. This is, *prima facie*, reliable audit evidence, being from an **independent source** and in **documentary** form. The confirmation of receivables on a test basis should not be regarded as replacing other normal audit tests, such as the testing in-depth of sales transactions, but the results may influence the scope of such tests.

3.2 Client's mandate

Confirmation is essentially an act of the **client**, who alone can authorise third parties to divulge information to the auditors.

The ISA outlines what the auditors' response should be when management refuses permission for the auditors to contact third parties for evidence. If management asks the auditor not to seek the confirmation, the auditor shall inquire about management's reasons for the refusal and seek audit evidence regarding the validity and reasonableness of the reasons. They shall also evaluate the implications of the refusal on the assessment of the risk of material misstatement and on the nature, timing and extent of other audit procedures. The auditor shall perform alternative audit procedures to obtain relevant and reliable audit evidence. If the auditor concludes that the refusal is unreasonable, or the auditor cannot obtain relevant and reliable audit evidence elsewhere, the auditor shall communicate with those charged with governance in accordance with ISA 260 and consider the implications for the auditor's report.

3.3 Positive v negative confirmation

Key terms

A **positive confirmation request** is one in which the confirming party responds directly to the auditor indicating whether they agree or disagree with the information in the request or provides the requested information.

A **negative confirmation request** is one in which the confirming party responds directly to the auditor only if they disagree with the information in the request.

When confirmation is undertaken the method of requesting information from the customer may be either **positive** or **negative**.

- Under the **positive** method the customer is requested to confirm the accuracy of the balance shown or state in what respect he is in disagreement.
- Under the **negative** method the customer is requested to reply only if the amount stated is disputed.

The positive method is generally preferable as it is designed to encourage definite replies from those contacted.

The negative method provides less persuasive audit evidence and shall not be used as the sole substantive procedure to audit receivables unless all of the following are present:

- The **risk** of material misstatement has been assessed as **low**.
- The auditor has obtained sufficient appropriate audit evidence on the operating effectiveness of relevant **controls**.
- The population consists of a **large number of small, homogeneous account balances**.
- A **very low exception rate** is expected.
- The auditor is not aware of circumstances or conditions that would cause customers to **disregard the requests**.

A specimen 'positive' confirmation letter is shown below.

The statements will normally be prepared by the client's staff, from which point the auditors, as a safeguard against the possibility of fraudulent manipulation, must maintain **strict control** over the preparation and dispatch of the statements.

Precautions must also be taken to ensure that undelivered items are returned, not to the client, but to the auditors' own office for follow-up by them.

MANUFACTURING CO LIMITED
15 South Street
London

Date

Messrs (customer)

In accordance with the request of our auditors, ABC Co, we ask that you kindly confirm to them directly your indebtedness to us at [insert date] which, according to our records, amounted to $.......... as shown by the enclosed statement.

If the above amount is in agreement with your records, please sign in the space provided below and return this letter direct to our auditors in the enclosed stamped addressed envelope.

If the amount is not in agreement with your records, please notify our auditors directly of the amount shown by your records, and if possible detail on the reverse of this letter full particulars of the difference.

Yours faithfully,

For Manufacturing Co Limited

Reference No: ....

....

(Tear-off slip)

The amount shown above is/is not * in agreement with our records as at

Account No	....	Signature	....
Date	....	Title or position	....

* The position according to our records is shown overleaf.

Notes

- The letter is on the client's paper, signed by the client.
- A copy of the statement is attached.
- The reply is sent directly to the auditor in a pre-paid envelope.

3.4 Sample selection

Auditors will normally only contact a **sample** of accounts receivable. If this sample is to yield a meaningful result it must be based upon a **complete list** of all accounts receivable. In addition, when constructing the sample, the following classes of account should receive special attention:

- **Old, unpaid** accounts
- Accounts **written-off** during the period under review
- Accounts with **credit balances**
- Accounts settled by **round sum payments**
- Accounts with **nil balances**
- Accounts which have been **paid** by the date of the examination

3.5 Follow-up procedures

ISA 505 states that the auditor may send an additional confirmation request when a reply to a previous request has not been received within a **reasonable time**. For example, the auditor may send an additional or follow-up request having rechecked the accuracy of the original address.

3.5.1 Exceptions and non-responses

y terms

An **exception** is a response that shows a difference between the information requested to be confirmed, or contained in the entity's records, and information provided by the confirming party.
A **non-response** is a failure of the confirming party to respond, or fully respond, to a positive confirmation request, or a confirmation request returned undelivered.

Auditors will have to carry out further work in relation to those receivables who:

- **Disagree** with the **balance stated** (positive and negative confirmation), resulting in **exceptions**
- **Do not respond**, resulting in **non-responses**

In the case of disagreements, the customer response should have identified specific amounts which are disputed. These give rise to exceptions and may indicate misstatements or potential misstatements in the financial statements. When a misstatement is identified, the auditor must evaluate whether this is indicative of fraud (in accordance with ISA 240). Exceptions might also indicate a deficiency in internal control. Some exceptions of course do not represent misstatements, as they may be due to timing, measurement or clerical errors in the confirmation procedures. The table below outlines some reasons for exceptions occurring.

REASONS FOR EXCEPTIONS
There is a **dispute** between the client and the customer. The reasons for the dispute would have to be identified, and provision made if appropriate against the debt.
Cut-off problems exist, because the client records the following year's sales in the current year or because goods returned by the customer in the current year are not recorded in the current year. Cut-off testing may have to be extended (see below).
The customer may have sent the **monies before** the year-end, but the monies were **not recorded** by the client as receipts until **after** the year-end. Detailed cut-off work may be required on receipts.
Monies received may have been posted to the **wrong account** or a cash-in-transit account. Auditors should check if there is evidence of other mis-posting. If the monies have been posted to a cash-in-transit account, auditors should ensure this account has been cleared promptly.
Customers who are also suppliers may **net-off balances** owed and owing. Auditors should check that this is allowed.
Teeming and lading, stealing monies and **incorrectly posting** other receipts so that no particular customer is seriously in debt is a **fraud** that can arise in this area. If auditors suspect teeming and lading has occurred, detailed testing will be required on cash receipts, particularly on prompt posting of cash receipts.

In the case of **non-responses**, the ISA states that the auditor shall perform **alternative audit procedures** to obtain relevant and reliable audit evidence. These could include reviewing subsequent cash receipts, shipping documentation and sales near the period-end.

3.6 Reliability of responses

The ISA states that the auditor shall obtain further audit evidence to resolve any **doubts about the reliability** of a response to a confirmation request. This could include contacting the confirming party.

If the auditor concludes that a response to a request is **not reliable**, he shall evaluate the impact of this on the assessment of the risk of material misstatement (including the risk of fraud), and on the related nature, timing and extent of other audit procedures.

4 Sales

FAST FORWARD

Sales comprise a material figure in the statement of comprehensive income that is often audited by analytical review as it should have predictable relationships with other figures in the financial statements.

Accounts' receivable will often be tested in conjunction with sales. Auditors are seeking to obtain evidence that sales pertain to the entity (occurrence), and are **completely** and **accurately recorded**. This will involve carrying out certain procedures to test for **completeness** of sales and also testing **cut-off.**

4.1 Completeness and occurrence of sales

Analytical review is important when testing completeness. A client is likely to have a great deal of information about company sales and should be able to explain any fluctuations and variances. Auditors should consider the following.

- The **level of sales** over the year, compared on a month-by-month basis with the previous year
- The effect on sales value of **changes in quantities** sold
- The effect on sales value of **changes in products** or **prices**
- The level of **goods returned, sales allowances** and **discounts**
- The **efficiency of labour** as expressed in sales or profit per tax per employee

In addition auditors must record reasons for changes in the **gross profit margin**. Analysis of the gross profit margin should be as detailed as possible, ideally broken down by **product area** and **month or quarter**.

As well as analytical review, auditors may feel that they need to carry out a directional test on **completeness of recording** of individual sales in the accounting records. To do this, auditors should start with the documents that first record sales (**goods dispatched notes** or **till rolls** for example), and trace sales recorded in these through intermediate documents such as sales summaries to the **sales ledger**.

Auditors must ensure that the population of documents from which the sample is originally taken is itself complete, by checking for example the **completeness** of the **sequence** of goods dispatched notes.

Exam focus point

You must remember the direction of this test. Since we are checking the completeness of recording of sales in the sales ledger, we cannot take a sample from the ledger because the sample would not include what has not been recorded.

Sherwood Textiles, a listed company, manufactures knitted clothes and dyes these clothes and other textiles. You are carrying out the audit of the accounts of the company for the year ended 30 September 20X6 which show a revenue of about $10 million, and a profit before tax of about $800,000.

You are attending the final audit in December 20X6 and are commencing the audit of trade accounts receivables, which are shown in the draft accounts at $2,060,000.

The interim audit (tests of control) was carried out in July 20X6 and it showed that there was a good system of internal control in the sales system and no serious errors were found in the audit tests. The company's sales ledger is maintained on a computer, which produces at the end of each month:

(i) A list of transactions for the month
(ii) An aged list of balances
(iii) Open item statements which are sent to customers. (Open item statements show all items which are outstanding on each account, irrespective of their age.)

Required

(a) List and briefly describe the audit tests you would carry out to verify trade accounts receivable at the year-end. You are not required to describe how you would carry out a direct confirmation of receivables.

(b) Describe the audit work you would carry out on the following replies to a receivables' circularisation:

 (i) Balance agreed by customer.
 (ii) Balance not agreed by customer.
 (iii) Customer is unable to confirm the balance because of the form of records kept by the customer.
 (iv) Customer does not reply to the confirmation letter.

Answer

(a) The auditors will carry out the following tests on the list of balances.

 (i) Agree the balances from the individual sales ledger accounts to the list of balances and vice versa.
 (ii) Agree the total of the list to the sales ledger control account.
 (iii) Cast the list of balances and the sales ledger control account.

 Other general tests auditors will carry out will be to:

 (i) Agree the opening balance on the sales ledger control account to ensure that last year's audit adjustments were recorded.
 (ii) Inspect ledger balances for unusual entries.
 (iii) Perform analytical procedures on trade receivables as follows

 – Compare receivables' turnover and receivables' days to the prior year and/or to industry data.
 – Perform an age analysis on trade receivables and compare this to the prior year.
 – Compare the bad debt expense as a % of sales to the prior year and/or to industry data.
 – Examine large customer accounts individually and compare them to the prior year.

 The determination of whether the company has made reasonable provision for bad and doubtful debts will be facilitated as the company produces an aged listing of balances.

Auditors will carry out the following procedures to audit bad debts.

(i) Debts against which specific allowance has been made (and debts written-off) should be examined in conjunction with correspondence, lawyers'/debt collection agencies' letters, liquidators' statements and so on, and their necessity or adequacy confirmed.

(ii) A general review of relevant correspondence may reveal debts where an allowance is warranted, but has not been made.

(iii) Where specific and/or general allowances have been determined using the aged analysis, the auditors should ensure that the analysis has been properly prepared by comparing it with the dates on invoices and matching cash receipts against outstanding invoices. They should check the reasonableness and consistency of any formula used to calculate general allowances.

(iv) Additional tests that should be carried out on individual balances will include ascertaining the subsequent receipt of cash, paying particular attention to round sum payments on account, examination of specific invoices and, where appropriate, goods received notes, and enquiry into any invoices that have not been paid when subsequent invoices have been paid.

(v) Excessive discounts should be examined, as should journal entries transferring balances from one account to another and journal entries that clear customer balances after the year-end.

(vi) Credit notes issued after the year-end should be reviewed and allowances checked where they refer to current period sales.

In order to audit cut-off and hence completeness, the auditors should, during the physical inventory count, have obtained details of the last serial numbers of goods outwards issued before the commencement of the count. The following substantive procedures are designed to test that goods taken into inventory are not also treated as sales in the year under review and, conversely, goods dispatched are treated as sales in the year under review and not also treated as inventory.

(i) Review goods outwards and returns inwards notes around year-end to ensure that:

    (1) Invoices and credit notes are dated in the correct period.

    (2) Invoices and credit notes are posted to the sales ledger and nominal ledger in the correct period.

(ii) Reconcile entries in the sales ledger control around the year-end to daily batch invoice totals ensuring batches are posted in correct year.

(iii) Review sales ledger control account around year end for unusual items.

(iv) Review material after-date invoices and ensure that they are properly treated as following year's sales.

(b) The verification of trade receivables by direct confirmation is the normal means of providing audit evidence to prove that receivables represent *bona fide* amounts due to the company (existence and rights and obligations).

The audit work required on the various replies to a receivables' circularisation would be as follows.

(i) *Balances agreed by customer*

All that is required would be to ensure that the debt does appear to be collectable, by reviewing cash received after-date or considering the adequacy of any allowance made for a long outstanding amount.

(ii) *Balances not agreed by customer*

All balance disagreements must be followed up and their effect on total receivables evaluated. Differences arising that merely represent invoices or cash-in-transit generally do not require adjustment, but disputed amounts, and errors by the client, may indicate that further substantive work is necessary to determine whether material adjustments are required.

(iii) *Customer is unable to confirm the balance because of the form of records maintained*

Certain companies, often computerised, operate systems which make it impossible for them to confirm the balance on their account. Typically in these circumstances their purchase ledger is merely a list of unpaid invoices. However, with sufficient information the customer will be able to confirm that any given invoice is outstanding. Hence the auditors can circularise such enterprises successfully, but they will need to break down the total on the account into its constituent outstanding invoices.

(iv) *Customer does not reply to confirmation letter*

When the positive request method is used the auditors must follow up by all practicable means those customers who fail to respond. Second requests should be sent out in the event of no reply being received within two or three weeks and if necessary this may be followed by telephoning the customer with the client's permission.

After two, or even three attempts to obtain confirmation, a list of the outstanding items will normally be passed to a responsible independent company official who will arrange for them to be investigated.

Alternative audit procedures might include the following.

(1) Check receipt of cash after-date by reviewing post year-end bank statements.

(2) Verify valid purchase orders, if any.

(3) Examine the account to see if the balance represents specific outstanding invoices.

(4) Obtain explanations for invoices remaining unpaid after subsequent ones have been paid.

(5) Observe whether the balance on the account is growing, and if so, find out why by discussions with management.

(6) Test the company's control over the issue of credit notes and the write-off of bad debts.

xam focus oint

The receivables' confirmation provides good audit evidence of the existence of receivables, but not necessarily of their valuation. Therefore, in a question on the audit of receivables, remember to include other audit procedures such as analytical procedures.

Chapter Roundup

- Receivables are usually audited using a combination of **tests of details** and **analytical procedures**.
- **Existence**, **completeness** and **valuation** are key assertions relating to the audit of receivables.
- A **confirmation of receivables** is a major procedure, usually achieved by **direct contact** with customers. There are two methods of confirmation: **positive** and **negative**.
- Sales comprise a material figure in the statement of comprehensive income that is often audited by analytical review as it should have predictable relationships with other figures in the financial statements.

Quick Quiz

1 The negative method of receivables' confirmation should only be used if the client has good internal controls and a small number of large customer accounts.

True ☐

False ☐

2 State four types of account which should receive special attention when picking a sample for a receivables confirmation.

(1) ....

(2) ....

(3) ....

(4) ....

3 Complete the following tests which aim to confirm the valuation of bad debts.

(a) Confirm adequacy of allowance by reviewing correspondence with

(i) ....

(ii) ....

(b) Examine .... issued after the year-end for allowances that should be made against current period balances.

4 List three things that can be considered when undertaking an analytical review on sales.

(1) ....

(2) ....

(3) ....

5 Give two examples of tests to verify prepayments.

(1) ....

(2) ....

Answers to Quick Quiz

1 False

2 From:

- Old unpaid accounts
- Accounts written-off during the period under review
- Accounts with credit balances
- Accounts settled by round sum payments
- Accounts with nil balances
- Accounts which have been paid by the date of the examination

3 (a) (i) customers, (ii) solicitors
(b) credit notes

4 (1) Level of sales, month by month
(2) Price
(3) Goods returned

5 From:

- Verify by reference to invoices, cash book, correspondence.
- Check calculations by reperformance.
- Review detailed statement of financial position to ensure all likely prepayments have been included.
- Use analytical procedures to review reasonableness.

Now try the question below from the Exam Question Bank

Number	Level	Marks	Time
Q19	Examination	20	36 mins

15

Cash and bank

Topic list	Syllabus reference
1 Introduction	E3
2 Bank	E3
3 Cash	E3

Introduction

Work on cash and bank will concentrate on the completeness and valuation using the bank reconciliation, bank confirmation letter and counting of cash as key audit tests.

Study guide

		Intellectual level
E3	**The audit of specific items: (d) bank and cash** (i) Bank confirmation reports used in obtaining evidence in relation to bank and cash (ii) Other evidence in relation to bank and cash, and (iii) The related income statement entries	
•	Explain the purpose of substantive procedures in relation to financial statement assertions	2
•	Explain the substantive procedures used in auditing each balance	2
•	Tabulate those substantive procedures in a work program	2

Exam guide

In the exam you may be asked to list and explain audit procedures you would perform to confirm specific assertions relating to cash and bank. The June 2008 paper had a three mark part at the end of question 3 on the procedures necessary to obtain a bank confirmation letter.

1 Introduction

'Cash' in the financial statements represents cash in-hand and cash on deposit in bank accounts. Most accounting transactions pass through the cash account so cash is affected by all of the entity's business processes, and is particularly impacted by the sales and purchases processes. We looked at the controls relating to cash in Chapter 10. In this chapter, we will consider the substantive audit testing applied to the year-end cash figure.

1.1 Audit objectives for cash

The following table demonstrates the audit objectives for cash balances and how these are related to the financial statement assertions relevant to this account area. The audit procedures described in the remainder of this chapter are undertaken to provide audit evidence to support these financial statement assertions.

Financial statement assertion	Audit objective
Existence	Recorded cash balances exist at the period-end
Completeness	Recorded cash balances include the effects of all transactions that have occurred
Rights and obligations	The entity has legal title to all cash balances shown at the period-end
Valuation	Recorded cash balances are realisable at the amounts stated
Assertions relating to presentation and disclosure (classification and understandability, occurrence and rights and obligations, accuracy and valuation, completeness)	Disclosures relating to cash are adequate and in accordance with accounting standards and legislation

2 Bank

June 08

Bank balances are usually **confirmed directly** with the bank in question.

2.1 Bank confirmation procedures

The audit of bank balances will need to cover **completeness**, **existence**, **rights and obligations and valuation**. All of these assertions can be audited directly by obtaining third party confirmations from the client's banks and reconciling these with the accounting records, having regard to **cut-off**.

The audit objectives linking these assertions are as follows:

- Recorded cash balances exist at the year-end **(existence)**
- Recorded cash balances include the effects of all transactions that occurred **(completeness)**
- Year-end transfers are recorded in the correct period **(cut-off)**
- Recorded balances are realisable at the amounts stated **(valuation and allocation)**
- The entity has legal title to all cash balances shown at the year-end **(rights and obligations)**

This type of audit evidence is valuable because it comes directly from an **independent source** and, therefore, provides greater assurance of reliability than that obtained solely from the client's own records. The bank letter is mentioned as a source of external third party evidence in ISA 505 *External confirmations*, and guidance to auditors is provided in IAPS 1000 *Inter-bank confirmation procedures.*

2.2 Confirmation requests

The **bank confirmation letter** can be used to ask a variety of questions, including queries about outstanding interests, contingent liabilities and guarantees.

The auditors should decide from which bank or banks to request confirmation, having regard to such matters as **size of balance**, **volume of activity**, **degree of reliance** on **internal control**, and **materiality** within the context of the financial statements.

The auditors should determine which of the following approaches is the most appropriate in seeking confirmation of balances or other information from the bank:

- **Listing balances** and other information, and requesting confirmation of their accuracy and completeness, or
- **Requesting details of balances** and other information, which can then be compared with the requesting client's records

In determining which of the above approaches is the most appropriate, the auditors should weigh the **quality** of **audit evidence** they require in the particular circumstances against the **practicality** of obtaining a reply from the confirming bank.

Difficulty may be encountered in obtaining a satisfactory response even where the client company submits information for confirmation to the confirming bank. It is important that a response is sought for **all** confirmation requests. Auditors should not usually request a response only if the information submitted is incorrect or incomplete.

2.2.1 Preparation and dispatch of requests and receipt of replies

Control over the content and dispatch of confirmation requests is the responsibility of the auditors. However, it will be necessary for the request to be **authorised** by the client entity. Replies should be returned directly to the auditors and to facilitate such a reply, a pre-addressed envelope should be enclosed with the request.

2.2.2 Content of confirmation requests

The form and content of a confirmation request letter will depend on the purpose for which it is required and on local practices.

The most commonly requested information is in respect of balances due to or from the client entity on **current, deposit, loan and other accounts**. The request letter should provide the account description number and the type of currency for the account.

It may also be advisable to request information about **nil balances** on accounts, and accounts which were **closed** in the 12 months prior to the chosen confirmation date. The client entity may ask for confirmation not only of the balances on accounts but also, where it may be helpful, other information, such as the maturity and interest terms on loans and overdrafts, unused facilities, lines of credit/standby facilities, any offset or other rights or encumbrances, and details of any collateral given or received.

The client entity and its auditors are likely to request confirmation of **contingent liabilities**, such as those arising on guarantees, comfort letter, bills and so on.

Banks often hold **securities** and other items in safe custody on behalf of customers. A request letter may thus ask for confirmation of such items held by the bank.

The procedure is simple but important, and outlined below.

(a) The banks will require **explicit written authority** from their client to disclose the information requested.

(b) The **auditors' request** must **refer** to the **client's letter** of authority and the date thereof. Alternatively it may be countersigned by the client or it may be accompanied by a specific letter of authority.

(c) In the case of joint accounts, **letters of authority** signed by all **parties** will be necessary.

(d) Such **letters of authority** may either **give permission** to the bank to disclose information for a specific request or grant permission for an indeterminate length of time.

(e) The request should **reach** the **branch manager** at least **one month in advance** of the client's **year-end** and should state both that year-end date and the previous year-end date.

(f) The **auditors** should themselves **check** that the bank response covers all the information in the standard and other responses.

2.3 Cut-off

Care must be taken to ensure that there is no **window dressing**, by auditing **cut-off** carefully. Window dressing in this context is usually manifested as an attempt to overstate the liquidity of the company by:

(a) Keeping the cash book open to take credit for **remittances actually received** after the year-end, thus enhancing the balance at bank and reducing receivables

(b) **Recording cheques paid in** the period under review which are not actually dispatched until after the year-end, thus decreasing the balance at bank and reducing liabilities

A combination of (a) and (b) can contrive to present an artificially healthy looking current ratio.

With the possibility of (a) above in mind, where lodgements have not been cleared by the bank until the new period, the auditors should **examine the paying-in slip** to ensure that the amounts were actually paid into the bank on or before the period-end date.

As regards (b) above, where there appears to be a particularly **large number of outstanding cheques** at the year-end, the auditors should check whether these were **cleared within a reasonable time** in the new period. If not, this may indicate that dispatch occurred after the year-end.

2.4 Audit plan for bank

AUDIT PLAN: BANK (to confirm completeness, valuation, existence, cut-off and assertions related to disclosure)
• **Obtain standard bank confirmations** from each bank with which the client conducted business during the audit period. • **Reperform** arithmetic of bank reconciliation. • **Trace cheques shown as outstanding** from the bank reconciliation to the cash book prior to the year-end and to the **after-date bank statements** and **obtain explanations** for any **large or unusual items** not cleared at the time of the audit. • **Compare cash book(s)** and **bank statements** in detail for the last month of the year, and **match items outstanding** at the reconciliation date to bank statements. • **Review bank reconciliation** previous to the year-end bank reconciliation and test whether **all items** are **cleared** in the last period or **taken forward** to the year-end bank reconciliation. • Obtain satisfactory explanations for **all items** in the **cash book** for which there are **no corresponding entries** in the **bank statement** and vice versa by **discussion** with finance staff. • **Verify contra items** appearing in the cash books or bank statements with original entry. • Verify by **inspecting** paying-in slips that **uncleared bankings** are **paid in** prior to the year-end. • **Examine all lodgements** in respect of which payment has been refused by the bank; ensure that they are cleared on representation or that other appropriate steps have been taken to effect recovery of the amount due. • Verify balances per the cash book according to the bank reconciliation by **inspecting** cash book, bank statements and general ledger. • **Verify** the **bank balances** with reply to **standard bank letter** and with the **bank statements**. • **Inspect** the cash book and bank statements before and after the year-end for **exceptional entries** or **transfers** which have a material effect on the balance shown to be in-hand. • Identify whether any **accounts** are **secured** on the **assets** of the company by **discussion** with management. • **Consider** whether there is a **legal right** of **set-off** of overdrafts against positive bank balances. • Determine whether the bank accounts are **subject** to any **restrictions** by **inquiries** with management. • **Review draft accounts** to ensure that disclosures for bank are complete and accurate and in accordance with accounting standards.

Exam focus point

Remember that the bank confirmation letter contains the balance held by the client at the bank **per the bank's records**. This must be **reconciled** to the balance held with the bank **per the client's records.**

Question — Bank letter

(a) Explain the importance of the bank letter and describe the procedures used to obtain confirmations from the bank.

(b) Describe how you would test a client's bank reconciliation.

Answer

(a) The bank letter is important because it is independent confirmation of a number of significant matters in the client's financial statements. It confirms cash and bank balances which may well be a significant asset. It also provides confirmation of customers' assets held as security, customers' other assets held (as custodian) and contingent liabilities. Auditors also ask the bank to give details of other banks and branches that the respondent bank is aware have a relationship with the client.

Audit procedures

(i) Obtain written authority from the client to the bank to disclose the necessary information.

(ii) Send a bank letter in standard form to the bank in sufficient time for it to arrive at least a month before the year-end. The letter should state both the year-end date and the previous year-end date, and should refer to the client's granting of authority.

(iii) If additional information over and above what is in the standard letter is requested, send a separate letter requesting that information.

(iv) When confirmation is received from the bank, check that the bank has answered all the questions in the letter.

(v) Follow up all points disclosed in the bank letter.

(b) The following procedures should be carried out on the bank reconciliation.

(i) Obtain standard bank confirmations from each bank with which the client conducted business during the period.

(ii) Test arithmetic of bank reconciliation by recasting.

(iii) Trace cheques shown as outstanding from the bank reconciliation to the cash book prior to the year-end and to the after-date bank statements and obtain explanations for any large or unusual items not cleared at the time of the audit.

(iv) Verify by checking paying-in slips that uncleared bankings are paid in prior to the year-end, and review whether uncleared bankings are cleared quickly after the year-end.

(v) Verify balances per cash book according to the reconciliation with cash book and general ledger.

(vi) Verify the bank balances with reply to standard bank letter and with the bank statements.

(vii) Scrutinise the cash book and bank statements before and after the period-end for exceptional entries or transfers which have a material effect on the balance shown to be in hand.

(viii) Identify whether any accounts are secured on the assets of the company.

(ix) Consider whether there is a legal right of set-off of overdrafts against positive bank balances.

(x) Determine whether the bank accounts are subject to any restrictions.

3 Cash

FAST FORWARD

Cash balances should be verified if they are **material** or **irregularities** are suspected.

Cash balances/floats are often individually immaterial but they may require some audit emphasis because of the opportunities for fraud that could exist where internal control is weak and because they may be material in total.

However in enterprises such as hotels and retail organisations, the amount of cash-in-hand at the period-end could be considerable. Cash counts may be important for internal auditors, who have a role in fraud prevention.

Auditors will be concerned that the cash **exists**, is **complete**, and belongs to the company (**rights and obligations**) and is stated at the correct **value**.

Where the auditors determine that cash balances are potentially material they may conduct a **cash count**, ideally at the period-end. Rather like attendance at an inventory count, the conduct of the count falls into three phases: planning, the count itself, and follow-up procedures.

3.1 Planning the cash count

Planning is an essential element, as it is important that all cash balances are counted at the same time as far as possible. Cash in this context may include unbanked cheques received, IOUs and credit card slips, in addition to notes and coins.

As part of their planning procedures the auditors will need to determine the **locations** where cash is held and which of these locations warrant a count.

Planning decisions will need to be recorded on the current audit file including:

- The **precise time** of the count(s) and location(s)
- The **names** of the **audit staff** conducting the counts
- The **names** of the **client staff** intending to be present at each location

Where a location is not visited it may be appropriate to obtain a letter from the client confirming the balance.

3.2 Cash count

The following matters apply to the count itself.

- All cash/petty cash **books** should be **written up** to date in **ink** (or other permanent form) at the time of the count.
- All **balances** must be **counted** at the **same time**.
- All **negotiable securities** must be **available** and **counted** at the time the cash balances are counted.
- At **no time** should the **auditors** be **left alone** with the cash and negotiable securities.
- **All cash** and securities **counted** must be **recorded** on working papers subsequently filed on the current audit file. **Reconciliations** should be prepared where applicable (for example, imprest petty cash float).

AUDIT PLAN: CASH COUNT (to confirm completeness, valuation, existence and disclosure)

- **Count cash balances** held and agree to petty cash book or other record:
  - Count all balances simultaneously
  - All counting to be done in the presence of the individuals responsible
  - Enquire into any IOUs or cashed cheques outstanding for a long period of time
- **Obtain certificates** of cash-in-hand from responsible officials.
- **Confirm** that bank and cash **balances** as reconciled above are **correctly stated** in the financial statements.

Follow up

- Obtain **certificates of cash-in-hand** as appropriate.
- Verify **unbanked cheques/cash receipts** have subsequently been **paid in** and agree to the bank reconciliation by **inspection** of the relevant documentation.
- Ensure **IOUs** and cheques cashed for employees have been **reimbursed**.
- Review whether **IOUs or cashed cheques outstanding** for **unreasonable periods** of time have been provided for.
- Verify the **balances** as counted are reflected in the accounts (subject to any agreed amendments because of shortages and so on) by **inspection** of draft financial statements.

Chapter Roundup

- **Bank balances** are usually **confirmed directly** with the bank in question.
- The **bank confirmation letter** can be used to ask a variety of questions, including queries about outstanding interests, contingent liabilities and guarantees.
- **Cash balances** should be verified if they are **material** or **irregularities** are suspected.

Quick Quiz

1 What are the relevant financial statement assertions for cash in the statement of financial position?

2 Summarise the procedure for obtaining confirmation from a client's bank of the year-end bank balance.

(1) ....

(2) ....

(3) ....

(4) ....

(5) ....

(6) ....

3 Complete the following two audit tests performed to verify the bank reconciliation.

(a) Trace cheques shown as outstanding on the .... to the .... prior to the year-end and ....

(b) Obtain satisfactory explanations for all items in the .... for which there is no corresponding entry in the .... and ....

4 Give two examples of businesses where cash floats could be considerable.

....

....

5 What planning matters relating to a cash count should be recorded in the current audit file?

....

....

....

Answers to Quick Quiz

1 Existence, completeness, valuation and allocation

2 (1) The banks will require **explicit written authority** from their client to disclose the information requested.

(2) The **auditors' request** must **refer** to the **client's letter** of authority and the date thereof. Alternatively it may be countersigned by the client or it may be accompanied by a specific letter of authority.

(3) In the case of joint accounts, **letters of authority** signed by all **parties** will be necessary.

(4) Such letters of authority may either give **permission** to the bank to disclose information for a **specific request** or grant permission for an **indeterminate length of time.**

(5) The request should **reach** the **branch manager** at least **one month in advance** of the client's **year-end** and should state both that year-end date and the previous year-end date.

(6) The **auditors** should themselves **check** that the bank **answers all the questions** and, where the reply is not received direct from the bank, be responsible for establishing the authenticity of the reply.

3 (a) bank reconciliations, cash book, after-date bank statements

(b) bank statements, cash book, bank reconciliation

4 Hotels
Retail operations

5 Time of count
Names of client staff attending
Names of audit staff attending

Now try the question below from the Exam Question Bank

Number	Level	Marks	Time
Q20	Examination	10	18 mins

16

Liabilities and capital

Topic list	Syllabus reference
1 Introduction	E3
2 Audit procedures for trade payables and purchases	E3
3 Non-current liabilities	E3
4 Provisions and contingencies	E3
5 Capital and other issues	E3

Introduction

In this chapter, we examine the audit of liabilities including payables and accruals, provisions and other long-term liabilities.

When auditing payables, the auditor must test for understatement (ie completeness). Rather than circularising payables, it is more common to obtain audit evidence from suppliers' statements.

The audit of provisions can be particularly complex due to the accounting treatment and the degree of judgement involved in calculating the provision.

This chapter ends with a brief look at the audit of share capital and reserves.

Study guide

		Intellectual level
E3	**The audit of specific items: (c) payables and accruals; (e) long-term liabilities** (c) Payables and accruals: (i) Supplier statement reconciliations and direct confirmation of accounts payable (ii) Obtain evidence in relation to payables and accruals, and (iii) The related income statement entries (e) Long-term liabilities: (ii) Evidence in relation to non-current liabilities, and (iii) The related income statement entries	
•	Explain the purpose of substantive procedures in relation to financial statement assertions	2
•	Explain the substantive procedures used in auditing each balance	2
•	Tabulate those substantive procedures in a work program	2

Exam guide

You may be asked to list and explain audit procedures you would perform to confirm specific assertions relating to liabilities. The pilot paper had 20 marks in question 1 on the substantive audit of purchases and trade payables. Similarly, the December 2007 paper had 12 marks in question 1 on the audit of purchases.

1 Introduction

In this chapter we will examiner the substantive audit of trade payables and accruals, long-term liabilities and provisions and end with a brief look at capital. Purchases are often tested in conjunction with the audit of trade payables and so are included in the section on trade payables. The following table sets out the financial statement assertions to which audit testing is directed.

Assertions about classes of transactions	– All purchase transactions recorded have occurred and relate to the entity **(occurrence)** – All purchase transactions that should have been recorded have been recorded **(completeness)** – Amounts relating to transactions have been recorded appropriately **(accuracy)** – Purchase transactions have been recorded in the correct period **(cut-off)** – Purchase transactions are recorded properly in the accounts **(classification)**
Assertions about period-end account balances	– Trade payables and accrued expenses are valid liabilities **(existence)** – Trade payables and accrued expenses are the obligations of the entity **(rights and obligations)** – All liabilities have been recorded **(completeness)** – All liabilities are included in the accounts at appropriate amounts **(valuation and allocation)**

Assertions about presentation and disclosure	– All disclosed events and transactions relating to liabilities have occurred and relate to the entity **(occurrence and rights and obligations)** – All disclosures required have been included **(completeness)** – Financial information is appropriately presented and described and disclosures clearly expressed **(classification and understandability)** – Financial information is disclosed fairly and at appropriate amounts **(accuracy and valuation)**

2 Audit procedures for trade payables and accruals

Pilot paper, Dec 07

FAST FORWARD

The largest figure in **current liabilities** will normally be **trade accounts payable** which are generally audited by comparison of **suppliers' statements** with **purchase ledger accounts.**

2.1 Audit procedures

As with accounts receivable, accounts payable are likely to be a material figure in the statement of financial position of most enterprises. The tests of controls on the purchases cycle (Chapter 10) will have provided the auditors with some assurance as to the completeness of liabilities.

Auditors should however be particularly aware, when conducting their work on the statement of financial position, of the possibility of **understatement** of **liabilities** to improve liquidity and profits (by understating the corresponding purchases). The primary objective of their work will therefore be to ascertain whether **liabilities** existing at the year-end have been **completely** and **accurately recorded**.

As regards **trade accounts payable**, this primary objective can be subdivided into two detailed objectives.

- Is there a **satisfactory cut-off** between goods received and invoices received, so that purchases and trade accounts payable are recognised in the correct year?
- Do trade accounts payable represent the ***bona fide*** amounts due by the company?

Before we ascertain how the auditors design and conduct their tests with these objectives in mind, we need to establish the importance of the list of balances.

The following table sets out audit procedures to test trade accounts payables and accruals.

AUDIT PLAN: ACCOUNTS PAYABLES AND ACCRUALS	
COMPLETENESS	• Obtain a listing of trade accounts payables and **agree** the total to the general ledger by casting and cross-casting. • Test for unrecorded liabilities by **inquiries of management** on how unrecorded liabilities and accruals are identified and examining post year-end transactions. • Obtain selected suppliers' statements and **reconcile** these to the relevant suppliers' accounts (see section 2.3 for details of suppliers' statements). • Examine files of unmatched purchase orders and supplier invoices for any **unrecorded liabilities**. • Perform a **confirmation of accounts payables** for a sample (see section 2.2 for details of the accounts payables' confirmation) • Complete the **disclosure checklist** to ensure that all the disclosures relevant to liabilities have been made. • **Compare** the current year balances for trade accounts payables and accruals to the previous year.

AUDIT PLAN: ACCOUNTS PAYABLES AND ACCRUALS	
	• **Compare** the amounts owed to a sample of individual suppliers in the trade accounts payables listing to amounts owed to these suppliers in the previous year. • **Compare** the payables' turnover and payables' days to the previous year and industry data. • **Reperform casts** of **payroll records** to confirm completeness and accuracy. • **Confirm** payment of net pay per payroll records to cheque or bank transfer summary. • **Agree** net pay per cashbook to payroll. • **Inspect** payroll for **unusual items** and **investigate** them further by **discussion** with management. • Perform **proof-in-total (analytical review)** on payroll and compare to figure in draft financial statements to assess reasonableness.
EXISTENCE	• **Vouch** selected amounts from the trade accounts payables listing and accruals listing to supporting documentation such as purchase orders and suppliers' invoices. • Obtain selected suppliers' statements and **reconcile** these to the relevant suppliers' accounts. • Perform a **confirmation of accounts payables** for a sample. • Perform **analytical procedures** comparing current year balances to the previous year to confirm reasonableness, and also calculating payables' turnover and comparing to the previous year.
RIGHTS AND OBLIGATIONS	• **Vouch** a sample of balances to supporting documentation such as purchase orders and suppliers' invoices to obtain audit evidence regarding rights and obligations.
VALUATION AND ALLOCATION	• **Trace** selected samples from the trade accounts payables listing and accruals listing to the supporting documentation (purchase orders, minutes authorising expenditure, suppliers' invoices etc). • Obtain selected suppliers' statements and **reconcile** these to the relevant suppliers' accounts. • For a sample of **accruals, recalculate** the amount of the accrual to ensure the amount accrued is correct. • **Compare** the current year balances for trade accounts payables and accruals to the previous year. • **Compare** the amounts owed to a sample of individual suppliers in the trade accounts payables listing to amounts owed to these suppliers in the previous year. • **Compare** the payables' turnover and payables' days to the previous year and industry data.
CUT-OFF	• For a sample of vouchers, **compare the dates** with the dates they were recorded in the ledger for application of correct cut-off. • **Test transactions** around the year-end to determine whether amounts have been recognised in the correct financial period. • **Perform analytical procedures** on purchase returns, comparing the purchase returns as a % of sales or cost of sales to the previous year.

ACCURACY	• **Recalculate** the mathematical accuracy of a sample of suppliers' invoices to confirm the amounts are correct. • **Recast** calculation of **remuneration.** • **Reperform** calculation of **statutory deductions** to confirm whether correct. • Confirm validity of **other deductions** by **agreeing** to supporting documentation. • **Recast** calculation of **other deductions**.
OCCURRENCE	• For a sample of vouchers, **inspect** supporting documentation such as authorised purchase orders. • **Agree individual remuneration** per payroll to personnel records, records of hours worked, salary agreements etc. • Confirm **existence** of employees on payroll by meeting them, attending wages payout, inspecting personnel and tax records, and confirmation from managers. • **Agree benefits** on payroll to supporting correspondence.
CLASSIFICATION AND UNDERSTANDABILITY	• **Review** the trade accounts payables listing to identify any large debits (which should be reclassified as receivables or deposits) or long-term liabilities which should be disclosed separately. • **Read** the disclosure notes relevant to liabilities in the draft financial statements and review for understandability.
ACCURACY AND VALUATION	• **Read** the disclosure notes to ensure the information is accurate and properly presented at the appropriate amounts.

2.2 Confirmation of trade payables

We have already discussed the receivables' confirmation procedure in Chapter 14. It is also possible to undertake confirmation of trade payables, although this is not used a great deal in practice because the auditor can test trade payables by examining **reliable, independent evidence** in the form of suppliers' invoices and suppliers' statements. However, where an entity's internal controls are weak, suppliers' statements may not be available and in this situation, it may be relevant to undertake confirmation procedures. Confirmation of trade payables provides evidence primarily for the **completeness** assertion.

Where the entity has **strong controls** in place to ensure that all liabilities are recorded, the confirmation will focus on **large balances**.

Where the auditor is **concerned** about the presence of **unrecorded liabilities**, regular suppliers with **small or zero balances** on their accounts and a sample of **other accounts** will be confirmed as well as **large balances**.

Auditors use a **positive confirmation** referred to as a **blank or zero-balance confirmation**. This confirmation **does not state** the balance owed but requires the supplier to declare the amount owed at the year-end and to provide a detailed statement of the account. When the confirmation is received back, the amount must be **reconciled** with the entity's records.

The selection and sending out of accounts payables' confirmations should be controlled using the same procedures as for the receivables' confirmation that we discussed in Chapter 14.

2.3 Reconciliations of accounts payables with suppliers' statements

Many suppliers provide **monthly statements** to their customers. These may therefore be available in the entity for examination. Because they are a source of documentary evidence originating outside of the entity, they are a **reliable** source of evidence to support suppliers' balances and provide evidence as to the **existence, completeness** and **valuation** of balances.

Having said this, auditors do still need to be **cautious** when using them as they may have been **tampered** with by the entity. The auditor should not rely on **photocopies or faxed statements**. If there is any doubt, the auditor should request a copy **directly** from the supplier or confirm the balance with the supplier (see above).

When selecting accounts for testing, the auditor should consider the **volume of business** during the year, not the balance outstanding at the year-end, because the risk is understatement of balances. Most differences between balances on suppliers' statements and the year-end accounts payables' listing are likely to be due to goods and cash-in-transit and disputed amounts, however all differences need to be investigated thoroughly.

Question

Trade payables and accruals

You have been assigned to the audit of Carter Brandon Co (CBC), and you are drafting the audit programme for payables and accruals for the year ended 31 December 20X7.

The company operates from a site in West Wendon. All raw materials are received in the stores and all deliveries are checked to the delivery note and purchase order. The stores supervisor raises a goods received note and is also responsible for raising credit requests if there are any problems with the raw materials delivered.

When the purchase ledger department staff receive the purchase invoices, they match them to the relevant goods received notes and purchase orders, and post them to the computerised purchase ledger. Suppliers are paid on the last day of each month.

Other payables and accruals consist of tax, wages and other statutory deductions, accruals and time-apportioned expenses such as electricity and telephone.

Required

Describe the audit work you will carry out:

(a) To compare suppliers' statements with balances recorded on the purchase ledger
(b) To check that purchases cut-off has been applied correctly
(c) To confirm that other payables and accruals have been accurately stated.

Answer

(a) Audit work

(i) Select a sample of balances and **compare suppliers' statements with purchase ledger balances**. The extent of the sample will depend on the results of tests of controls and assessment of the effectiveness of controls within the purchases system.

(ii) **Select** the **sample on a random basis**. Selection of only large balances or those with many transactions will not yield an appropriate sample as understatement of liabilities is being tested for. Nil and negative balances will also need to be included in the sample.

(iii) If **no statement** was **available** for the supplier, **confirmation** of the balance **from the supplier** should be requested.

If the balance **agrees exactly**, no further work needs to be carried out.

Where differences arise these need to be categorised as either in-transit items or other (including disputed) items. In-transit items will be either goods or cash.

(iv) If the difference relates to goods-in-transit, **ascertain** whether the **goods** were **received** before the year-end by reference to the GRN and that they are included in year-end inventory and purchase accruals. If not, a cut-off error has occurred and should be

investigated. If the goods were received after the year-end, the difference with the suppliers' accounts is correct.

(v) Similarly, cash-in-transit would arise where the payment to the supplier was made by cheque before the year-end but was not received by him until after the year-end. The **date** the **cheque** was **raised** and its subsequent **clearing** through the bank account after the year-end should be **verified by inspecting the cash book** and the post year-end bank statements.

(vi) However, if the cheque clears after the year-end date, it may indicate that the cheque, though raised before the year-end was not sent to the supplier until after the year-end. The relevant amount should be added back to year-end accounts payable and to the end of year bank balance.

(vii) Differences which do not arise from in-transit items need to be investigated and **appropriate adjustments** made where necessary.

These differences may have arisen due to **disputed invoices**, where for example the client is demanding credit against an invoice which the supplier is not willing to agree. The client may decide not to post the invoice to the supplier account as he does not consider it to be a liability of the company. However, differences may also arise because **invoices** have been **held back** in order to reduce the level of year-end accounts payable.

(viii) If significant unexplained differences are discovered it may be necessary to **extend** my **testing**. There may also be a problem if sufficient suppliers' statements are not available. Alternative procedures, eg a circularisation may then be required.

(b) Audit work

(i) From the inventory count working papers, the **number** of the **last GRN** that was issued before the year-end will have been noted. **Select a sample** of **GRNs** issued in the period immediately before and immediately after the year-end. The period to be covered would be at least two weeks either side of the year-end.

(ii) **Concentrate** the sample on **high value items**, and more on those GRNs from before the year-end as these represent the greatest risk of cut-off error.

(iii) Check that the **GRNs** have a **correct number**, according to the last GRN issued in the year and whether the **goods** were **received before or after the year-end**.

(iv) For **GRNs** issued **before the year-end**, check whether the **inventory** has been included in the year-end inventory total. Also check whether the **payable** is either **included** in **trade payables** or **purchase accruals** by **inspecting** the relevant documentation.

(v) For **GRNs** issued **after the year-end**, to ensure that the **inventory** is **included** in the inventory records **after the year-end**. In addition, review the **purchase ledger** to ensure that the relevant **invoice** has been **posted** to the supplier account after the year-end.

(c) Audit work

(i) **Assess the system of control** instituted by management to identify and quantify accruals and accounts payable.

(ii) From the client's sundry payables and accruals listing, check that **accruals** are **calculated correctly** and verify them by reference to subsequent payments. Check that **all time apportionments** have been made correctly (for example, for electricity) by **recalculation**.

(iii) **Taxation balances**

(1) Check the **amount paid to the tax authorities** by inspecting relevant documentation. The balance at the year-end would normally represent one month's deductions and can be verified to the payroll records. The payment should be traced from the cash book to the payment book (if used) and subsequent bank statements.

(2) For the sales tax balance, **review** for **reasonableness** to the **next return. Ensure** that the **payment** for the **previous return** was for the **correct** amount and has cleared through the bank.

(iv) **Review the statement of comprehensive income** and **prior year figures** (for any accruals which have not appeared this year or which did not appear last year) and consider liabilities inherent in the trade (eg weekly wages) to ensure that all likely accruals have been provided.

(v) **Scrutinise payments** made after the year-end to ascertain whether any payments made should be accrued. This will include consideration of any payments relating to the current year which are made a long time after the year-end.

(vi) **Consider and document** the basis for **round sum accruals** and ensure it is consistent with prior years.

(vii) **Ascertain** why any **payments on account** are being made and **ensure** that the full **liability** is **provided**.

(viii) **Accrued interest** and basic **charges on loans** or overdrafts can be **agreed** to the **bank letter** received for audit purposes.

3 Non-current liabilities

FAST FORWARD

Non-current liabilities are usually authorised by the board and should be well documented.

We are concerned here with non-current liabilities comprising debentures, loan inventory and other loans **repayable** at a date **more than one year after the year-end**.

Auditors will primarily try and determine:

- **Completeness**: whether all non-current liabilities have been disclosed
- **Accuracy**: whether interest payable has been calculated correctly and included in the correct accounting period
- **Classification and understandability**: whether long-term loans and interest have been correctly disclosed in the financial statements

The major complication for the auditors is that debenture and loan agreements frequently contain conditions with which the company must comply, including restrictions on the company's total borrowings and adherence to specific borrowing ratios.

AUDIT PLAN: NON-CURRENT LIABILITIES

- **Obtain/prepare schedule of loans** outstanding at the year-end date showing, for each loan: name of lender, date of loan, maturity date, interest date, interest rate, balance at the end of the period and security.
- **Compare opening balances** to previous year's papers.
- **Test the clerical accuracy** of the analysis.
- **Compare balances** to the **general ledger**.
- **Agree name** of **lender** etc, to **register** of **debenture holders** or equivalent (if kept).
- **Trace additions** and **repayments** to **entries** in the **cash book**.
- **Confirm repayments** are in accordance with **loan agreement**.
- **Examine cancelled cheques** and **memoranda of satisfaction** for **loans repaid**.
- **Verify** that **borrowing limits** imposed by agreements are **not exceeded**.
- **Examine signed Board minutes** relating to **new borrowings/repayments**.

AUDIT PLAN: NON-CURRENT LIABILITIES

- **Obtain direct confirmation** from **lenders** of the amounts outstanding, accrued interest and what security they hold.
- **Verify interest charged** for the period and the adequacy of accrued interest.
- **Confirm assets charged** have been **entered** in the **register of charges** and **notified** to the **Registrar**.
- **Review restrictive covenants** and provisions relating to default:
  - **Review** any **correspondence** relating to the loan
  - **Review confirmation** replies for non-compliance
  - If a **default** appears to exist, determine its **effect**, and schedule findings
- **Review minutes, cash book** to confirm that all **loans have been recorded**.
- **Review draft accounts** to ensure that **disclosures** for non-current liabilities are correct and in accordance with accounting standards. Any elements repayable within one year should be classified under current liabilities.

4 Provisions and contingencies

AST FORWARD

The accounting treatments for provisions and contingencies are complex and involve judgement and this can make them difficult to audit.

4.1 Accounting issues

ey terms

A **provision** is a liability of uncertain timing or amount.

A **liability** is a present obligation of the entity arising from past events, the settlement of which is expected to result in an outflow from the entity of resources embodying economic benefits.

An **obligating event** is an event that creates a legal or constructive obligation that results in an entity having no realistic alternative to settling that obligation.

A **legal obligation** is an obligation that derives from:

(a) A contract (through its explicit or implicit terms),
(b) Legislation, or
(c) Other operation of law

A **constructive obligation** is an obligation that derives from an entity's actions where:

(a) By an established pattern of past practice, published policies or a sufficiently specific current statement, the entity has indicated to other parties that it will accept certain responsibilities, and
(b) As a result, the entity has created a valid expectation on the part of those other parties that it will discharge those responsibilities.

A **contingent liability** is:

(a) A possible obligation that arises from past events and whose existence will be confirmed only by the occurrence or non-occurrence of one or more uncertain future events not wholly within the control of the entity, or
(b) A present obligation that arises from past events but is not recognised because:
  (i) It is not probable that an outflow of resources embodying economic benefits will be required to settle the obligation, or
  (ii) The amount of the obligation cannot be measured with sufficient reliability.

A **contingent asset** is a possible asset that arises from past events and whose existence will be confirmed only by the occurrence or non-occurrence of one or more uncertain future events not wholly within the control of the entity.

Under IAS 37 *Provisions, contingent liabilities and contingent assets*, an entity should not recognise a contingent asset or a contingent liability. However if it becomes probable that an outflow of future economic benefits will be required for a previous contingent liability, a provision should be recognised. A contingent asset should not be accounted for unless its realisation is virtually certain; if an inflow of economic benefits has become probable, the asset should be disclosed.

Examples of the principal types of contingencies disclosed by companies are:

- **Guarantees** (for group companies, of staff pension schemes, of completion of contracts)
- **Discounted bills of exchange**
- **Uncalled liabilities** on shares or loan inventory
- **Lawsuits** or claims pending
- **Options** to purchase assets

4.2 Obtaining audit evidence of contingencies

Part of ISA 501 *Audit evidence – specific considerations for selected items* covers contingencies relating to litigation and legal claims, which will represent the major part of audit work on contingencies. Litigation and claims involving the entity may have a material effect on the financial statements, and so will require adjustment to/disclosure in those financial statements.

The auditor shall design and perform procedures in order to identify any litigation and claims involving the entity which may give rise to a risk of material misstatement. Such procedures would include the following.

- **Make appropriate inquiries of management** and others including in-house legal advisers.
- **Review minutes of meetings** of those charged with governance and **correspondence** between the entity and its external legal advisers.
- **Review legal expense** accounts.
- **Use any information** obtained regarding the entity's business including information obtained from discussions with any in-house legal department.

When litigation or claims have been identified or when the auditor believes they may exist, the auditor shall seek **direct communication** with the entity's external legal advisers through a **letter of inquiry** that is prepared by management and sent by the auditor, requesting the legal adviser to communicate directly with the auditor. This assists the auditor in obtaining sufficient appropriate audit evidence as to whether potentially material litigation and claims are known and management's estimates of the financial implications, including costs, are reasonable. The letter may be one of **general inquiry** or one of **specific inquiry**.

A letter of **general inquiry** requests the entity's external legal advisers to inform the auditor of any litigation and claims that they are aware of, together with an assessment of the outcome of the litigation and claims, and an estimate of the financial implications, including costs involved.

However, if it is considered **unlikely** that the entity's external legal advisers will respond appropriately to a letter of general inquiry, the auditor may seek direct communication through a letter of **specific inquiry**. This will include:

- A **list** of litigation and claims
- Where available, **management's assessment** of the outcome of each of the identified litigation and claims and its **estimate** of the financial implications, including costs involved
- A request that the entity's external legal advisers **confirm the reasonableness** of management's assessments and provide the auditor with **further information** if they consider the list to be incomplete or incorrect.

In certain circumstances (the matter is a significant risk, the matter is complex, there is disagreement between management and legal advisers), the auditor also may judge it necessary to **meet** with the entity's external legal advisers to discuss the likely outcome of the litigation or claims. These meetings require management's permission and a member of management will be present at the meeting.

If management **refuses** to give the auditor permission to communicate or meet with the entity's external legal advisers, or the entity's external legal advisers refuse to respond appropriately to the letter of inquiry, or are prohibited from responding, and the auditor is unable to obtain sufficient appropriate audit evidence by performing alternative audit procedures, the auditor shall modify the opinion in the auditor's report in accordance with ISA 705 *Modifications to the opinion in the independent auditor's report.*

The auditor shall request management and, where appropriate, those charged with governance to provide **written representations** that all known actual or possible litigation and claims whose effects should be considered when preparing the financial statements have been disclosed to the auditor and accounted for and disclosed in accordance with the applicable financial reporting framework.

4.3 The audit of provisions

The following audit plan can be used in the audit of provisions.

AUDIT PLAN: PROVISIONS/CONTINGENCIES

- **Obtain details** of all **provisions** which have been included in the **accounts** and all **contingencies** that have been disclosed.
- **Obtain** a **detailed analysis** of all **provisions** showing opening balances, movements and closing balances.
- **Determine** for each material provision whether the company has a **present obligation** as a result of past events by:
  - **Review** of **correspondence** relating to the item
  - **Discussion** with the **directors**. Have they created a valid expectation in other parties that they will discharge the obligation?
- **Determine** for each material provision **whether** it is **probable** that a **transfer of economic benefits** will be required to settle the obligation by:
  - Checking whether any **payments** have been made in the post year-end period in respect of the item by reviewing after-date cash
  - **Review of correspondence** with solicitors, banks, customers, insurance company and suppliers both pre and post year-end
  - **Sending** a **letter** to the **solicitor** to obtain his views (where relevant)
  - **Discussing** the **position** of similar **past provisions** with the directors. Were these provisions eventually settled?
  - **Considering** the **likelihood** of **reimbursement**
- **Recalculate** all provisions made.
- **Compare** the **amount provided** with any post year-end payments and with any amount paid in the past for similar items.
- In the event that it is not possible to estimate the amount of the provision, check that a **contingent liability** is **disclosed** in the accounts.
- **Consider** the **nature** of the **client's business**. Would you expect to see any other provisions eg warranties?
- Consider the adequacy of **disclosure** of provisions, contingent assets and contingent liabilities in accordance with IAS 37.

am focus
int

The audit of provisions is notoriously complex because of the degree of judgement used and the availability of sufficient appropriate audit evidence. This is likely to be tested in a mini scenario type question so you must be able to apply your knowledge to the circumstances in the question.

5 Capital and other issues

FAST FORWARD

The main concern with share capital and reserves is that the company has complied with the law.

The issued share capital as stated in the accounts must be **agreed** in total with the **share register**. An examination of transfers on a test basis should be made in those cases where a company handles its own registration work. Where the registration work is dealt with by independent registrars, auditors will normally examine the reports submitted by them to the company, and obtain from them at the year-end a certificate of the share capital in issue.

Auditors should check carefully whether clients have complied with local legislation about share issues or purchase of own shares. Auditors should take particular care if there are any movements in reserves that cannot be distributed, and should confirm that these movements are **valid**.

AUDIT PLAN: CAPITAL AND RELATED ISSUES	
SHARE EQUITY CAPITAL	• **Agree** the **authorised share capital** with the statutory documents governing the company's constitution. • **Agree changes** to **authorised share capital** with **properly authorised resolutions**.
ISSUE OF SHARES	• **Verify any issue** of share capital or other changes during the year with general and **board minutes**. • **Ensure issue or change** is within the **terms** of the **constitution**, and directors possess appropriate **authority** to issue shares. • **Confirm** that **cash** or **other consideration** has been **received** or **receivable(s) is included** as called-up share capital not paid.
TRANSFER OF SHARES	• **Verify transfers of shares** by reference to: – Correspondence – Completed and stamped transfer forms – Cancelled share certificates – Minutes of directors' meeting • **Review the balances** on **shareholders' accounts** in the register of members and the total list with the amount of issued share capital in the general ledger.
DIVIDENDS	• **Agree dividends** paid and proposed pre year-end to **authority** in minute books and **reperform calculation** with **total share capital** issued to ascertain whether there are any outstanding or unclaimed dividends. • **Agree dividend payments** with **documentary evidence** (say, the returned dividend warrants). • Test that **dividends do not contravene** distribution provisions by reviewing the legislation. • **Inspect** tax returns to insure that **imputed tax** has been accounted for to the taxation authorities and correctly treated in the accounts.
RESERVES	• Agree **movements on reserves** to supporting authority. • **Ensure that movements on reserves do not contravene** the **legislation** and the company's constitution by reviewing the legislation • **Confirm** that the **company** can **distinguish distributable** reserves from those that are **non-distributable**. • **Ensure appropriate disclosures** of movements on reserves are made in the company's accounts by **inspection** of the financial statements.

Chapter Roundup

- The largest figure in **current liabilities** will normally be **trade accounts payable** which are generally audited by comparison of **suppliers' statements** with **purchase ledger accounts.**
- Non-current liabilities are usually authorised by the board and should be well documented.
- The accounting treatments for provisions and contingencies are complex and involve judgement and this can make them difficult to audit.
- The main concern with **share capital and reserves** is that the company has complied with the law.

Quick Quiz

1 What are the two primary objectives of year-end work on liabilities?

(1) ....

(2) ....

2 Give two instances where trade accounts payables' confirmation is required.

(1) ....

(2) ....

3 State four issues auditors should consider when carrying out analytical review on wages and salaries.

(1) ....

(2) ....

(3) ....

(4) ....

4 Complete the definition

Non-current liabilities comprise ...., ...-........................ and other loans .... at a date .... a year .... the year-end.

5 What are the audit objectives relating to share capital?

(1) ....

(2) ....

(3) ....

Answers to Quick Quiz

1 To ensure (1) completely and (2) accurately recorded.

2 (1) Supplier statements are unavailable
(2) Weak internal controls

3 (1) Salary rate changes
(2) Average wage by month over the year
(3) Sale/employee
(4) Payroll proof in total

4 debentures, loan-inventory, repayable, more than, after.

5 Share capital has been (1) properly classified and (2) disclosed in the financial statements and changes are (3) properly authorised.

Now try the question below from the Exam Question Bank

Number	Level	Marks	Time
Q21	Examination	30	54 mins

17

Not-for-profit organisations

Topic list	Syllabus reference
1 Objectives of not-for-profit organisations	E6
2 Audit planning	E6
3 Audit evidence	E6
4 Audit reporting	E6

Introduction

This chapter looks at the audit of not-for-profit organisations. Such entities may or may not be required to have a statutory audit under legislation. They may choose to have a non-statutory audit under the terms of a charitable deed or as part of good practice.

The points made in this chapter about the issues inherent in these entities are relevant for any kind of assurance work in not-for-profit organisations. These entities will have particular features, the most obvious being the difference in objectives of the entity, which will affect the way the work is carried out.

In this chapter we look specifically at the aspects of audit planning, evidence and reporting in not-for-profit organisations and how these differ from for-profit organisations.

Study guide

		Intellectual level
E6	**Not-for-profit organisations**	
(a)	Apply audit techniques to small not-for-profit organisations	2
(b)	Explain how the audit of small not-for-profit organisations differs from the audit of for-profit organisations	1

Exam guide

An exam question on not-for-profit organisations may come up as a scenario-based question on audit planning or evidence. In this case, use your knowledge of not-for-profit organisations as well as the clues given in the scenario to generate ideas for your answer. The December 2008 paper had a question on audit planning for a charity – there were 12 marks for identifying inherent risk areas and four marks on the control environment.

1 Objectives of not-for-profit organisations

FAST FORWARD

There are various types of organisations such as charities which do not exist for the purpose of maximising shareholder wealth but which may still require an audit.

1.1 Not-for-profit organisations

Before considering what a not-for-profit organisation's audit will entail, it will be helpful to consider the types of entities that might exist with objectives other than to make a profit and their objectives, as these will impact on the way that they report and the audit that is carried out.

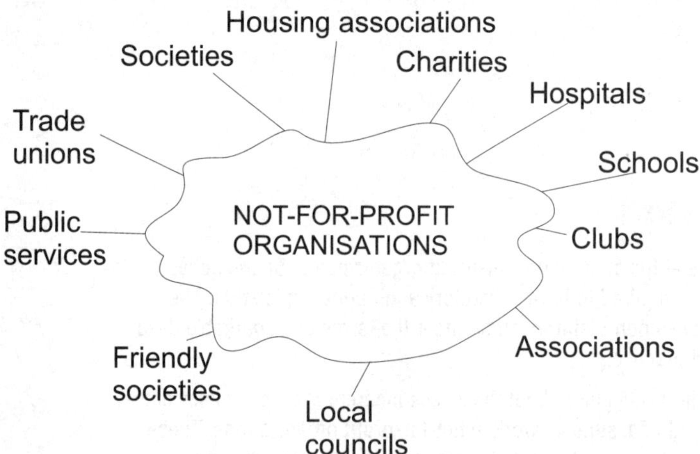

1.2 Objectives of not-for-profit organisations

A hospital could operate at a profit by not spending all the money it receives in its budget. However, the key objective of a hospital is to provide health services to the public, not to make a profit. As its income is fixed, it is more likely to focus on **cost-saving** so that it can operate within its budget.

Question **Objectives**

Identify the key objectives and focus of the types of association listed above.

Answer

Charities and friendly societies	To carry out the charitable purpose. May involve fund-raising, receiving donations, managing invested funds, controlling costs.
Schools	To provide education. Likely to involve managing a tight budget (either from fees or government funds).
Clubs, associations, societies, unions	To further the aims of the club, provide a service to members. May include managing subscriptions paid and keeping costs of running the club down.
Housing associations	Managing the related houses and providing facilities for residents. May involve rent collection and maintenance costs or even building costs of future developments.
Local councils, public services	To provide local services to a budget based on public money. Likely to be focused on value for money as they are in the public eye.

1.3 Reporting

We noted in Chapter 1 that many not-for-profit organisations are legislated for and the acts which relate to them may specify how they are to report their results.

Many of the organisations mentioned above may be companies (often companies limited by guarantee) and so are required to prepare financial statements and have them audited under companies legislation.

In the UK, some of the entities will have associated **Statements of Recommended Practice** (SORPs). SORPs are recommendations on accounting practices for specialised industries or sectors. They supplement accounting standards and other legal and regulatory requirements. For example, there is a SORP for charities (*Accounting and reporting by charities*) outlining what a charity's accounts should comprise.

1.4 Audit

Where a statutory audit is required, the auditors will be required to produce the statutory audit opinion concerning the truth and fairness of financial statements.

Where a statutory audit is not required, it is possible that the organisation might have one anyway for the benefit of interested stakeholders, such as the public or people who donate to a charity.

It is also possible that such entities will have special, additional requirements of an audit. These may be required by a regulator, or by the constitution of the organisation. For example, a charity's constitution may require an audit of whether the charity is operating in accordance with its charitable purpose. The Charity Commission for England and Wales has been established by law as the regulator and registrar for charities in England and Wales, for example.

1.5 Conclusion

An audit of a not-for-profit organisation may vary from a 'for profit audit' due to:

- Its objectives and the impact on operations and reporting
- The purpose for which an audit is required

When carrying out an audit of a not-for-profit organisation, it is vital that the auditor establishes:

- Whether a statutory audit is required
- If a statutory audit it not required, what the objectives of the engagement are
- What the engagement is to report on
- To whom the report should be addressed
- What form the report should take

Exam focus point

> You should think around the issues raised for the audit in relation to all the following entities, and be able to apply similar facts and reasoning to any not-for-profit organisation which comes up in the exam. Remember, the issues relating to small companies that we have discussed in this Study Text may also apply to small not-for-profit organisations as well. There is a useful article on not-for-profit organisations in the September 2009 edition of *Student Accountant*, which you can also access on the ACCA's website.

2 Audit planning

FAST FORWARD

> The audit risks associated with not-for-profit organisations may well be different from other entities.

2.1 Small charity audit

When planning the audit of a charity, the auditors should particularly consider the following:

- The **scope** of the audit
- Recent **recommendations** of the regulatory bodies
- The **acceptability of accounting policies** adopted
- **Changes in circumstances** in the sector in which the charity operates
- **Past experience** of the effectiveness of the charity's accounting system
- **Key audit areas**
- The **amount of detail included** in the financial statements on which the auditors are required to report

The scope of the audit is two-fold. The auditors have to report on the truth and fairness of the financial statements for the benefit of the trustees and also on whether the charity is meeting its objectives. The auditors should therefore establish what the objectives are and consider how they are to identify whether the objectives are being met. In order to identify the key audit areas, the auditors will have to consider **audit risk**.

2.1.1 Audit risk

FAST FORWARD

> **Cash** may be significant in small not-for-profit organisations and **controls** are likely to be **limited**. Income may well be a risk area, particularly where money is donated or raised informally.

There are certain risks applicable to charities that might not necessarily be applicable to other small companies. The auditors should consider the following:

Issue	Key factors
Inherent risk	• The complexity and extent of regulation • The significance of donations and cash receipts • Difficulties of the charity in establishing ownership and timing of voluntary income where funds are raised by non-controlled bodies • Lack of predictable income or precisely identifiable relationship between expenditure and income • Uncertainty of future income • Restrictions imposed by the objectives and powers given by charities' governing documents • The importance of restricted funds • The extent and nature of trading activities must be compatible with the entity's charitable status • The complexity of tax rules (whether income, capital, sales or local rates) relating to charities

Issue	Key factors
	• The sensitivity of certain key statistics, such as the proportion of resources used in administration • The need to maintain adequate resources for future expenditure whilst avoiding the build up of reserves which could appear excessive
Control risk	• The amount of time committed by trustees to the charity's affairs • The skills and qualifications of individual trustees • The frequency and regularity of trustee meetings • The form and content of trustee meetings • The independence of trustees from each other • The division of duties between trustees • The degree of involvement in, or supervision of, the charity's transactions on the part of individual trustees
Control environment	• A recognised plan of the charity's structure showing clearly the areas of responsibility and lines of authority and reporting • Segregation of duties • Supervision by trustees of activities of staff where segregation of duties is not practical • Competence, training and qualification of paid staff and any volunteers appropriate to the tasks they have to perform • Involvement of the trustees in the recruitment, appointment and supervision of senior executives • Access of trustees to independent professional advice where necessary • Budgetary controls in the form of estimates of income and expenditure for each financial year and comparison of actual results with the estimates on a regular basis • Communication of results of such reviews to the trustees on a regular basis

2.1.2 Internal controls

Small charities will generally suffer from internal control weaknesses common to small enterprises, such as **lack of segregation of duties** and the use of **unqualified staff**. Shortcomings may arise from the staff's lack of training and also, if they are volunteers, from their attitude, in that they may resent formal procedures.

The auditors will have to consider particularly carefully whether they will be able to obtain adequate assurance that the accounting records do reflect all the transactions of the enterprise and bear in mind whether there are any related statutory reporting requirements.

The following types of internal control might be typical of a number of charities.

Cash donations	
Source	**Examples of controls**
Collecting boxes and tins	Numerical control over boxes and tins Satisfactory sealing of boxes and tins so that any opening prior to recording cash is apparent Regular collection and recording of proceeds from collecting boxes Dual control over counting and recording of proceeds
Postal receipts	Unopened mail kept securely Dual control over mail opening Immediate recording of donations on opening of mail or receipt Agreement of bank paying-in slips to record of receipts by an independent person

Cash donations	
Source	**Examples of controls**
Deeds of covenant	Regular checks and follow-up procedures to ensure due amounts are received Regular checks to ensure all tax repayments have been obtained
Legacies	Comprehensive correspondence files maintained in respect of each legacy Regular reports and follow-up procedures undertaken in respect of outstanding legacies
Donations in kind	In case of charity shops, separation of recording, storage and sale of inventory

Other income	
Source	**Examples of controls**
Fund-raising activities	Records maintained for each fund-raising event Other appropriate controls maintained over receipts Controls maintained over expenses as for administrative expenses
Central and local government grants and loans	Regular checks that all sources of income or funds are fully utilised and appropriate claims made Ensuring income or funds are correctly applied by adequate monitoring

Use of resources	
Resource	**Examples of controls**
Restricted funds	Separate records maintained of relevant income, expenditure and assets Terms controlling application of funds Oversight of application of fund monies by independent personnel or trustees
Grants to beneficiaries	Records maintained, as appropriate, of requests for material grants received and their treatment Appropriate checks made on applications and applicants for grants, and that amounts paid are in accordance with legislation Records maintained of all grant decisions, checking that proper authority exists, that adequate documentation is presented to decision-making meetings, and that any conflicts of interest are recorded Controls to ensure grants made are properly spent by the recipient for the specified purpose

Question

Audit risks

The Midvale League is a small association. It runs several local football leagues for various ages and stages. It employs a general administrator and some casual bar staff. Any player who appears in more than 30% of a team's games for the season is required to pay a subscription to the association. The subscriptions pay for the administrator's wages, the referee's fees, team coaches' expenses and a lease on a sport's club comprising a clubhouse, changing facilities and three football pitches. The administrator also acts as groundsman. There is a bar in the clubhouse which is run for the benefit of members at a profit which covers bar staff wages and contributes to other expenses of the club. The association pays a local firm of accountants to prepare management accounts every quarter and to produce annual financial statements which it then audits for the benefit of members of the club.

Required

Identify any audit risks arising from The Midvale League.

Answer

Inherent risks

The classification of the sport's club **lease** may be problematic. It is certainly likely to be their biggest financial commitment. The auditor will need to determine whether the terms of the lease mean that it should be included on the statement of financial position as an asset, showing the corresponding liability or whether it does not qualify. If the terms of the lease agreement imply that the lease is merely an operating lease, the auditors should consider whether this has implications for the **going concern** of the association, as if it obtains no long-term benefit from the lease, it might be faced with the situation where it has nowhere to operate in the foreseeable future, in which case, the purpose of the association is gone.

The auditors will also have to consider the role of the general administrator, who fulfils a number of roles. He is clearly a **key man** to the association, and it might find that it had difficulties if he was incapacitated, not least perhaps in affording a replacement and any sickness benefit they were required to pay by law.

It is unclear what degree of financial record keeping the administrator takes on. The audit firm is hired to produce **quarterly management accounts**. It will gain some assurance from the fact that it prepares the accounts, but there is also a risk that day to day transactions are not **properly recorded**, as there appears to be nobody with financial expertise 'at the coal face'. Given that the administrator will record or maintain the relevant records to be passed on to the accountancy firm, there is also an issue of **segregation of duties** here.

The auditors should be aware of any legal issues relating to the bearing of a licence for the bar, particularly perhaps the danger that the licence might be jeopardised by the sale of liquor to underage drinkers. The loss of the licence to serve alcohol could severely diminish the income of the club to the point where it could no longer function.

The auditors will also need to pay attention to the membership of the association from the point of view of completeness of income.

3 Audit evidence

FAST FORWARD

Obtaining audit evidence may be a problem, particularly where organisations have informal arrangements and this may impact on the auditor's report.

3.1 Small charity

When designing substantive procedures for charities the auditors should give special attention to the possibility of:

- **Understatement or incompleteness** of the **recording of all income** including gifts in kind, cash donations, and legacies
- **Overstatement of cash grants or expenses**
- **Misanalysis** or misuse in the application of funds
- **Misstatement** or omission of **assets** including donated properties and investments
- The existence of **restricted or uncontrollable funds** in foreign or independent branches

Completeness of income can be a particularly problematic area. Areas auditors may check include:

- Loss of income through fraud
- Recognition of income from professional fund raisers
- Recognition of income from branches, associates or subsidiaries
- Income from informal fundraising groups
- Income from grants

3.1.1 Overall review of financial statements

The auditors must consider carefully whether the **accounting policies** adopted are **appropriate** to the activities, constitution and objectives of the charity, and are consistently applied, and whether the financial statements adequately disclose these policies and present fairly the state of affairs and the results for the accounting period.

In particular the auditors should consider the basis of disclosing income from fund-raising activities (for example, net or gross), accounting for income and expenses (accruals or cash), the capitalising of expenditure on non-current assets, apportioning administrative expenditure and recognising income from donations and legacies.

Charities without significant endowments or accumulated funds will often be dependent upon future income from voluntary sources. In these circumstances auditors may question whether a going concern basis of accounting is appropriate.

Question

Charity audit

You have recently been appointed auditor of Links Famine Relief, a small registered charity which receives donations from individuals to provide food in famine areas around the world.

The charity is run by a voluntary management committee, which has monthly meetings and it employs the following full-time staff:

(a) A director, Mr Roberts, who suggests fund raising activities and payments for relief of famine, and implements the policies adopted by the management committee

(b) A secretary and bookkeeper, Mrs Beech, who deals with correspondence and keeps the accounting records

You are planning the audit of income of the charity for the year ended 5 April 20X7 and are considering the controls which should be exercised over this area.

The previous year's accounts, to 5 April 20X6 (which have been audited by another firm) show the following income.

	$	$
Gifts under non-taxing arrangements		14,745
Tax reclaimed on gifts under non-taxing arrangements		4,915
		19,660
Donations through the post		63,452
Autumn Fair		2,671
Other income		
Legacies	7,538	
Bank deposit account interest	2,774	
		10,312
		96,095

Notes

(a) Income from gifts under non-taxing arrangements is stated net. Each person who pays by deed of covenant has filled in a special tax form, which is kept by the full-time secretary, Mrs Beech.

(b) All gifts under non-taxing arrangements are paid by banker's order – they are credited directly to the charity's bank account from the donor's bank. Donors make their payments by deed of covenant either monthly or annually.

(c) The tax reclaimed on these gifts is 1/3 of the net value of the gifts, and relates to income received during the year – as the tax is received after the year-end, an appropriate amount recoverable is included in the statement of financial position. The treasurer, who is a voluntary (unpaid) member of the management committee, completes the form for reclaiming the income tax, using the special tax forms (in (a) above) and checks to the secretary's records that each donor has made the full payment in the year required by the arrangement.

(d) Donations received through the post are dealt with by Mrs Beech. These donations are either cheques or cash (bank notes and coins). Mrs Beech prepares a daily list of donations received,

which lists the cheques received and total cash (divided between the different denominations of bank notes and coins). The total on this form is recorded in the cash book. She then prepares a paying-in slip and banks these donations daily. When there is a special fund-raising campaign, Mrs Beech receives help in dealing with these donations from voluntary members of the management committee.

(e) The Autumn Fair takes place every year on a Saturday in October – members of the management committee and other supporters of the charity give items to sell (for example food, garden plants, clothing). A charge is made for entrance to the fair and coffee and biscuits are available at a small charge. At the end of the fair, Mrs Beech collects the takings from each of the stalls and she banks them the following Monday.

(f) Legacies are received irregularly, and are usually sent direct to the director of the charity, who gives them to Mrs Beech for banking – they are stated separately on the daily bankings form (in (d) above).

(g) Bank deposit account interest is paid gross of income tax by the bank, as the Links Famine Relief is a charity.

Required

List and briefly describe the work you would carry out on the audit of income of the charity, the controls you would expect to see in operation and the problems you may experience for the following sources of income, as detailed in the statement above.

(a) Gifts under non-taxing arrangements
(b) Tax reclaimed on gifts made under non-taxing arrangements
(c) Donations received through the post
(d) Autumn Fair

Answer

The audit consideration in relation to the various sources of income of the Links Famine Relief charity would be as follows.

(a) *Gifts made under non-taxing arrangements*

This type of income should not present any particular audit problem as the donations are made by banker's order direct to the charity's bank account and so it would be difficult for such income to be 'intercepted' and misappropriated.

Specific tests required would be as follows.

(i) Agree a sample of receipts from the bank statements to the cash book to ensure that the income has been properly recorded.

(ii) Agree a sample of the receipts to the special tax forms to ensure that the full amount due has been received.

Any discrepancies revealed by either of the above tests should be followed up with Mrs Beech.

(b) *Tax reclaimed on gifts made under non-taxing arrangements*

Once again this income should not pose any particular audit problems. The auditors should inspect the claim form submitted to the tax authorities and calculate whether the amount of the claim represents 1/3 of the net value of the covenants recorded as having been received.

(c) *Donations received through the post*

There is a serious problem here as the nature of this income is not predictable and also because of the lack of internal checks, with Mrs Beech being almost entirely responsible for the receipt of these monies, the recording of the income and the banking of the cash and cheques received. The auditors may ultimately have to express a qualified opinion in this area.

Notwithstanding the above reservations, specific audit tests required would be as follows.

(i) Agree the details on the daily listings of donations received to the cash book, bank statements and paying-in slips, observing whether the details agree in all respects and confirming that there is no evidence of any delay in the banking of this income.

(ii) Agree the donations received by reference to any correspondence which may have been received with the cheques or cash.

(iii) Consider whether the level of income appears reasonable by performing analytical procedures to make comparison with previous years and in light of any special appeals that the charity is known to have made during the course of the year.

(iv) Carry out, with permission from the management committee, surprise checks to vouch the completeness and accuracy of the procedures relating to this source of income.

(d) *Autumn Fair*

Once again there is a potential problem here because of the level of responsibility vested in one person, namely Mrs Beech.

Specific work required would be as follows.

(i) Attend the event to observe the proper application of laid down procedures and count the cash at the end of the day.

(ii) Agree any records maintained by individual stallholders to the summary prepared by Mrs Beech.

(iii) Inspect the vouchers supporting any expenditure deducted from the proceeds in order to arrive at the net bankings.

(iv) Agree the summary prepared by Mrs Beech to the entry in the cash book and on the bank statement.

4 Audit reporting

FAST FORWARD

The nature of the report will depend on statutory and entity requirements, but it should conform to the criteria in ISA 700 *Forming an opinion and reporting on financial statements.*

For not-for-profit audits where a statutory audit report is required, the auditors should issue the same report that we have considered briefly in Chapter 1. They should also consider whether any additional statutory requirements fall on the audit report.

Where an association or charity is having an audit for the benefit of its members or trustees, the standard audit report may not be required or appropriate. The auditor should bear in mind the objectives of the audit and make suitable references in the audit report. However, the ISA 700 format will still be relevant.

The auditor should ensure that he makes the following matters clear:

- The addressees of the report
- What the report relates to
- The scope of the engagement
- The respective responsibilities of auditors and management/trustees/directors
- The work done
- The opinion drawn

Chapter Roundup

- There are various types of organisations such as charities which do not exist for the purpose of maximising shareholder wealth but which may still require an audit.
- The audit risks associated with not-for-profit organisations may well be different from other entities.
- **Cash** may be significant in small not-for-profit organisations and **controls** are likely to be **limited**. Income may well be a risk area, particularly where money is donated or raised informally.
- Obtaining audit evidence may be a problem, particularly where organisations have informal arrangements and this may impact on the auditor's report.
- The nature of the report will depend on statutory and entity requirements, but it should conform to the criteria in ISA 700 *Forming an opinion and reporting on financial statements.*

Quick Quiz

1 List five examples of not-for-profit organisations.

2 All not-for-profit organisations must have a statutory audit.

True ☐

False ☐

3 Explain why income can be a problem when auditing charities.

4 Complete the table, giving two examples of controls in each area.

Cash donations	Other donations	Other income

5 Explain why the control environment in a small charity might be weak.

Answers to Quick Quiz

1 Any five from charities, hospitals, schools, clubs, associations, friendly societies, local councils, public services, trades unions, societies, housing associations

2 False

3
- Loss of income through fraud
- Recognition of income from professional fund raisers
- Recognition of income from branches, associates or subsidiaries
- Income from informal fundraising groups
- Income from grants

4

Cash donations	Other donations	Other income
Numerical control over boxes and tins	Regular checks and follow-up procedures to ensure due amounts are received	Records maintained for each fundraising event
Satisfactory sealing of boxes and tins so that any opening prior to recording cash is apparent	Regular checks to ensure all tax repayments have been obtained	Other appropriate controls maintained over receipts
Regular collection and recording of proceeds from collecting boxes	Comprehensive correspondence files maintained in respect of each legacy	Controls maintained over expenses as for administrative expenses
Dual control over counting and recording of proceeds	Regular reports and follow-up procedures undertaken in respect of outstanding legacies	Regular monitoring that all sources of income or funds are fully utilised and appropriate claims made
Unopened mail kept securely	In case of charity shops, separation of recording, storage and sale of inventory	
Dual control over the opening of mail		
Immediate recording of donations on opening of mail or receipt		
Agreement of bank paying-in slips to record of receipts by an independent person		

5
- Lack of segregation of duties
- Unqualified staff
- Lack of staff training
- Voluntary staff so unclear responsibilities
- High staff turnover
- Lack of internal audit department

Now try the question below from the Exam Question Bank

Number	Level	Marks	Time
Q22	Examination	20	36 mins

P

A

R

T

F

Review

18

Audit review and finalisation

Topic list	Syllabus reference
1 Subsequent events	F1
2 Going concern	F2
3 Written representations	F3
4 Overall review of financial statements	F4

Introduction

This chapter will consider the reviews that take place to complete the audit, which include subsequent events and going concern. These are both important disclosure issues in the financial statements, because if the disclosures are not correct, this will impact on the auditor's report.

In this chapter, we also consider the use and reliability of written representations from management as audit evidence.

Financial reporting knowledge is particularly important at the review stage of the audit. Auditors need to be able to interpret accounts and understand the requirements of specific accounting standards. Analytical procedures must be used when undertaking the final review of the financial statements.

Study guide

		Intellectual level
F1	**Subsequent events**	
(a)	Explain the purpose of a subsequent events review	1
(b)	Discuss the procedures to be undertaken in performing a subsequent events review	2
F2	**Going concern**	
(a)	Define and discuss the significance of the concept of going concern	2
(b)	Explain the importance of and the need for going concern reviews	2
(c)	Explain the respective responsibilities of auditors and management regarding going concern	1
(d)	Discuss the procedures to be applied in performing going concern reviews	2
(e)	Discuss the disclosure requirements in relation to going concern issues	2
(f)	Discuss the reporting implications of the findings of going concern reviews	2
F3	**Management representations**	
(a)	Explain the purpose of and procedure for obtaining management representations	2
(b)	Discuss the quality and reliability of management representations as audit evidence	2
(c)	Discuss the circumstances where management representations are necessary and the matters on which representations are commonly obtained	2
F4	**Audit finalisation and the final review**	
(a)	Discuss the importance of the overall review of evidence obtained	2
(b)	Explain the significance of unadjusted differences	1

Exam guide

The review stage of the audit is very important and highly likely to come up in the exam. It is very important that you understand the difference between the review stage of the audit and the earlier testing stage. A question on subsequent events was set in the pilot paper in a scenario-based question which was also linked to the potential impact on the audit report. The December 2007 paper contained a five mark knowledge-based question on going concern.

The June 2008 paper had a three mark knowledge-based question on items to be included in the representation letter, as well as 16 marks on going concern in a scenario context. The December 2008 had a 20 mark scenario question on subsequent events. The June 2009 paper had a similar requirement in question 5.

1 Subsequent events — Pilot paper, Dec 08, June 09

FAST FORWARD

Subsequent events are events occurring between the period-end and the date of the auditor's report and also include facts discovered after the auditor's report has been issued. Auditors shall consider the effect of such events on the financial statements and on their audit opinion.

Key term

Subsequent events are events occurring between the date of the financial statements and the date of the auditor's report, and facts that become known to the auditor after the date of the auditor's report.

IAS 10 *Events after the reporting period* deals with the treatment in the financial statements of events, both favourable and unfavourable, occurring after the period-end. There are two types of event defined by IAS 10:

- Those that provide evidence of conditions that existed at the year-end date (**adjusting events**)
- Those that are indicative of conditions that arose after the year-end date (**non-adjusting events**)

You should be familiar with adjusting and non-adjusting events from your financial reporting studies. Here are some examples.

Adjusting events	Non-adjusting events
Settlement of a court case	Dividends declared after the year-end
Sale of inventory after year-end providing evidence of its NRV at year-end	Fire causing destruction of major plant
Fraud or error showing the accounts are incorrect	Announcement of a major restructuring

ISA 560 *Subsequent events* provides guidance to auditors in this area. The objectives of the auditor are:

- To obtain sufficient appropriate audit evidence about whether events occurring between the date of the financial statements and the date of the auditor's report that need adjustment or disclosure in the financial statements are properly reflected in the financial statements
- To respond appropriately to facts that become known to the auditor after the date of the auditor's report which may have caused the auditor to amend the auditor's report if they were known to the auditor at the date of the report

1.1 Procedures

FAST FORWARD

Auditors have a **responsibility** to **review subsequent events** before they sign the auditor's report, and may have to take action if they become aware of subsequent events between the date they sign the auditor's report and the date the financial statements are issued.

The following time line is helpful when considering subsequent events and the auditor's responsibilities concerning them.

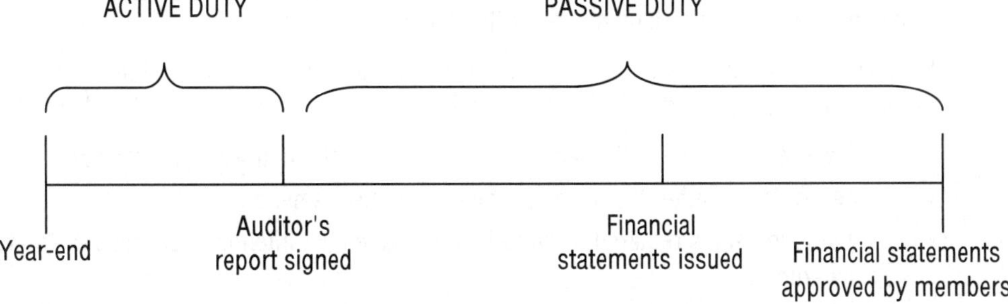

1.1.1 Events occurring up to the date of the auditor's report

The auditor shall perform procedures designed to obtain sufficient appropriate audit evidence that all events up to the date of the auditor's report that may require adjustment of, or disclosure in, the financial statements have been identified.

These procedures should be applied to any matters examined during the audit which may be susceptible to change after the year-end. They are in addition to tests on specific transactions after the period end, eg cut-off tests.

ISA 560 lists procedures to identify subsequent events which may require adjustment or disclosure. They should be performed as near as possible to the date of the auditors' report.

AUDIT PROCEDURES TO TEST SUBSEQUENT EVENTS	
Inquiries of management	Status of items involving **subjective judgement** Status of items accounted for using **preliminary or inconclusive** data Whether there are any new **commitments, borrowings or guarantees** Whether there have been any: • **Sales** or destruction of **assets** • **Issues** of **shares/debentures** or changes in business structure • **Developments** involving **risk areas, provisions** and **contingencies** • **Unusual accounting adjustments** • **Major events** (eg going concern problems) affecting appropriateness of accounting policies for estimates • Litigations or claims
Other procedures	**Review** management procedures for identifying subsequent events to ensure that such events are identified. **Read minutes** of general board/committee meetings and enquire about unusual items. **Review latest available interim financial statements** and budgets, cash flow forecasts and other management reports. **Obtain evidence** concerning any litigation or claims from the company's solicitors (only with client permission). Obtain **written representation** that all events occurring subsequent to the period-end which need adjustment or disclosure have been adjusted or disclosed.

1.1.2 Facts discovered after the date of the auditor's report but before the financial statements are issued

The financial statements are the management's responsibility. They should therefore inform the auditors of any material subsequent events between the date of the auditors' report and the date the financial statements are issued. The auditor does **not** have any obligation to perform procedures, or make enquires regarding the financial statements, **after** the date of the report.

However if the auditor becomes aware of a fact that had it been known to the auditor at the date of the report may have caused the auditor to amend the auditor's report, the auditor shall:

- **Discuss** the matter with management and those charged with governance.
- **Determine** whether the financial statements need amendment.
- If amendment is required, **inquire** how management intends to address the matter in the financial statements.

If amendment is required to the financial statements and management makes the necessary changes, the auditor must carry out a number of procedures:

- Undertake any **necessary audit procedures** on the changes made.
- **Extend audit procedures** for identifying subsequent events that may require adjustment of or disclosure in the financial statements to the date of the new auditor's report.
- Provide a **new auditor's report** on the amended financial statements.

If management does not amend the financial statements:

- If the auditor's report has not yet been provided to the entity, the auditor shall **modify the opinion** and then provide the auditor's report.
- If the auditor's report has already been provided to the entity, the auditor shall notify management and those charged with governance **not to issue** the financial statements before the amendments are made; but if the financial statements are issued anyway, the auditor shall take action to seek to **prevent reliance** on the auditor's report.

1.1.3 Facts discovered after the financial statements have been issued

Auditors have **no obligations** to perform procedures or make enquiries regarding the financial statements **after** they have been issued.
However if the auditor becomes aware of a fact that had it been known to the auditor at the date of the report may have caused the auditor to amend the auditor's report, the auditor shall:

- **Discuss** the matter with management and those charged with governance.
- **Determine** whether the financial statements need amendment.
- If amendment is required, **inquire** how management intends to address the matter in the financial statements.

If management amends the financial statements, the auditor shall carry out procedures necessary on the amendment and review the steps taken by management to ensure that anyone in receipt of the previously issued financial statements is **informed**.

The auditor shall also issue a **new or amended auditor's report** which will include an **explanatory paragraph** (known as an **emphasis of matter paragraph** or **other matter paragraph** – we discuss these further in Chapter 19) that refers to a note in the financial statements that discusses the reason for the amendment. Audit procedures will be extended to the date of the new report.

If management does not take the necessary steps, the auditor shall **notify** management and those charged with governance that the auditor will **seek to prevent future reliance** on the report. If management still does not act, the auditor shall take appropriate action to **seek to prevent reliance** on the auditor's report.

2 Going concern — Dec 07, June 08

FAST FORWARD

If the entity has inappropriately used the going concern assumption or a material uncertainty exists, this may impact on the auditor's report.

Key term

Under the **going concern assumption**, an entity is viewed as continuing in business for the foreseeable future. When the use of the going concern assumption is appropriate, assets and liabilities are recorded on the basis that the entity will be able to realise its assets and discharge its liabilities in the normal course of business.

ISA 570 *Going concern* provides guidance to auditors in this area. The objectives of the auditor are:

- To obtain sufficient appropriate audit evidence regarding the **appropriateness** of management's use of the going concern assumption
- To conclude whether a **material uncertainty** exists related to events or conditions that may cast significant doubt on the entity's ability to continue as a going concern
- To determine the **implications** for the auditor's report

ISA 570 includes examples of events or conditions that may cast doubt about the going concern assumption. These fall under three headings: 'financial', 'operating' and 'other', and are shown in the table below.

Events or conditions that may cast doubt about the going concern assumption	
Financial	• Net liability or net current liability position • Fixed-term borrowings approaching maturity without realistic prospects of renewal or repayment • Excessive reliance on short-term borrowings to finance long-term assets • Withdrawal of financial support by creditors • Negative operating cash flows

Events or conditions that may cast doubt about the going concern assumption	
	• Adverse key financial ratios • Substantial operating losses or significant deterioration in the value of assets used to generate cash flows • Arrears or discontinuance of dividends • Inability to pay creditors on due dates • Inability to comply with terms of loan agreements • Change from credit to cash-on-delivery transactions with suppliers • Inability to obtain financing for essential new product development or other essential investments
Operating	• Management intentions to liquidate or cease operations • Loss of key management without replacement • Loss of a major market, key customers, licence, or principal suppliers • Labour difficulties • Shortages of important supplies • Emergence of a highly successful competitor
Other	• Non-compliance with capital or other statutory requirements • Pending legal or regulatory proceedings against the entity • Changes in law or regulations that may adversely affect the entity • Uninsured or under-insured catastrophes when they occur

2.1 Management's responsibilities for going concern

Management has specific responsibilities relating to going concern that may be set out in law or regulation and in the financial reporting framework. IAS 1 *Presentation of financial statements*, for example, contains a specific requirement that management makes an assessment of an entity's ability to continue as a going concern.

Regardless of this, because general purpose financial statements are prepared on a going concern basis, the going concern assumption is a **fundamental principle** in the preparation of financial statements. Therefore management's responsibility for the preparation and presentation of the financial statements also encompasses a responsibility to assess the entity's ability to continue as a going concern even if there is no explicit requirement to do so in the financial reporting framework.

Management's assessment involves making a **judgement** about inherently uncertain future outcomes of events or conditions. This judgement is affected by the following:

- **Degree of uncertainty** which increases the further into the future an event/condition/outcome occurs
- **Size and complexity** of the entity
- **Nature and condition** of the business
- Judgement about the future is based on **information available** at the time the judgement is made but **subsequent events** may result in **inconsistent outcomes**

This section highlights why audit work on going concern is crucial – because of the **judgements** used by management in making its assessment of going concern.

2.2 Management's assessment

Management may have performed a **preliminary assessment** of whether the entity can continue as a going concern. If it has, the auditor shall discuss it with management. If the assessment has not been performed, the auditor shall discuss with management the basis for the intended use of the going concern assumption.

The auditor shall **remain alert** throughout the audit for evidence of events or conditions that may cast significant doubt on the entity's ability to continue as a going concern.

The auditor shall **evaluate** management's assessment of the entity's ability to continue as a going concern. However, if this assessment covers less than 12 months from the date of the financial statements, the auditor shall ask management to extend its assessment period to **at least 12 months** from that date.

The auditor shall also inquire of management its knowledge of events or conditions beyond the period of the assessment that may cast significant doubt on the entity's ability to continue as a going concern.

2.3 Events or conditions identified

If events or conditions are identified that may cast significant doubt on the entity's ability to continue as a going concern, the auditor shall obtain sufficient appropriate audit evidence to determine whether a material uncertainty exists by:

- Requesting management to make its **assessment** where this has not been done
- Evaluating management's **plans for future action**
- Evaluating the **reliability of underlying data** used to prepare a cash flow forecast and considering the **assumptions** used to make the forecast
- Considering whether any **additional facts or information** have become available since the date management made its assessment
- Requesting **written representations** from management and those charged with governance about plans for future action and the feasibility of these plans

Specific audit procedures the auditor might carry out could include the following:

- **Analyse and discuss cash flow**, profit and other relevant forecasts with management.
- **Analyse and discuss** the entity's latest available **interim financial statements** (or management accounts).
- **Review the terms of debentures and loan agreements** and determine whether they have been breached.
- **Read minutes** of the meetings of shareholders, the board of directors and important committees for reference to financing difficulties.
- **Inquire** of the entity's lawyer regarding **litigation and claims.**
- **Confirm the existence, legality and enforceability** of arrangements to provide or maintain financial support with related and third parties.
- **Assess** the **financial ability** of such parties to **provide additional funds.**
- **Consider the entity's position** concerning unfulfilled customer orders.
- **Review events after the period-end** for items affecting the entity's ability to continue as a going concern.

2.4 Audit reporting

The auditor shall consider whether a **material uncertainty** exists related to events or conditions which may cast doubt on the entity's ability to continue as a going concern, as this will impact on the opinion issued in the auditor's report because the uncertainty must be disclosed.

The following table summarises the possible scenarios that could arise following the auditor's review of going concern. We discuss audit reporting in detail in chapter 19 so you may wish to revisit this section again after having studied chapter 19. ISA 570 does provide example extracts in respect of the following scenarios and these are presented below the table.

Scenario	Impact on audit report
1 Going concern assumption appropriate but material uncertainty which is adequately disclosed	Unmodified opinion and explanatory emphasis of matter paragraph
2 Going concern assumption appropriate but material uncertainty which is not adequately disclosed	Qualified or adverse opinion (ie modified opinion)
3 Use of going concern assumption inappropriate	Adverse opinion (ie modified opinion)
4 Management unwilling to make or extend its assessment	Qualified or disclaimer of opinion (ie modified opinion)

Scenario 1: Going concern assumption appropriate but material uncertainty which is adequately disclosed

In this situation, the opinion on the financial statements will be **unmodified** but the auditor's report will include an **emphasis of matter paragraph** which is an explanatory paragraph detailing the uncertainty. The ISA contains an example of such an extract from the auditor's report:

> *Emphasis of Matter*
>
> Without qualifying our opinion, we draw attention to Note X in the financial statements which indicates that the Company incurred a net loss of ZZZ during the year ended December 31, 20X1 and, as of that date, the company's current liabilities exceeded its total assets by YYY. These conditions, along with other matters as set forth in Note X, indicate the existence of a material uncertainty that may cast significant doubt about the Company's ability to continue as a going concern.

Scenario 2: Going concern assumption appropriate but mater uncertainty which is not adequately disclosed

In this situation, as inadequate disclosure has been made of the material uncertainty, the auditor's opinion will be modified – either a qualified or adverse opinion will be issued depending on the magnitude of the uncertainty. An extract from the auditor's report where a qualified opinion is issued is provided by the ISA and set out below:

> *Basis for Qualified Opinion*
>
> The Company's financing arrangements expire and amounts outstanding are payable on March 19, 20X1. The Company has been unable to re-negotiate or obtain replacement financing. This situation indicates the existence of a material uncertainty that may cast significant doubt on the Company's ability to continue as a going concern and therefore the Company may be unable to realise its assets and discharge its liabilities in the normal course of business. The financial statements (and notes thereto) do not fully disclose this fact.
>
> *Qualified Opinion*
>
> In our opinion, except for the incomplete disclosure of the information referred to in the Basis for Qualified Opinion paragraph, the financial statements present fairly, in all material respects (or "give a true and fair view of") the financial position of the Company as at December 31, 20X0, and of its financial performance and its cash flows for the year then ended in accordance with …

Scenario 3: Use of going concern assumption inappropriate

When the going concern assumption has been used but this is considered inappropriate by the auditor, an adverse opinion must be issued, regardless of whether or not the financial statements include disclosure of the inappropriateness of management's use of the going concern assumption.

> *Basis for Adverse Opinion*
>
> [Provide explanation of inappropriate use of going concern assumption]
>
> *Adverse Opinion*
>
> In our opinion, because of the omission of the information mentioned in the Basis for Adverse Opinion paragraph, the financial statements do not present fairly (or "give a true and fair view of") the financial position of the Company as at December 31, 20X0, and of its financial performance and its cash flows for the year then ended in accordance with …

Scenario 4: Management unwilling to make or extend its assessment

In some circumstances, the auditor may ask management to make or extend its assessment. If management does not do this, a qualified opinion or a disclaimer of opinion in the auditor's report may be appropriate, because it may not be possible for the auditor to obtain **sufficient appropriate audit evidence** regarding the use of the going concern assumption in the preparation of the financial statements. Examples of auditor's reports with a disclaimer of opinion are provided in chapter 19 which looks at modifications to the auditor's opinion in detail.

2.5 Communicating to those charged with governance

The auditor shall **communicate with those charged with governance** events or conditions that may cast doubt on the entity's ability to continue as a going concern. This will include:

- Whether the events or conditions constitute a material uncertainty
- Whether the use of the going concern assumption is appropriate in the preparation and presentation of the financial statements
- The adequacy of related disclosures

3 Written representations — June 08

FAST FORWARD

> The auditor obtains **written representations** from management concerning its responsibilities and to support other audit evidence where necessary.

Key term

> **Written representations** are written statements by management provided to the auditor to confirm certain matters or to support other audit evidence. They do not include the financial statements, assertions or supporting books and records.

ISA 580 *Written representations* provides guidance to auditors in this area. The objectives of the auditor are:

- To obtain written representations that management believes that it has fulfilled the fundamental responsibilities that constitute the premise on which an audit is conducted
- To support other audit evidence relevant to the financial statements if determined by the auditor or required by other ISAs
- To respond appropriately to written representations or if management does not provide written representations requested by the auditor

There are three areas in which written representations are necessary – to **confirm management's responsibilities**, where they are **required by other ISAs** and to **support other audit evidence**. We discuss these below in more detail.

3.1 Written representations about management's responsibilities

The auditor shall request management to provide written representations on the following matters:

- That management has fulfilled its responsibility for the **preparation and presentation of the financial statements** as set out in the terms of the audit engagement and whether the financial statements are prepared and presented in accordance with the applicable financial reporting framework

- That management has provided the auditor with all **relevant information** agreed in the terms of the audit engagement and that all transactions have been recorded and are reflected in the financial statements

3.2 Other written representations

Other ISAs require written representations on specific issues but if the auditor considers it necessary to obtain representations in addition to these to support other audit evidence, the auditor shall request these other written representations.

The following table includes examples of other written representations.

Other written representations
Whether the selection and application of accounting policies are appropriate
Plans or intentions that may affect the carrying value or classification of assets and liabilities
Liabilities, both actual and contingent
Title to, or control over, assets, liens or encumbrances on assets and assets pledged as collateral
Aspects of laws, regulations and contractual agreements that may affect the financial statements, including non-compliance
All deficiencies in internal control that management is aware of have been communicated to the auditor
Written representations about specific assertions in the financial statements
Significant assumptions used in making accounting estimates are reasonable
All subsequent events requiring adjustment or disclosure have been adjusted or disclosed
The effects of uncorrected misstatements are immaterial, both individually and in aggregate
Disclosed the results of management's assessment of the risk that the financial statements may be materially misstated as a result of fraud
Disclosed all information in relation to fraud or suspected fraud involving management, employees with significant roles in internal control, and others where fraud could have a material effect on the financial statements
Disclosed all information in relation to allegations of fraud or suspected fraud communicated by employees, former employees, analysts, regulators or others
Disclosed all instances of non-compliance or suspected non-compliance with laws or regulations

3.3 Quality and reliability of written representations as audit evidence

Written representations are a form of audit evidence, however **on their own** they **do not provide sufficient appropriate audit evidence** about the issues they relate to.

In addition, the fact that management has provided reliable written representations does not affect the nature or extent of other audit evidence obtained by the auditor regarding the fulfilment of management's responsibilities, or about specific assertions in the financial statements.

You will have noted at the start of section 3 on the objectives of the auditor regarding written representations that the second objective is 'To **support** other audit evidence...' This is because although

written representations are necessary, they cannot provide sufficient appropriate audit evidence when they stand alone.

3.4 Form of written representations

The written representations shall be in the form of a representation **letter** addressed to the auditor. ISA 580 includes an example representation letter in an appendix. The date of the representation letter must be as near as practicable to, **but not after**, the date of the auditor's report on the financial statements and must be for all the financial statements and period(s) referred to in the auditor's report.

Written representations are requested from those responsible for the preparation of the financial statements – **management** is usually the responsible party. They can therefore be requested from the chief executive officer and chief financial officer, or equivalent. In some cases though, it may be that those charged with governance are also responsible for the preparation of the financial statements.

3.5 Doubt about the reliability of written representations

If written representations are **inconsistent** with other audit evidence, the auditor shall perform audit procedures to try to resolve the matter. If the matter cannot be resolved, the auditor shall reconsider the assessment of the competence, integrity and ethical values of management, and the effect this may have on the reliability of representations and audit evidence in general.

If the auditor concludes that written representations are not reliable, the auditor shall take appropriate actions, including determining the impact on the auditor's report.

3.6 Written representations not provided

If management does not provide one or more requested written representations, the auditor shall:

- **Discuss** the matter with management.
- **Re-evaluate** the integrity of management and evaluate the effect this may have on the reliability of representations and audit evidence in general.
- Take **appropriate actions**, including determining the **impact** on the auditor's report.

4 Overall review of financial statements

FAST FORWARD

The auditors must perform and document an **overall review** of the financial statements by undertaking **analytical procedures** before they can reach an opinion.

Once most of the substantive audit procedures have been carried out, the auditors will have a draft set of financial statements which should be supported by appropriate and sufficient audit evidence. At the beginning of the end of the audit process, it is usual for the auditors to undertake an **overall review** of the financial statements.

This review of the financial statements, in conjunction with the conclusions drawn from the other audit evidence obtained, gives the auditors a reasonable basis for their opinion on the financial statements. It should be carried out by a senior member of the audit team, with appropriate skills and experience.

4.1 Compliance with accounting regulations

The auditors should consider whether:

(a) The information presented in the financial statements is in accordance with local/national statutory requirements.

(b) The accounting policies employed are in accordance with accounting standards, properly disclosed, consistently applied and appropriate to the entity.

When examining the **accounting policies**, auditors should consider:

(a) Policies **commonly adopted in particular industries**

(b) Policies for which there is **substantial authoritative support**

(c) Whether any **departures from applicable accounting standards** are necessary for the financial statements to give a true and fair view

(d) Whether the **financial statements reflect the substance** of the underlying transactions and not merely their form

When compliance with local/national statutory requirements and accounting standards is considered, the auditors may find it useful to use a **checklist**.

4.2 Review for consistency and reasonableness

The auditors should consider whether the financial statements are **consistent** with their knowledge of the entity's business and with the results of other audit procedures, and the manner of disclosure is fair. This can be done by applying **analytical procedures** at or near the end of the audit in accordance with ISA 520 *Analytical procedures* which states that the auditor shall design and perform analytical procedures near the end of the audit that assist in forming an overall conclusion as to whether the financial statements are consistent with the auditor's understanding of the entity.

The principal considerations are as follows.

(a) Whether the financial statements adequately reflect the **information** and **explanations** previously obtained and conclusions previously reached during the course of the audit

(b) Whether it reveals any **new factors** which may affect the presentation of, or disclosure in, the financial statements

(c) Whether **analytical procedures** applied when completing the audit, such as comparing the information in the financial statements with other pertinent data, **produce results** which assist in arriving at the overall conclusion as to whether the financial statements as a whole are consistent with their knowledge of the entity's business

(d) Whether the **presentation** adopted in the financial statements may have been unduly influenced by the **directors' desire** to present matters in a favourable or unfavourable light

(e) The potential impact on the financial statements of the **aggregate of uncorrected misstatements** (including those arising from bias in making accounting estimates) identified during the course of the audit and the preceding period's audit, if any

The analytical review at the final stage should cover the following:

- Important accounting ratios
- Related items
- Changes in products/customers
- Price and mix changes
- Wages changes
- Variances
- Trends in production and sales
- Changes in material and labour content of production
- Other expenditure in the statement of comprehensive income
- Variations caused by industry or economy factors

As at other stages of the audit process, significant fluctuations and unexpected relationships must be investigated by **inquiries of management** and obtaining appropriate audit evidence relevant to **management's responses**, and **performing other audit procedures** considered necessary.

4.3 Accounting treatment issues

As noted in the previous section auditors review the financial statements to assess whether the **accounting policies are consistently applied**. Auditors should therefore consider whether new accounting policies are appropriate, whether matters in financial statements are consistent with each other, and whether the financial statements give a true and fair view.

4.4 Treatment of misstatements

Key terms

> A **misstatement** is a difference between the amount, classification, presentation, or disclosure of a reported financial statement item and the amount, classification, presentation, or disclosure that is required for the item to be in accordance with the applicable financial reporting framework. It can arise from error or fraud.
> An **uncorrected misstatement** is a misstatement accumulated during the audit by the auditor which has not been corrected.

ISA 450 *Evaluation of misstatements identified during the audit* requires the auditor to accumulate misstatements identified during the audit, other than those that are clearly trivial. The ISA distinguishes between **factual misstatements** (misstatements about which there is no doubt), **judgemental misstatements** (misstatements arising from management's judgement concerning accounting estimates or accounting policies) and **projected misstatements** (the auditor's best estimate of misstatements arising from sampling populations).

ISA 450 requires the auditor to communicate all misstatements accumulated during the audit with the appropriate level of management on a timely basis and to request management to correct those misstatements. If management refuses, the auditor must establish the reasons why and consider this when evaluating whether the financial statements as a whole are free from material misstatement.

As part of their completion procedures, auditors shall consider whether the **aggregate of uncorrected misstatements** in the financial statements is **material**, having first reassessed materiality in accordance with ISA 320 *Materiality in planning and performing an audit* to confirm that it is still appropriate. When determining whether uncorrected misstatements are material (individually or in aggregate), the auditor shall consider the size and nature of the misstatements and the effect of uncorrected misstatements related to prior periods on the financial statements as a whole.

4.4.1 Communication of uncorrected misstatements

ISA 450 requires the auditor to **communicate uncorrected misstatements** and their effect to those charged with governance, with material uncorrected misstatements being identified individually. The auditor shall request uncorrected misstatements to be corrected. The auditor shall also communicate the effect of uncorrected misstatements relating to prior periods.

The auditor shall request a **written representation** from management and those charged with governance whether they believe the effects of uncorrected misstatements are immaterial (individually and in aggregate) to the financial statements as a whole. A summary of these items shall be included in or attached to the representation.

4.4.2 Documentation

ISA 450 requires the auditor to document the following information:

- The amount below which misstatements would be regarded as clearly trivial
- All misstatements accumulated during the audit and whether they have been corrected
- The auditor's conclusion as to whether uncorrected misstatements are material and the basis for that conclusion

Exam focus point

> The audit review and finalisation stage of the external audit is very important. It could come up in a scenario-based question or in the knowledge-based question 2 of the paper. It is vital that you are completely comfortable with this stage of the audit process, and can distinguish it from the audit testing stage.

Chapter Roundup

- **Subsequent events** are events occurring between the period-end and the date of the auditor's report and also include facts discovered after the auditor's report has been issued. Auditors shall consider the effect of such events on the financial statements and on their audit opinion.
- Auditors have a **responsibility** to **review subsequent events** before they sign the auditor's report, and may have to take action if they become aware of subsequent events between the date they sign the auditor's report and the date the financial statements are issued.
- If the entity has inappropriately used the going concern assumption or a material uncertainty exists, this may impact on the auditor's report.
- The auditor obtains **written representations** from management concerning its responsibilities and to support other audit evidence where necessary.
- The auditors must perform and document an **overall review** of the financial statements by undertaking **analytical procedures** before they can reach an opinion.

Quick Quiz

1 State three inquiries that should be made of management to test subsequent events.

1 ....
2 ....
3 ....

2 Complete the definition, using the words given below.

Under the .... assumption, an entity is viewed as .... in business for the ....

future	going	continuing	foreseeable	concern

3 The auditors must satisfy themselves that the use of the going concern basis in the financial statements is appropriate.

True ☐

False ☐

4 List four examples of what areas analytical review at the final stage should cover.

1 ....
2 ....
3 ....
4 ....

5 In evaluating whether the financial statements give a true and fair view, auditors shall assess the materiality of uncorrected misstatements.

True ☐

False ☐

Answers to Quick Quiz

1 From:

- What the status is of items involving subjective judgement
- Whether there are any new commitments, borrowings or guarantees
- Whether any assets have been sold or destroyed
- Whether any new shares/debentures have been issued
- Whether there have been any developments in risk areas
- Any unusual accounting adjustments
- Any major events

2 going concern, continuing, foreseeable future

3 True

4 From:

- Important accounting ratios
- Related items
- Changes in products/customers
- Price and mix changes
- Wages changes
- Variances
- Trends in production and sales
- Changes in material and labour content of production
- Other income statement expenditure
- Variations caused by industry or economy factors

5 True

Now try the questions below from the Exam Question Bank

Number	Level	Marks	Time
Q23	Examination	20	36 mins
Q24	Examination	10	18 mins

PART G

Reporting

19

Reports

Topic list	Syllabus reference
1 The auditor's report on financial statements	G1
2 Reports to management	G2

Introduction

The auditor's report is the means by which the external auditors express their opinion on the truth and fairness of a company's financial statements. It is for the benefit principally of the shareholders, but also for other users as the audit report is usually kept on public record with the filed financial statements.

Many of the contents of the auditor's report are prescribed by statute. They are also subject to professional requirements in the form of ISA 700 *Forming an opinion and reporting on financial statements.* The auditor's report may be unqualified or modified and these are considered in detail in this chapter. We also look at circumstances in detail which may impact on the auditor's report: other information in documents containing audited financial statements, and opening balances and comparatives.

We end this chapter by looking at the report to management submitted to the directors and management of a company. This is also known as a letter of weakness or management letter or letter on internal control and is submitted at the end of the audit as a by-product of the audit.

Study guide

		Intellectual level
G1	**Audit reports**	
(a)	Describe and analyse the format and content of unmodified audit reports	2
(b)	Describe and analyse the format and content of modified audit reports	2
G2	**Reports to management**	
(a)	Identify and analyse internal control and system weaknesses and their potential effects and make appropriate recommendations to management	2

Exam guide

You will not be expected to reproduce a full audit report in the exam, however you may be required to describe different types of modification either in a knowledge-based part of a question or in a scenario-based situation. Questions on the report to management setting out deficiencies in internal control are highly likely to come up in a scenario-based context.

The pilot paper had three marks in question 2 on modifications to the audit report. There were eight marks available in question 3 on weaknesses in a company's wages system and recommendations to overcome the weaknesses. Question 5 was on subsequent events but contained a six mark part on the impact on the audit report.

The December 2007 paper had 12 marks in question 1 on weaknesses in the inventory counting system and recommendations to overcome the weaknesses. Question 5 had 14 marks relating to the audit report in a scenario context.

Question 1 of the December 2008 paper had 14 marks available for writing a management letter regarding a wages system.

Question 2 of the June 2009 paper had two marks for explaining the term 'modified'.

1 The auditor's report on financial statements

Pilot paper, Dec 07, June 09

The auditor is required to produce an **audit report** at the end of the audit which sets out his **opinion** on the truth and fairness of the financial statements. The report contains a number of **consistent elements** so that users know the audit has been conducted according to **recognised standards**.

Objective 18 of the PER performance objectives is to evaluate and report on audit. The knowledge you gain in this key chapter will assist you in demonstrating the achievement of this objective in practice.

ISA 700 *Forming an opinion and reporting on financial statements* establishes standards and provides guidance on the form and content of the auditor's report issued as a result of an audit performed by an independent auditor on the financial statements of an entity. It states that the auditor shall form an opinion on whether the financial statements are prepared, in all material respects, in accordance with the **applicable financial reporting framework**.

In order to form the opinion, the auditor needs to conclude as to whether reasonable assurance has been obtained that the financial statements are free from material misstatement. The auditor's conclusion needs to consider the following.

- Whether **sufficient appropriate audit evidence** has been obtained (ISA 330)
- Whether **uncorrected misstatements are material** (ISA 450)

- **Qualitative aspects of the entity's accounting practices**, including indicators of **possible bias** in management's judgements
- Whether the financial statements **adequately disclose the significant accounting policies selected and applied**
- Whether the accounting policies selected and applied are **consistent** with the applicable financial reporting framework and are **appropriate**
- Whether **accounting estimates** made by management are **reasonable**
- Whether **the information** in the financial statements is **relevant, reliable, comparable and understandable**
- Whether the financial statements provide **adequate disclosures** to allow users to understand the effect of material transactions and events on the information presented in the financial statements
- Whether the **terminology** used in the financial statements is **appropriate**
- The **overall presentation, structure and content** of the financial statements
- Whether the financial statements represent the underlying transactions and events so as to achieve **fair presentation**
- Whether the financial statements **adequately refer to or describe the applicable financial reporting framework**

1.1 Unmodified auditor's report

y term

An **unmodified opinion** is the opinion expressed by the auditor when the auditor concludes that the financial statements are prepared, in all material respects, in accordance with the applicable financial reporting framework.

ISA 700 states that the auditor shall express an unmodified opinion when the auditor concludes that the financial statements are prepared, in all material respects, in accordance with the applicable financial reporting framework.

If the auditor concludes that the financial statements as a whole are not free from material misstatement or cannot obtain sufficient appropriate audit evidence to make this conclusion, the auditor must modify the opinion in accordance with ISA 705 *Modifications to the opinion in the independent auditor's report.* We discuss modifications to the opinion later in this section.

The following extract from an audit report shows an example of the opinion paragraph for an unmodified report, in accordance with ISA 700, which contains illustrations of unmodified auditors' reports in its appendix. The full unmodified report was also set out in Chapter 1 of this Study Text.

In our opinion, the financial statements present fairly, in all material respects, (or *give a true and fair view of*) the financial position of ABC Company as of December 31, 20X1, and (*of*) its financial performance and its cash flows for the year then ended in accordance with International Financial Reporting Standards.

1.2 Basic elements of the auditor's report

A measure of **consistency** in the form and content of the auditor's report is desirable because it **promotes credibility** in the global marketplace and also helps to promote the **reader's understanding** and to **identify unusual circumstances** when they occur.

The auditor's report must be **in writing** and includes the following basic elements, usually in the following layout.

Basic elements of audit report	Explanation
Title	The auditor's report must have a title that clearly indicates that it is the report of the independent auditor. This signifies that the auditor has met all the ethical requirements concerning independence and therefore distinguishes the auditor's report from other reports.
Addressee	The addressee will be determined by law or regulation, but is likely to be the shareholders or those charged with governance.
Introductory paragraph	This shall identify the entity being audited, state that the financial statements have been audited, identify the title of each statement that comprises the financial statements being audited, refer to the summary of significant accounting policies and other explanatory notes, and specify the date or period covered by each statement comprising the financial statements.
Management's responsibility for the financial statements	This part of the report describes the responsibilities of those who are responsible for the preparation of the financial statements. The report shall include a section headed 'Management's responsibility for the financial statements' and describe management's responsibility including the following: • Management is responsible for the preparation of the financial statements in accordance with the applicable financial reporting framework. • Management is responsible for such internal control necessary to enable the preparation of financial statements that are free from material misstatement, whether due to error or fraud. • Reference shall be made to 'the preparation and fair presentation of these financial statements' (or' the preparation of financial statements that give a true and fair view') where the financial statements are prepared in accordance with a fair presentation framework.
Auditor's responsibility	The report shall include a section entitled 'Auditor's responsibility'. The report must state that the auditor is responsible for expressing an opinion on the financial statements based on the audit. This section must also state that the audit was conducted in accordance with International Standards on Auditing and ethical requirements and that the auditor planned and performed the audit so as to obtain reasonable assurance that the financial statements are free from material misstatement. The report must describe an audit by stating that: • An audit involves performing procedures to obtain audit evidence about the amounts and disclosures in the financial statements. • The procedures chosen depend on the auditor's judgement of risks of material misstatements, and the auditor considers internal control relevant to the preparation of the financial statements in order to design appropriate audit procedures (but not to express an opinion on the effectiveness of internal control). • An audit includes evaluation of the appropriateness of the accounting policies used, the reasonableness of accounting estimates made by management, and the overall presentation of the financial statements.

Basic elements of audit report	Explanation
	This part of the report shall also state whether the auditor believes that the audit evidence obtained is sufficient and appropriate to provide a basis for the opinion.
Opinion paragraph	If the auditor expresses an unmodified opinion on financial statements prepared in accordance with a fair presentation framework, the opinion shall use one of the following equivalent phrases: • The financial statements present fairly, in all material respects,…in accordance with [the applicable financial reporting framework]; or • The financial statements give a true and fair view of … in accordance with [the applicable financial reporting framework].
Other reporting responsibilities	If the auditor is required by law to report on any other matters, this must be done in an additional paragraph below the opinion paragraph which is titled 'Report on other legal and regulatory requirements' or otherwise as appropriate.
Auditor's signature	The report must contain the auditor's signature, whether this is the auditor's own name or the audit firm's name or both.
Date of the report	The report must be dated no earlier than the date on which the auditor has obtained sufficient appropriate audit evidence on which to base the auditor's opinion on the financial statements.
Auditor's address	The location where the auditor practises must be included.

1.3 Modified opinions

FAST FORWARD

There are three types of **modified opinion**: a **qualified opinion**, an **adverse opinion**, and a **disclaimer of opinion**.

ISA 705 *Modifications to the opinion in the independent auditor's report* sets out the different types of modified opinions that can result. It identifies three possible types of modifications:

- A **qualified** opinion
- An **adverse** opinion
- A **disclaimer** of opinion

1.3.1 Types of modifications

Key term

Pervasiveness is a term used to describe the effects or possible effects on the financial statements of misstatements or undetected misstatements (due to an inability to obtain sufficient appropriate audit evidence). There are three types of pervasive effect:

– Those that are not confined to specific elements, accounts or items in the financial statements
– Those that are confined to specific elements, accounts or items in the financial statements and represent or could represent a substantial portion of the financial statements
– Those that relate to disclosures which are fundamental to users' understanding of the financial statements

The type of modification issued depends on the following:

- The **nature of the matter** giving rise to the modifications (i.e. whether the financial statements **are materially misstated** or whether they **may be misstated** when the auditor cannot obtain sufficient appropriate audit evidence)
- The auditor's judgement about the **pervasiveness** of the effects/possible effects of the matter on the financial statements

A modified opinion is required when:

- The auditor concludes that the financial statements as a whole are not free from material misstatements or
- The auditor cannot obtain sufficient appropriate audit evidence to conclude that the financial statements as a whole are free from material misstatement.

1.3.2 Qualified opinions

A qualified opinion must be expressed in the auditor's report in the following two situations:

(1) The auditor concludes that misstatements are material, but not pervasive, to the financial statements.

Material misstatements could arise in respect of:

- The appropriateness of selected accounting policies
- The application of selected accounting policies
- The appropriateness or adequacy of disclosures in the financial statements

(2) The auditor cannot obtain sufficient appropriate audit evidence on which to base the opinion but concludes that the possible effects of undetected misstatements, if any, could be material but not pervasive.

The auditor's inability to obtain sufficient appropriate audit evidence is also referred to as a limitation on the scope of the audit and could arise from:

- Circumstances beyond the entity's control (e.g. accounting records destroyed)
- Circumstances relating to the nature or timing of the auditor's work (e.g. the timing of the auditor's appointment prevents the observation of the physical inventory count)
- Limitations imposed by management (e.g. management prevents the auditor from requesting external confirmation of specific account balances)

1.3.3 Adverse opinions

An adverse opinion is expressed when the auditor, having obtained sufficient appropriate audit evidence, concludes that misstatements are both **material and pervasive** to the financial statements. For example, an adverse opinion might be issued if there is a material uncertainty in respect of going concern which has not be adequately disclosed or use of the going concern assumption is inappropriate (we discussed this in Chapter 18).

1.3.4 Disclaimers of opinion

An opinion must be disclaimed when the auditor **cannot obtain sufficient appropriate audit evidence** on which to base the opinion and concludes that the **possible effects** on the financial statements of undetected misstatements, if any, **could be both material and pervasive**.

The opinion must also be disclaimed in situations involving **multiple uncertainties** when the auditor concludes that, despite having obtained sufficient appropriate audit evidence for the individual uncertainties, it is not possible to form an opinion on the financial statements due to the **potential interaction of the uncertainties and their possible cumulative effect** on the financial statements.

An example of when a disclaimer of opinion is used could be in relation to going concern if management is unwilling to make or extend its assessment (see Chapter 18).

1.3.5 Impact on the auditor's report

When the auditor has had to modify the auditor's report, the report must include a paragraph before the opinion paragraph, which provides a description of the matter giving rise to the modification. This paragraph will be entitled 'Basis for qualified opinion' or 'Basis for adverse opinion' or 'Basis for disclaimer of opinion' depending on the type of modification.

The section of the auditor's report containing the opinion will be headed either 'Qualified opinion', 'Adverse opinion' or 'Disclaimer of opinion', again depending on the type of modification.

When the auditor expresses a qualified or adverse opinion, the section of the report on the auditor's responsibilities must be amended to state that the auditor believes that the audit evidence obtained is sufficient and appropriate to provide a basis for the auditor's modified audit opinion.

When the auditor disclaims an opinion due to being unable to obtain sufficient appropriate audit evidence, the section on the auditor's responsibilities must be amended to include the following: 'Because of the matter(s) described in the Basis for Disclaimer of Opinion paragraph, however, we were not able to obtain sufficient appropriate audit evidence to provide a basis for an audit opinion'.

We will now look at some examples of extracts from modified auditor's reports for each of the situations we have discussed above.

Example 1: Qualified opinion due to material misstatement of inventories

Basis for qualified opinion

The company's inventories are carried in the balance sheet at xxx. Management has not stated inventories at the lower of cost and net realisable value but has stated them solely at cost, which constitutes a departure from International Financial Reporting Standards. The company's records indicate that had management stated the inventories at the lower of cost and net realisable value, an amount of xxx would have been required to write the inventories down to their net realisable value. Accordingly, cost of sales would have been increased by xxx, and income tax, net income and shareholders' equity would have been reduced by xxx, xxx and xxx, respectively.

Qualified Opinion

In our opinion, except for the effects of the matter described in the Basis for Qualified Opinion paragraph, the financial statements present fairly, in all material respects, (or *give a true and fair view of*) the financial position of ABC Company as at December 31, 20X1, and (*of*) its financial performance and its cash flows for the year then ended in accordance with International Financial Reporting Standards.

Example 2: Adverse opinion due to material misstatement because of non-consolidation of a subsidiary

Basis for adverse opinion

As explained in Note X, the company has not consolidated the financial statements of subsidiary XYZ Company it acquired during 20X1 because it has not yet been able to ascertain the fair values of certain of the subsidiary's material assets and liabilities at the acquisition date. This investment is therefore accounted for on a cost basis. Under International Financial Reporting Standards, the subsidiary should have been consolidated because it is controlled by the company. Had XYZ been consolidated, many elements in the accompanying financial statements would have been materially affected. The effects on the consolidated financial statements of the failure to consolidate have not been determined.

Adverse Opinion

In our opinion, because of the significance of the matter discussed in the Basis for Adverse Opinion paragraph, the consolidated financial statements do not present fairly (or *do not give a true and fair view of*) the financial position of ABC Company and its subsidiaries as at December 31, 20X1, and (*of*) their financial performance and their cash flows for the year then ended in accordance with International Financial Reporting Standards.

Example 3: Qualified opinion due to inability to obtain sufficient appropriate audit evidence about an investment in a foreign affiliate (material but not pervasive)

> **Basis for qualified opinion**
>
> ABC Company's investment in XYZ Company, a foreign associate acquired during the year and accounted for by the equity method, is carried at xxx on the balance sheet as at December 31, 20X1, and ABC's share of XYZ's net income of xxx is included in ABC's income for the year then ended. We were unable to obtain sufficient appropriate audit evidence about the carrying amount of ABC's investment in XYZ as at December 31, 20X1 and ABC's share of XYZ's net income for the year because we were denied access to the financial information, management, and the auditors of XYZ. Consequently, we were unable to determine whether any adjustments to these amounts were necessary.
>
> **Qualified Opinion**
>
> In our opinion, except for the possible effects of the matter described in the Basis for Qualified Opinion paragraph, the financial statements present fairly, in all material respects, (or *give a true and fair view of*) the financial position of ABC Company as at December 31, 20X1, and (*of*) its financial performance and its cash flows for the year then ended in accordance with International Financial Reporting Standards.

Example 4: Disclaimer of opinion due to inability to obtain sufficient appropriate audit evidence about a single element of the financial statements (financial information of a joint venture investment representing over 90% of company's net assets – material and pervasive)

> **Basis for disclaimer of opinion**
>
> The company's investment in its joint venture XYZ (Country X) Company is carried at xxx on the company's balance sheet, which represents over 90% of the company's net assets as at December 31, 20X1. We were not allowed access to the management and the auditors of XYZ, including XYZ's auditors' audit documentation. As a result, we were unable to determine whether any adjustments were necessary in respect of the company's proportional share of XYZ's assets that it controls jointly, its proportional share of XYZ's liabilities for which it is jointly responsible, its proportional share of XYZ's income and expenses for the year, and the elements making up the statement of changes in equity and cash flow statement.
>
> **Disclaimer of Opinion**
>
> Because of the significance of the matter described in the Basis for Disclaimer of Opinion paragraph, we have not been able to obtain sufficient appropriate audit evidence to provide a basis for an audit opinion. Accordingly, we do not express an opinion on the financial statements.

Example 5: Disclaimer of opinion due to inability to obtain sufficient appropriate audit evidence about multiple elements of the financial statements (inventories and accounts receivable – material and pervasive)

> **Basis for disclaimer of opinion**
>
> We were not appointed as auditors of the company until after December 31, 20X1 and thus did not observe the counting of physical inventories at the beginning and end of the year. We were unable to satisfy ourselves by alternative means concerning the inventory quantities held at December 31, 20X0 and 20X1 which are stated in the balance sheet at xxx and xxx, respectively. In addition, the introduction of a new computerized accounts receivable system in September 20X1 resulted in numerous errors in accounts receivable. As of the date of our audit report, management was still in the process of rectifying the system deficiencies and correcting the errors. We were unable to confirm or verify by alternative means accounts receivable included in the balance sheet at a total amount of xxx as at December 31, 20X1. As a result of these matters, we were unable to determine whether any adjustments might have been found necessary in respect of recorded or unrecorded inventories and accounts receivable, and the elements making up the income statement, statement of changes in equity and cash flow statement.

> **Disclaimer of Opinion**
>
> Because of the significance of the matters described in the Basis for Disclaimer of Opinion paragraph, we have not been able to obtain sufficient appropriate audit evidence to provide a basis for an audit opinion. Accordingly, we do not express an opinion on the financial statements.

1.3.6 Communication with those charged with governance

ISA 705 states that when the auditor expects to express a modified opinion, the auditor must **communicate with those charged with governance** the circumstances leading to the expected modification and the proposed wording of the modification in the auditor's report.

This allows the auditor to give **notice** to those charged with governance of the intended modification and the reasons for it, to **seek agreement or confirm disagreement** with those charged with governance with respect to the modification, and to give those charged with governance an **opportunity to provide further information and explanations** in respect of the matter giving rise to the expected modification.

1.3.7 Summary of modifications and impact on the auditor's report

The following table summarises the different types of modified opinion that can arise.

Nature of circumstances	*Material but not pervasive*	*Material and pervasive*
Financial statements are materially misstated	QUALIFIED OPINION	ADVERSE OPINION
Auditor unable to obtain sufficient appropriate audit evidence	QUALIFIED OPINION	DISCLAIMER OF OPINION

Question — Modified reports

During the course of your audit of the non-current assets of Eastern Engineering Inc at 31 March 20X4, two problems have arisen.

(a) The calculations of the cost of direct labour incurred on assets in the course of construction by the company's employees have been accidentally destroyed for the early part of the year. The direct labour cost involved is $10,000.

(b) The company incurred development expenditure of $25,000 spent on a viable new product which will go into production next year and which is expected to last for ten years. The direct labour cost involved is $10,000.

(c) Other relevant financial information is as follows.

	$
Profit before tax	100,000
Non-current asset additions	133,000
Assets constructed by company	34,000
Non-current asset at net book value	666,667

Required

(a) List the general forms of modification available to auditors in drafting their report and state the circumstances in which each is appropriate.

(b) State whether you feel that a modified audit report would be necessary for each of the two circumstances outlined above, giving reasons in each case.

(c) On the assumption that you decide that a modified audit report is necessary with respect to the treatment of the revaluation, draft the section of the report describing the matter (the whole report is not required).

Answer

(a) ISA 705 *Modifications to the opinion in the independent auditor's report* suggests that the auditor may need to modify the opinion under one of two main circumstances:

- The auditor concludes that the financial statements as a whole are not free from material misstatements or
- The auditor cannot obtain sufficient appropriate audit evidence to conclude that the financial statements as a whole are free from material misstatement.

For both circumstances there can be two 'levels' of modified opinion:

(i) *Material but not pervasive,* where the circumstances prompting the misstatement or possible misstatement are material.

(ii) *Material and pervasive* to the overall view shown by the financial statements, ie the financial statements are or could be misleading. These will result in an adverse opinion (financial statements are misstated) or a disclaimer of opinion (the auditor is unable to obtain sufficient appropriate audit evidence).

(b) Whether a qualification of the audit opinion would be required in the circumstances described would depend on whether or not the auditors considered either of them to be material to the financial statements as a whole. An item is likely to be considered material in the context of a company's financial statements if its omission, misstatement or non-disclosure would prevent a proper understanding of those statements on the part of a potential user.

(i) *Loss of records relating to direct labour costs for assets in the course of construction*

The loss of records supporting one of the asset figures in the statement of financial position would cause a limitation in scope of the auditor's work because the auditor would be unable to obtain sufficient appropriate audit evidence. The $10,000 represents 29.4% of the expenditure incurred during the year on assets in course of construction but only 6% of total additions to non-current assets during the year and 1.5% of the year-end net book value for non-current assets. The total amount of $10,000 represents 10% of pre-tax profit but, as in relation to asset values, the real consideration by the auditor should be the materiality of any over- or under-statement of assets resulting from error in arriving at the $10,000 rather than the total figure itself.

Provided there are no suspicious circumstances surrounding the loss of these records and the total figure for additions to assets in the course of construction seems reasonable in the light of other audit evidence obtained, then it is unlikely that this matter would be seen as sufficiently material to merit any modification of the audit opinion. If other records have been lost as well, however, it may be necessary for the auditor to comment on the directors' failure to maintain proper books and records.

(ii) *Development cost debited to the income statement*

The situation here is one of misstatement in the financial statements, since best accounting practice as laid down by IAS 38 requires that development costs should be taken to the statement of comprehensive income over the useful life of the product to which they relate.

This departure from IAS 38 does not seem to be justifiable and would be material to the reported pre-tax profits for the year, representing 22.5% of that figure.

Whilst this understatement of profit (and corresponding overstatement of undistributable reserves) would be material to the financial statements, it is not likely to been seen as pervasive and therefore a qualified opinion would be appropriate.

(c) *Qualified audit opinion extract*

Basis for qualified opinion

As explained in note ... development costs in respect of a potential new product have been deducted in full against profit instead of being spread over the life of the relevant product as required by IAS 38; the effect of so doing has been to decrease profits before and after tax for the year by $25,000.

Qualified opinion

In our opinion, except for the effects of the matter described in the Basis for Qualified Opinion paragraph, the financial statements present fairly, in all material respects, (or *give a true and fair view of*) the financial position of Eastern Engineering Inc as at March 31, 20X4, and (*of*) its financial performance and its cash flows for the year then ended in accordance with International Financial Reporting Standards.

xam focus oint

If you are given a scenario in a question on audit reports and asked whether the report should be modified and on what basis, always remember to calculate materiality and comment on it in the context of its impact on the type of modification (ie qualified opinion, adverse opinion or disclaimer of opinion).

1.4 Emphasis of matter paragraphs and other matter paragraphs in the auditor's report

FAST FORWARD

Emphasis of matter paragraphs and **other matter paragraphs** can be included in the auditor's report under certain circumstances. Their use does not modify the auditor's opinion on the financial statements.

ISA 706 *Emphasis of matter paragraphs and other matter paragraphs in the independent auditor's report* provides guidance to auditors on the inclusion of paragraphs in the auditor's report that either draw users' attention to a matter that is of such importance that it is **fundamental** to their understanding or that is **relevant** to their understanding of the audit, the auditor's responsibilities or the auditor's report.

1.4.1 Emphasis of matter paragraphs

ey term

An **emphasis of matter paragraph** is a paragraph included in the auditor's report that refers to a matter appropriately presented or disclosed in the financial statements that, in the auditor's judgement, is of such importance that it is fundamental to users' understanding of the financial statements.

Emphasis of matter paragraphs are used to draw readers' attention to a matter **already presented or disclosed** in the financial statements that the auditor feels is **fundamental** to their understanding, provided that the auditor has obtained sufficient appropriate audit evidence that the matter is **not materially misstated**.

When an emphasis of matter paragraph is included in the auditor's report, it comes **immediately after the opinion paragraph** and is entitled 'Emphasis of matter' (or appropriate). The paragraph must contain a **clear reference** to the matter being emphasised and to where relevant disclosures that fully describe it can be found in the financial statements. The paragraph must state that **the auditor's opinion is not modified** in respect of the matter emphasised.

The following are examples of situations in which the auditor might include an emphasis of matter paragraph in the auditor's report:

- An uncertainty relating to the future outcome of **exceptional litigation or regulatory action**
- **Early application of a new accounting standard** that has a **pervasive effect** on the financial statements

- A **major catastrophe** that has had, or continues to have, **a significant effect** on the entity's financial position

ISA 706 contains an example auditor's report that contains an emphasis of matter paragraph, relevant extracts of which are shown below.

> **Emphasis of Matter**
>
> We draw attention to Note X to the financial statements which describes the uncertainty related to the outcome of the lawsuit filed against the company by XYZ Company. Our opinion is not qualified in respect of this matter.

1.4.2 Other matter paragraphs

Key term

> An **other matter paragraph** is a paragraph included in the auditor's report that refers to a matter other than those presented or disclosed in the financial statements that, in the auditor's judgement, is relevant to users' understanding of the audit, the auditor's responsibilities or the auditor's report.

Other matter paragraphs are used where the auditor considers it necessary to draw readers' attention to a matter that is relevant to their understanding of the audit, the auditor's responsibilities or the auditor's report.

The other matter paragraph must be included immediately after the opinion paragraph and any emphasis of matter paragraph, or elsewhere in the auditor's report if the content of it is relevant to the other reporting responsibilities section. The content of the other matter paragraph must reflect clearly that the other matter is not required to be presented and disclosed in the financial statements, and does not include information that the auditor is prohibited from providing by law and regulations or other standards, or information that is required to be provided by management.

1.4.3 Communication with those charged with governance

ISA 706 states that when the auditor expects to include an emphasis of matter paragraph or an other matter paragraph, the auditor must **communicate with those charged with governance** the circumstances and the proposed wording of the paragraph in the auditor's report.

1.5 Reporting on Compliance with International Financial Reporting Standards

As we have discussed above, the objective of an audit is to enable the auditor to express an opinion on whether the financial statements are prepared, in all material respects, in accordance with an **applicable financial reporting framework**. The auditor's report must indicate the financial reporting framework that has been used to prepare the financial statements.

IAPS 1014 *Reporting by auditors on compliance with International Financial Reporting Standards* provides additional guidance to auditors when the auditor expresses an opinion on financial statements that are prepared:

- Solely in accordance with IFRSs
- In accordance with IFRSs and a national financial reporting framework or
- In accordance with a national financial reporting framework with disclosure of the extent of compliance with IFRSs

The following table summarises the guidance in the IAPS in each of these situations

Basis of preparation of financial statements	Impact on audit report
Solely in accordance with IFRSs	Qualified, disclaimed or adverse opinion if auditor concludes financial statements are not prepared in accordance with IFRSs
In accordance with IFRSs and a national financial reporting framework	Consider each framework separately. If failure to comply with either or both frameworks, issue a qualified opinion or adverse opinion on either one framework or both.
In accordance with a national financial reporting framework with disclosure of the extent of compliance with IFRSs	If financial statements fail to comply with national reporting framework because disclosures on compliance with IFRSs are misleading, express a qualified opinion or adverse opinion.

1.6 Other information in documents containing audited financial statements

FAST FORWARD

Auditors shall review the **other information** in documents containing audited financial statements for material inconsistencies and misstatements of fact.

ISA 720 *The auditor's responsibilities relating to other information in documents containing audited financial statements* provides guidance to auditors in this area. The objective of the auditor is to respond appropriately when documents containing audited financial statements include other information that could **undermine the credibility** of the financial statements and the auditor's report.

Key terms

Other information is financial and non-financial information, other than the financial statements and the auditor's report, which is included, either by law, regulation or custom, in a document containing audited financial statements and the auditor's report.

An **inconsistency** means the other information contradicts information contained in the audited financial statements. A material inconsistency may raise doubt about the audit conclusions drawn from audit evidence previously obtained and possibly also the basis for the auditor's opinion on the financial statements.

A **misstatement of fact** is when the other information that is unrelated to matters appearing in the audited financial statements is incorrectly stated or presented. A material misstatement of fact may undermine the credibility of the document containing audited financial statements.

Examples of other information include the following:

- A report by management or those charged with governance on operations
- Financial summaries or highlights
- Employment data
- Planned capital expenditures
- Financial ratios
- Names of officers and directors
- Selected quarterly data

1.6.1 Material inconsistencies

ISA 720 states that the auditor shall **read** the other information to identity **material inconsistencies** with the audited financial statements. If a material inconsistency is identified, the auditor shall determine whether the audited financial statements or other information needs to be **revised**.

If the **financial statements** need to be revised but management refuses, the auditor shall **modify** the audit opinion.

If the **other information** needs to be revised but management refuses, the auditor shall **communicate** this matter to those charged with governance and:

- Include an **emphasis of matter paragraph** in the auditor's report that describes the material inconsistency or
- **Withhold** the auditor's report or
- **Withdraw** from the engagement (where this is legally permitted)

1.6.2 Material misstatements of fact

If the auditor becomes aware that the other information includes an apparent material misstatement of fact, he shall **discuss** this with management.

If, after the discussions, the auditor still considers there is an apparent material misstatement of fact, he shall request management to consult a **qualified third party** such as a lawyer and the auditor shall consider the advice received.

If management refuses to correct the other information, the auditor shall **notify those charged with governance** and take any **appropriate further action**, such as consulting the auditor's lawyer.

1.7 Opening balances and comparative information

FAST FORWARD

Auditors must ensure that the **opening balances** and **comparative information** are fairly stated in the financial statements.

1.7.1 Opening balances

Key terms

Opening balances are those account balances that exist at the beginning of the period. They are based on the closing balances of the prior period and reflect the effects of transactions of prior periods and accounting policies applied in the prior period. They also include matters requiring disclosure that existed at the beginning of the period, such as contingencies and commitments.

An **initial audit engagement** is one in which either the financial statements for the prior period were not audited or one in which the financial statements for the prior period were audited by a predecessor auditor.

ISA 510 *Initial audit engagements – opening balances* provides guidance to auditors on the audit of opening balances when conducting an initial audit engagement.

The ISA states that for initial audit engagements the auditor's objective is to obtain sufficient appropriate audit evidence whether:

- Opening balances contain **misstatements** that **materially** affect the current period's financial statements.
- **Appropriate accounting policies** are **consistently** applied or changes have been properly accounted for and adequately presented and disclosed.

1.7.2 Audit evidence for opening balances

ISA 510 states that the auditor shall **read** the most recent financial statements and the predecessor auditor's report for information relevant to opening balances.

The auditor shall obtain sufficient appropriate audit evidence about whether opening balances contain misstatements that materially affect the current period's financial statements by:

- Determining whether the prior period's closing balances have been correctly brought forward or restated
- Determining whether the opening balances reflect the application of appropriate accounting policies

- Performing one or more of the following:
  - Where the prior period's financial statements were audited, reviewing the predecessor auditor's working papers
  - Evaluating whether audit procedures performed in the current period provide evidence relevant to opening balances
  - Performing specific audit procedures to obtain evidence regarding opening balances

1.7.3 Opening balances – audit conclusions and reporting

If the auditor cannot obtain **sufficient appropriate audit evidence** for opening balances, the auditor shall express a qualified opinion or a disclaimer of opinion.

If the opening balances contain misstatements that could **materially affect** the current year's financial statements, the auditor shall express a qualified opinion or an adverse opinion.

If the auditor concludes that the current period's **accounting policies** are not consistently applied in relation to opening balances or changes have not been properly accounted for and adequately presented and disclosed, the auditor shall express a qualified opinion or an adverse opinion.

If a prior period modification remains **relevant and material** to the current period's financial statements, the auditor shall modify the auditor's opinion on the current period's financial statements accordingly.

1.7.4 Comparative information

ey terms

Comparative information is amounts and disclosures included in the financial statements in respect of one or more prior periods in accordance with the applicable financial reporting framework. There are two methods of presentation: **corresponding figures**, where amounts and other disclosures for the prior period are included as an integral part of the current period financial statements, and are intended to be read only in relation to the amounts and other disclosures relating to the current period; and **comparative financial statements** where amounts and other disclosures for the prior period are included for comparison with the financial statements of the current period but, if audited, are referred to in the auditor's report.

ISA 710 *Comparative information – corresponding figures and comparative financial statements* provides guidance to auditors on comparatives, both corresponding figures and comparative financial statements. Whether corresponding figures or comparative financial statements are required is usually dictated by law or regulation but may also be specified in the terms of engagement.

In terms of audit reporting, for corresponding figures, the auditor's opinion refers to the current period only. For comparative financial statements, the auditor's opinion refers to each period for which financial statements are presented.

1.7.5 Auditor's responsibilities for comparative information

The ISA states that the auditor must determine whether the financial statements include the comparative information required by the applicable financial reporting framework and whether it is appropriately classified. This includes an evaluation of whether:

- The **accounting policies** used for corresponding figures or comparative financial statements are consistent with the current period.
- The corresponding figures or comparative financial statements **agree** with the amounts and other disclosures presented in the prior period.

If the auditor becomes aware of a possible material misstatement regarding the comparative information, the auditor must perform additional audit procedures to obtain sufficient appropriate audit evidence to determine whether a material misstatement exists.

ISA 710 requires the auditor to obtain a **written representation** for all periods referred to in the auditor's opinion and a specific written representation regarding any restatements made to correct a material misstatement in prior period financial statements that affect the comparative information.

1.7.6 Corresponding figures - reporting

In terms of reporting, the audit report does not specifically refer to the corresponding figures because the opinion is on the current period's financial statements as a whole, and this includes the corresponding figures. The following table summarises the impact on the auditor's report in particular circumstances.

Scenario	Impact on auditor's report
Prior period report modified and matter unresolved and results in modification of current period report	Modified regarding current period's financial statements
Prior period report unmodified but evidence of material misstatement and figures not restated	Modified (qualified opinion or adverse opinion) regarding corresponding figures
Prior period financial statements audited by a predecessor auditor	Other matter paragraph stating that financial statements audited by predecessor auditor, type of opinion expressed, date of the report
Prior period financial statements not audited	Other matter paragraph stating that corresponding figures unaudited

1.7.7 Comparative financial statements – reporting

The auditor's opinion must refer to each period for which financial statements are presented and on which an audit opinion is expressed. The following table summarises the impact on the auditor's report in particular circumstances.

Scenario	Impact on auditor's report
Opinion on prior period financial statements different from opinion previously expressed	Other matter paragraph to explain different opinion
Prior period financial statements audited by a predecessor auditor	Other matter paragraph stating that prior period financial statements audited by a predecessor auditor, type of opinion expressed, date of the report
Material misstatement affecting prior period financial statements on which predecessor auditor had expressed an unmodified opinion	If predecessor auditor is informed and financial statements are amended and new report issued, auditor reports only on current period
Prior period financial statements not audited	Other matter paragraph stating that comparative financial statements not audited

1.8 The audit report as a means of communication

1.8.1 Implied information

Unmodified audit reports may not appear to give a great deal of information. The report says much, however, by implication. Remember that the auditors report *by exception*, so an unmodified report tells the user that, for example:

- **Adequate accounting** records have been **kept**.
- The **accounts agree** with the **records.**
- The **auditors** have **received** all **necessary information**.
- All **directors' transactions** have been **disclosed**.
- The **directors' report** is consistent with the **accounts**.

The real problem here is that, unfortunately, most users do not know that this is what an unmodified audit report tells them. This issue is also confused by the fact that many users do not understand the responsibilities of either the auditors or the directors in relation to the financial statements.

1.8.2 Expectations gap

This difference between the actual and the public perception is part of what is called the '**expectations gap**', defined as the difference between the apparent public perceptions of the responsibilities of auditors on the one hand (and hence the assurance that their involvement provides) and the legal and professional reality on the other. The question remains: how can we make the **meaning** of an unqualified audit report clear to the user?

The above definition of the expectations gap is not definitive but we can highlight some specific issues.

(a) **Misunderstandings of the nature of audited financial statements**, for example that:
- The statement of financial position provides a fair valuation of the reporting entity.
- The amounts in the financial statements are stated precisely.
- The audited financial statements will guarantee that the entity concerned will continue to exist.

(b) **Misunderstanding as to the type and extent of work undertaken by auditors**

(c) **Misunderstanding about the level of assurance provided by auditors**, for example that:
- An unmodified auditor's report means that no frauds have occurred in the period.
- The auditors provide absolute assurance that the figures in the financial statements are correct (ignoring the concept of materiality and the problems of estimation).

Different countries have tackled this problem in different ways. The role of auditors has been included in the debate on corporate governance in many western countries, leading to further rules which are nevertheless voluntary, not mandatory, as we discussed in Chapter 3.

2 Reports to management **Pilot paper, Dec 07, Dec 08**

FAST FORWARD

Reports to management can be sent by external auditors after both the interim and final audits. They set out deficiencies in internal control, the implications of those deficiencies on the business and suggested recommendations to mitigate them.

ISA 265 *Communicating deficiencies in internal control to those charged with governance and management* sets out guidance on internal control deficiencies. We covered the requirements of this standard in detail in Chapter 9 of this Study Text. Many external auditors produce a **report to management** as a by-product of an external audit, listing any deficiencies they have found in systems and making recommendations for improvements. The report to management may also be referred to as the management letter, letter of weakness or letter on internal control.

One of the PER performance objectives is to 'communicate effectively'. Examples of this in practice would be to compile written reports for management or clients. This would therefore include a report to management. The knowledge you attain in this section of the Study Text will help you in situations where you are asked to draft a report to management, and therefore assist you in achieving this particular PER objective. At the same time it applies also to objective 18 ('evaluate and report on audit') – examples under this objective include drafting and presenting reports to management.

2.1 The report to management

Recommendations regarding internal control are a by-product of the audit of the financial statements, not a primary objective, but nonetheless are frequently of great value to a client. The auditors shall communicate with those charged with governance any material deficiencies in the design, implementation or operating effectiveness of internal control which have come to their attention during the course of the audit. This shall be done on **timely basis**.

When auditors prepare a written communication on internal control matters, the following points should be considered:

(a) It should not **include language** that **conflicts** with the **opinion** expressed in the auditor's report.

(b) It should state that the **accounting and internal control** system were **considered only** to the **extent necessary** to **determine** the **auditing procedures** to report on the financial statements and not to determine the adequacy of internal control for management purposes or to provide assurances on the accounting and internal control systems.

(c) It will state that it **discusses only deficiencies** in internal control which have **come to the auditors' attention** as a result of the **audit** and that other deficiencies in internal control may exist.

(d) It should also include a statement that the **communication is provided for use only by management** (or another specific named party).

After the above items and the auditors' suggestions for corrective action are communicated to management, the auditors will usually ascertain the actions taken, including the reasons for those suggestions rejected. The auditors may encourage management to respond to the auditors' comments in which case any response can be included in the report.

The significance of findings relating to the accounting and internal control systems may change with the passage of time. Suggestions from previous years' audits which have not been adopted, if any, should normally be repeated or referred to.

2.1.1 Example report to management

This is an example of a report to management or letter on internal control which demonstrates how the principles described above might be put into practice.

ABC & Co
Certified Accountants
29 High Street

The Board of Directors
Manufacturing Ltd
15 South Street

1 April 20X8

Members of the board,

Financial statements for the year ended 31 May 20X8

We set out in this letter certain matters which arose as a result of our review of the accounting systems and procedures operated by your company during our recent interim audit. The matters dealt with in this letter came to our notice during the conduct of our normal audit procedures which are designed primarily for the purpose of expressing our opinion on the financial statements. Consequently our work did not encompass a detailed review of all aspects of the system and cannot be relied on necessarily to disclose defalcations or other irregularities or to include all possible improvements in internal control.

Purchases: ordering procedures

Deficiency
During the course of our work we discovered that it was the practice of the stores to order certain goods from X Co orally without preparing either a purchase requisition or purchase order.

Implication
There is therefore the possibility of liabilities being set up for unauthorised items and at a non-competitive price.

Recommendation
We recommend that the buying department should be responsible for such orders and, if they are placed orally, an official order should be raised as confirmation.

Payables ledger reconciliation

Deficiency
Although your procedures require that the payables ledger is reconciled against the control account on the nominal ledger at the end of every month, this was not done in December or January.

Implication

The balance on the payables ledger was short by some $2,120 of the nominal ledger control account at 31 January 20X8 for which no explanation could be offered. This implies a serious breakdown in the purchase invoice and/or cash payment batching and posting procedures.

Recommendation

It is important in future that this reconciliation is performed regularly by a responsible official independent of the day-to-day payables ledger, cashier and nominal ledger functions.

Receivables ledger: credit control

Deficiency

As at 28 February 20X8 trade receivables accounted for approximately 12 weeks of sales, although your standard credit terms are cash within 30 days of statement, equivalent to an average of about 40 days (6 weeks) of sales.

Implication

This has resulted in increased overdraft usage and difficulty in settling some key suppliers' accounts on time.

Recommendation

We recommend that a more structured system of debt collection be considered using standard letters and that statements should be sent out a week earlier if possible.

Preparation of payroll and maintenance of personnel records

Deficiency

Under your present system, just two members of staff are entirely and equally responsible for the maintenance of personnel records and preparation of the payroll. Furthermore, the only independent check of any nature on the payroll is that the chief accountant confirms that the amount of the wages cheque presented to him for signature agrees with the total of the net wages column in the payroll. This latter check does not involve any consideration of the reasonableness of the amount of the total net wages cheque or the monies being shown as due to individual employees.

Implication

It is a serious weakness of your present system that so much responsibility is vested in the hands of just two people. This situation is made worse by the fact that there is no clearly defined division of duties as between the two of them. In our opinion, it would be far too easy for fraud to take place in this area (eg by inserting the names of 'dummy workmen' into the personnel records and hence on to the payroll) and/or for clerical errors to go undetected.

Recommendations

(i) Some person other than the two wages clerks be made responsible for maintaining the personnel records and for periodically (but on a surprise basis) checking them against the details on the payroll.

(ii) The two wages clerks be allocated specific duties in relation to the preparation of the payroll, with each clerk independently reviewing the work of the other.

(iii) When the payroll is presented in support of the cheque for signature to the chief accountant, he should be responsible for assessing the reasonableness of the overall charge for wages that week.

Our comments have been discussed with your Finance Director and the Chief Accountant and these matters will be considered by us again during future audits. We look forward to receiving your comments on the points made.

This letter has been produced for the sole use of your company. It must not be disclosed to a third party, or quoted or referred to, without our written consent. No responsibility is assumed by us to any other person.

We should like to take this opportunity of thanking your staff for their co-operation and assistance during the course of our audit.

Yours faithfully

ABC & Co

Exam focus point

> You may be asked to draft paragraphs for a letter on internal control in the exam, given a specific scenario in the question. Your recommendations should be specific to the circumstances in the scenario – vague statements will not score good marks.

Chapter Roundup

- The auditor is required to produce an **audit report** at the end of the audit which sets out his **opinion** on the truth and fairness of the financial statements. The report contains a number of **consistent elements** so that users know the audit has been conducted according to **recognised standards.**
- There are three types of **modified opinion**: a **qualified opinion**, an **adverse opinion** and a **disclaimer of opinion**.
- **Emphasis of matter paragraphs** and **other matter paragraphs** can be included in the auditor's report under certain circumstances. Their use does not modify the auditor's opinion on the financial statements.
- Auditors shall review the **other information** in documents containing audited financial statements for material inconsistencies and misstatements of fact.
- Auditors must ensure that the **opening balances** and **comparative information** are fairly stated in the financial statements.
- **Reports to management** can be sent by external auditors after both the interim and final audits. They set out deficiencies in internal control, the implications of those deficiencies on the business and suggested recommendations to mitigate them.

Quick Quiz

1 The statement of management's responsibilities is always included in the auditors' report.

True ☐

False ☐

2 Draw a table that summarises the different modified opinions that can arise in the auditor's report.

3 The inclusion of an emphasis of matter paragraph in the auditor's report does not affect the auditor's opinion on the financial statements.

True ☐

False ☐

4 Give three examples of misunderstandings which contribute to the expectations gap.

(1) ....

(2) ....

(3) ....

5 Which of the following are examples of other information in documents containing audited financial statements?

- Employment data
- Information contained on the entity's website
- Representation letter
- Financial ratios
- Names of officers and directors

Answers to Quick Quiz

1 False

2 Modification table

Nature of circumstances	*Material but not pervasive*	*Material and pervasive*
Financial statements are materially misstated	QUALIFIED OPINION	ADVERSE OPINION
Auditor unable to obtain sufficient appropriate audit evidence	QUALIFIED OPINION	DISCLAIMER OF OPINION

3 True

4 (1) The nature of the financial statements
(2) The type of extent of work undertaken by auditors
(3) The level of assurance given by auditors

5 Employment data, financial ratios, and the names of officers and directors are all examples of other information in documents containing audited financial statements.

Now try the questions below from the Exam Question Bank

Number	Level	Marks	Time
Q25	Introductory	n/a	n/a
Q26	Examination	20	36 mins

Exam question and answer bank

Examination standard questions are indicated by mark and time allocations.

1 Objectives, characteristics and responsibilities

Your client, Mr Neville, has written to you saying he has been considering setting up an internal audit department but has heard from his brother that he would be better off abandoning this idea and getting the external auditor to do some assurance work instead. His brother also claimed that if the external auditor does some work for the company, there would be no need to have an external audit.

Required

Write a letter to Mr Neville explaining the objectives, characteristics and responsibilities of internal audit, external audit and assurance.

2 Audit and assurance engagements

(a) Explain the difference between negative and positive assurance in the context of the external audit and review engagements. State some of the limitations of the external audit. **(4 marks)**

(b) The audit opinion sets out explicit opinions which must be stated in the audit report. State what these are and outline the possible implied opinions, which are only reported on by exception. **(3 marks)**

(c) Auditors have certain rights to allow them to carry out their duties. State and explain what these rights are, using the UK as an example. **(3 marks)**

(Total = 10 marks)

3 Standards

Discuss the advantages and disadvantages of auditing standards to auditors and the consequences of them being enforceable by statute.

4 Corporate governance

The objective of a system of corporate governance is to secure the effective, sound and efficient operation of companies. This objective transcends any legislation or voluntary code. Good corporate governance embraces not only making the company prosper but also doing business in a legal and ethical manner. A key element of corporate governance is the audit committee. The audit committee is a committee of the board of directors and is of a voluntary nature regulated by voluntary codes.

Required

(a) Explain how an audit committee could improve the effectiveness of the external auditor's work.

(b) Discuss the problems of ensuring the 'independence' of the members of the audit committee.

(c) Discuss the view that the role of the audit committee should not be left to voluntary codes of practice but should be regulated by statute.

5 Independence

It has been suggested that the most important matter affecting the credibility of the auditor is that of 'independence'.

Required

(a) Discuss, giving examples, matters other than independence, which might be relevant in relation to the credibility of the auditor and steps that the accounting profession has taken or might take in relation to them.

(b) Discuss the following situations in the context of the independence of the auditor, showing clearly the principles involved:

(i) The audit manager in charge of the audit assignment of Andrew Co holds 1,000 $1 ordinary shares in the company (total shares in issue – 100,000). The audit partner holds no shares.

(ii) The audit fee receivable from Janet Co, a private company is $100,000. The total fee income of the audit firm is $700,000.

(iii) The audit senior in charge of the audit of Margot Bank Co has a personal loan from the bank of $2,000 on which she is currently paying 13% interest.

(iv) The audit partner is responsible for two audit assignments, Harry Co and Jean Co. Harry Co has recently tendered for a contract with Jean Co for the supply of material quantities of goods over a number of years. Jean Co has asked the audit partner to advise on the matter.

6 Objectivity **36 mins**

(a) Explain the concept of objectivity, with reference to

(i) External auditors
(ii) Internal auditors, who are members of ACCA,

outlining any general threats to objectivity that exist. **(8 marks)**

(b) *Scenario 1*

Bakers Co is an audit client of Hinkley Innes, a firm of Chartered Certified Accountants. The firm has had the audit of Bakers for 17 years and the fee represents 7% of firm income. Bakers is considering a major new project and has asked the firm if it would be happy to undertake some one-off consultancy work for the firm. It is possible that the fee income for this contract would represent 10% of that year's income for Hinkley Innes. The new business services partner, who heads up a new division of the firm, is keen to take on the work, as this would represent his best contract yet.

Scenario 2

Peter works in the purchasing department of Murphy Manufacturing Co. He has been instrumental in setting up control systems in the purchasing department as part of a recent risk management exercise. He has a poor relationship with his immediate supervisor, the Purchasing Director. Murphy Manufacturing has just advertised the post of trainee internal auditor. Peter is interested in the work that internal audit do, having liased substantially with the department during the recent controls exercise. No formal accountancy qualifications are required for the post, because the successful candidate will be put through accountancy training. Peter has had a chat with the head of internal audit concerning the post and is seriously considering making an application.

Required

Discuss the threats and the safeguards to objectivity that could be implemented in the two situations given above. **(12 marks)**

(Total = 20 marks)

7 Role of internal audit **36 mins**

(a) You are a member of the internal audit team at Golden Holdings, a listed company. The board of directors wants to raise the profile of the internal audit department in the company. They have asked the internal audit department to give a series of seminars on corporate governance and the role of internal audit in achieving corporate objectives to other members of staff.

The head of internal audit has asked you to prepare some notes on this subject.

Required

Prepare the notes which the head of internal audit wants. **(12 marks)**

You should cover the following matters:

(i) The Board of Directors
(ii) Accountability
(iii) The meaning of risk management

(b) After the seminars, the various departments of Golden Holdings have been asked to carry out risk management brainstorming sessions to identify risks in each of their departments and to design internal control systems to reduce those risks. The Sales Director, Wayne, has asked you if you will attend the brainstorming session in the sales department and whether you will assist them in the risk identification and management process.

Required

Prepare a memorandum to the Sales Director, answering his questions. **(8 marks)**

You should cover the following matters:

(i) Whether you will attend the meeting, and in what capacity

(ii) Whether you attend the meeting or not, what involvement you, as a member of the internal audit team, will have in the risk management exercise

(Total = 20 marks)

8 Glo **36 mins**

Glo-Warm Co, a limited liability company, manufactures various heating products which it sells to both High Street and catalogue retailers.

The statement of financial position for the years ended 20X7 and 20X6 are set out below. Last year, materiality was set at $10,000.

	20X7		*20X6*	
	$'000	$'000	$'000	$'000
Non-current assets				
Tangible non-current assets		20		21
Investments		2		2
Current assets				
Inventory	52		179	
Receivables	78		136	
Cash at bank	12		34	
Cash in hand	1		1	
	143		350	
Total assets		165		373
Current liabilities				
Trade payables	121		133	
Bank loan	5		5	
	126		138	
Long-term liabilities				
Bank loan		20		25
Provision*		20		–
Capital and reserves				
Share capital		2		2
Reserves		(3)		208
Total liabilities		165		373

*The provision of $20,000 consists entirely of a warranty provision.

Required

(a) Discuss whether the materiality level used in 20X6 will be appropriate for this year's audit, giving reasons for your answer. **(3 marks)**

(b) Explain audit risk. **(3 marks)**

(c) Review the statement of financial position given above and state the areas in which audit work should be concentrated, giving reasons in each case. **(14 marks)**

(Total = 20 marks)

9 Audit planning and documentation **18 mins**

(a) Explain the difference between the overall audit strategy and the audit plan and state the key contents of the overall audit strategy document. **(4 marks)**

(b) Briefly explain the reasons for auditors documenting their work. **(3 marks)**

(c) Many audit firms use standardised working papers. List the advantages and disadvantages of audit firms using standardised working papers to document their audit work. **(3 marks)**

(Total = 10 marks)

10 Audit evidence considerations **18 mins**

(a) Discuss how analytical procedures can be used as substantive audit procedures to provide audit evidence. Illustrate your answer with an example. **(5 marks)**

(b) ISA 500 *Audit evidence* requires auditors to obtain sufficient appropriate audit evidence to be able to draw reasonable conclusions on which to base their audit opinion. Discuss the different sources of evidence available to auditors and assess their relative appropriateness. **(5 marks)**

(Total = 10 marks)

11 Knits **54 mins**

Knits Co is a small company which manufactures and sells high quality knitwear. Its customers are mainly fashion boutiques.

Knits Co has two directors, one who is non-executive and the other who is involved in the day-to-day administration of the company. There are ten other employees. Six of these work in the factory, one works in the warehouse, one is a sales representative and two are accounts staff. The accounts staff consist of Miss Jones, who is responsible for processing sales and receivables, and Mrs Singh, who is the purchases and wages clerk. Mrs Singh works part-time, five mornings a week.

The company's sales representative visits shops throughout the region. He takes orders from customers which he records on a pre-numbered two-part order form. He passes the completed forms to the accounts department. Miss Jones files one copy of the order form in numerical sequence and passes the other to the warehouse.

The completed order is despatched from the warehouse by carrier, accompanied by one copy of a despatch note. The other copy is sent to Miss Jones, who prepares an invoice based on the information it contains and on the company's price list. She sends one copy of the invoice to the customer, and a second copy of the invoice is retained.

Each Friday, Miss Jones inputs the week's invoices to the computerised sales ledger. She then files the invoices alphabetically by customer name. Despatch notes are not retained because filing space is limited.

Miss Jones opens the post daily and lists remittances received from credit customers. Every Friday, she inputs the information listed to the sales ledger. Cheques received are banked daily by the executive director.

Miss Jones reviews the sales ledger balances every month and writes to customers who have not paid within 90 days of receiving goods. The sales ledger is printed out annually for year-end purposes. Otherwise no hard copy is printed and Miss Jones reviews the sales ledger on the computer screen.

The company's computer package includes the facility to produce a sales day book and sales ledger control account. These are not used because Miss Jones considers that the low volume of transactions (10-15 invoices per week) makes them unnecessary.

Required

(a) Explain the particular issues relating to controls which would affect the audit of a small company such as Knits. **(4 marks)**

(b) List six control objectives of a sales system. **(6 marks)**

(c) State, with reasons, what you consider to be the potential deficiencies in Knits Co's present system of accounting for sales and receivables. **(10 marks)**

(d) List and explain the controls that a small firm such as Knits Co could feasibly adopt to overcome the deficiencies you have identified. **(10 marks)**

(Total = 30 marks)

(*Note*: You are not required to consider the system for dealing with returns and credit notes.)

12 Fenton Distributors **54 mins**

Fenton Distributors Co is a small company which maintains its sales, purchase and nominal ledgers on a small PC, using a standard computerised accounting package. The company buys products from large manufacturers and sells them to shops which either sell or hire them to the general public. The products include drain clearing machines, portable generators, garden cultivators and wallpaper strippers.

You have been asked to carry out an audit of the nominal ledger system to verify that items are accurately recorded in the year. At the end of the year, the nominal ledger produces a trial balance, which is used to prepare the annual accounts.

The company employs a bookkeeper, who is responsible for posting the sales and purchase ledgers, and maintaining the nominal ledger. Data is posted to the nominal ledger as follows.

(a) At the start of the financial year, all the balances on the nominal ledger accounts are set to zero (using the standard year-end procedure of the computer package).

(b) The following procedures relate to purchase transactions.

  (i) When invoices are posted to the purchase ledger, the purchase analysis code (for the nominal ledger), the purchases value and the sales tax value are entered. The total invoice value is posted to the purchase ledger.

  (ii) At the end of the month, the computer posts the following items to the nominal ledger.

    (1) The total of each category of invoice expense and sales tax for purchase invoices and credit notes posted in the month (at the same time the computer prints details of the individual invoices making up the total of each invoice expense and sales tax for the month).

    (2) The total of purchase ledger cash payments, discount received and adjustments posted to the purchase ledger in the month (the computer prints details of the individual items comprising the total cash discount and adjustments for the month).

    (3) Where there is no account in the nominal ledger relating to the items being posted, the computer posts the items to a payables suspense account. Also, all adjustments are posted to the suspense account.

(c) Sales ledger data is posted to the nominal ledger in a similar way to purchase ledger data.

(d) Journals are posted manually to the nominal ledger for:

  (i) The opening balances at the start of the year
  (ii) Other cash book items (other than sales and purchase ledger cash)
  (iii) Petty cash payments
  (iv) Wages analysis (details are obtained from the computerised payroll system)
  (v) Adjustments, which include:

    (1) Correction of errors

    (2) Dealing with items in the sale and purchase ledger suspense accounts (adjustments posted to the ledger, and items where there is no account in the nominal ledger)

  All these journals are written manually in an accounts journal book, and they must be authorised by the managing director before posting. The opening balances are posted to the nominal ledger when the previous year's accounts have been approved by the auditors. Although the employee wages are calculated using another computer package, the total wages expense is posted to the nominal ledger manually. The wages expense is calculated from the payroll's monthly summary, using a spreadsheet package, and the wages expense is analysed into directors, sales, warehouse and office wages (or salaries).

Required

(a) List three control objectives of a sales system and three control objectives of a purchases system. **(6 marks)**

(b) List and describe the audit work you would perform on the computerised nominal ledger system, and in particular:

(i) The audit procedures you would perform to verify the accuracy of purchases transactions which are posted to the nominal ledger. **(5 marks)**

(ii) The audit procedures you would perform to verify the validity and accuracy of journals posted to the nominal ledger. Also, you should briefly describe any other tests you would perform to verify the accuracy of the year-end balances on the nominal ledger. **(15 marks)**

(*Note*. You should assume that sales transactions are accurately recorded and correctly posted to the nominal ledger.)

(c) Explain the auditor's responsibilities in respect of opening balances. **(4 marks)**

(Total = 30 marks)

13 Cheque payments and petty cash — 36 mins

Mr A Black has recently acquired the controlling interest in Quicksand Co, who are importers of sportswear. In his review of the organisational structure of the company Mr Black became aware of weaknesses in the procedures for the signing of cheques and the operation of the petty cash system. Mr Black engages you as the company's auditor and requests that you review the controls over cheque payments and petty cash. He does not wish to be a cheque signatory himself because he feels that such a procedure is an inefficient use of his time. In addition to Mr Black, who is the managing director, the company employs 20 personnel including four other directors, and approximately three hundred cheques are drawn each month. The petty cash account normally has a working balance of about $300, and $600 is expended from the fund each month. Mr Black has again indicated that he is unwilling to participate in any internal control procedures which would ensure the efficient operation of the petty cash fund.

Required

(a) Prepare a letter to Mr Black containing your recommendations for good internal control procedures for:

(i) Cheque payments **(9 marks)**
(ii) Petty cash **(7 marks)**

(Marks will be awarded for the style and layout of the answer.)

(b) Discuss the audit implications, if any, of the unwillingness of Mr Black to participate in the cheque signing procedures and petty cash function. **(4 marks)**

(Total = 20 marks)

14 Using the work of a management's expert — 36 mins

You are carrying out the audit of Ravenshead Construction a quoted company. The company's business includes large civil engineering contracts (the construction of buildings and roads). It also owns investment properties which are let to third parties and these comprise offices and industrial buildings.

During the year ended 31 October 20X6 the company received a substantial claim for damages from Netherfield Manufacturing for faults in a building it had constructed. This claim includes the cost of repairs and damages, as the customer alleges that the building cannot be used because of the faults, so alternative accommodation has had to be found. The company has obtained advice on the likely outcome of this claim from a local solicitor.

In the year-end financial statements the properties had been revalued by an independent valuer and the work in progress has been valued by an employee of the company who is a qualified valuer.

Required

Describe the matters you would consider and the other evidence you would obtain to enable you to assess the reliability of the work of experts in the following cases:

(a) Legal advice obtained from the local solicitor on the outcome of the claim by Netherfield Manufacturing **(7 marks)**

(b) Valuation of the properties by the independent valuer **(7 marks)**

(c) Valuation of the work in progress by the internal valuer **(6 marks)**

(Total = 20 marks)

15 Elsams — 36 mins

You are the auditor of Elsams Co which operates a chain of retail shops throughout the country selling a wide range of electrical goods. Each branch has computerised cash registers linked into the central computerised sales, receivables and inventory records. At the point of sale, the information keyed in includes the following: branch reference, product number, inventory location, unit selling price, date of sale.

The file of inventory records is updated daily for sales and receipts. It contains both cost (on a FIFO basis) and selling price information. The only regular printed output is sales summaries analysed by value, product and branch.

Required

(a) Explain the ways in which you, as the auditor of Elsams Co, could use computer programs to assist in the verification of inventory at the year-end, and indicate their limitations. **(8 marks)**

(b) Without particular reference to Elsams Co, describe the objectives and principles of using test data and comment on the areas where it can be of most use in an audit, and on the difficulties of this technique. **(5 marks)**

(c) Describe the following different methods of sample selection:

(i) Random selection
(ii) Systematic selection
(iii) Haphazard selection
(iv) Block selection **(7 marks)**

(Total = 20 marks)

16 Boston Manufacturing — 36 mins

You are the audit assistant assigned to the audit of Boston Manufacturing. The audit senior has asked you to plan the audit of non-current assets. He has provisionally assessed materiality at $72,000.

Boston Manufacturing maintains a register of non-current assets. The management accountant reconciles a sample of entries to physical assets and vice versa on a three-monthly basis. Authorisation is required for all capital purchases. Items valued less than $10,000 can be authorised by the production manager, items costing more than $10,000 must be authorised by the Managing Director. The purchasing department will not place an order for capital goods unless it has been duly signed.

The company has invested in a large amount of new plant this year in connection with an eight year project for a government department.

The management accountant has provided you with the following schedule of non-current assets:

	Land and buildings	*Plant and equipment*	*Computers*	*Motor vehicles*	*Total*
	$	$	$	$	$
Cost					
At 31 March 20X6	500,000*	75,034	30,207	54,723	659,964
Additions		250,729	1,154		251,883
At 31 March 20X7	500,000	325,763	31,361	54,723	911,847
Accumulated depreciation					
At 31 March 20X6	128,000	45,354	21,893	25,937	221,184
Charge for the year	8,000	28,340	2,367	13,081	51,788
At 31 March 20X7	136,000	73,694	24,260	39,018	272,972
Net realisable value					
At 31 March 20X7	364,000	252,069	7,101	15,705	638,875
At 31 March 20X6	372,000	29,680	8,314	28,786	438,780

*Of which, $100,000 relates to land.

Required

(a) Without undertaking any calculations, assess the risk of the tangible non-current assets audit, drawing reasoned conclusions. **(6 marks)**

(b) State the audit procedures you would undertake on non-current assets in respect of the following assertions:

(i) Existence **(3 marks)**
(ii) Valuation (excluding depreciation) **(4 marks)**
(iii) Completeness **(3 marks)**

(c) Describe how you would assess the appropriateness of the depreciation rates. **(4 marks)**

(Total = 20 marks)

17 Wandsworth Wholesalers **36 mins**

Your firm is the auditor of Wandsworth Wholesalers Co, and you have been asked to carry out audit checks on cut-off and verifying inventory quantities at the year-end.

The company maintains details of inventory quantities on its computer. These inventory quantities are updated from goods received notes, and sales invoices. The company carries out inventory counts each month, when all the fast moving and high value inventory is counted, and a third of the remaining inventory is counted in rotation so that all items are counted at least four times a year.

You attend the inventory count on Sunday 13 October, and a further inventory count was carried out on Sunday 10 November. The company's year-end was Thursday 31 October 20X1, and the inventory quantities at that date, as shown by the computer, have been used in the valuation of the inventory. No inventory was counted at the year-end.

Required

List and describe:

(a) The principal matters you should have checked and the matters you should have recorded when you attended the company's inventory count on Sunday 13 October **(8 marks)**

(b) The tests you will perform in ensuring that sales and purchases cut-off has been correctly carried out:

(i) At the date of inventory count on 13 October 20X1
(ii) At the year-end **(4 marks)**

(c) The work you will carry out to test whether the book inventory records have been correctly updated from the counts at the inventory count **(4 marks)**

(d) The work you will carry out to satisfy yourself that the inventory quantities used in the valuation of the inventory at the year-end are correct **(4 marks)**

(Total = 20 marks)

(*Note*. You should assume that the price per unit of inventory is correct.)

18 Sitting Pretty **36 mins**

Sitting Pretty Co is a small, family-run company that makes plastic chairs in a variety of shapes and colours for children and 'fun at heart' adults. It buys in sheets of plastic which can be cut and bent into the correct shape and a plastic leg that is custom made by another company to Sitting Pretty's requirements. All off-cut plastic is sent back to the supplier who melts it down and re-uses it, for which Sitting Pretty receive a 10% discount off their purchase price.

For the inventory count, the factory manager ensures that no work-in-progress is outstanding and closes down production for the day. The factory workers come in early on the day of the inventory count to count the inventory, and they are entitled to go home as soon as inventory is counted. Good controls have always been maintained over the inventory count in previous years. There are no perpetual inventory records. Raw materials are all kept in the stores and are only taken out when they are required for production. Finished goods are kept in the end of the factory, near the delivery exit.

You are the audit assistant assigned to attend the inventory count. You have just rung the factory manager and he has mentioned that on the day of the inventory count a large consignment of plastic is going to be delivered. It is the only day that his supplier can make the delivery, and he needs the material to continue with production on the day after the count.

The audit engagement partner has told you that he is aware that Sitting Pretty changed the specification of their customised leg recently, after a series of complaints over the stability of their chairs. Last year's inventory was valued at $200,000 in the statement of financial position, of which $30,000 related to raw material inventory.

Finished goods are all carried at the same valuation as each other as there is very little difference between the inventory ranges. Planning materiality for this year has been set at $5,000 on the grounds, at this stage, that the figures are expected to be similar to last year.

Required

(a) Explain the importance of the inventory count in this situation. **(3 marks)**

(b) Prepare notes for your audit supervisor detailing the procedures you propose to undertake in relation to your inventory count attendance. **(7 marks)**

(c) State the procedures which should be taken in relation to cut-off at the final audit. **(5 marks)**

(d) List the audit procedures you would carry out on the valuation of inventory at the final audit. **(5 marks)**

(Total = 20 marks)

19 Bright Sparks **36 mins**

Bright Sparks, a limited liability company, distributes domestic electrical equipment from one warehouse. Customers are mainly installers of such equipment, but there is a 'cash and carry' counter in the warehouse for retail customers. The warehousemen are responsible for raising invoices and credit notes relating to credit sales as well as handling cash sales.

You have carried out your interim audit in respect of the year ending 31 December 20X0 which included a circularisation of 80 trade accounts receivable as at 30 September 20X0 selected from a total credit customer list of 1,000. Replies were received from all customers circularised. The interim audit work disclosed the following.

(a) Of the 80 customers' accounts circularised, eight disagreed but could be reconciled by bringing into account payments stated by the customers concerned to have been made before 30 September 20X0 but which in each case were recorded in Bright Sparks' books between 14 and 18 days after the dates stated by the customers as the date of payment.

(b) Your tests suggested that some 25% of credit customers were allowed settlement discounts of 2.5% although payments were consistently received after the latest date eligible for discount.

(c) A large number of credit notes were raised representing approximately 12% of the total number of invoices raised. A review of the copy credit notes indicated that they usually arose from arithmetical and pricing errors on invoices raised.

You are required to explain the conclusions you would draw as a result of the interim audit and describe the work you would plan to carry out at the final audit on trade receivables at 31 December 20X0 based upon those conclusions. **(20 marks)**

20 Audit of cash and bank **18 mins**

(a) State the characteristics of a bank confirmation letter. **(3 marks)**
(b) List six examples of items requested in the bank confirmation letter. **(3 marks)**
(c) Explain the purpose and importance of the bank reconciliation. **(4 marks)**

(Total = 10 marks)

21 Understatement **54 mins**

Research into the distribution of errors in accounts has shown that for most items on the statement of financial position the errors are normally distributed. However, with payables the distribution is skewed, and there is a greater risk that payables will be understated than overstated. Understatement of payables will lead to overstatement of profit, so auditors must design their tests to ensure that payables are not understated.

You have been asked by the manager in charge of the audit of Heanor Wholesale Co to verify trade payables and accruals at the company's year-end of 30 April 20X2. The company maintains its purchase ledger on a microcomputer, using a standard purchase ledger accounting package. Purchase invoices are posted to the purchase ledger after they have been checked to the delivery note and the purchase order and have been authorised by either the financial director or the managing director.

The purchase ledger can show for each purchase ledger account:

(a) The unpaid invoices and credit notes
(b) An ageing of the balance into current month, one month, two months and three or more months
(c) The total balance on the account

Also, the system is able to provide the total of the balances of all the accounts on the purchase ledger.

Your audit of the purchases system has revealed that the system for recording receipt of goods is relatively weak. The company does not use goods received notes, but the supplier's delivery note should be dated by the goods received department when the goods are received. Your audit tests have revealed that some delivery notes are not dated by the goods received department. The delivery note is filed with the purchase invoice in alphabetical order (by supplier).

A full inventory count was carried out at the company's year-end and you are satisfied that it was counted accurately.

In the company's draft financial statements the value of trade payables and accruals at 30 April 20X2 are as follows.

	$
Trade payables	509,200
Purchase accruals	27,050
	536,250
Sundry payables and accruals	59,480
Current liabilities	595,730

Heanor's annual revenue figure is about $3.5 million and its profit before tax is $190,000. The age of payables at 30 April 20X2 is 3.4 months, which is similar to the previous year. Sundry payables and accruals comprise mainly wages accruals (including income tax and other deductions) and a sales tax liability of $20,000.

Required

(a) Consider and discuss the reasons why:

(i) It is more likely that payables will be understated than overstated.

(ii) It is difficult for auditors to ensure that payables are not understated. **(6 marks)**

(b) Describe the audit work you will perform to verify trade payables and purchase accruals. Your answer should include consideration of:

(i) Tests using suppliers' statements

(ii) Why most auditors do not carry out a payables' circularisation, and the circumstances when a payables' circularisation should be carried out

(iii) Audit tests which are designed to detect understatement of payables **(14 marks)**

(c) Describe the audit procedures you will perform to verify sundry payables and accruals, including the sales tax liability. **(10 marks)**

(Total = 30 marks)

22 'Tap!' 36 mins

You are an audit assistant in the firm Rogers and Smith. You have been asked to plan the audit of 'Tap!' for the year ended 30 June 20X4. It is the first time your audit firm has audited the charity, which has not been audited previously. The trustees have expressed interest in receiving a 'value added' audit and are particularly interested in business advice, especially in the area of systems controls.

'Tap!' is a registered charity that raises money for projects building wells in Africa through musical entertainment. The group consists of volunteers who travel around the country, putting on variety shows of music and dance, the proceeds of which are put towards building the wells. The main show is a tap dance production, acting out the difficulties many people face when they are not near a clean water supply.

The administrative offices of 'Tap!' are located in a large provincial town. It owns a house, donated by legacy in the past, where the administration is carried out and where the volunteers stay during off periods.

A large proportion of 'Tap!'s income comes from box office receipts which are taken by the theatre at which they are performing. The theatres usually waive their standard terms for use of the premises and merely take a 10% commission on ticket receipts to cover light and heat and other such expenses. Income usually comes in after every booking in the form of a lump sum cheque from the theatre, together with a break down of takings and commission.

'Tap!' also receives donations towards the work. These come from a variety of sources:

- Cash donations from buckets passed around at the interval of each performance
- Cash donations on the (rare) occasion that the team does street performances
- Cash donations made over the phone or by post by interested donors

The troupe consists largely of volunteers so they are only paid expenses for their work. The cost of housing the group while they are on the road is borne by the charity. The charity employs an administrator who organises bookings, handles publicity and co-ordinates all the finances.

Required

(a) Discuss the risks arising for the audit of the year ending 30 June 20X4. **(8 marks)**

(b) State the audit procedures you would undertake in respect of cash income in the financial statements. **(6 marks)**

(c) List some controls over cash which the charity should implement. **(6 marks)**

(Total = 20 marks)

Approaching the answer

You should read through the requirement before working through and annotating the question as we have so that you are aware of what things you are looking for.

You are an audit assistant in the firm Rogers and Smith. You have been asked to plan the audit of 'Tap!' for the year ended 30 June 20X4. It is the first time your audit firm has audited the charity, which has not been audited previously. The trustees have expressed interest in receiving a 'value added' audit and are particularly interested in business advice, especially in the area of systems controls.

First time audit for firm so little cumulated knowledge and experience.

Impact on opening balances and comparatives.

Not just a simple audit. This may make the engagement too risky – given the potential bad publicity that could result if there were problems with the audit.

High degree of regulation. Do we have any experience in this field?

'Tap!' is a registered charity that raises money for projects building wells in Africa through musical entertainment. The group consists of volunteers who travel around the country, putting on variety shows of music and dance, the proceeds of which are put towards building the wells. The main show is a tap dance production, acting out the difficulties many people face when they are not near a clean water supply.

Where is the audit evidence? Also, is expenditure in line with the Trust Deed?

The administrative offices of 'Tap!' are located in a large provincial town. It owns a house, donated by legacy in the past, where the administration is carried out and where the volunteers stay during off periods.

Is this common? Are there restrictions on expenditure? Also ensure accounts are correct for disclosures.

Trust?

A large proportion of 'Tap!'s income comes from box office receipts which are taken by the theatre at which they are performing. The theatres usually waive their standard terms for use of the premises and merely take a 10% commission on ticket receipts to cover light and heat and other such expenses. Income usually comes in after every booking in the form of a lump sum cheque from the theatre, together with a break down of takings and commission.

Cash income – risky

How accounted?

Trust for completeness?

Again cash. Also, poor in future years for analytical evidence. Lack of good evidence available.

'Tap!' also receive donations towards the work. These come from a variety of sources:

Again cash. Also, what are the controls here? Completeness may be a problem.

- Cash donations from buckets passed around at the interval of each performance
- Cash donations on the (rare) occasion that the team does street performances
- Cash donations made over the phone or by post by interested donors

The troupe consists largely of volunteers so they are only paid expenses for their work. The cost of housing the group while they are on the road is borne by the charity. The charity employs an administrator who organises bookings, handles publicity and co-ordinates all the finances.

No salaries

Expenditure issues again.

Not a specialist? But drafting complex accounts.

Required

You should have been noticing and annotating risks as you have worked through the scenario. Try and categorise them in your mind (inherent, control, detection).

(a) Discuss the risks arising for the audit of the year ending 30 June 20X4. **(8 marks)**

Note you are looking specifically for **audit** risks.

You must tailor your answer to the scenario.

(b) State the audit procedures you would undertake in respect of cash income in the financial statements. **(6 marks)**

Only cash income!!

(c) List some controls over cash which the charity should implement. **(6 marks)**

Think of control objectives and then design reasonable controls that meet the objective. There are more control problems in the scenario than you need to identify/solve for the marks.

Answer plan

(a) Audit risks

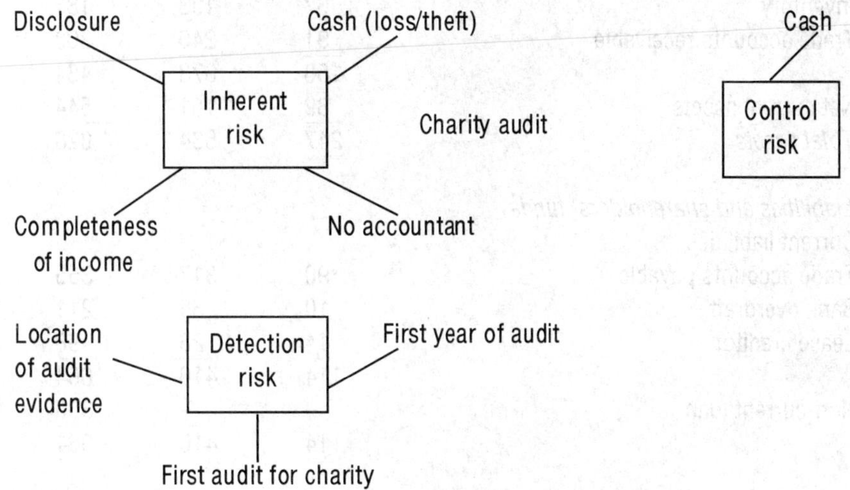

(b) Audit procedures

- Income from box office
- Income from buckets
- Income from other donations

(c) Controls

- Schedule of seats
- Two people to collect
- Pre-numbered forms

Security of cash during collection and between banking?

Other income

Use pre-numbered forms

Periodic reviews of work by Trustees

23 Going concern **36 mins**

Carrington Joinery, a private company, owned by its directors, manufactures wooden window frames, doors and staircases for domestic houses. It has prepared draft accounts for the year ended 30 September 20X6 and you are concerned that they indicate serious going concern problems. The statements of comprehensive income and statements of financial position for the last five years (each ended 30 September) are given below.

STATEMENT OF COMPREHENSIVE INCOME

	20X2	*20X3*	*20X4*	*20X5*	*20X6*
	$'000	$'000	$'000	$'000	$'000
Sales	625	787	1,121	1,661	1,881
Cost of sales	(478)	(701)	(962)	(1,326)	(1,510)
Gross profit	147	86	159	335	371
Other expenses	(88)	(86)	(161)	(240)	(288)
Interest	(6)	(9)	(58)	(90)	(117)
Net profit/(loss)	53	(9)	(60)	5	(34)

STATEMENT OF FINANCIAL POSITION

	20X2	20X3	20X4	20X5	20X6
	$'000	$'000	$'000	$'000	$'000
Assets					
Current assets					
Inventory	67	133	181	307	449
Trade accounts receivable	91	240	303	313	364
	158	373	484	620	813
Net current assets	89	161	544	600	587
Total assets	247	534	1,028	1,220	1,400
Liabilities and shareholders' funds					
Current liabilities					
Trade accounts payable	90	317	355	490	641
Bank overdraft	10	65	211	269	365
Lease creditor	14	28	98	92	59
	114	410	664	851	1,065
Non-current loan	–	–	300	300	300
	114	410	964	1,151	1,365
Shareholders' funds					
Share capital	17	17	17	17	17
Reserves	116	107	47	52	18
	133	124	64	69	35
Total liabilities and shareholders' funds	247	534	1,028	1,220	1,400

The company has been in business for about fifteen years. In January 20X3 it decided to build a new factory on a site leased from the local authority which would allow a major increase in sales. This new factory with new equipment was completed a year later. The factory was financed by a non-current loan of $300,000 from a merchant bank and an increase in the bank overdraft.

The loan from the merchant bank is secured by a fixed charge on the leasehold factory and the bank overdraft is secured by a second charge on the leasehold factory, a fixed charge on the other non-current assets and a floating charge on the current assets.

The company purchases its main raw material, wood, from timber wholesalers. It sells around 75% of its production to about 12 local and national builders of new domestic houses. The remaining sales are mainly to smaller builders with a very few sales to local builders merchants.

Required

(a) In relation to the financial statements above, list and briefly describe the factors which indicate that the company may not be a going concern. You should also highlight certain figures and calculate relevant ratios in the accounts. **(13 marks)**

(*Note.* You will only be given credit for going concern problems which can be determined from the accounts above.)

(b) Describe the investigations and tests you would carry out, in addition to those described in part (a) above, to determine whether the company is a going concern. **(7 marks)**

(Total = 20 marks)

24 Audit review and finalisation **18 mins**

(a) ISA 560 *Subsequent events* provides guidance on the responsibilities of auditors regarding subsequent events. Briefly explain the responsibilities of auditors for facts discovered up to the date of the auditor's report, facts discovered after the date of the auditor's report but before the accounts are issued and for facts discovered after the financial statements have been issued.

(4 marks)

(b) ISA 580 *Written representations* explains the purpose and use of written representations as audit evidence. State six items that could be included in a written representation letter.

(3 marks)

(c) Briefly discuss the use of analytical procedures at the review stage of the audit. **(3 marks)**

(Total = 10 marks)

25 Wiseguys National Bakeries

Your firm acts as auditor of Wiseguys National Bakeries Co. The finance director has prepared financial statements of the company for year to 31 December 20X9 which show a pre-tax profit of $450,000. You have been advised that the board of directors has approved the financial statements and decided that no amendments should be made thereto.

As partner responsible for the audit you have noted the following matters during your review of the financial statements and the audit working papers:

(a) The freehold property which was included at cost in previous years' statement of financial position, has now been restated at a professional valuation of $1,250,000 carried out during the year. You are satisfied with the valuation, the relevant figures have been correctly adjusted and the necessary information disclosed in the notes to the financial statements.

(b) An amount of $45,000 due from a customer in respect of sales during the year is included in receivables but, from information made available to you, you conclude that no part of this debt will be recovered. No allowance has been made against this amount.

(c) The financial statements do not disclose the fact that a director was indebted to the company for an amount of $22,000 during a period of six weeks commencing 1 February 20X9.

Required

Explain how each of the above will impact on the auditor's report.

26 Builders Merchants **36 mins**

You are the auditor of Builders Merchants, a listed company which distributes materials to the construction industry from eight depots in the south of the country, and you are currently finalising the audit for the year ended 31 March 20X1. Your audits tests have proved satisfactory with the exception of the following four matters.

(a) The physical inventory count sheets for one of the depots were lost before they were made available to you, and you have not been able to confirm the inventory quantities and values for this depot by alternative methods. The directors have valued this part of the inventory at $75,000 and this figure is included in the overall inventory valuation of $640,000.

(b) Included in trade receivables, which total $580,000, is a debt amounting to $45,000 from a customer which went into liquidation on 15 June 20X1. You have ascertained from the liquidator that your client is unlikely to receive a distribution. The statement of comprehensive income for the year shows a pre-tax profit of $100,000 but the directors are not prepared to provide for this debt.

(c) The financial statements of Builders Merchants do not contain a statement of cash flows.

(d) A substantial claim has been lodged against the company by a major customer. The matter is fully explained in the notes to the accounts, but no provision has been made for legal costs or compensation payable as it is not possible to determine with reasonable accuracy the amounts, if any, which may become payable. The directors have received legal advice which appears to be reliable in indicating that the claim can be successfully defended.

Required

Explain how the above items will influence the auditor's report you will issue. **(20 marks)**

1 Objectives, characteristics and responsibilities

Bird & Co
1 Old Street
New Town
M1 3WQ

1 January 20X1
Mr G Neville
1 Any Street
New Town
M2 5LM

Dear Mr Neville

In response to your queries I have produced some information on the difference between statutory audit, assurance work and internal audit. I have included this information in an appendix. However, it is important to note that the external audit is a legal requirement for many companies and cannot be avoided by employing the auditor to do other work.

If you require any further details please do not hesitate to contact me.

Yours sincerely

A N Accountant

Enclosure: Appendix

External audit	**Assurance work**	**Internal audit**
Characteristics and objectives		
The external audit is a legal requirement for limited liability companies above a certain size. Partnerships and sole traders do not normally need to have any audit, though some may opt to do so to give independent credibility to their financial statements.	Assurance work is voluntary for companies. Management can employ the external auditor to report on any specific areas. Directors may employ the external auditor when they feel a specific investigation or some specific work needs to be done, e.g. in support of an insurance claim or loan application.	Internal audit departments are not a legal requirement, though the *Combined Code on Corporate Governance* recommends them as best practice for listed companies in the UK and other countries are following this model.
In an external audit the auditor gives an independent opinion on whether the financial statements are true and fair. Implied opinions may also be given on issues such as whether the financial statements agree with the underlying records and all information and explanations which are relevant to the audit have been received.	The scope of assurance work is determined by management.	Internal auditors are employees of the company. They report on the internal controls, identifying problems and suggesting improvements. They may also report on the effectiveness of efficiency of operations.
External audits are performed annually, and the auditor is paid based on hours worked. The audit fee is normally disclosed in a set of financial statements.	Assurance work is a one-off specific assignment; fees are normally agreed with management and based on hours worked.	Internal auditors are full-time employees, and as such there are ongoing costs involved with setting up an internal audit department.

External audit	Assurance work	Internal audit
Characteristics and objectives		
The auditor's report is a formal report with standard wording, prepared for shareholders. An unqualified auditor's report indicates that the auditor believes the financial statements are true and fair.	Reports are tailored to the scope of work, and addressed to management.	Reports are prepared for management. There is no guidance governing the wording of reports, though companies may have their own internal guidelines.
Responsibilities		
Work and procedures are governed by International Standards on Auditing, produced by the International Auditing and Assurance Standards Board of IFAC. Compliance with these Standards is a good defence should the auditor end up in court.	The *International Framework for Assurance Engagements* provides guidance on the nature of assurance engagements. ISAE 3000 *Assurance Engagements* provides standards for assurance engagements other than audits or reviews of historical financial information. Auditors are expected to comply with this standard for both reasonable and limited assurance engagements.	There are no International Standards on Auditing to govern internal audit work.

2 Audit and assurance engagements

(a) Assurance engagements are engagements in which a professional accountant expresses a conclusion which provides the intended user with a level of assurance about a particular subject matter. External audits and review engagements are examples of assurance engagements.

An external audit provides only reasonable assurance because of the inherent limitations of the audit such as the fact that not all the transactions in the accounts can be tested and that judgement is required in the audit of provisions, for example.

Review engagements only provide negative assurance – this means that nothing has come to the attention of the auditor which indicates that the accounts have not been prepared according to the applicable framework.

Limitations of the external audit:

- Not all items in the financial statements are tested.
- Judgement is required.
- There are limitations in the accounting and control systems.
- The audit report is issued a while after the balance sheet date.

(b) The explicit opinions stated in the audit report:

- The state of the company's affairs at the end of the financial year in the statement of financial position.
- The company's profit or loss for the financial year in the statement of comprehensive income.

Implied opinions are reported on in the audit report only by exception, and could include the following:

- Adequate accounting records have been kept.
- Returns adequate for the audit have been received from branches not visited.
- The accounts are in agreement with the accounting records and returns.
- All information and explanations have been received by the auditors and they have had access at all times to the company's books, accounts and records.
- Details of directors' emoluments and other benefits have been correctly disclosed in the accounts.
- Particulars of loans and other transactions in favour of directors and others have been correctly disclosed in the accounts.

(c) Using the UK as an example, auditors have the following rights:

- Access to records: Auditors have a right of access at all times to the books, accounts and vouchers of the company.
- Information and explanations: Auditors have a right to require from the company's officers any information and explanations that they consider necessary for the performance of their duties.
- Attendance at and notices of general meetings: Auditors have a right to attend any general meetings of the company and to receive all notices of and communications relating to such meetings which any member of the company is entitled to receive.
- Right to speak at general meetings: Auditors have a right to be heard at general meetings which they attend on any part of the business that concerns them as auditors.
- Rights in relation to written resolutions: Auditors have a right to receive a copy of any written resolution proposed.
- Right to require laying of accounts: Auditors have a right to give notice in writing that a general meeting is held for the purpose of the laying of accounts and reports before the company.

3 Standards

The major advantages and disadvantages of auditing standards can be summarised as follows.

Advantages
They give a framework for all audits around which a particular audit can be developed.
They help to standardise the approach of all auditors to the common objective of producing an opinion.
They assist the court in interpretation of the concept of 'due professional care' and may assist auditors when defending their work.
They increase public awareness of what an audit comprises and the work behind the production of an audit report.
They provide support for auditors in potential disputes with clients regarding the audit work necessary.

Disadvantages
It may appear that they impinge on, rather than assist, professional judgement.
They are considered by some to stifle initiative and developments of new auditing methods.
They may create additional and unnecessary work and thus raise fees, particularly in the audit of small companies.

If auditing standards were to be enforceable by statute it would mean that there would be government intervention in areas currently controlled solely by the profession itself. This might ultimately lead to a diminished role in self-regulation. To be enforceable by statute the standards would have to be applicable to all circumstances and thus need to be very general and broad in their instructions. This might reduce their usefulness to the auditors. Auditors might spend unnecessary time ensuring that they have complied with the law rather than considering the quality of service to their clients.

Finally, it should be considered whether full statutory backing for standards would force auditors into narrow views and approaches which might gradually impair the quality of accounting and auditing practices.

4 Corporate governance

(a) **Improving the effectiveness of audit**

- Increasing assurance from stronger corporate governance and internal controls
- Providing an opportunity to discuss the terms and scope of external audit in an impartial way
- Strengthening the ability of the external auditor to request changes in control systems
- Ensuring that there is minimal duplication of work where internal auditors are involved, by discussing the audit plan with the external auditors via the audit committee
- Ensuring that directors' statements on internal control as required by Cadbury are reviewed by the audit committee
- Reviewing going concern issues and ensuring that appropriate disclosures are made
- Acting as a forum for resolving problems between the directors and the external auditors
- Resolving difficulties over the availability of information and key client personnel
- Reviewing draft financial statements before presentation to the auditors and the executive board

(b) **Independence of audit committees**

- The members should be **independent** and declare any interests in the company.
- Non-executive directors often sit on several boards, so **conflicts of interest** can easily arise.
- Salaries are paid by the company so **financial independence** can be compromised.
- Members of the audit committee tend to have **other roles** at the client, eg personnel. They act in several capacities and **independence may be impaired.**
- Members may have had **previous involvement** in executive positions and could have share options or pension schemes, again **compromising independence.**

(c) **Statutory regulation**

Statutory regulation could impose additional costs and regulatory burdens, which might not justify the end in all cases and could sometimes be detrimental to shareholders.

However, an argument in favour of statutory regulation is that **voluntary codes of practice** may not be applied consistently by companies. Another is that the non-executive audit committee may not feel able to criticise management unless they have **statutory backing**.

Shareholders do not readily understand the role of the audit committee. If it was appointed by statute and governed this role might be better understood, but this is not necessarily the case. There is no evidence that shareholders understand legal regulations any better than voluntary ones in many cases. It is difficult to arrive at a **'model' audit committee** suitable for all entities, as would be required if statutory regulation were introduced. Companies are unique and have unique requirements.

A **statutory monitoring report** upon the audit committee would be required. This would further increase costs for the company. It would be very difficult to set **standards for non-executive directors** on audit committees.

5 Independence

(a) If an auditor is to have credibility then it is vital that he should be seen to be independent of any concern on which he is required to report. However, independence is but one of a number of qualities which the modern auditor must possess if he is to be accepted as suitable for his role.

Outside of independence, perhaps the two most important qualities required of an auditor are:

(i) *Integrity*

The auditor must be seen as honest. Having formed his opinion, based on the audit evidence he has collected, he will not allow others to sway his judgement to suit their own ends. It is the auditor's integrity which will allow interested parties to place reliance on his reports.

IFAC and national supervisory bodies do a great deal to try and ensure that the integrity of the profession as a whole, as well as that of individual members, is maintained. This is done by laying down ethical guidelines which all members are required to follow (disciplinary proceedings are taken against any member known to have breached such guidelines). The accounting bodies also assist in this area by providing a broad framework for the training and examination of prospective new members, such as the ACCA's *Code of Ethics and Conduct*.

(ii) *Professional competence*

Clearly the auditor must be in possession of certain technical skills. This fact is clearly recognised so far as statutory audits are concerned, as only suitable qualified accountants are recognised as being competent to hold office as auditor. Examples of some of the skills required of the modern auditor are that he must be:

- Aware of and understand audit objectives
- Able to interpret systems
- Able to communicate well with others
- Conversant with required techniques such as sampling
- Able to cope with the impact of modern technology on accounting and internal control systems

The accounting profession is only too well aware of the need to maintain and improve standards of professional competence and for this reason has issued and recently revised a number of International Standards on Auditing. In addition the accounting bodies are heavily involved in running courses to assist members in maintaining and improving their technical skills.

(b) Independence on the part of the auditor as a reporting accountant is seen by many to be a fundamental concept of auditing. It has been said that it would never be sufficient for an auditor to claim that he was independent. In fact, he must always be clearly seen to be independent in practice. Given this situation, it would be almost impossible to draw up a set of rules to cover every conceivable situation where an auditor's independence might be called into question.

Whilst not able to provide an exhaustive list of recommendations, the main principles which should be applied when considering the question of independence may be found in the relevant section of the ACCA's *Code of Ethics and Conduct*. With this in mind, the following comments could be made in relation to the situations specified in the question:

(i) The audit partner has no shareholdings in the client company and so, all other things being equal, he could be seen as giving an objective audit opinion. However, the audit manager does have a shareholding in the client company which, whilst not material to the company (at 1% of issued share capital), could be material to the audit manager and certainly might be seen to influence his ability to give an impartial opinion in relation to the company's affairs. As the partner will inevitably have to rely upon the work completed and controlled by the audit manager it is clearly undesirable for the manager to have such a financial involvement in the client's affairs.

(ii) The code suggests that under normal circumstances no more that 15% of the gross fee income of a practice should come from any one client source. The reason for this is that the fear of losing a major client, and thus a substantial proportion of fee income, could prejudice the auditor's objectivity and make him more likely to bow to pressures from the client.

The audit fee from Janet Co contributes some 14.3% of the total fees income of the practice and so is within the 15% recommended limit. It would be necessary to consider whether any other fee income was received from this client, as this could result in the 15% limit being exceeded. However, perhaps the most important point to note is that the 15% is merely a guide. If the figure is slightly exceeded it does not automatically mean that independence is impaired and it must also be appreciated that even if the level of fee income is below 15% the auditor's independence could still be seen as being prejudiced. The firm would need to keep this situation under constant review.

(iii) As another instance of where financial involvement in a client's affairs could be seen to impair an auditor's objectivity, the code recommends that between an auditor and a client, there should be no loans or guarantees in respect of loans either way. Any such financial involvement could be seen to impair the auditor's judgement either because of a client putting pressure on the auditor or because of the auditor's own fear of suffering some financial loss.

However, the code does allow for one exception in making the above recommendation and that is where the loan is 'in the normal course of business and on normal commercial terms', providing it is not to the engagement partner (i.e. allowed for other audit staff members and practice partners). It is part of a bank's normal business to make personal loans and if the rate of interest being paid by the audit senior is the normal commercial rate of interest, this transaction is unlikely to be seen as impairing the auditor's independence.

(iv) The code also considers the problems that can be created when conflicts of interest arise between different clients and between clients and the auditor's own business interests. It concludes that every effort should be made to avoid conflicts of interest arising and that it would be highly unethical for an accountant to act in a situation where he knew that a conflict of interest existed.

The situation described in the question is a good example of the type of conflict of interest with which the code is concerned. The audit partner should not advise Jean Co with regard to the contract tender received from Harry Co. The auditor should explain the professional reasons why he is unable to act on this occasion and suggest that Jean Co seek advice from another firm of accountants.

6 Objectivity

(a) **Objectivity**

Objectivity is defined by the ACCA as being 'a state of mind which has regard to all considerations relevant to the task in hand but no other. It pre-supposes intellectual honesty.'

(i) *External auditors.* Objectivity is usually hallmarked by 'independence' in the case of external auditors. The auditor must be, and be seen to be, independent. ACCA provides a number of guidelines as to how an auditor should maintain his independence.

(ii) *Internal auditors.* Internal auditors are usually employees of the people they report to, so independence is a more difficult issue to understand here. However, it is vital that they maintain objectivity towards their tasks within a company, so they must avoid conflicts of interest and maintain integrity in their relationships with other staff members.

In particular, as an ACCA member, an internal auditor is bound by the ACCA's *Code of Ethics and Conduct.* Objectivity is a fundamental principle of this code.

Threats to objectivity

The following are all threats to objectivity:

- Personal interest (for example, fear of losing fees or a good relationship with a client/fellow staff member)
- Review of own work (for example, if an auditor audits financial statements he has compiled, or an internal auditor monitors systems he has designed)
- Disputes (for example, with a client, or where an audit firm advocates for its client, or where an internal auditor has a personal issue with a staff member)
- Long association or undue sympathy (for example, through close personal relationships)
- Intimidation (this is linked to self-interest, for example, fear of losing a client or an internal auditor losing his job)

(b) **Two situations**

Scenario 1

(i) **Threats**

The situation raises three potential threats to objectivity.

The first is the issue that the firm has had a long association with the audit client. It is unclear whether the same engagement staff have been associated with the entity in that time.

The second is that the firm has been offered the opportunity to carry out work other than audit for the firm. ACCA guidance states that provision of other services can affect objectivity.

Connected to the previous point is the fact that a self-interest threat arises through the substantial fee income that this client may generate in the current year. ACCA's guideline in respect to recurring income is that 15% of office income from one client is likely to adversely affect objectivity (for an unlisted company). The income in this year is likely to be 17%, but much of that is not recurring. However, the firm should consider that the result of the consultancy might be that the business expands and the audit fee might rise in the future. They should lay down contingency plans.

(ii) **Safeguards**

In relation to the other services, the key inherent safeguard is that it is a one-off project, as stated above. It appears that it will also be carried out by a department other than the audit department, which will help to maintain objectivity.

In terms of the audit, as the client has been associated with the audit firm for a number of years, the firm should consider laying out procedures for rotation of the engagement partner in relation to the client, so that the relationship cannot become too close over time.

If this is considered inappropriate, it might consider instituting a second partner review as another measure to maintain objectivity.

Scenario 2

(i) **Threats**

If Peter was to get the job in the internal audit department, there would be considerable threat of self-review, as he would have to monitor the systems which he has set up in the purchasing department.

As Peter is a current employee of the company, there is also a risk that his objectivity towards an internal audit role would be affected by his relationships with fellow employees.

This is particularly the case with regard to his relationship with his current boss, the Purchasing Director, as he has a poor relationship with him. As a member of the internal audit department, Peter would in all likelihood have to report directly on matters relating to this director.

(ii) **Safeguards**

If Peter gets the job, an important safeguard would be that he did not work on matters relating to the purchasing department for a period of time, or perhaps until the systems have been reviewed again and/or the Purchasing Director moves on.

It would also be important to address the issue of objectivity as part of the recruitment process. The issue of relationships with staff would have to be discussed and understood.

Lastly, it is important to have objectivity in the recruitment process. As Peter has had an informal discussion with the head of Internal Audit, the head of Internal Audit should ensure that other staff members are included in the recruitment process.

7 Role of internal audit

(a) **Notes on the role of internal audit**

(i) *Requirements in relation to the Board of Directors*

As a listed company, Golden Holdings should implement the following:

- The Board must meet regularly
- There should be a clearly accepted division of responsibilities
- Positions of Chief Executive and Chairman should be distinct
- A formal schedule of matters for referral to the Board should exist
- There should be a balance of executive and non-executive directors

Companies should also set up remuneration committees consisting of non-executive directors to determine executive remuneration. The Committee should report annually to the shareholders setting out the company's policy on remuneration and making disclosures about director's remuneration packages.

(ii) *Requirements in relation to accountability*

They should also consider the following matters in relation to accountability:

- Directors must explain their responsibility for preparing accounts
- Directors must report on the going concern status of the company
- The Board should establish an audit committee

In addition, the financial statements are likely to be required to be audited by an independent auditor who qualifies for the position under legislation.

(iii) *Risk management*

Directors should review the effectiveness of internal control systems at least annually.

Internal control systems are maintained to enable the business to operate efficiently, to ensure that assets are safeguarded and that reliable records are maintained. An internal control system reduces risk to a company.

As such, an internal control system is part of a company's risk management. Directors are required to review the system as part of their risk management exercise, to ensure that the system is still reducing risks, and that all risks have been considered.

The directors are also required to appraise the need for an internal audit department annually. Internal audit have a role in monitoring the risk management of an entity.

(b) **Sales department brainstorming session**

MEMORANDUM

To: Sales director

(i) I should be able to come along to your brainstorming session in July. However, it is probably best that I attend in an **advisory and interested capacity** only.

As we shall be involved in monitoring the systems which the sales department puts into place to mitigate risks in the business, it is i**nappropriate** for me to get **too involved** in the initial systems **design stage**, as this will **impair my future objectivity** when **monitoring** how the system is operating and achieving its objectives.

(ii) In terms of **assessing risks**, I am not best qualified to undertake this role. **You are the specialists** and should be able to identify the major risks arising in the department.

Just to give you a better idea of what my role can be, internal audit are able to provide three things:

- **Objective assurance** on the operation of systems once you have them up and running
- Assistance in **setting up a process to help you identify risks**
- Assistance in **strengthening the control process** once you have identified risks

In other words, if you are struggling to identify risks at the meeting, I can give you some pointers on how to go about it, but after that my job will be looking at the systems you come up with, and helping you improve them continually.

Internal auditor

8 Glo

(a) **Materiality**

It is **never appropriate** to apply the prior year's materiality figure to the current year figures. Materiality should be assessed in each year.

If the financial position has not changed much, and the results are very comparable with the prior year, it is possible that the materiality assessed year-on-year is very similar, but this does not mean that the auditors should not assess it for each audit. When assessing materiality, the auditor must consider **all known factors at the current date**. In this case, the position has changed considerably, increasing the risk of the audit, which may lower materiality itself.

As the **position** on the statement of financial position has **changed considerably**, when materiality is assessed, it is unlikely that it will be similar to the prior year. Using the information available, **materiality is likely to be assessed extremely low** in monetary terms, due to the overall decrease in assets and the loss that appears to have been made in the year. It is also possible that given the current position, the figures on the statement of financial position will not be used to assess materiality in this year.

(b) **Audit risk**

Audit risk is the risk that the auditor will give an inappropriate opinion on financial statements. It is made up of three different elements of risk:

- **Inherent risk**: the risks arising naturally in the business and specific accounts/transactions
- **Control risk**: the risk that the accounting system will fail to detect and prevent errors
- **Detection risk**: the risk that the auditors will not detect material misstatements

Detection risk comprises **sampling risk** (the risk that the auditors' conclusion drawn from a sample is different to what it would have been, had the whole population been tested) and **non-sampling risk** (the risk that auditors may use inappropriate procedures or misinterpret evidence).

Inherent and control risk are assessed by the auditors. Detection risk is then set at a level which makes overall audit risk acceptable to them.

(c) **Specific audit areas of risk**

A review of this statement of financial position suggests that audit work should be directed to the following areas:

Going concern

Total assets have fallen from $373,000 to $165,000. Although the statement of comprehensive income has not been reviewed, the statement of financial position shows a **retained loss** for the year of $211,000.

Net assets show a **reduction in both inventory and receivables**, which **suggests a decrease in activity**, although trade payables do not seem to have fallen so considerably. However, this could be accounted for by Glo-Warm not paying its suppliers in a similar fashion to the previous year. It will be **necessary to review** the **statement of comprehensive income** to substantiate whether activity has reduced.

The **cash position has also worsened**, with cash falling by $22,000. The statement of cash flows should reveal more detail about this fall. However, the company has paid off $5,000 of its bank loan, reducing overall net debt.

In summary, audit work should be directed at going concern as **several indicators of going concern problems** exist on the statement of financial position. This will be further amplified when the statement of comprehensive income is available.

Inventory

Inventory has been mentioned above in the context of going concern. Audit work should be directed at inventory specifically as this **balance has fallen significantly** from the previous year, which seems **odd in a manufacturing company**. There is no suggestion on the statement of financial position for why this should be so (for example, receivables are not correspondingly high, suggesting high pre-year end sales, and payables are not correspondingly low, suggesting low pre-year end purchases). It may be that the inventory count did not include every item of inventory. Alternatively it could simply point to a fall in activity (discussed above).

Warranty provision

A provision of $20,000 has been included in 20X6 for warranties. The reasons for this must be investigated and the auditors must check that it has been accounted for correctly.

It seems **odd that a warranty provision should suddenly appear on a statement of financial position**. It suggests a change in the terms of contracts given to customers, or a change in the customers themselves (with different terms then applying). Alternatively it suggests that **IAS 37** has been **wrongly applied in the current year, or should have been applied in the previous year**, and was not.

Other material items

As stated above, given the indications of loss and the reduction in total asset value, it is likely that materiality will be assessed low in monetary terms. In this case, most balances on the statement of financial position are likely to be material (excluding investments and cash-in-hand which appear to be very low risk).

However, as the bank loan is likely to be substantiated by good audit evidence, the most risky of the other balances are **trade receivables** and **trade payables**, for reasons discussed above in going concern. More detail is required to make a judgement about the risk of tangible non-current assets.

9 Audit planning and documentation

(a) The overall audit strategy is a document that outlines the general strategy of the audit. It sets the direction of the audit, describes the expected scope and conduct of the audit and provides guidance for the development of the audit plan.

The audit plan is a more detailed document than the overall audit strategy and includes instructions to the audit team that set out the audit procedures the auditors intend to adopt. The audit plan may also contain references to other matters such as audit objectives, timing, sample sizes and the basis of selection for each account area. It also serves as a means to control and record the proper execution of the audit work.

Key contents of an overall audit strategy:

- Section on understanding the company's environment.
- Section on understanding the company's accounting and internal control system.
- Risk and materiality considerations.
- Nature, timing and extent of audit procedures.
- Section on co-ordination, direction, supervision and review.
- Any other matters.

(b) ISA 230 *Audit documentation* requires auditors to document their audit work. Audit work needs to be documented for a number of reasons which are outlined below.

Audit documentation provides evidence of the auditor's basis for a conclusion about the achievement of the auditor's objectives and evidence that the audit was planned and performed in accordance with ISAs and other applicable legal and regulatory requirements.

It also assists the engagement team to plan and perform the audit; it assists team members responsible for supervision to direct and supervise the audit work; it enables the team to be accountable for its work; it allows a record of matters of continuing significance to be retained; and it allows for the conduct of quality control reviews and inspections (both internal and external).

(c) Standardised audit working papers

Advantages

- May improve efficiency of audit work, through the use of checklists and specimen letters, for example.
- Automated working paper packages may make documenting audit work easier, because they include features such as automatic cross-referencing, for example.
- Facilitate review.
- Can lead to time saving.

Disadvantages

- May lead to a mechanical approach without applying audit judgement.
- May not be applicable to all clients.
- New audit staff will require training to use the audit documentation system used by the audit firm.

10 Audit evidence considerations

(a) Analytical procedures can be used at the planning stage, as substantive procedures, and at the review stage of the audit. Analytical procedures consist of the analysis of significant ratios and trends including the resulting investigations of fluctuations and relationships that are inconsistent with other relevant information or which deviate from predictable amounts. Analytical procedures include comparisons with similar information from prior periods, comparisons to budgets and forecasts, comparisons with predictions prepared by auditors, and comparisons with industry information.

When using analytical procedures as substantive tests, auditors need to consider the information available in terms of its availability, relevance and comparability. They also need to consider the plausibility and predictability of the relationships they are testing. Other factors to consider include materiality, other audit procedures, the accuracy with which the expected results can be predicted, the frequency with which a relationship is observed and the assessments of inherent and control risks.

An example of an analytical procedure that can be used as a substantive test is a proof in total test on depreciation and amortisation. In this test, the auditor predicts the expected charge for the year for depreciation and amortisation by using the client's accounting policy for depreciation and applying this to the brought forward figures for non-current assets from the prior year audited financial statements, factoring in additions and disposals for the year. The figure obtained can be compared to the charge in the draft financial statements to assess its reasonableness and accuracy.

(b) Audit evidence is available to auditors in a variety of forms. These include auditor-generated evidence (e.g. analytical procedures), external sources of evidence from third parties (e.g. solicitors' correspondence, valuation reports from surveyors for land and buildings), internal sources of evidence from within the entity being audited (e.g. minutes of meetings from the Board of directors, reports generated from the accounting system), and oral or written evidence. Another factor to consider is whether the evidence, if written, is from an original document or a copy.

Audit evidence from external sources to the entity is more reliable than that obtained from the entity's records. Evidence from the entity's records is more reliable when the related internal control system is operating effectively. Auditor-generated evidence is more reliable than that obtained indirectly or by inference. Evidence in the form of documents or written representations is more reliable than oral representations. Where evidence is written, original documents are more reliable than photocopies which can be altered by the client relatively easily.

11 Knits

(a) The audit of a small company such as Knits poses particular problems for an auditor because of the following reasons:

- A single individual/small number of individuals running the business
- Lack of segregation of staff
- Few internal controls in place
- Informal controls that can be overridden by management

Knits has two directors, one who is involved in the everyday running of the company. This means that internal controls can be overridden easily and may not be in place in any case. Although the other director is a non-executive, this individual may not feel confident in discussing any control issues, particularly if the director running the business is a strong individual.

It can also be seen that in the accounts department, there are only two members of staff so segregation of duties may not be possible – this also can result in fraud being easy to perpetrate.

In terms of the audit, this may mean that the auditor cannot rely on the internal controls in place, so would undertake a fully substantive audit consisting of tests of detail and analytical procedures.

(b) *Control objectives of a sales system*

- Goods and services ate only supplied to customers with good credit ratings.
- Customers are encouraged to pay promptly.
- Orders are recorded correctly.
- Orders are fulfilled.
- All dispatches are recorded.
- All goods and services sold are correctly invoiced.
- All invoices raised relate to goods and services supplied by the business.
- Credit notes are only issued for valid reasons.
- All sales that have been invoiced are recorded in the accounting system.

- All entries in the sales ledger are made to the correct accounts.
- Potentially doubtful debts have been identified.

(*Note.* Only six were required.)

(c)

	Internal control deficiency	*Reason*
1	There does not appear to be any list of regular customers to be visited or timetable of regular visits.	Potential sales may be lost if customer goodwill is lost through inventory not being ordered promptly.
	There is no credit check for accepting an order.	Goods may be issued to a bad credit risk.
2	The order form set has insufficient copies.	The customer has no copy of the accepted order, disputes at a later date when the goods are despatched may become difficult to resolve.
3	The copy of the order for use in the warehouse is not sent directly to the warehouse.	The accounts department, who generate and post the sales invoice have the ability to adjust the order before it is sent to the warehouse.
4	The order form is filed before being matched to a despatch note and sales invoice.	Poor monitoring of accurate and timely completeness of sales orders.
5	No copy of the despatch note is retained in the warehouse.	No documentation is available within the warehouse to support inventory movements and prepare inventory records.
6	The sales ledger is only updated weekly.	Customers are being given an additional weeks credit which does not help Knits Co's cash flow.
7	Mrs Jones has control over most stages of the sales cycle from passing the order to despatch, raising and posting the sales invoice to receiving and posting the cash.	Sales transactions may be manipulated and company funds lost.
8	Written customer statements are only produced for balances over 90 days old.	The company is giving a very long credit period before chasing for payment. This causes cash flow problems for the company and given the nature of the customers business could easily become bad debts within a 90 day period.
9	There is no monthly reconciliation of a receivables listing to a control account balance.	Errors in updating sales invoices and cash may go undetected until a customer complains.
	This is exacerbated by the fact that hard copy printouts of sales ledger balances are not retained.	Lack of audit trail poses problems for the company in dealing with complaints but also in making year-end provisions and providing audit evidence for the external auditor.

Additional valid points

1	The sales representative does not monitor the completeness of orders.	Customer goodwill may be lost as a result of errors or time delay in completing orders.
2	There is no customer confirmation of receipt of goods.	Any dispute regarding receivables arising from goods delivered may be difficult to resolve.
3	There is no independent review of the sales invoices prepared by Mrs Jones.	Errors in terms of prices to be charged, any discounts due to arithmetical errors may go undetected.
4	Sales invoices are filed away, without retaining the despatch note, before the customer has paid.	Any customer disputes arising may be difficult to resolve without evidence of the goods despatched. Bad debts may arise.
5	The executive director does not appear to check the cheques received and being banked to a remittances list.	Errors in recording and banking receipts may go undetected.

(d) Controls to overcome the internal control deficiencies stated in part (a)

1 A schedule of planned visits should be prepared by the sales representative and completed with details of sales orders taken.

This schedule should be reviewed by the executive director on a weekly basis, comparing sales made to budgeted sales.

Any customers who are bad credit risks should be notified to the sales representative before his scheduled visit.

2,3,4 A four-part order form should be prepared at the customers premises, with evidence of approval by the customer.

The parts should be distributed as follows:

(1) Remain with customer
(2) To the warehouse
(3) To accounts to match with the sales invoice and despatch note
(4) Remain with the sales representative, to be used to monitor the progress of orders.

5 A three part despatch note system should be used as follows:

(1) Copy with the goods
(2) Filed with a copy of the order in the warehouse
(3) Sent to Accounts

6 Sales invoices should be posted to the sales ledger daily.

7 The sending of a copy of the despatch note directly to the warehouse and the monitoring of the completion of the order by the sales representative would help to introduce segregation of duties into the system.

In addition, cash and cheque receipts received in the morning could be recorded by Mrs Singh if she was given the additional morning duty of opening the post.

8 Statements should be sent on a monthly basis. In addition the company should investigate whether the company's computer package could produce them automatically.

9 Printouts of sales invoice and cash receipts postings should be retained, to provide adequate audit trail.

In addition the individual sales ledger balances should be listed monthly and reconciled to the nominal ledger sales ledger control account.

This account reconciliation should be performed by the executive director.

Additional points

- A schedule of goods being despatched should be prepared and the courier company should sign for the goods being taken to customers.
- The executive director should review a sample of invoices per week, comparing details to despatch notes, price lists and orders and checking numerical calculations.
- The copy of the sales invoice retained by Knits Co should be matched to the order and despatch note before being filed away.
- Mrs Singh should prepare a list of remittances detailing the customers name, specific invoices being paid and the net and gross amounts. A copy of the form should be sent to Mrs Jones and a second copy sent to the executive director alongside the cheques for banking. The executive director should evidence the form on banking the cheques to the form filed in date order.

12 Fenton Distributors

(a) Control objectives

Sales system

- Goods and services ate only supplied to customers with good credit ratings.
- Customers are encouraged to pay promptly.
- Orders are recorded correctly.
- Orders are fulfilled.
- All dispatches are recorded.
- All goods and services sold are correctly invoiced.
- All invoices raised relate to goods and services supplied by the business.
- Credit notes are only issued for valid reasons.
- All sales that have been invoiced are recorded in the accounting system.
- All entries in the sales ledger are made to the correct accounts.
- Potentially doubtful debts have been identified.

Purchases system

- All orders for goods and services are properly authorised and are for goods and services that are actually received and are for the company.
- Orders are only made to authorised suppliers and at competitive prices.
- Goods and services are only accepted if they have been ordered and the order has been authorised.
- All goods and services received are accurately recorded.
- Liabilities are recorded for all goods and services that have been received.
- All credit notes received are recorded in the nominal and purchase ledger.

(*Note*. Only three were required for each.)

(b) (i) To verify the accuracy of the purchases transactions posted to the nominal ledger I would perform the following tests.

- I would verify that the bookkeeper was up to date with the monthly posting of all purchases transactions to the nominal ledger.
- Specific tests on purchase transactions will include the following.

  (1) Purchase transactions will be traced from the invoice to the nominal ledger and the analysis and analysis code will be checked.

  (2) The total invoice value will be traced to the nominal ledger.

  (3) The category of invoice expense and the expense amount will be examined to confirm that it appears correctly on the detailed computer list for the month concerned.

(4) The total of the items on the detailed list will be matched to the nominal ledger.

(5) Transactions will also be traced backwards from the entries in the nominal ledger making up the monthly total posted to the purchase ledger back to both the detailed analysis and the individual invoice.

(6) The amount of the invoice expense will be agreed with the amount posted to the nominal ledger.

The tests above check accounting entries forwards and backwards within the system and any errors would be fully investigated as to their type, cause, materiality and pattern.

- The tests on the detailed list and total postings of cash payments, discounts received and adjustments will follow the same procedure as for invoices and credit notes. The monthly cash book total will be agreed to the total posted from the purchase ledger to the nominal ledger.

- An examination of the analysis and coding of purchase invoices will be carried out to establish the level of accuracy achieved. Particular care will be taken to see that the expense category 'purchases' is correctly identified and coded from invoices and is not confused with other categories, for example stationery, rates, gas and telephone. Incorrect analysis and/or coding may be indicated where the expense category is high or low in comparison with its budget to date.

  Large variations between actual and budget on expense categories should be examined further to verify that they are not due to errors in analysis, coding or posting.

(ii) To verify the validity and accuracy of the journals posted to the nominal ledger I would carry out the following tests.

- Firstly, I would check the opening balances at the start of the financial year from the opening trial balance back to the closing entries on the previous year's accounts. After this, each item would be agreed to the nominal ledger ensuring that both the value and analysis are correct. These opening postings should be the first entries in the new year as all nominal ledger balances should have been set to zero, and this should be confirmed.

- Other cash book items would be agreed to the nominal ledger to confirm that postings are correct as to value and expense category. Large items would require a larger sample size and large, unusual or suspicious items should all be checked and evidenced by supporting documentation or Board approval.

- The year-end balances of cash and bank on the nominal ledger should be agreed with the year-end balances in the cash book. This would require the last month to be scrutinised as the closing balances at all previous month-ends will have been agreed already.

- The tests on petty cash payments transactions would include the following.

  (1) Check that transactions are supported by vouchers and correctly posted to the right nominal ledger account. This would include checking that transactions are valid and coded to the correct expense category.

  (2) Check that petty cash transactions are within any limits, regarding the type of expenditure or maximum value, established by management.

  (3) Agree that the petty cash balance in the nominal ledger at the end of each month and at the financial year-end matches with the balance in the petty cash book.

- The wages expense is posted manually to the nominal ledger from the monthly payroll summaries by means of a journal. To verify that the journals are correctly posted I would select several journals and check the following matters.

  (1) The totals of the analysis columns on the monthly summary shown on the spreadsheet should be posted to the journal, and forward to the nominal ledger.

  (2) The breakdown of wages expense into directors and the several departmental categories will be checked. The correct identification of directors' pay is important as this requires statutory disclosure. I would obtain the current list of directors. I would add up the totals in the analysis columns to confirm the summary total, and consider its reasonableness.

  (3) Amounts owing at the year-end for income tax, accrued pay and other deductions will be verified and any reconciliation drawn up by the bookkeeper agreed.

  (4) Any additions to, or amendments of, weekly wages records posted to the nominal ledger through the adjustments journal will be fully investigated and their validity established.

  (5) The analysis of wages expense for the year will be compared with the budget and an explanation will be sought for any significant variances.

- Adjustment journals are potentially a high-risk area and any tests would include the following.

  (1) Check that all the manually written adjustment journals were authorised by the managing director and supported by documentation and proper narratives.

  (2) Check journals are posted in numerical order and there should be no missing numbers gaps in the postings.

  (3) Examine all large adjustments and the reasons given for the errors. These will be traced to the nominal ledger to ensure that postings do correct the errors.

  (4) Investigate closely recurring errors to establish their cause and whether these can be avoided in future by management action.

  (5) Examine the purchase ledger suspense account (payables suspense) and trace all postings in and out.

  (6) Where there was no account in the nominal ledger, agree back to the purchase invoice, establish the account number and verify that the item has been posted from the suspense account to the correct account.

  (7) Where the adjustment is due to the wrong account number being used, agree that the journal correctly transfers the item to the right account.

  (8) Where the bookkeeper has created contra entries between the purchase ledger and the sales ledger, check that the supplier/customer company concerned is posted with a purchase ledger and sales ledger contra of the same value.

  (9) All other adjustments will be checked for validity and supporting documentation.

  Reasons will be established for postings that increase or reduce purchase ledger balances.

- Year-end balances on the nominal ledger would be further tested as follows.

  (1) Any balances remaining on the purchase ledger and sales ledger suspense accounts should be itemised on a supporting schedule and the existence of each item justified.

  (2) Nominal ledger balances for the cash book, petty cash book, sales ledger and purchase ledger should agree to, or be reconciled to, the cash book, petty cash book, total sales ledger and total purchase ledger balances at the year-

end. I will investigate further to confirm that any difference is reconciled and explained. It may be that further adjustments are required to reduce or eliminate a difference.

(3) All non-current asset movements should be checked, including purchases, sales, revaluations and depreciation.

(4) All outstanding liabilities should be verified and their size reviewed for reasonableness.

(5) The bank reconciliation should establish the correctness of balances on all types of bank account, ie loan, current, deposit, special transactions and so on.

(6) A review of the financial statements would be carried out to ensure that material changes in assets, expenses, revenues, liabilities and share capital are justified and explained. Justification would be sought in both relative and absolute terms.

(c) *Opening balances*

In accordance with ISA 510 *Initial audit engagements – opening balances*, the auditor shall read the most recent financial statements and the previous auditor's report for information relevant to opening balances.

The auditor shall obtain sufficient appropriate audit evidence about whether the opening balances contain misstatements that materially affect the current period's financial statements, and whether the accounting policies reflected in the opening balances have been consistently applied in the current period's financial statements.

If the auditor obtains audit evidence that the opening balances contain misstatements that materially affect the current period's financial statements, he shall perform additional appropriate audit procedures to determine the effect on the current period's financial statements.

If the auditor concludes that such misstatements exist in the current period's financial statements, they shall be communicated to the appropriate level of management and those charged with governance.

13 Cheque payments and petty cash

(a) A Black
Managing Director
Quicksand Co
12 Kelvin Street
Anytown

MNO & Co
3 Green Street
Anytown

Date

Dear Mr Black

You recently requested that we should advise you on good internal controls over cheque payments and petty cash.

The main objectives of control over payments are to ensure that payments are made only in respect of valid transactions and that they are suitably authorised. The following control procedures will contribute toward attaining these objectives.

Cheque payments

(i) Cheques should be raised only on the basis of authorisation, for example a purchase invoice which has been suitably authorised.

(ii) Cheques should be signed by people other than those who approve invoices.

(iii) There should be two independent signatories for each cheque, for instance, two directors might act as signatories. Signatories should inspect the documents supporting the cheque to ensure that the details agree. They should also mark the document so that it cannot be reused.

(iv) Cheques should be restrictively crossed.

(v) Unused cheques should be kept in a secure place. Blank cheques should never be signed.

(vi) Cheques should be under sequential control and all numbers should be accounted for. Spoilt cheques should therefore be retained.

(vii) When cheques have been signed, they should be despatched immediately.

Petty cash

(i) Petty cash payments should be made only on the basis of suitably authorised vouchers, which should be under sequential control. Vouchers should be retained for subsequent references. Where independent evidence is also available, for example invoices and receipts, this should be retained.

(ii) An imprest system should be used to control petty cash. This means that the petty cash float is maintained at a specific amount and is reimbursed at regular intervals on the basis of vouchers showing the payments which have been made. It is suggested that the float should be kept at a level of $300 and be reimbursed on a weekly basis.

(iii) The petty cash float should be subject to periodic surprise counts by a responsible person not involved with the petty cash system. The balance in-hand should be reconciled to the imprest account by reference to the vouchers not yet reimbursed.

(iv) The size of individual payments out of petty cash should be subject to a maximum to be agreed by the directors.

(v) Staff should not be allowed to cash personal cheques or borrow from petty cash.

I hope that the above information is useful to you in designing your systems of internal control. If you require any more information, please let me know.

Yours sincerely,

A Smith

(b) Mr Black presumably feels that involvement in cash and cheque controls will be time-consuming, and that he is too busy to be involved in it. He may feel that he does not want to play a direct part in the petty cash function. Because of the small amounts involved, he may wish to delegate this function to another director. He should appreciate, however, that involvement at least in the authorisation of cheque payments would help to ensure that he is aware of major transactions in his business. He might consider the possibility of authorising cheques in excess of a given amount; this would minimise the demands on his time, while exercising control and keeping him informed of significant outgoings from the business.

Auditors may wish to consider whether Mr Black's lack of involvement may be symptomatic of insufficient attention being given to financial matters by the board.

14 Using the work of a management's expert

(a) In assessing the reliability of the legal advice obtained from a local solicitor on the outcome of the claim by Netherfield Manufacturing, the auditors shall consider the following.

(i) The materiality of the claim is important as the significance to the company of the amount involved would clearly affect the extent of the audit work required.

(ii) The qualification, experience, reputation and standing of the local solicitor would be relevant. Presumably the solicitor would be qualified, but it would also be necessary to consider his suitability to advise on this type of claim. The experience of the solicitor and his firm and their reputation in this field of litigation would be an important factor in determining the extent of reliance to be placed on the solicitor's advice. In particular, consideration should be given as to whether the solicitor had advised the company in

respect of similar litigation in the past and how reliable his advice had proved to be on those earlier occasions.

(iii) The independence of the solicitor must be checked as any suggestion that the solicitor or his firm had any direct connection with the company or its management would tend to reduce somewhat the reliability of the evidence provided.

(iv) The nature and extent of the evidence provided by the company to the solicitor, and on which he has based his opinion, should be carefully reviewed to ensure that the solicitor's decision appears to have been based upon all relevant facts available to the company.

(v) The solicitor's opinion should be examined and its reasonableness assessed, in the light of the auditor's knowledge and experience of similar cases against both Ravenshead and other clients engaged in similar activities.

(vi) If the auditors consider the amount of the claim to be material, and there is uncertainty in relation to the outcome of the claim and/or the solicitor's evidence, they should consider recommending to the client that a second opinion from an independent specialist in the field be obtained. If the client was not agreeable to this action or if the auditors still considered there to be material uncertainty, then a qualification of the audit report would probably be required.

(b) The factors to be considered by the auditors in assessing the reliability of the valuation of properties by an independent valuer would be as follows.

(i) The independence of the valuer should be considered in a similar way to that of the local solicitor, and for the same reasons.

(ii) The qualification, reputation and experience of the valuer should be considered. The valuer should be a qualified member of a professional valuation body with experience of valuing similar properties within the same geographical area as the properties owned by Ravenshead. If the valuer does not have experience of the type of properties held by the company or of the areas in which they are located, then the importance of his evidence is likely to be considerably reduced. The reputation of the valuer or his firm would also affect the reliability of his evidence so far as the auditors are concerned, with the likelihood that more reliance could be placed on a valuation made by a large firm with a good reputation, than one obtained from a little-known small firm.

(iii) The actual valuation of the properties by the valuer should be carefully examined. The auditors would need to satisfy themselves that a reasonable basis for the valuation had been adopted. Typically, an open market value based upon existing usage would be expected.

(iv) Any change in the valuation of the properties since the time of the previous valuation should be assessed. The validity of any significant changes in the valuation of the properties should be considered in the light of any statistical or other evidence available for similar properties.

(v) The reasonableness of the valuations should be considered against any profits or losses made on any properties disposed of in recent times, as this could be a good indication of any tendency to over or under value the properties to a material extent, either being likely to distort the truth and fairness of the financial statements.

(vi) The reasonableness of the valuations could also be considered by the auditors comparing the valuations with those used by other clients holding similar properties in the same locations.

(c) The matters to be considered when assessing the valuation of the work-in-progress by an internal valuer would be as follows.

(i) How material is this asset in the financial statements: as it is likely to be highly material, it needs to be valued accurately.

(ii) The basis of the valuation should be carefully checked to consider the extent to which it appears to comply with the requirements of IAS 2 *Inventories*.

(iii) Recognition needs to be made of the fact that, as the valuer is an employee of Ravenshead, this will reduce the reliability of the evidence provided. However this may be countered to a certain extent by the fact that the valuer should have a more detailed knowledge of the

work-in-progress than it would perhaps ever be possible for an independent valuer to obtain.

(iv) Confirmation should be sought that the valuer had actually visited all of the relevant sites, or otherwise obtained satisfactory evidence as to the stage of completion of the inventory in order to provide himself with a reliable basis for its valuation.

(v) The valuer's basis of determining costs should be ascertained and the auditor would need to be satisfied as to the reliability of the company's records in this respect and, in particular, that a consistently applied satisfactory basis of overhead recognition had been employed.

15 Elsams

(a) *Use of computer programs to verify inventory*

If physical inventory counting takes place at the year-end, it may be assumed that the results of the physical inventory count are entered into, and valued by, the computer. If so, then it is important to compare the results of the physical count with the book quantities. The client may have a computer program to make this comparison. It would be possible for the auditor to check this comparison by re-performance using his own specially written computer audit program or a computer audit package. The auditor's computer audit program or package, when run against the file of book inventory, might also be used to carry out the following tasks.

- Select a monetary unit or random sample of book inventory items for the auditor to check the physical count quantities.
- Select items with specific characteristics, e.g. no sale since a specific date, unit selling price over a specified figure for further testing (test counts or obsolescence enquiries).
- Prepare an aged analysis of inventory items.
- Re-perform calculation of the FIFO cost of each inventory item, compare with the book inventory figure and print details if there is a discrepancy.
- Cast the file of book inventory and print the total.
- Print details (product number, supplier, quantity, cost, date of supply) for a sample of recent inventory receipts contained on the file of book inventory for substantiation against suppliers' invoices.
- Prepare summaries of inventory by branch, product number and location to assist in analytical procedures on the inventory figure, especially when comparing with previous years.
- Compare the unit FIFO cost of each inventory item with the unit selling price and print details of all inventory items where unit selling price is the lower to assist in evaluating net realisable value.

Limitations

Computer audit programs specific to the client are expensive to write. Computer audit packages which are tailored to the client's computer and file structure are less expensive. However, packages are often only compatible with certain makes of computer. The audit software can work only with the information contained in the computer files. For example, an inventory ageing cannot be produced if the dates of inventory movements are not available. Clearly audit software cannot perform audit tests where an element of judgment is involved. For example, it can produce an inventory ageing analysis but the auditor must decide, on the basis of all available evidence, what level of obsolescence provision is reasonable. Audit software requires the auditor to have a detailed knowledge of the software and of the computer files to be used.

(b) *Test data*

Audit test data consists of data submitted by the auditor for processing by the enterprise's computer-based accounting system. It may be processed during a normal production run (live test data) or during a special run separate from the normal cycle (dead test data). The auditor predicts the results of processing the data and compares the prediction with the actual results. The primary objective of test data is to test programmed controls. For example, if the program contains a control which rejects overtime hours greater than 20 per week, then the test data might include the case of 21 hours overtime to see if it is rejected. The basic principle of using test data is that if the program processes the test data correctly, then the logic of the program and the program coding works and will process the actual data correctly.

Difficulties

- When live test data is used there is difficulty in ensuring that the dummy data does not become included in the actual data.
- When dead test data is used it may be difficult to ensure that the program tested is identical with that used for the actual data.
- The initial time spent designing the test data is excessive in relation to the benefit it brings – many auditors would rather devote that time to substantive audit work.

(c) *Audit sampling*

(i) Random selection ensures that all items in the population have an equal chance of selection, e.g. by use of random number tables or computerised generator.

(ii) Systematic selection involves selecting items using a constant interval, the first interval having a random start. When using this method, the auditor must be sure that the population is not structured in such a way that the sampling interval corresponds with a particular pattern in the population.

(iii) Haphazard selection is an alternative to random selection, as long as the auditor is satisfied that the sample is representative of the whole population. This method requires care to guard against making a selection that is biased. It should not be used if statistical sampling is being carried out.

(iv) Block selection can be used to check whether certain items have particular characteristics. However it may produce samples that are not representative of the population as a whole, especially if errors only occurred during a certain part of the period and hence the errors found cannot be projected onto the rest of the population.

16 Boston Manufacturing

(a) **Risk in the tangible non-current asset audit**

Control risk

The controls over non-current assets at Boston Manufacturing appear to be strong. The company maintains and reconciles a non-current asset register and there are authorisation procedures in operation. These controls should be tested, and if they prove effective, control risk could be assessed low.

Inherent risk

The tangible non-current assets are material on the basis of the proposed materiality level. There has been a substantial movement on the plant and equipment account this year, but this appears to be supported by the information given by the management accountant. There appear to be no disposals in the year, which may indicate that they have been omitted, or that obsolete items are included in the register. It is also unclear whether land is being depreciated. It would be inappropriate if it was being depreciated. Overall, the inherent risk seems to be medium.

Detection risk

Given that inherent risk has been assessed as moderate and control risk has been assessed as low, detection risk will be assessed as higher. However, there is usually good evidence in relation to the existence and valuation of non-current assets and these are the key assertions which the auditors

are interested in. There will also be scope to carry out good analytical procedures, such as proof-in-total of depreciation.

Conclusion

The audit of non-current assets appears to be medium to low risk.

(b) **Audit procedures**

(i) **Existence**

In many cases it is self-evident that land and buildings exist. However, it is important for the auditors to verify all components of land and buildings contained within the statement of financial position, if they are on a site different to the one which the auditors are primarily attending, for example. Land and buildings should also be verified to **title deeds** to ensure that they **not only exist**, but that **they are owned** by the client.

The other classes of asset should be **inspected**. A sample of assets from the **register should be agreed to the physical asset**. There may be scope to rely on the work that the management accountant has undertaken here. The auditor should check a reconciliation which the accountant has performed. The auditors should make use of any identification marks on assets recorded in the register, for example, security tags or bar codes which are kept on assets to distinguish them. The auditor should inspect the **condition** of the assets and ensure that they are **in use**.

The motor vehicles should be **reconciled in terms of number of vehicles existing at the opening and closing positions**. Again, to ensure that they not only exist, but are owned by the company, the auditors should check the **registration documents** to ensure that the company is the registered owner.

For all the above assets, the external auditor should also review the insurance provision for the assets. This gives **third party evidence** of the existence of assets as the insurer would not insure an asset which did not exist.

(ii) **Valuation (excluding depreciation)**

Land and buildings appear to be stated at historic **cost** as the schedule does not contain the words 'at valuation'. The auditors should **confirm** that this is the case with the management accountant. The cost can then be **agreed to brought forward figures** as there have been no additions in the year. These figures will have been audited in the previous year. If the assets are held at valuation, the auditors must ensure that the requirements of IAS 16 in relation to revaluations are being complied with.

Similarly, as there have been no movements in the year, **motor vehicles** can be agreed to the **opening position**.

To audit the valuation of **plant and computers**, the auditors should **agree the opening position**. They should then **obtain a schedule of additions** to non-current assets, which can be **agreed to purchase invoices** to verify valuation.

Lastly, the auditors should investigate whether the cost figures include any **fully-written down assets**. This is implied by the fact that the depreciation charge on plant excluding additions is low. If so, the auditor should find out whether these assets **are still in use**, and if not, consider whether they **should be excluded** from the cost and accumulated depreciation figures contained within the notes to the accounts. Excluding them would have a net effect on the reported figure of $0.

(iii) **Completeness**

The schedule of non-current assets prepared should be reconciled to:

- The **opening position** (that is, the previous statement of financial position)
- The **closing position** (what is disclosed in the financial statements)
- The **underlying records** (the nominal ledger)

If the non-current asset register contains details of the cost and accumulated depreciation of each asset, the **register should also be reconciled to the schedule**. Explanations should be sought for any differences.

The additions of the schedule should also be checked to ensure that the opening and closing positions reconcile within the schedule.

The auditors should also carry out a test on some of the **individual additions**, tracing the transaction through the system, from purchase orders to delivery notes and invoices and through the ledgers to the financial statements to ensure that additions have been included completely.

(c) **Depreciation**

(i) **Appropriateness**

The appropriateness of the rates should be considered and discussed with management. **Relevant factors** to consider are matters such as:

- The **replacement policy** for the asset
- The pattern of **usage** in the business
- The **purpose of the asset** being owned

In this instance, the auditors should establish the rationale behind the depreciation rates applied, particularly in the case of plant. In the case of the plant purchased this year, the depreciation rate applied is 10%. However, the assets have been purchased in relation to an 8 year project, so 12.5% might be a more appropriate rate.

(ii) **Audit procedures**

Depreciation on **buildings** can be verified by agreeing the purchase date of the buildings to last year's file or historic invoices/purchase documents and the valuation applied to the building portion.

For the other classes of asset, depreciation should be agreed for individual assets, as it is not possible to agree them in total. The auditors should obtain a **breakdown of the charges** for the year. They should be able to **recalculate the depreciation** from details in the non-current asset register and compare the results.

17 Wandsworth Wholesalers

(a) I would have checked the following matters at the pre-year end inventory count.

(i) Counting staff, although not the usual custodians of the inventory, were competent. They were briefed before the count and given sufficiently detailed written instructions. They were assigned marked areas to count.

(ii) No inventory was moved during the count. If inventory had to be moved, then the count supervisor would make a detailed note of quantities, inventory numbers and goods dispatched notes.

(iii) The inventory was clearly identified and well laid out. The counters should work in an organised way, with one counting and one checking. Each inventory line or area should be marked or tagged when counted to avoid any double counting.

(iv) Count sheets should be pre-numbered if possible, to ensure that they are all returned. Numbers should be in ink, not pencil.

(v) Management (or internal audit) should perform test counts throughout the inventory count. Any discrepancies should be investigated and resolved, usually by a recount.

(vi) Slow moving, obsolete and damaged inventory should be marked as such on the inventory count sheets in as much detail as possible to highlight inventory which possibly should be valued at net realisable value.

(vii) The management present should initial all the inventory sheets after performing random tests to check that all items of inventory have been counted.

I should record the following matters during my attendance at the inventory count.

(i) Perform test counts, selecting items from the floor to check to the sheets and vice versa. I would record all these tests (including inventory numbers, inventory sheets and so on) and any discrepancies I find should be investigated by the count staff and management present at the time.

(ii) Record all the inventory sheet numbers used in the count.

(iii) Record the last goods received note number received and the last goods dispatched note number issued prior to the inventory count.

(iv) Complete an inventory count checklist.

(v) Record any problems or unresolved discrepancies. This would include obsolete, slow moving or damaged inventory and any inventory movements during the inventory count.

(b) (i) To test cut-off at the inventory count on 13 October I would perform the following checks.

(1) *Sales cut-off.* Select a few goods dispatched notes from immediately both before and after the inventory count. Check that they have been recorded in the book inventory records in the appropriate period as being dispatched before or after the inventory count date.

(2) *Purchases cut-off.* Select a few goods received notes from immediately both before and after the inventory count. Check that they have been recorded as received in the appropriate period, either before or after the inventory count date.

(ii) At the year end it will be necessary to perform full *cut-off* tests, rather than just a check on the computerised book records as in (b)(i) above. After performing these tests for transactions about the year-end, the following additional tests will be carried out.

(1) *Sales cut-off.* Trace the goods from the GDNs to the relevant sales invoices and check that those invoices were posted to the sales ledger either before or after the year-end, as appropriate.

(2) *Purchases cut-off.* Trace the goods from the GRNs to the relevant purchase invoices and check that the invoices have been recorded in the purchase ledger in the correct period, as appropriate. Invoices which relate to the period prior to the year-end may not have been received in time to be posted in the ledger. In these cases such invoices should be included in the purchase accruals at the year-end.

(c) The following checks are relevant.

(i) Trace the check counts I performed at the inventory count to the inventory sheets, and from there to the book records. Some small adjustments may have been made to the book inventory. These discrepancies, if not material, may be explained by small differences found at the inventory count.

(ii) Investigate any material discrepancies between the inventory-sheet quantities counted at the inventory count and the book inventory records. Adjustments between the inventory count date and the year-end should also be investigated.

Large differences should be explained by the results of the inventory count. Evidence should be seen that further check counts were performed to ensure the inventory counts were correct. There should also be evidence that the management of the company have investigated large differences.

(d) As well as the tests detailed above in relation to the inventory count and cut-off, I would perform the following checks.

(i) Vouch the quantities used in the year and valuation to the book inventory records. This test should also be performed in reverse.

(ii) An overall check of complete book inventory against the amounts used in the valuation might be attempted using a computer program if the book inventory records are held on file. The program might produce all material discrepancies.

(iii) Investigate all material adjustments to the book inventory records at the year-end.

(iv) Investigate the level of adjustments made to book inventory records throughout the year. Consider whether the adjustments are small enough to give comfort that the book inventory records are reasonably accurate.

(v) Review the inventory counts from throughout the year to ensure that all inventory lines have been counted at least once during the year.

(vi) Review the book inventory records at the year-end and check for any negative inventory quantities. Where such negative figures have occurred, there should be evidence that the managers of the company have investigated the reasons for them, and that the figures have been adjusted to the actual physical amount.

18 Sitting Pretty

(a) **Importance of the inventory count**

The inventory count provides important **audit evidence** as to the **existence** and **completeness** of inventory included in the financial statements.

In this case, the inventory count is particularly important because the **company does not maintain perpetual inventory records**. As no perpetual records are maintained, the only basis for the inventory entries in the financial statements is the result of this inventory count.

Inventory is **generally material** to the statement of financial position of a manufacturing company and is also one of the **higher risk areas** on the statement of financial position. The inventory count provides important audit evidence reducing the risk of material misstatement in relation to inventory.

(b) **Planning for attendance**

Gain knowledge: I must review the notes of last year's inventory count and I must contact the factory manager to obtain details of this year's. I must review this year's details to ensure that the inventory count appears to be planned efficiently and effectively.

Assess key factors: There are various key factors given in the scenario:

(i) **Nature and volume of the inventory**. There should be no WIP, so I will count raw materials (approximately 10% of the inventory) and finished goods. However, raw material plastic should be low because a delivery is required to continue with production.

(ii) **Possible obsolescence**. I must make a note of the number of old chair legs maintained in raw materials as these are now obsolete, a new specification having been agreed.

(iii) **Cut-off issues**. I need to ensure that the delivery on the day is isolated and that I obtain details of the delivery made during the inventory count. I need to determine whether this should be included as deliveries for the year, but most of all ensure that it does not get counted twice (as it arrives, and if it is put into stores). I should also obtain copies of the relevant documents, for example, the last invoices in the year and the last goods received and despatched notes.

(iv) **Off-cuts**. I need to consider whether any off-cuts are maintained on site and whether these are being included in the inventory count. As the company receives a discount relating to them, they are unlikely to be considered Sitting Pretty's legally and so should not be included.

(v) **Staff issues**. It appears that the inventory count is undertaken by the people who work in the factory and handle the inventory on a daily basis. This is not best practice, although in practical terms it is difficult to avoid. However, I should discuss this with the factory

manager to assess whether staff can be allocated to counting inventory they have not produced. Also, as the staff are allowed to go home as soon as the inventory count is completed, there is a risk that the inventory count will be rushed and mistakes will be made.

Plan procedures: I need to determine my sample sizes and whether there is a need for expert assistance at this inventory count.

(i) **Procedures**. I will carry out test counts, checking from a sample of physical items to the count sheets and a sample of count sheet items to the physical items.

(ii) **Samples**. There are no higher value items that I should concentrate particularly on. Materiality for the year has been set at $5,000 currently. Dividing last year's figures for inventory by this materiality level would give a sample size of six items for raw materials and 34 items for finished goods. I need to determine the batches in which inventory is valued to ensure that I count the correct items. I need to assess the levels of inventory when I arrive to ascertain whether this remains appropriate.

(c) **Cut-off at final audit**

General procedures

The audit team should take a **sample of delivery notes** for sales and purchases on either side of the year-end and **trace** these to **invoices** and **ledgers** and **inventory** records to ensure that **sales and purchases have been included in the correct period** and that **inventory is accounted for where appropriate** (that is, sales have not been counted twice and purchases have been included in inventory). As the factory has been shut down, there is a lower risk that sales cut-off is inappropriate than purchases cut-off.

Inventory count delivery

Once it is determined whether this delivery should count as this year's inventory (which it should if the inventory count was the year-end date), the delivery information should be traced to purchase invoices and ledgers to ensure that the purchase is recorded in the year and that the creditor is accounted for in the year. The inventory should then also be included.

Other matters

If **inventory returns** are material, the returns after the year-end should be reviewed to ensure that items are not included as sales in the year and that the inventory is added to the inventory figure unless it is now obsolete, whereupon it should be written-off.

(d) **Valuation of inventory**

The auditors should obtain the client's working papers relating to the valuation of inventory. Items which the auditor sampled at the inventory count should already have been verified to the inventory count records as part of the verification of existence.

Cost

The auditors should then **trace a sample of items to purchase invoices** to ensure that **cost has been correctly applied**. Cost of purchase excludes trade discounts and rebates, so the auditors should ensure that the valuation **cost excludes the 10% discount** received for returning the off-cuts of plastic.

The auditors should then ensure that for a sample of finished goods items, **costs of conversion** (comprising costs of labour and overheads) have been included. This should be on a comparable basis to the previous year and therefore can be audited by analytical review.

Net realisable value

The auditors should ensure that **cost is lower than net realisable value** by tracing their sample to **after-date sales**. If no invoices are yet available, the auditors can make confirmations by reviewing sales orders and price lists.

Obsolete

Lastly, the auditors should ensure by review and by discussion with management that inventory which has been identified as **obsolete** at the inventory count has **not been attributed value** and has been **scrapped**.

Analytical procedures

The auditors will undertake general analytical procedures to ensure that the inventory figure stacks up. This could include calculating ratios such as inventory turnover and ensuring that they tally with the facts that have been presented them in the course of the inventory audit.

19 Bright Sparks

(a) *Conclusions to be drawn as a result of the interim audit*

The following weaknesses exist in the company's systems.

(i) In any system of internal control, one person should not be able to process a whole transaction from start to finish:

(1) Authorisation
(2) Execution
(3) Recording

The most serious deficiency in the company's system is that warehousemen can:

(1) Sell goods
(2) Receive cash from cash sales
(3) Raise sales invoices for credit sales
(4) Raise credit notes

Moreover, there appears to be no procedures in place for checking any of their work. Since the accounting records are written up on the evidence of these invoices and credit notes, any errors made by the warehousemen will be carried into the records. It may also be the case that the issue of credit notes is not authorised by a senior member of staff.

Possible consequences

(1) Errors on invoices may not be detected except by customers

(2) Risk of unauthorised or fraudulent invoices or credit notes being raised without detection

(3) Risk of goods leaving the premises without being invoiced, whether through error or fraud (this is particularly dangerous in a business such as this, with a variety of high-value items)

(4) Time wasted by needless disagreements with customers about amounts owing

(ii) There appears to be a weakness in the recording of cash received by the company. The dates recorded in the books are presumably the dates when the entries were written up. If so, there is clearly an excessive delay in recording cash received, and possibly also in banking it. There may also be no record of cash received made when incoming mail is opened.

Possible consequences

(1) Errors and defalcations can arise where a cash received system is weak.

(2) The longer the gap between receipt and recording, the more likely it is that discrepancies can occur.

(3) Specific possibilities:

- Falsification of records leading to misappropriation of cash (teeming and lading)

- Mislaying of cheques if not banked promptly
- Errors in the records, especially concerning dates

(iii) Stricter control is needed over the granting of cash discounts (assuming that it is the actual receipt of cash which is later than the due date, not merely the late recording of same).

Possible consequence

Discounts given to a standard list of customers who may be friends of staff or regular customers, not necessarily prompt payers.

(b) *Audit work on trade accounts receivable at the final audit*

(i) *Second circularisation*

(1) Consider circularising all trade receivables accounts, or at least a larger sample than before of accounts not circularised at 30 September.

(2) Circularise and investigate disagreeing replies. Discover if reasons are similar to those given at 30 September circularisation.

(ii) To gain further evidence about the rights and obligations and existence of receivables

(1) Check the sales invoices which make up the balances with backing documentation, for example purchase orders and despatch notes (if the latter exist)

(2) Ascertain extent of cash received from customers after the year-end; reconcile the individual invoices to ensure that no discrepancies exist

(3) Obtain explanations for invoices remaining unpaid after subsequent invoices have been paid

To gain evidence about the valuation of receivables, I would review the cash received after-date and would also carry out the following tests.

(1) Check calculation of outstanding invoices

(2) Carry out further tests on settlement discounts and ascertain whether the position has improved or deteriorated since the time of the interim audit

(3) Confirm necessity/adequacy of provision against write-off of specific debts by review of correspondence, solicitors' debt collection, agencies' letters, liquidation statements

(4) Consider whether amounts owed may be not recovered where there have been round sum payments on account or invoices unpaid after subsequent invoices paid

(5) Review customer files/correspondence from solicitors and circularisation results for evidence of potential bad debts

(6) Confirm any general provisions for bad debts, considering how well previous year's provision considering predicted actual bad debts and whether the formula used is reasonable and consistent with previous years

I would check the completeness of receivables by carrying out cut-off tests at 31 December to ensure that all goods leaving the premises by that date (and only those) have been included in sales. I would also check that all returns of goods after the year-end relating to 20X0 sales have been correctly recorded.

Other general tests include:

(1) Agree the opening balance on the sales ledger control account with the previous year's working papers to ensure all the necessary adjustments were put through last year

(2) Scrutinise sales ledger control for unusual entries

(3) Check list of trade account receivables balances to and from sales ledger, and reconcile with sales ledger control account

(4) Carry out analytical procedures, particularly reviewing changes in the receivables turnover period, and changes in the age profile of receivables

(5) Check that trade receivables have been separately disclosed in the notes to the accounts

20 Audit of cash and bank

(a) Characteristics of bank confirmation letter

- The client must give its permission in writing to the bank for disclosure of information to the auditors.
- The bank letter must refer to the client's letter of authority and the date of that letter.
- The bank letter should reach the bank at least two weeks before the year-end date and should state the year-end date and the previous year-end date.

(b) Items requested in the bank confirmation letter

- Balances due to or from the client on current, deposit and loan accounts
- Nil balances on accounts
- Accounts closed during the year
- Maturity and interest terms on loans and overdrafts
- Confirmation of contingent liabilities on guarantees etc
- Confirmation of securities and other items in safe custody
- Any offset or other rights or encumbrances
- Collateral given or received

(*Note:* Only six were required.)

(c) The bank reconciliation is carried out because the balance on a company's general ledger cash account is unlikely to match the figure in the year-end bank statement because of timing differences for cheques and other payments and receipts clearing. The bank reconciliation is an exercise to compare the balance per the ledger and the balance per the bank statement and therefore to confirm the accuracy of the figure on the company's statement of financial position.

21 Understatement

(a) (i) It is more likely that payables will be understated than overstated because of the nature of the evidence available to indicate that liabilities exist.

It is relatively simple to ensure whether a recorded liability has been correctly accrued at the year-end. However it is more difficult to identify liabilities which have been omitted from payables.

(ii) The auditor's difficulty in ensuring that payables are not understated arise precisely because of the circumstances described above. The auditor can test accrued invoices to ensure that they are a valid liability of the company at the year-end date. However, identifying liabilities which have been omitted at the year-end presents a more difficult problem. As there may be no direct evidence of the liability (say an invoice) understatement may have to be identified using indirect evidence for example unmatched pre-year end goods received notes, post-year end cash book entries.

(b) Audit work to verify trade payables and purchase accruals would be as follows.

(i) *Purchases cut-off*

As goods received notes are not used the normal procedures for auditing cut-off will need to be adapted.

(1) Examine purchase invoices on either side of the year-end to dated suppliers delivery note to ensure invoices have been correctly accrued. (Where the goods received

department have not date-stamped the delivery date it will be necessary to use the suppliers despatch date.)

(2) Enquire if the goods received department or bought ledger department are holding any unmatched delivery notes (those without an invoice) relating to the period before the year-end.

(ii) Completeness, existence and ownership

(1) Select invoices from the trade payables listing and trace to supporting documentation to ensure that the purchase was for the purpose of the business.

(2) Reconcile a sample of suppliers' statements with purchase ledger balances. This will highlight any purchases that have been omitted. Where there are major accruals for which statements are not available it may be necessary to carry out a payables' circularisation. (A circularisation is not normally the primary procedure to be selected as the supplier's statement provides more effective evidence and a reconciliation is simpler to carry out than a circularisation.)

(3) Review balances for unusually low balances with major suppliers.

(4) Compare the ratio of trade payables to purchases and inventory with the previous year's figures.

(5) Match cash payments posted in purchase ledger accounts before and after the year-end to cash records to ensure they were posted in the right period.

(iii) Trade payables listing

(1) Agree the total unpaid invoices and credit notes to balances on the aged payables listing.

(2) Agree the total of balances on the aged payables listing to the purchase ledger control account.

(3) Agree the list of balances to individual ledger accounts and vice versa.

(4) Review the listing for large payable balances and enquire into reasons for them and action being taken.

(5) Review the control account around the year-end for unusual items.

(c) Sundry payables and accruals is an area that lends itself to analytical review and reconciliation techniques, except for liabilities such as income tax and sales tax which should be checked in detail.

(i) From the sundry payables and accruals listing confirm that the calculation of accruals is reasonable and verify to subsequent payments. Income tax and related deductions liabilities should also be verified to payroll.

(ii) Scrutinise post year-end payments/invoices received to check for understatement of sundry payables and accruals.

(iii) Ascertain whether any expenditure is likely to be invoiced a long time after the goods or services are received.

(iv) Compare sundry payable and accruals with prior year balances and inquire into significant variations.

(v) Check that the sales tax accrual is disclosed at correct amount by vouching to returns and accounting records.

(vi) Ensure that no non-deductible tax is reclaimed on the return, by scrutinising it.

(vii) Vouch payments or refunds of sales tax to cash book from sales tax returns.

(viii) Obtain sales tax returns for the period and check that they have been properly prepared and filed promptly.

(ix) Test sales tax totals from prime records to monthly/quarterly summaries and test cast summaries and scrutinise for unusual items.

(x) Review correspondence with taxation authority and results of any recent control visits.

22 'Tap!'

(a) **Audit risks**

There is a higher audit risk associated with a charity as in the event of problems arising and litigation taking place, the audit firm could experience a significant amount of bad publicity.

Inherent risks

(i) **Cash**. The charity operates with a high number of cash and cheque transactions. A substantial part of their **income** comes from cash donations. Put another way, it is likely that very little of their income comes from direct bank transfers. Also, it is likely that many of the **expenses** which 'Tap!' incurs are also cash expenses. Cash is **risky for audit purposes** because it is **susceptible to loss, miscounting or misappropriation**.

(ii) **Charity**. The theatre company is a charity, and is therefore subject to a high degree of **regulation**. This raises the risk for our audit.

(iii) **Accounting specialist**. The charity employs an administrator, but there is no mention of an accountant. It is **unclear who is going to draft the charity accounts** (which must comply with specialist requirements) but it does not appear that a specialist exists to undertake this job. This increases the risk of errors existing in the accounts.

(iv) **Completeness of income**. As the charity appears to have **no control** over the primary collection of income from box office receipts, there is a significant **risk that income is understated** and that the theatres have not accounted properly to the theatre.

(v) **Disclosure of income**. The disclosure of income must be considered. It is unlikely to be appropriate to show the 'net income from theatres' figure. Rather, the gross income less commission should probably be disclosed.

(vi) **Expenditure**. The charity expenses may be well-recorded, or they may be **difficult to substantiate** – this is not clear. It may also be difficult to substantiate payments made to build wells in Africa. We currently have no knowledge about how that aspect of the charity operates. It will be important to check that expenditure is made in accordance with the trust deed. Some essential administrative expense will not necessarily be conducive to the aims of the charity. We must ensure that it is all analysed correctly.

Control

There currently appear to be **no controls over cash** in the charity.

Detection

This is a **first year audit**, so there is little knowledge of the business at present. It is also the **first ever audit** of the charity, so the comparatives are unaudited. We must make this clear in our report, and we will need to undertake more detailed work on the **opening balances**. As the charity is to a large degree **peripatetic**, we may find audit evidence difficult to obtain, if it has not been properly returned to the administrative offices.

Conclusion

This appears to be a high risk first year audit. It is likely to result in a modified audit opinion.

(b) **Audit procedures**

Income from box office takings

Income from box office takings can be **verified to the statement from the theatre** and the **bank statements** to ensure that it is complete. The **commission** can be agreed by **recalculation**.

It might be necessary to **circularise** a number of the theatres and request **confirmation of the seats sold** for each performance to ensure that income is completely stated on the return from the theatre. (However, if theatres have been defrauding the charity, they are unlikely to confirm this to the auditors. This may have to be an area which is aided by stronger controls over income.)

Income from buckets (theatres and streets)

We must discover whether the charity fills out 'counting sheets' when the buckets of money are originally counted. If so, the **money in buckets can be verified from the original sheet to the banking documentation**.

However, in the **absence of strong controls** over the counting, it will be **impossible to conclude that this income is complete**.

Income from other donations

Donations made over the phone should have been noted on documents and then retained at the administrative offices. Donations made by post should have **original documents**. A sample of these should be **traced to banking documentation** and bank statements.

Again, in the **absence of originating documentation**, it will be **difficult to conclude that income is fairly stated**.

(c) **Controls over cash**

Income from box office takings

It would be a good control over completeness of income to request a **schedule of seats sold** from the theatres for every night a performance is given. This is likely to be information that theatres can print off their systems with no trouble. This will lead to the theatre company having more assurance as to the completeness of income.

Income from buckets

As this income is highly susceptible to loss or misappropriation, strong controls should be put in place:

(i) **Number of people**. If possible, the charity should assign **two people** to each bucket during the collection phase and two people should count the money in the bucket at the end of the day. These people will act as a **check on each other** to ensure that cash is kept more secure.

(ii) **Security**. The security arrangements for buckets should be strong. The charity could invest in a **transportable safe** in which to store the money between collection and banking. It might also be wise to use **collecting tins** rather than buckets, as this simple measure would ensure that the cash was less open to the public. The cash should also be **banked frequently**. It should not be kept unbanked for longer than 24 hours after collection.

(iii) **Recording**. A record should be made of cash counts and it should be signed by both the people that undertook the count. These can provide an initial record of the cash takings.

Other income

The controls over other income will be restricted by the number of staff at the provincial office. It appears that only the administrator may work there regularly. If this is the case, it is going to be difficult to introduce supervision into the cash operations.

All phone donations should be **recorded on pre-numbered documentation** so as to give evidence of completeness.

As the administrator largely works alone, it would be a good idea for the Board of Trustees to carry out a cyclical review of the work of the administrator. This would provide useful protection from problems for both the charity and the administrator.

23 Going concern

Workings

The following significant accounting ratios are based on the accounts provided in the question.

	20X2	*20X3*	*20X4*	*20X5*	*20X6*
Gross profit (%)	23.50	10.90	14.20	20.20	19.70
Other expenses: sales (%)	14.10	10.90	14.40	14.40	15.30
Interest: sales (%)	0.90	1.10	5.20	5.50	6.20
Net profit (%)	8.50	(1.10)	(5.40)	0.30	(1.80)
Current ratio	1.39	0.91	0.73	0.73	0.76
Liquidity ratio	0.80	0.59	0.46	0.37	0.34
Leverage (%)	84.71	57.14	9.52	9.45	4.83
Inventory (months)	1.68	2.28	2.26	2.77	3.57
Receivables (months)	1.75	3.66	3.24	2.26	2.32
Payables (months)	2.26	5.43	4.43	4.43	5.09

Notes

$$\text{Inventory age} = \frac{\text{Year-end inventory}}{\text{Cost of sales}} \times 12$$

$$\text{Receivables' age} = \frac{\text{Year-end receivables}}{\text{Sales}} \times 12$$

$$\text{Payables' age} = \frac{\text{Year-end payables}}{\text{Sales}} \times 12$$

$$\text{Leverage} = \frac{\text{Shareholders' equity} + \text{Long-term loans} + \text{Bank overdraft} + \text{Lease}}{\text{Shareholders' equity}}$$

(a) The various factors in the accounts which may be indicative of going concern problems are as follows.

(i) Only losses or low profits are being made and the company is not generating sufficient funds to finance the expansion required

(ii) There has been a dramatic increase in the level of overdraft over the last year and there seems little prospect of the borrowing being reduced and the security is threatened.

(iii) There are signs of overtrading as the expansion has been financed by borrowings and the increase in current assets is being financed by trade accounts payable.

(iv) The leverage is low and decreasing, with very little security being available for the loans.

(v) There is a low current ratio and short-term funds are being used to finance long-term assets.

(vi) The liquidity ratio is low and decreasing and the company's ability to meet its liabilities on demand must be very questionable.

(vii) Inventory levels are increasing, suggesting that one or more of the following problems may exist: deteriorating sales, poor inventory control, obsolete or slow-moving inventories.

(viii) The value and age of trade accounts payable are increasing: some suppliers must be having to wait a considerable time before being paid and it can only be a matter of time before pressure is put on the company by one or more of its creditors.

(ix) High and increasing interest charges make the company very vulnerable, especially in a period of recession and high interest rates.

(x) The fluctuating gross profit would suggest that the company's profit margins are under pressure. The present level of gross profit does not seem sufficient given the company's high level of expenses.

(b) The other important steps to be taken by the auditors in determining whether or not the company may be properly regarded as a going concern at the year-end would include:

(i) Review carefully the cash and profit forecasts for the next year to see if they suggested any improvement in the company's position

(ii) Seek some evidence that the company's bank is prepared to continue supporting the company

(iii) Review the level of post year-end trading to see if this supports the forecasts and show any signs of improvement in the company's position

(iv) Examine correspondence files for any evidence that suppliers might be putting pressure on the company for repayment of monies owing

(v) Consider how the company's position compares with similar companies in the same business

(vi) Discuss generally the situation with management and review any recovery plans which they may have in mind

24 Audit review and finalisation

(a) The auditor shall perform audit procedures designed to obtain sufficient appropriate audit evidence that all events up to the date of his report that may require adjustment or disclosure in the financial statements have been identified. These procedures should take place as near as possible to the date of the auditor's report. They would include, for example, reading minutes of meetings with shareholders and audit committee meetings, reviewing the entity's latest interim accounts, and reviewing procedures that management have for identifying subsequent events. The auditor shall request management and those charged with governance to provide a written representation that all subsequent events requiring adjustment or disclosure have been adjusted or disclosed.

The auditor has no obligation to undertake audit procedures or make inquiries regarding the financial statements after the date of the auditor's report. Between this date and the date of issue of the financial statements, it is the management's responsibility to inform the auditors of any facts that might affect the financial statements. If such facts do arise which the auditor becomes aware of, he shall consider whether the financial statements need amending, discuss the matter with management and take appropriate action. If the financial statements are amended, a new audit report must be issued. If management refuses to make any amendments required, the auditor shall modify the opinion.

After the financial statements have been issued, the auditor has no obligation to make any inquiry regarding the financial statements. Where the auditor becomes aware of facts that may affect the financial statements after they have been issued, he shall consider whether they need to be revised and shall discuss with management and take appropriate action. If amendments are made to the financial statements, the auditor shall issue a new audit report which shall include an emphasis of matter paragraph referring to a note in the financial statements that discusses the reason for the revised financial statements in more detail.

(b) Written representation letter:

- Addressed to the auditor.
- Signed and dated, normally the date of the auditor's report.
- Acknowledgement from management for the design and implementation of internal control to prevent and detect error.
- A statement that management believes that the effects of uncorrected misstatements are immaterial, both individually and in aggregate. The letter should contain a summary of these items.

- A statement confirming the completeness of information provided regarding the identification of related parties.
- A statement that the financial statements are free from material misstatements, including omissions.
- A statement that the management have made available to the auditors all books of account and supporting documentation and all meetings of minutes of shareholders and the Board of directors.
- A statement that the entity has satisfactory title to all assets and there are no liens or encumbrances on the entity's assets, except where disclosed in the notes to the accounts.
- A statement that all liabilities, both actual and contingent, have been disclosed in the accounts, as well as any guarantees to third parties.
- A statement that there have been no events subsequent to the year-end which require adjustment or disclosure in the accounts, other than where specifically disclosed in the accounts.

(c) The auditors must perform and document an overall review of the financial statements before they can reach an opinion. This review gives the auditors a reasonable basis for their opinion on the financial statements. At the review stage, the auditors consider compliance with accounting regulations, consistency and reasonableness and application of accounting policies.

Analytical procedures are a very useful tool at this stage of the audit. They can be used to calculate important accounting ratios, changes in products or customers, price and mix changes, variances, trends in production and sales and variations caused by industry or economic factors. Any significant fluctuations and unexpected relationships must be investigated through inquiries with management and obtaining appropriate audit evidence relevant to **management's responses**, and **performing other audit procedures** considered necessary in the circumstances.

25 Wiseguys National Bakeries

(a) *Freehold property*

In past years this property has been shown in the statement at its original cost, whereas it is now restated at $1,250,000 as professionally valued during the year. The auditor is satisfied as to the basis of the revaluation, adjustment to and disclosure made in the financial statements. As a result of the audit evidence obtained no further reference to the property revaluation will be required in the auditor's report.

(b) *Allowance for doubtful debts*

No part of the debt of $45,000 due from XYZ Co will be recovered by the company. Since the financial statements which the directors have approved include no allowance for this debt, it will be necessary for the auditor's report to state that:

(i) No allowance has been made against an amount of $45,000 owing by the customer.

(ii) They believe such amount to be irrecoverable.

(iii) In their opinion, except for the failure to make such allowance, a true and fair view of the state of the company's affairs and its results is given by the financial statements.

(c) *Loan to a director*

Since the director's indebtedness of $22,000 which subsisted during a six week period, has not been disclosed in the financial statements in accordance with IAS 24 *Related party disclosures*, the auditors are obliged to include in their report an explanatory paragraph giving the required disclosure.

The particulars include:

(i) The amount of the loan and any interest

(ii) The zero outstanding balance at the year-end

(iii) Terms and conditions

The auditor's report will conclude with the statement of their opinion that the financial statements, except for the information specified above, give a true and fair view.

26 Builders Merchants

(a) This represents a potential material limitation on scope because the 'missing' inventory represents 12% of the total. The auditor would expect all inventory counting sheets to be available. The auditor's opinion would be modified.

The auditor's report would include a basis of qualified opinion paragraph before the opinion paragraph which would refer to the fact that the inventory counting sheets for this depot were lost. The qualified opinion paragraph would state that "except for" adjustments that may have been necessary in relation to this inventory, the financial statements present fairly, in all material respects (or give a true and fair view).

The auditor's report would also state that in relation to inventory quantities:

- All information and explanations considered necessary were not obtained; and
- The auditor was unable to determine whether proper accounting records were kept.

(b) This represents a material misstatement. The debt represents 8% of the total receivables balance and 45% of the profit for the year.

The auditor's opinion would be qualified.

The basis of qualified opinion paragraph would refer to the fact that the customer is in liquidation and there is little prospect of payment. It would also state that net assets and profits are overstated by $45,000.

The qualified opinion paragraph would state that "except for" the absence of this allowance the financial statements present fairly, in all material respects (or give a true and fair view).

(c) As the client is listed, its financial statements should include a statement of cash flows.

The auditor's opinion should therefore be qualified as the financial statements are materially misstated. This disagreement is not pervasive to the financial statements, it is limited to the statement of cash flows, so this would be a qualified opinion.

The basis of qualified opinion paragraph will refer to the fact that the financial statements do not contain a statement of cash flows and include the figures required, and the qualified opinion paragraph will state that the financial statements give a true and fair view and have been properly prepared in accordance with an applicable financial reporting framework except for the omission of a statement of cash flows.

(d) The auditors need to determine whether the legal claim is a material matter and even whether it is pervasive to the financial statements as a whole. For example, if the customer involved is a major customer, it could be that an adverse outcome could affect the going concern basis of the company.

It appears that the disclosure in the financial statements is adequate and there appears to be no basis on which to make a provision in the financial statements. However, the auditor's report will be affected by the fact that there is an uncertainty affecting the business. The auditor will have to decide whether the inherent uncertainty is fundamental to users' understanding. If so, the auditor's report should include an emphasis of matter paragraph beneath the opinion paragraph with details of this matter. It should also state that the auditor's opinion on the financial statements is not modified in relation to this matter.

Index

Note. Key Terms and their references are given in **bold**.

Notes

Review Form & Free Prize Draw – Paper F8 Audit and Assurance (International) (9/09)

All original review forms from the entire BPP range, completed with genuine comments, will be entered into one of two draws on 31 January 2010 and 31 July 2010. The names on the first four forms picked out on each occasion will be sent a cheque for £50.

Name: ____________________ **Address:** ____________________

How have you used this Text?
(Tick one box only)

- ☐ Home study (book only)
- ☐ On a course: college __________
- ☐ With 'correspondence' package
- ☐ Other __________

Why did you decide to purchase this Text? *(Tick one box only)*

- ☐ Have used BPP Texts in the past
- ☐ Recommendation by friend/colleague
- ☐ Recommendation by a lecturer at college
- ☐ Saw advertising
- ☐ Saw information on BPP website
- ☐ Other __________

During the past six months do you recall seeing/receiving any of the following?
(Tick as many boxes as are relevant)

- ☐ Our advertisement in *ACCA Student Accountant*
- ☐ Our advertisement in *Pass*
- ☐ Our advertisement in *PQ*
- ☐ Our brochure with a letter through the post
- ☐ Our website www.bpp.com

Which (if any) aspects of our advertising do you find useful?
(Tick as many boxes as are relevant)

- ☐ Prices and publication dates of new editions
- ☐ Information on Text content
- ☐ Facility to order books off-the-page
- ☐ None of the above

Which BPP products have you used?

Text	☑	*Success CD*	☐	*Learn Online*	☐
Kit	☐	*i-Learn*	☐	*Home Study Package*	☐
Passcard	☐	*i-Pass*	☐	*Home Study PLUS*	☐

Your ratings, comments and suggestions would be appreciated on the following areas.

	Very useful	*Useful*	*Not useful*
Introductory section (Key study steps, personal study)	☐	☐	☐
Chapter introductions	☐	☐	☐
Key terms	☐	☐	☐
Quality of explanations	☐	☐	☐
Case studies and other examples	☐	☐	☐
Exam focus points	☐	☐	☐
Questions and answers in each chapter	☐	☐	☐
Fast forwards and chapter roundups	☐	☐	☐
Quick quizzes	☐	☐	☐
Question Bank	☐	☐	☐
Answer Bank	☐	☐	☐
Index	☐	☐	☐

Overall opinion of this Study Text *Excellent* ☐ *Good* ☐ *Adequate* ☐ *Poor* ☐

Do you intend to continue using BPP products? *Yes* ☐ *No* ☐

On the reverse of this page are noted particular areas of the text about which we would welcome your feedback.
The BPP author of this edition can be e-mailed at: jaitindergill@bpp.com

Please return this form to: Lesley Buick, ACCA Publishing Manager, BPP Learning Media Ltd, FREEPOST, London, W12 8BR

Review Form & Free Prize Draw (continued)

Please note any further comments and suggestions/errors below

Free Prize Draw Rules

1 Closing date for 31 January 2010 draw is 31 December 2009. Closing date for 31 July 2010 draw is 30 June 2010.

2 Restricted to entries with UK and Eire addresses only. BPP employees, their families and business associates are excluded.

3 No purchase necessary. Entry forms are available upon request from BPP Learning Media Ltd. No more than one entry per title, per person. Draw restricted to persons aged 16 and over.

4 Winners will be notified by post and receive their cheques not later than 6 weeks after the relevant draw date.

5 The decision of the promoter in all matters is final and binding. No correspondence will be entered into.